SIR JOHN WOODROFFE, TANTRA AND BENGAL

SIR JOHN WOODROFFE, TANTRA AND BENGAL

'An Indian Soul in a European Body'?

Kathleen Taylor

CURZON

First Published in 2001
by Curzon Press
Richmond, Surrey
http://www.curzonpress.co.uk

Typeset in Bembo by LaserScript Ltd, Mitcham, Surrey
Printed and bound in Great Britain by
Biddles Ltd, Guildford and King's Lynn

British Library Cataloguing in Publication Data
A catalogue record of this book is available from the British Library

Library of Congress Cataloguing in Publication Data
A catalogue record for this book has been requested

ISBN 0–7007–1345–X

To the memory of my mother, who wanted very much to see this book, and of James Edward Woodroffe, who did not like talking about his family but became a dear friend.

For the one thing that strikes a close reader of his exposition is that he is truly an Indian Soul in a European body . . .

(M.P. Pandit: *A Commentary on Sir John Woodroffe's: the Serpent Power*)

CONTENTS

ILLUSTRATIONS

PREFACE

This book began one day in the college library when I looked at the books of Arthur Avalon, alias Sir John Woodroffe, in a long row in red bindings on the shelf. I can only describe it as a powerful feeling that I *ought* to know more about this British judge who had also been a scholar of Tantra. I could not tell why, and I did not, at that time, specially want to. Probably the name 'Arthur Avalon' had tapped into subliminal memories from many years previously, in India in the 1960s, when many young western travellers did seem to think they knew him, on some level.

At any rate, when I chose Woodroffe as the subject of a PhD thesis, the conviction remained for a long time (and despite proofs to the contrary) that everyone knew more about him than I did. At first I was astonished to discover there was no biography. I soon discovered why: no-one, however interesting, can survive their death if they do not leave a record of themselves behind. The thesis had to start with a search for papers. I went to Calcutta armed with another name, and an address of eighty years before. A second vivid memory is of one Sunday afternoon in the company of Mr Keshab Sarkar, of the Ramakrishna Mission Institute of Culture, as we went from door to door in the back roads and gullies of the north of the city making enquiries about the family of Atal Bihari Ghose. It was a fascinating and delightful introduction to a wonderful city. When we eventually found the house we wanted it had two wings and one of them, the one to which I most wanted access, was locked up. The owner had gone to live in Pondicherry. So I bought a rail ticket to Madras, and then a bus journey.

Pondicherry in early March was hot and humid, but from my balcony in the ashram guest house I could look straight out east, to the dawn over the sea. Mr Sobhun Ghose was an interesting and, I instinctively felt, deeply spiritual person. He gave me what I wanted most of all in the world at that moment: a letter of permission to his family for me to enter his house and search in his grandfather's library. It was like being given a golden key. What the search unlocked was evidence of a fascinating collaboration between two very different personalities, who had merged to create the figure of Arthur Avalon.

Nevertheless, this book remains essentially a study of Woodroffe. If, as some say, the scholarly monograph is dying in the age of the internet, one devoted to a particular individual is even more unfashionable. But I offer no apologies. In this single person's story, many different themes converge: relationships and choices of individuals against the background of colonialism and nationalism; the debate over the nature of 'orientalism'; the relationship of western enquirer and Indian knowledge in the encounter with Hinduism; the ever-fascinating subject of Tantrism. Unlike more dominating and better known personalities of his day (such as Annie Besant) Woodroffe reflected his social surroundings more than he stamped his image upon them. This, to my mind, makes him even more interesting. We meet less of the individual and more of his world. We find that the fault-lines of his social environment are reflected in internal conflicts and inconsistencies in his personality.

Many generations of people in the West as well as in India have been influenced by 'Arthur Avalon' and fascinated by the figure of Woodroffe. This study has been written in a way that I hope will offer something of interest to the academic, while also not presenting itself as 'a closed book' to the more general reader.

ACKNOWLEDGEMENTS

First of all I owe thanks to the two long-suffering supervisors of my PhD: Dr Avril Powell, and Dr John Marr at the School of Oriental and African Studies in London. To Avril Powell especially for her patience and faith that this work would be completed one day – which helped to ensure that it did; to John Marr (and his wife Wendy) without whose warm support, interest, generosity and above all inspiration, it would probably not have been begun. The thesis was made possible by a grant from the British Academy; and my second research visit to Calcutta was financed by a travelling fellowship from the Royal Asiatic Society. I thank also Lindsay Whittome of the SOAS computer centre, for very patiently helping me print copy from my antiquated computer programme.

I owe, as already mentioned, a great debt to Mr Sobhun Ghose for his kindness and support, and for giving me most of the originals of the correspondence between Woodroffe and his grandfather; also to Mrs Sumita Guha and her son Jayadip who gave me much patient help when I was allowed to browse in her grandfather's library; to Mr Krishna Ghose their cousin, who first welcomed me to the house and who had a print made for me of the photograph reproduced in plate 6, and to all the members of the Ghose family. I am equally grateful to Mr T.T. Samdup, son of the Lama Kazi Dawasamdup, who lives at Kalimpong, for giving me the originals of his father's correspondence with Woodroffe and others, and for his and his family's hospitality. Both sets of correspondence are now with the Oriental and India Office Collections of the British Library. Most of the photographs of Woodroffe and his wife were given to me by his son, the late James Edward Woodroffe, to whose memory I am grateful for these and many other kindnesses. Another person who died while this book was being written, and to whom I owe a debt of gratitude is the late retired Justice Mr Somarendranath Bagchi, for giving me copies of his articles on Woodroffe and for sharing his useful interpretation of his story.

I also thank Mr R.A. Ali, son of Sir Torick Ameer Ali, for allowing me to quote from his father's unpublished memoirs; and the Prior and community of Downside Abbey, near Bath, Somerset, for allowing me to research in their archives and to quote from Woburn Park school's journal *The Amoeba*. I also thank Father B.A. Rossiter of St George's School Weymouth for introducing me to the work of Father Stewart Foster of the Servite Order, and to Father Foster himself for allowing me to use the sources he had gathered for the interesting story of Woburn Park school.

I thank warmly Mr Satyakam Sengupta for his long friendship, support and invaluable help, especially, but not only, with translation; and Mr Keshab Sarkar who is mentioned in my preface, who also helped me with translation. I must also mention Mr Gautam Sengupta of All India Radio Archives, Calcutta, who with great patience found the important tape of an interview on West Bengal Radio which is mentioned in chapter 10. I would like to thank Dr Debabrata Sen Sarma and Dr Tapati Guha-Thakurta, for several helpful conversations in Calcutta; and the Mishra family who made me welcome in Darbhanga; also for their support and helpful suggestions many other friends and colleagues, especially: Indira Chowdhury, Francesca Fremantle, Jeanne Openshawe and Singharaja Delgoda.

Parts of chapters 8 and 11 have been published previously in Julia Leslie (ed.) *Myths and Mythmaking*, London, Curzon Press 1996. Quotations from India Office Records appear with the permission of the custodians of the Oriental and India Office Collections, the British Library. Extracts from the letters of Sir E. Denison Ross appear with the permission of the archives of the School of Oriental and African Studies, London. Quotations from all the works published under the name of Woodroffe or Arthur Avalon are in the copyright of Ganesh and Co. (Pvt) Ltd, Madras, including those from the 6th edition of *Shakti and Shakta* which were published under an arrangement with Dover Press, New York.

ABBREVIATIONS

BS	*Bhārata Shakti* 1) 1917, 2) 1918, 3) 1921.
CWN	*Calcutta Weekly Notes*, High Court of Calcutta.
DP	Dover Press edition (of *Shakti and Shākta*).
EIED	Bhattacharje, S.B. *Encyclopedia of Indian Events and Dates* New Delhi, Sterling, 1995.
ER	Eliade (ed.) *Encyclopedia of Religion*, New York, MacMillan, 1987.
GLb	*The Great Liberation* (English translation of MNT) 6th ed. Madras, Ganesh & Co., 1985.
GOL or *Garland*	*Garland of Letters*, 9th ed. Madras, Ganesh, 1989.
GOL (1)	1st ed.(1922) Madras, Ganesh; London, Luzacs.
HTSL	Goudriaan T. and Gupta S. *Hindu Tantric and Śākta Literature* Wiesbaden, Harrassowitz, 1981.
IIC	*Is India Civilized?* (1918, 1919, 1922).
IIC(3)	*Is India Civilized?* 1922 Madras, Ganesh & Co.
IOR	India Office Records (at the British Library, London).
ISOA	Indian Society of Oriental Art.
ITS	*An Introduction to Tantra Śastra* (The Introduction to MNT published separately): 8th ed. Madras, Ganesh, 1990.
JASB	*Journal of the Asiatic Society of Bengal.*
JISOA	*Journal of the Indian Society of Oriental Art.*
JRAS	*Journal of the Royal Asiatic Society.*
KKV	*Kāma-kalā-vilāsa.*
KT	*Kulārṇava tantra.*
MNT	*Mahānirvāṇa tantra.*
NAI	National Archives of India (at the Nehru Memorial Museum and Library, New Delhi).
OIOC	Oriental and India Office Collections of the British Library, London.
PST	*Prapañcasāra tantra.*

PT/1 & 2	*Principles of Tantra* (translation of Sivacandra Vidyarnava's *Tantratattva*) in 2 Volumes 6th ed. Madras, Ganesh, 1986.
SCN	*Ṣaṭ-cakra-nirūpaṇa.*
SOR	*Seed of Race* 1) 1919, 2) 1921 Madras, Ganesh.
SP or *Serpent*	*The Serpent Power*, 14th ed. Madras, Ganesh, 1989.
SS & SS(DP)	*Śhakti and Śhākta*, New York, Dover Press, 1978. (paperback). Unless an edition number is specified this is always the edition referred to. When more than one edition is mentioned, this one is indicated by SS(DP).
SS(1)	*Shakti and Shākta* 1918,
SS(2)	*Shakti and Shākta* 1920, London, Luzacs; Calcutta, Thacker Spink & Co.
SS(3)	*Śakti and Śākta* 3rd ed. Madras, Ganesh, 1927.
ST	*Śāradā tilaka.*
Studies	*Studies in the Mantra Shāstra* (Central portion of *Garland of Letters* originally published separately).
TRT	*Tantrarāja tantra.*
TT	*Tantrik Texts*. Volume numbers are indicated TT/1 etc.
VRS	Varenda Research Society.
WAP	*The World As Power*, 6th ed. Madras, Ganesh, 1981.

NOTE ON REFERENCING

References to Arthur Avalon's or Woodroffe's books on Tantra are placed in square brackets in the text. Editions are as stated in this list. Note that SS (followed by a page number only) indicates the Dover Press edition of *Śakti and Śākta* and *not* the latest edition. All general references, including those to Woodroffe's non-tantric books, are placed in endnotes under each chapter at the end of the book.

INTRODUCTION

> ... the opinion is expressed that there is in the body of the Scripture called Tantra a nucleus only of Tantrik teaching properly so called, which nucleus is defined as "black art of the crudest and filthiest kind, with a rough background of the Śiva Śakti cult" ... It is of them that the author cited says: "The highly coloured Yogic imagination pales beside the doctrines of the infamous Tantras in which a veritable Devil's mass is purveyed in various forms to a swarm of sects, mostly of the Śivaite persuasion". [*Principles of Tantra*, vol 1, p. 6]

In this passage a hitherto unknown orientalist called Arthur Avalon is quoting another Western scholar, the Sanskritist L.D. Barnett.[1] The year is 1913, when the first translations and editions of tantric texts under the name of Arthur Avalon were published. He appeared on the scene quite suddenly in the second decade of the twentieth century as an expert on Hindu Tantra which he claimed was abused and misunderstood because of what today we would call the orientalist discourse. Barnett's was only one of several examples he gave in the preface from which I have quoted. In line with Edward Said and others in more recent times,[2] Arthur Avalon attacked Western orientalist 'knowledge' which shaped the self-perception of the English-educated in India, and claimed this was particularly so in relation to the tantric tradition within Hinduism. He believed that the influence of foreign orientalists was almost solely responsible for the extremely negative reputation of Tantra among members of the English-educated Indian middle class. His books set out to re-educate both groups, but primarily the latter.

Those books of Arthur Avalon which are still in print have been published for many years under the name of Sir John Woodroffe, a British judge at the High Court of Calcutta who won popularity with many among the Indian public not only for instigating a revival of the tantric tradition, but also as a defender of Hindu culture as a whole. Although written initially for an Indian readership, his work soon became popular and extremely influential in the West as well, where Woodroffe became an early role model for Western converts to Hinduism or Buddhism. He emphasised the mystical and metaphysical aspects of Tantra, towards which most previous European orientalist scholars had been sceptical.

This made his books controversial at first, for in Tantra there seemed to be much to offend. A large array of divinities, among whom goddesses were more important than their male consorts, were worshipped by complicated rituals strongly focused upon figurative or geometric images and *mantras*. Then the 'infamous' *pañcatattva* rite included sex and alcohol as well as meat and fish among its 'five substances' for worship. With all these elements, plus a reputation for black magic, Tantra represented everything that the notions of 'paganism', 'idolatry' or 'witchcraft' summoned up for Europeans of the nineteenth and early twentieth centuries. In more recent times its always highly sexualized image has led to a reversal of values, so that 'Tantra' evokes popular notions of a romantic cult associated with erotic temple imagery, or 'spiritual sex'.[3] But in India, as well as being sexualized, Tantra also still evokes fear because of its association with magic.

In the Avalon/Woodroffe books *Tantrasāstra*, the doctrine contained in the Tantras, emerges as a refined subtle philosophy, its erotic and magic elements either marginalized or reinterpreted in an ethical or rational light; and their author insisted on its place within general Hinduism, rather than on an exotic fringe. Through his influence on contemporary and subsequent scholars he radically affected the study of Tantra for a long time, while his books also had a popular appeal that helped to make Tantra fashionable.

In India however, Woodroffe's significance was wider than that of a tantric scholar. He also wrote and spoke publicly on the more general theme of Hindu culture and the threat of westernization. Although not overtly political, the best known of his books on this theme, *Is India Civilized?*, made Woodroffe especially popular with the Indian public at a particularly sensitive time politically; his name was associated among his contemporaries with this book as much as with his tantric writings. As a British supporter of Indian nationalism, Woodroffe stands alongside more famous contemporaries such as Annie Besant, Nivedita and C.F. Andrews.

Although 'Arthur Avalon' presented his work as that of an independent outsider investigating Tantra impartially, there is evidence that Woodroffe was more personally involved, even to the extent of taking tantric initiation. Exactly how he was first drawn to it is not known for certain, though there are many stories. We find few traces of the process in his writings, which were produced within a relatively short period of time, and there is little chronological development within his work. Its different strata have more to do with the influence of his collaborators.

It is well-known and has been generally accepted for a long time that 'Arthur Avalon' was Sir John Woodroffe's pseudonym. In fact the matter was not so straightforward. Woodroffe claimed that he used the pseudonym to cover the fact that he worked with 'others', especially one anonymous person whom in a previously published paper I identified as the Bengali vakil and scholar Atal Behari Ghose.[4] The second part of this book probes further the collaboration of these two people, who between them effectively created 'Arthur Avalon' as an imaginary character, combining the talents of both men but especially the public image of Woodroffe with the textual knowledge of Ghose.[5] The first part examines the role played by Woodroffe in contemporary colonial society in which his identity as 'Arthur Avalon' took on significance, and the mixture of nationalism and idealistic or romantic orientalism that inspired his circle.

'Orientalism'

It is necessary to clarify the different contexts in which I use the words 'orientalist' and 'orientalism'. Before Edward Said opened the debate on European constructions of the 'orient', *orientalist* in the context of Indian studies referred to those among the British administrators, and especially educationists in India, who favoured 'oriental' learning and culture, as opposed to the 'anglicists' (a paradoxical alliance of utilitarians, rationalists and some Christian missionaries) who wished to supplant the indigenous culture through English education. The word 'orientalist' also had an earlier meaning which denoted scholars of Asian languages and cultures, and especially the English scholars in India of the eighteenth and early nineteenth century who first revealed to Europe the richness of the Sanskritic tradition. Sir William Jones and his followers, who founded the Asiatic Society of Bengal (the quintessential 'orientalist' society) were also 'orientalists' in the ideological sense I have outlined, in that they placed high value upon the non-European culture they encountered; but their successors in 'oriental' studies often took the diametrically opposite view, and placed all non-European cultures at a lower level of development.[6] It was attitudes typical of the latter group which mostly came under scrutiny in Said's *Orientalism*, but for Said, *all* European writing on 'the orient' in the context of colonialism was characterised by projections upon an essentialized 'other' and the desire to shape and control that other. Hence it is less relevant to his argument whether these projections were romantic and idealized, or contemptuous and abusive as in the quotation with which this Introduction begins. In India, however, the two attitudes led to radically different conclusions politically as the former veered close to, and influenced, Indian nationalism (see below chapter 4).

Woodroffe was an 'orientalist' in the romantic, idealistic sense and I have used the term 'romantic orientalism' to refer to his values and those of his circle.[7] It is the contention of this book that he was not an 'orientalist' in the more literal sense of the term: a scholar of Asian languages, but that he posed as one – or at the very least allowed himself to be perceived as one. I would have liked to avoid the term 'orientalist' altogether in this latter context and substituted 'indologist' in its place, but that would have been to overthrow the fulcrum on which the whole story rests. Arthur Avalon in fact perceived Western orientalist 'knowledge' in a manner that sometimes approached Said's, and that he did so tends to uphold my central thesis: that Woodroffe in his role as Arthur Avalon was different from other Western scholars in being open to Indian influence to an unusual degree. Indian writers had attacked the assumptions and sense of racial superiority of certain Western commentators since the mid-nineteenth century.[8] 'Orientalism' connoting a body of scholarship claiming expertise and making certain (positive or negative) evaluations of Indian religion and society from an external and supposedly privileged position, forms the essential backdrop to the story of Arthur Avalon. It was that image of the 'orientalist' which Ghose and Woodroffe addressed, appropriated and successfully made use of. Hence I use the term in both senses: as scholarship of Asian languages and culture, and as an ideology. I hope these different senses will be clear from the contexts in which they are used.

SUMMARY

Woodroffe's life in Calcutta can be looked at through five roles, four public and one half-secret. His most significant role, that of Arthur Avalon the orientalist scholar, takes up the second part of the book which deals with his writings on Tantra. At the same time it forms the backdrop to the other roles which are the subject of part one: the judge of the High Court at a time of political ferment in the province of Bengal (chapter 3); the patron and connoisseur of Indian art, and friend of the Tagores (chapter 4); the prestigious foreigner who won popularity as a defender of Hinduism (chapter 5); and lastly, the secret Tantric, whose secret nevertheless was not well kept (chapter 6). By way of prologue we look at a sixth, unknown role: Woodroffe's youthful 'career' as a leading politician in the Parliament of his highly unusual public school (chapter 2).

Part Two begins with an outline of European attitudes to Tantra within the study of Hinduism and Buddhism prior to Arthur Avalon, followed by a summary of the works published under the Avalon and Woodroffe names (chapter 7). Chapter 8 concerns 'Arthur Avalon': the images the pseudonym evoked and the response to this new orientalist who seemed to have such profound textual knowledge of Tantra as well as an understanding that belonged to the 'insider', and who seemed a completely new kind of European scholar. This leads up to the appearance of Sir John Woodroffe in the public arena as a scholar of Tantra. The chapter moves on to discuss the choice and significance of the pseudonym. Finally it introduces Atal Bihari Ghose and presents arguments for his very significant involvement in the Arthur Avalon books, and raises questions around the degree of Woodroffe's Sanskrit knowledge.

The last three chapters focus on the Avalon/Woodroffe books. Chapter 9 outlines the area presented in them as *Tantraśāstra* and relates it to selected modern studies of Tantrism. Chapter 10 analyses some of Woodroffe's apologetic themes, especially against the background of Swami Vivekananda's neo-Vedanta, and closes with a study of how Woodroffe used fashionable western occultist and scientific concepts. This chapter focuses upon Woodroffe's lectures where we can be fairly sure he speaks in his own voice. The last chapter attempts to unravel different strands in the writings. Beginning with Woodroffe's correspondence with Ghose and with Lama Kazi Dawasamdup, it looks at his relationship with these two collaborators. Then it turns to Woodroffe's relationship with Sanskrit and Sanskrit texts, and with secondary literature. Finally it examines his use of the knowledge of Ghose and of other Indian people, arguing that the books put forward a modern 'insider's' re-interpretation of the tantric tradition presented under the name of a foreign 'orientalist'. I end by making some suggestions about how to distinguish the two chief voices, those of Woodroffe and Atal Bihari Ghose, who speak through 'Arthur Avalon'.

Throughout I refer to the author as 'Woodroffe' for passages originally put out under that name, usually because they occur in lectures delivered by him; 'Avalon' is used for passages published originally under the pseudonym; and Avalon/Woodroffe when referring to the whole body of writings. This is because Woodroffe did write under his own name in his lifetime and so 'Arthur Avalon' does not strictly cover all the books.

A NOTE ON SOURCES

Family

After Sir John Woodroffe's death, his widow Ellen lived until her own death in 1944 at Menton on the Italian border. According to their son James Edward Woodroffe, this house was looted twice during the war and he gave this as the reason why there were no family papers and no trace of the extensive art collection his father was said to have amassed. The Woodroffes had three children, two girls called Nancy and Barbara, and James who was born in 1909. None of these children married and so there are now no direct descendants. Barbara died young in 1925; Nancy died in 1973; James Woodroffe lived until 1995, in a caravan near the south coast of England where I first met him in 1989. Most of the information on the family has been provided by him.

Private Correspondence in India

'The correspondence between Woodroffe and Atal Bihari Ghose which is discussed in this book was discovered in the house of his grandchildren in Calcutta. It was apparently a random selection, found among his manuscript collection and in other places in the house.' Mostly this consisted of letters written to Ghose from England and France after Woodroffe's retirement from India. They were kindly donated to me by Sobhun Ghose and are now with the Oriental and India Office Collection of the British Library. Photocopies and typed versions of those letters which are discussed in this book are to be found in Appendix I, where the reference numbers assigned to them are my own.[9]

A larger collection of correspondence that was brought to light in India was that between Woodroffe and Lama Kazi Dawasamdup, who edited volume 7 of Avalon's *Tantrik Texts*. This was also kindly donated by the Lama's son Mr T.T. Samdup. As I deal in less depth with this correspondence, I have not reproduced any of it in the appendix. The originals are also now with the India Office collection in London.[10]

Public Archives

Among the records of the former India Office Library, information on Sir John Woodroffe's official career was to be found in the papers of the Judicial and Public Department, now in the British Library in London, and in the Home Department Judicial Proceedings, in the National Archives of India. Private papers of individuals contemporary with him in India yielded occasional references to him, but were mostly useful for providing background. Reconstruction of his judicial career is drawn from the *Calcutta Weekly Notes* published by the High Court, augmented by the India Office files, and reports on Indian newspapers.

Secondary Sources

Anecdotes about Woodroffe appeared in several memoirs and biographies. Those of Ordhendu Coomar Ganguly, art historian and member of the Indian Society of Oriental Art, have provided information for chapters 4 and 6.[11] A Bengali biography of the tantric guru Sivacandra Vidyarnava by his disciple Vasanta Kumar Pal provides significant information on Woodroffe intermixed with legend. This source is examined in depth in chapter 6.[12] In the many biographies and memoirs concerning the Tagores, Woodroffe is one of the background figures in a world of charismatic personalities. But among these are significant references to the tantric leanings of Woodroffe and some of his European friends. These sources are also discussed in chapter 6.

Because the nature of this study has been inter-disciplinary, some chapters owe much, especially in theoretical matters, to the work of others who have opened up particular fields. For the historical background to the period when Woodroffe was a judge in Calcutta, Sumit Sarkar's history of the 'swadeshi' years is invaluable.[13] My chapter 4 owes much to the work of Partha Mitter and Tapati Guha-Thakurta on the relationship between orientalism and nationalism in the aesthetic appreciation of Indian art.[14] Chapter 9, on Tantra, draws much upon André Padoux's book on the doctrine of the Word,[15] and on Alexis Sanderson's articles which reconstruct the historical development of the saivite and śākta tantric sects and their literature.[16] For the mystical and theological world of Kashmir Śaivism and Śāktism I am especially indebted to the work of Debabrata Sen Sarma,[17] and Gavin Flood.[18]

Periodicals

Reviews of Woodroffe's writings appeared in many contemporary papers and journals, and a large collection of extracts was reprinted in his books, especially in the third edition of *Shakti and Shākta* [SS(3) ps. iii–xxvi]. Woodroffe is mentioned from time to time in British and Indian-owned English language newspapers in Calcutta. The Calcutta journal *Modern Review* provided a vivid week-by-week entry into the political, social and cultural world of Calcutta from 1907 when the journal started, while *The Theosophist* provided a picture of the period through the views and opinions of the Theosophical Society, with whom Woodroffe had significant connections, even though he was not a member. *Bhārat Varṣa* and *Baśumati*, two illustrated Bengali literary journals, had editors who were linked to Sivacandra Vidyarnava, and contained significant articles and obituaries of Woodroffe.

Part One

SIR JOHN WOODROFFE 1865–1936

A biographical study

Chapter One

GLIMPSES OF A LIFE

Camera and pen

Sir John Woodroffe does not tell us much about himself. He left no (or at least no surviving) diaries, and his letters reveal few intimacies. His writings for the most part avoid self-reference. But we do have portraits of him in his many-faceted life – in both the literal and figurative sense: photographs, as well as pen-portraits showing how he was seen through the eyes of others, and actions revealing how he presented himself to the gaze of those others. There is the orientalist scholar lecturing on Tantra to an eminent audience; and the pseudonymous 'Arthur Avalon' proclaiming his identification with things Indian by his dress at a party (chapter 8); the popular figure at the High Court (chapter 3); the cultured scholar and art connoisseur (chapter 4); the defender of Hindu culture against its detractors (chapter 5); and the various pictures of Woodroffe as a Tantric – slightly eccentric in the eyes of some, the devoted disciple of the guru to others (chapter 6). In most of his photographs in the literal sense he appears enigmatic and unhappy, never looking at the camera but with eyes either down on the ground or gazing at something unseen in the distance. It is the face of a very sensitive, seemingly deeply introverted person [plate 1].

A family photograph of him as a young man shows him in riding clothes, standing in the entrance of what for a time was his parents' home in England [plate 2]. The house was called Frensham Heights, near Farnham in Surrey, and the site is now a school. Though the original building the Woodroffes lived in has been demolished, the magnificent view from the top of the Heights can still be enjoyed today, and gives a glimpse of the wealth and privilege of the family who once owned the site. Writing on the back of the photograph states that this is "Jack", taken by his younger brother Alban.

Jack was the eldest of a family of four sons and three daughters. He was born in Calcutta on 15 December 1865 and baptised in St Peter's Anglican Church there in January 1866.[1] His father, James Tisdall Woodroffe, was a barrister of the High Court who became extremely successful in his profession. At the beginning of the twentieth century he was Advocate

General of Bengal, and a member of the Viceroy's Council, until he resigned from it after a quarrel with Lord Curzon.[2] The elder Woodroffe was one of the great figures at the Calcutta bar and amassed great wealth.[3] The *Calcutta Weekly Notes* often refers to the high fees which barristers could command, something which made litigation a very expensive affair for the public.[4]

The Woodroffes were a family of Irish Protestant clergy and James Tisdall seems to have been the only member of the immediate family to work in India,[5] but his wife, Florence Hume, came from a family who had lived there for several generations. She was born in India, the youngest child of James Hume, a cousin of Alan Octavian Hume who was among the founding members of the Indian National Congress, and one of a small group of British people who supported it in its early phase.[6] James Hume was Presidency Magistrate of Calcutta. Someone of the same name founded the only Calcutta club in the 1850s which was open to both English and Indian members,[7] and this might have been Florence's father. There was also a James Hume who was editor of the *Star* newspaper, but it is not clear if all three were the same person.

Alan Octavian Hume, like his cousin's grandson, not only supported Indians politically but was also drawn to Theosophy and Hinduism,[8] but both John Woodroffe's parents converted to Roman Catholicism when he was still a child. His mother was probably the Mrs Woodroffe who visited Cardinal Newman in 1873 in the company of Lady Herbert of Lea,[9] for her husband was soon afterwards giving generous donations to Catholic projects in Bengal. James Tisdall's conversion was said to have taken place in 1875,[10] and led to a passionately-held devotion to his new faith.[11] John and his next brother Francis were sent to Woburn Park, an attractively unconventional Catholic public school which opened in 1878. Its headmaster, Monsignor Lord Petre, had views on education which strongly emphasized the autonomy and freedom of the child. As we shall see in the next chapter, John Woodroffe may have felt himself particularly fortunate in being able to stay there throughout most of its seven brief years of existence. Afterwards he attended University College Oxford from 1884–8, where he was one of the first undergraduates to study for the Bachelor's Degree in Law. Training for a profession at Oxford was an innovation at the time, when the prevailing ideal of a 'liberal education' was opposed to specialisation.[12] Although Catholics had been admitted to the university since the 1850s, in the 1880s they were still discouraged by their Church from going there. Woodroffe's progressive headmaster, however, held different views.[13] The great Max Muller was a prominent personality at Oxford in the 1880s – although retired from his Chair in Comparative Philology – and he entertained people from all over the world, especially from India.[14] Woodroffe would also have been present at Oxford when the university honoured the ninety year old Brian Houghton

Hodgson (see below, chapter 7).[15] But if Woodroffe was ever inspired by such famous figures of nineteenth century orientalism, there is nothing in his writings to suggest it: on the contrary he consciously ploughed a different furrow.

A more pertinent influence – although Woodroffe hardly ever expressly mentions them – would have been the British school of Idealist, or Neo-Hegelian philosophers. T.H. Green had just died when Woodroffe became an undergraduate but his influence was still paramount at Oxford in the 1880s. Overthrowing the dominance of Utilitarianism and Scientific Materialism, the Idealists posited the notion of the Absolute or what was termed 'the supra-relational unity of all reality' – which they distinguished from our normal partial apprehension of truth. 'There is no truth but the Whole', they declared. Similarities to Hindu Vedanta attracted many Indians to this school.[16] Woodroffe believed in the primacy of what he called 'the Full or Whole Experience' [WAP:16][17] as distinct from the partial and varied experiences of the world of ordinary perception. But he did not equate any of the Hindu systems with Idealism: on the contrary he emphasized their 'realism'.[18] The significance of Idealism perhaps lies not so much in its direct influence as in its atmosphere. Woodroffe's profound interest in metaphysical problems and their solutions is clearly manifest in his attraction both to Vedanta and Tantrism. Such metaphysical concern is not fashionable in modern Western culture (unless through the direct influence of non-Western gurus or teachers), and can even appear exotic. In the period between the late nineteenth century and the First World War, however, when the school of Idealism was dominant in Britain and Europe, metaphysical discourse in 'West' and 'East' would have seemed closer than it does today.[19]

Taking his BCL in 1888, John Woodroffe was called to the Bar at the Middle Temple in 1889, and joined his father at the Calcutta Bar the following year. He quickly established himself as an expert on Indian Law, his first two publications being his lectures as Tagore Law Professor of Calcutta University in 1897.[20] He was promoted to the judiciary at the comparatively young age of thirty-nine in 1904. Whether or not the influence of his famous father played any part in this, the younger Woodroffe had produced another important book on Indian Law by this time in collaboration with a senior Indian judge, Sir Sayeed Ameer Ali. *The Law of Evidence* was regarded as an authoritative textbook and remained in print for a very long time.[21]

James Tisdall Woodroffe seems to have been a dominating personality, which helped to make him one of the famous figures at the Bar in his day, but it seems also to have made him a formidably authoritarian father. He banished his third son, Alban, both from the family and from the country for an incident involving a relationship with a girl while at his cadet school. His nephew James recounted Alban's story of what happened when as a young man he was summoned into the presence of his father, who had a map of the world spread out on a table in front of him. Alban was ordered to select a country from the map, and then was given some money for his passage and sent away. He chose Argentina without knowing anything about it – he had just been drawn to its warm orange colour. Alban eventually did rather well in Argentina and was later on reconciled with his father and even inherited his father's estate instead of his elder brothers. But his nephew James described this uncle as an extremely unpleasant authoritarian character.

James Tisdall made arrangements in his Will for his second son, Francis, to lose his inheritance if he should enter a marriage that was not approved by the Catholic Church. Francis Woodroffe never married, and his Will reveals that he had a long friendship with a woman who was not a Catholic. His nephew described him as a failed actor and a rather restless and unsuccessful person.

James Tisdall Woodroffe's eldest son John seems to have retained his trust, for he was executor of his father's Will, and the father and son lived together at the Bengal Club and in various lodgings until 1900, though they did not share Chambers.[22] This son, at least, did not appear cowed by his awesome father, for there is an amusing account of how the two Woodroffes once appeared on opposite sides of the same case and how the younger demolished the elder in court. O.C. Ganguly, at the time a young solicitor's clerk, describes a courtroom crowded with those eager to watch the battle between '*baṛa*' and '*chhoṭo*' Woodroffe. The younger man roundly accused his father of using dishonest arguments, and for some time afterwards the Bar lounge resounded to James Tisdall's outraged protest: 'John calls me dishonest!' His friends are reported as replying: 'He has found you out at last!'[23] This is strong evidence of John's independent spirit.

Despite his ability to hold his own with his father, it is nevertheless extremely unlikely that John Woodroffe could have gone so far as to openly display an interest in Tantra before James Tisdall's retirement from India in 1904, without losing his father's favour and his inheritance. He may well have been secretly drawn to it, however, much earlier. In 1894 his mother died at the age of only forty-eight. There is a cryptic reference by Woodroffe to 'a man I know who had lost his mother,' who was told by Vama Khappa – a Bengali Tantric saint of the last century – to seek out the Mother of the Universe.[24] It is highly probable that Woodroffe, though he normally avoided personal references, was here writing about himself. His attraction towards 'the Mother' as divinity in Her own right is prominent in his books.

It may have been soon after his father's retirement, when the younger Woodroffe had just become a judge, that another tantric saint, Sivacandra Vidyarnava, initiated him into tantric rituals. The main source for this story is the Bengali biography of the saint discussed in chapter 6. No dates are given to the events in the account, but if Woodroffe met the guru soon after becoming a judge in 1904, this would fit in with reports of him practising tantric yoga with his friend the art historian E.B. Havell, who left India in 1906. In 1907, Woodroffe was one of several High Court judges who were among the founder members of the Indian Society of Oriental Art, in which he soon took a leading role. He was a close friend of Abanindranath and Gaganendranath Tagore, the artist nephews of Rabindranath. He may have started studying Sanskrit around this time, or a little later in 1911. 1912 might have been the year of a controversial photograph taken at Konarak temple where Woodroffe, Ghose and a European friend wore Indian dress [plate 6]. As we have seen, the first books of Arthur Avalon were published the following year, in 1913. Woodroffe was knighted in 1915. He retired from the High Court in 1922 and the following year returned to University College Oxford to lecture in Indian Law.[25] He finally retired to the south of France in 1930 and died at Beausoleil, a suburb of Monte Carlo, in January 1936.

In 1902 John Woodroffe was married at the age of thirty-seven, to Ellen Elizabeth Grimson, then aged twenty-five.[26] She was a concert pianist and belonged to an extremely talented family. Her father Samuel Grimson, a violinist, seems to have been very keen to promote the musical education of his large family, especially the girls. Three of Ellen's sisters pursued successful careers on the concert platform, having been trained by their father from an early age.[27] James Woodroffe told me his parents met when his father attended one of his mother's concerts and thereafter they shared a love of music as well as an attraction towards Indian philosophy.

PORTRAITS

Sir Torick Ameer Ali

A lively picture of Woodroffe can be found in the memoirs of the son of Sir Sayeed Ameer Ali, Woodroffe's elder colleague and his first collaborator who was co-author of his legal textbooks (see above). The elder Ameer Ali was an Indian Muslim nationalist who has in modern times been claimed as an early progenitor of Pakistan,[28] and would not seem at first sight a very likely friend of someone like Woodroffe. But that their friendship was real is attested by the son in his memoirs, who portrays Woodroffe as a loveable eccentric. This is how he saw him in 1917:

> In appearance small and sallow, he had never in his life played an outdoor game, but on the other hand he never missed a race meeting. In repose he wore the mask of a disillusioned gargoyle: when amused

> that of a delighted goblin. His two passions in life were classical music, played for him by his wife, an accomplished pianist, and the more abstruse forms of Tantric philosophy. He was at the time engaged on his great work 'Shakti and Shākta'. Due to his pre-eminence as a pandit, Woodroffe J. was yearly elected to be president of the All India Cow Conference, an office which he held with outward decorum and some inward amusement. All these sinister tendencies, together with his rooted objection to wearing night-clothes profoundly disturbed my more conventional father, but fortunately for me had not impaired the friendship between the two.[29]

The elder Ameer Ali achieved high positions in British India, from which he had retired to England in 1904. He was a member of the Viceroy's Legislative Council, but according to one account he was not fully accepted socially by either the British or the Muslim communities in India, largely because he had an English wife. The Arabic scholar E. Denison Ross worried that Ameer Ali 'would not receive the send-off he would have liked' on his retirement.[30] Woodroffe's warm friendship with this man whose personal interests were so distant from his own, attests to the width of his friendships with Indian people, something which is obvious from the wide popularity Woodroffe acquired. By contrast, Denison Ross himself expresses the stereotypical British aloofness: social contact with Indians was rare, and personal friendships seemed to him impossible.[31]

Sir Torick Ameer Ali's account continues: 'It was Woodroffe J's habit after court hours to meditate, bare-headed and semi-clothed in an attitude of yoga on the house roof.' This piece of information leads up to an amusing story: once when he was thus meditating a Calcutta kite had swooped upon his balding head, mistaking it for something shiny, and caused temporary concussion. 'The greatest of Greek dramatists, he told me, suffered the same or an even worse experience.' Woodroffe could tell a joke at his own expense.

The house, we are informed, was in Camac Street. This is situated in the heart of the city close to its two major thoroughfares, Park Street and Chowringhi. It was a select neighbourhood inhabited by high officials of the 'Raj'. Woodroffe had taken the house over from another High Court judge. Thacker's Directory informs us that it was number 4. Government offices now occupy the large site. Perhaps the compound was sufficiently large to conceal the rooftop meditator from the street, but we can guess that Woodroffe would not worry at thus disturbing British-India's sensibilities.[32]

Although he was related to Alan Octavian Hume, Sir Torick Ameer Ali commented that Woodroffe himself took no interest in politics, and made fun of the title 'trustee for the Dumb Millions', once bestowed upon

Hume – 'such cant phrases he abhorred'.[33] The remark suggests that Woodroffe did not identify with his distinguished relative despite some similarities in their sympathies and interests.

We see straightaway that it was a salient aspect of Sir Torick's image of his host that he should be involved in 'abstruse Tantric philosophy' and engaged on 'his great work Shakti and Shākta'. One interesting piece of information that follows the passage quoted, is that this guest perceived a contradiction between his host being 'a fine scholar in a dead language' and his apparently poor linguistic ability in a modern Indian one.[34] Woodroffe's scholarly and philosophical interests are seen as one with his championship of cow protection and his meditation practice, and are all assigned by his guest to the image of lovable eccentricity he casts him in. Woodroffe's joke at his own expense perhaps shows that he accepted and acted up to this image. Sir Torick reassures us that Woodroffe's more abstruse interests 'did not exclude a lively interest in ordinary human affairs' nor 'a warm appreciation of a pretty woman'. Like others did, he comments admiringly on the Woodroffes' home, describing his brief stay there as 'a week of gracious living'.[35]

James Woodroffe

A powerful and very sad contrast with this lively and loving picture of Woodroffe is given in the memories of his son James, who was mostly describing a slightly later period, when his parents had returned to England. James was the only living person who was able to give me direct information about his father, but unfortunately he did not like talking about his family, and no-one could penetrate far behind the veil he drew over his childhood. Several years before I began my own research James was interviewed by Dr Louisa Finn for a short article.[36] When I first contacted him he immediately stated his dislike of 'interrogation' and was much on his guard. This might have been because he wanted to cover up a loss of memory, but he displayed what seemed like a carefully constructed pose of indifference at the mention of any member of his family.

It was evident, however, that the Woodroffes were a most unhappy family, at least in the latter part of their parents' lives when they were living in England and France. James was not close to his father and seemed to have had little communication with him, and the father seemed to have passed on nothing at all of his knowledge and interests to his son. James's picture of him was of someone extremely withdrawn and depressed, disillusioned with his life and enjoying no sense of achievement. He recalled long walks which the father and son would sometimes take together during which neither of them spoke a single word.

James had only faint memories of the time he lived with his parents in Calcutta as a child during the First World War, when it is significant that he thought his parents had few European friends, but many Indian ones. He remembered the Ghoses, and holidays which the two families took together at Ranchi, then a forest area in Bihar. James absolutely refused to countenance the idea that his father was a Hindu (let alone a Tantric of which he seemed not to have heard). When I ventured one day to ask him about reports that his father had an image of the Goddess in his Oxford home, to which he performed rituals, he replied curtly: 'Who's been spreading rumours like that?' James managed to convince Louisa Finn that his father wrote only as an objective scholar, and was not 'a secret adept'.[37] James himself was a practising Catholic. He said his father rarely went to Mass, but the children were all brought up as Catholics, and this could not be due entirely to the influence of their grandfather James Tisdall, who died in 1908 when the girls were small and James was not yet born. The girls boarded at a convent school in England, and James eventually went to the Benedictine school at Downside Abbey. Only James was with his parents in India, and even he only for a few years.

James' picture of his father's extreme reserve was shared by Lady Sonya Wilson, daughter of Woodroffe's friend E.B. Havell. Having known each other in India, the Havells and Woodroffes lived near each other in Oxford for a time. Lady Wilson knew Sir John when she was a child of six and remembers him as 'an extremely cold man' who never spoke to her. Woodroffe's obituary in *The Times* of London alluded to his reserve, which was politely put down to 'the shyness of the absorbed scholar' which made him 'slow to reveal his mind to a casual acquaintance'. However 'he could talk much and well when in congenial company'.[38]

These last descriptions are in contrast to Woodroffe as we shall meet him in the following chapters, as the extremely energetic organiser who had extensive and very warm contacts with people in many areas of Indian life beyond his favourite fields of art and tantric studies. The change is perhaps evidence of greater personal unhappiness after his retirement, when it seems the shadows gathered quickly around him in the form of increased family tensions and his own and family illnesses. He looks unhappy in the photograph in Plate 1 which, James informed me, was taken soon after his return to England. Another photograph, taken in the garden at Oxford a few years later, James introduced by saying: 'This is my father in one of his silent moods'. His posture seems to express deep dejection [plate 3]. The two heaviest of all the burdens would have been the death of his daughter Barbara, and his own Parkinson's Disease from which he eventually died at the age of seventy-one.

The Woodroffes' Marriage: Ellen Woodroffe [plate 4]

James' memories of his mother were stronger than those of his father, though not more favourable. Ellen Grimson had never been to India before her marriage, but like many artistic and fashionable people of the day, she was a Theosophist and James believed it was she who influenced her husband to take an interest in Indian religion. It seemed to him that up until his marriage his father had been a more extrovert personality, interested only in horse-racing, for which he had a passion, and in foreign travel. As a young man he used to ride as a jockey and enjoyed steeplechasing. Before his marriage he used to spend his vacations from India exploring East and South East Asia and shortly after it, he and Ellen attempted their own brief incursion into Tibet, inspired by the example of the Younghusband expedition. (They were soon intercepted and quickly but politely sent home again.) Around this time James believed his father must have experienced some sort of religious conversion which changed his personality and he put this down to the influence of his marriage. But Ellen was not the main influence, for we shall see that Woodroffe's relations of friendship or discipleship with Indian men were probably a far stronger factor. It is interesting to see the early love of adventure and exploration in 'the orient' turning in middle life into an inner exploration into new areas of the spirit which belonged to the image of this 'mystic East'. It was an inner pilgrimage made by other Westerners before and since, especially Francis Younghusband himself, with whom he was acquainted in Calcutta and London. But Woodroffe otherwise presents a strong contrast to the 'great imperial adventurer'.[39]

Ellen shared her husband's attraction to Hindu philosophy. The couple began studying Sanskrit together, and the name 'Ellen Avalon', was given as co-author to the translation of *Hymns to the Goddess* in 1913, one of the first Avalon publications. According to several accounts the couple at first shared an interest in Tantra too and were initiated together. But according to the Ghose family, Ellen later grew increasingly anxious about her husband's deepening involvement, and urged him to return to England. At the end of her life she herself converted to Roman Catholicism quite independently of her husband's Catholic background; indeed James believed that in this too it was she who influenced him, leading to his being re-baptised the year before he died. (See below chapter 6).

Ellen continued to perform as a pianist in Calcutta, at both public and private concerts,[40] and the Woodroffes were highly thought of there for their taste in music, as in art. Denison Ross, who lived in Calcutta from 1902 till 1911,[41] was an amateur singer. In his letters of 1904 to his fiancée (also a concert pianist) he describes the great honour he felt at having been invited to sing at one of the Woodroffes' *soirées* and his anxiety to perform at his best. It was far more important for him than other singing engagements at the time. The Viceroy had lent the Woodroffes his band for the occasion.[42] A little later, he mentions a dinner at the Lieutenant Governor's where Mrs Woodroffe played the piano.[43] This was during the first decade of the century and indicates that at least at that time the

Woodroffes were well integrated into British society in Calcutta. The same seems true in 1912 when Alexandra David-Neel described a grand musical *soirée* at the Woodroffes where the guests were from both the European and Indian communities. According to the Ghose family, the Woodroffes were eventually socially ostracised by the British in Calcutta and they believed this was another reason why Ellen wanted her husband to retire early from India. Other sources suggested he had been forced to retire by official pressure.[44]

It seems that Ellen Woodroffe had a strong personality and identity of her own in Calcutta. Besides her music, she founded the French Literary and Artistic Society, at which Woodroffe gave a lecture in French in 1917.[45] But according to her son's description she was not a happy person. There were rumours of mental illness in the recollections of people I talked to at the High Court, though I have not been able to corroborate these. But her son James gave vivid testimony to her very bad relationship with his two sisters after she returned to England – something which he put down to the very difficult temperament of his mother. Barbara, the younger daughter, died of anorexia at the age of eighteen, in 1925. Over twenty years later, her elder sister Nancy gave away to a taxi-driver a marble bust of her deceased mother because she could not bear the thought of living with her memory. Amid great domestic turbulence, according to James, his father tried ineffectually to make peace when he did not withdraw completely. 'So that,' he told me 'was what life was like in the Woodroffe family.' Perhaps Ellen's unhappiness was due in part to the frustration of a very talented woman having to forgo a career on the concert platform, which, James said, would have been considered beneath her status as the wife of a judge.

It would seem that by far the happiest periods of Sir John Woodroffe's life were those he spent in India, where we shall see how significant were his relations with Indian male friends, admirers and mentors. But a strong early influence on him was perhaps that of another man: his headmaster Monsignor Lord Petre. It was not unusual for a Victorian headmaster to exert a powerful influence – but Woburn Park had a most unusual headmaster and was a most original school. We look in the next chapter at Woodroffe's first 'public' career there, and at Lord Petre's individual brand of Catholic Liberalism.

Chapter Two

THE YOUNG POLITICIAN

Woburn Park School

Monsignor Lord Petre was a dynamic, eccentric but attractive personality, a descendant of one of the few old Roman Catholic aristocratic families of England. He opened his school at the family estate of Woburn Park, near Weybridge in Surrey, in 1878. Jack Woodroffe and his younger brother Francis had been in England at least from 1872 for education by a private tutor. 'Dear Mama,' the 7 year old Jack wrote to his mother in that year, 'I am very sorry that you cannot come home just yet for I am longing to see you, and so is Frankie.' He wanted to have an ape: 'I should like you to ask Papa to send me one. I know that there are a lot out there.'[1]

He and Frankie joined Woburn Park in 1879, when Jack would have been 13 years old, and they stayed there until 1884 when he went to Oxford University, and when the school itself closed due to financial difficulties. Jack and Francis Woodroffe were among those who experienced longest its unusually benevolent atmosphere in comparison with most other contemporary public schools, whether catholic or protestant. It was a highly original educational experiment that attracted a lot of controversy in the catholic community.

Information on Lord Petre and Woburn Park School is to be found in nine issues of the school's journal, *The Amoeba*, which is preserved at Downside Abbey near Bath in Somerset; and in a chapter devoted to Woburn in *Schools* by Colonel Raleigh Chichester, which is an account of its author's inspection in 1881 of the major catholic public schools of his day.[2] Lord Petre's ideas on catholic education were presented in several pamphlets which he wrote just before he opened his school – writings which were part of a heated debate on the subject.[3] Drawing on these sources and on the contemporary catholic press, an article was published by Victor McClelland on the school and its headmaster in *Victorian Studies* in 1972.[4] A biography of a former pupil, the singer Gervase Elwes, describes Woburn Park and the personality of its headmaster.[5] I am indebted to research by Father Stewart Foster O.S.M. for first drawing my attention to these sources and the story of Woburn Park School.[6]

Lord Petre founded his school at a time of debate about catholic education. It was felt that catholic public schools compared unfavourably with the famous protestant institutions like Eton and Harrow and provided a narrower education; discipline was harsh; and the catholic aristocracy were suspicious of the strong monastic influence in their schools. Although Monsignor Petre was a priest and a celibate, he was not a monk and his school was not run by a religious order. Its atmosphere seems to have been more 'worldly' than that of other contemporary catholic institutions; nor did Petre envisage any part of its purpose as being to provide a recruiting ground for the priesthood or monastic orders.[7] On the contrary, it appears that the aim of Woburn Park was to produce a type of catholic gentleman, scholarly, cultured and urbane, who had benefitted from the same kind of 'liberal education' that was seen as the prerogative of the sons of the protestant aristocracy. Perhaps this was why the newly converted Woodroffes favoured it. Its moral aims were couched in the language of nineteenth century gentlemanly virtues: a sense of honour and self-reliance.[8]

Lord Petre's experiment, however, was more than merely an elitist attempt to appeal to the aristocracy. His educational reforms were quite original and aroused controversy because of his rejection of authoritarian discipline and because of the manner of his school's organisation. Its most original feature was its parliament modelled on Westminster, which governed many aspects of school life. The boys sat for imaginary constituencies, formed themselves into government and opposition, formed cabinets and framed the school rules through 'parliamentary' bills. In both decor and procedure it was an exact replica of the House of Commons. Raleigh Chichester gives us a colourful picture of the parliament at work, with all the panoply and regalia of the real thing, even though it was housed in an iron hut:

> . . . the general arrangement is as closely as possible a copy of that of the House of Commons. Looking up the room, one sees on each side three long rows of cushioned benches, dotted with boys wearing dark clothes and tall hats (the dress is de rigeur). On our left are the ministerial benches, on the right the Opposition . . . At the end of the room, on a raised platform, is the Speaker's chair under its canopy. In that chair sits the Speaker (Mr Petre) in flowing wig and robes over his usual clerical costume . . . The Sergeant-at-arms, in black suit, with knee-breeches, dress-sword and a gold collar across his shoulders, moves freely about the house and ushers Mr Speaker in, with all due pomp and ceremony, when, on his entry, the mace is borne in before him and placed on the table. The scene is one of sustained animation . . .[9]

It was not just an amateur debating society, for real power struggles took place in the parliament and the pupils were not always shielded from them.

Any discontent in the school gravitated towards the opposition, 'whose leader, a young gentleman who evinces Radical proclivities, sat for Birmingham', wrote Chichester. The school was divided into three age-bands. Senior pupils sat in the parliament by right; juniors were present only as observers; and the middle group, the junior-seniors were elected: one member for every four boys. He continued:

> The object of the whole scheme is governmental as well as educational ... It is pleasant to see little junior-seniors jumping perkily up addressing all kinds of Questions to the Captain of the School, the Games Captain – boys twice their size and weight, who have to answer in the deferential manner with which ministers disguise their real feelings.[10]

The parliament also acted as a court of justice. In Chichester's presence there was a trial at the bar of the House of a case of bullying, which led to the expulsion of two members.[11] Petre sought to control bullying by creating a public opinion in the school against it; and the system of 'fagging' at the more famous public schools was not practised at Woburn.

The visitor was clearly impressed by Woburn's system of government but he considered it depended very much upon Lord Petre's dynamic personality: 'In his mind is the battery,' wrote Chichester and 'the parliament and all else are but wires'. He noted the 'quite extraordinary' personal influence Petre had over the boys as individuals. In this respect at least, however, this headmaster was not unique in Victorian England.[12]

The Curriculum

Lord Petre's views on curriculum as he expressed them in his pamphlets also differed from those of other catholic educators, and in many respects from the Victorian ethos in general. He protested against the cult of manliness in public schools, declaring himself in favour of the cultivation of mind and spirit rather than the body. Although he encouraged outdoor games, he complained: 'How long are we to suffer the tyranny of muscular Christianity?' and averred that 'men of genius never have been, and never will be, famous as athletes.'[13]

Not only was the life of the mind to be set free from an excessive emphasis upon sport, but it was not to be cramped either by narrow educational aims. Pupils at Woburn were encouraged to read what they liked – a big departure from the system in other catholic schools. Classics were to be taught with an emphasis upon their literary aspects rather than the philological. Petre called for greater openness towards secular knowledge and considered that natural science should be given a dominating place in the curriculum. He pleaded: 'Let us not keep ourselves more aloof than we are already from the world's intellectual life by a too timorous attitude of mind.' He also insisted that the young should not be crammed with factual knowledge, but should have opportunities 'for reverie, for private reading, for the action of the many selective tendencies of the mind in youth . . .'[14]

These ideas were set out in pamphlets written by Petre before he opened his school. But a timetable printed in *The Amoeba* bears out Chichester's claim that there was less difference in practice between the curriculum of Woburn Park and that of other public schools. Science, for example, did not seem to have as prominent a place as Petre claimed for it in theory, while the whole of the afternoon, every day, was devoted to Games – mainly cricket or football. There does not appear to have been very much time left completely free, either, though there were several hours set aside for private study.[15] The upper forms were divided into a 'classical' and a 'modern' side. There was not very much difference between them: both spent most of their time on Latin, French, Mathematics and English composition; while the classical side also devoted much time to Greek, replaced on the modern side by German and English history. The latter had one session a week of Science, while for the classical side it was an optional additional subject. Both sides had just one session a week of Religious Instruction. Woodroffe's fluency in French in later life seems to have had its foundation in the prominence given to it in the Woburn curriculum. It seems he was very good at Latin – a visiting inspector's report picked him out for praise for one of his translation papers.[16]

THE PARLIAMENT AND WOODROFFE'S 'CAREER'

The Amoeba gives an intermittent but fascinating glimpse of the school's parliament at work, and shows us that Jack Woodroffe played an active role in it. In 1881 when the parliament was inaugurated he was already a senior, so he took his seat by right and adopted the imaginary constituency of Greenwich. He took little part in the earlier sessions, but by 1882 he was becoming prominent in the ranks of a radical opposition party – the group gathered around the radical 'member for Birmingham' noticed by Raleigh Chichester. Like some others who joined the opposition, however, he seems to have had conservative instincts at heart once he acquired power himself! In November 1883, during his final year, he became Prime Minister and Captain of the School and the last issue of *The Amoeba* contains his lengthy address to parliament in that capacity, which we will examine later. This was also, as it turned out, to be the final year of the school's existence, and *The Amoeba* leaves us with the scene of Woodroffe enjoying an apparently unrivalled supremacy after what seems to have been a chaotic power struggle. For the first time in the parliament's history there was a completely empty opposition bench! We do not know what happened after that in the parliament, but the school had closed by the summer of 1884.[17]

The parliament therefore existed for four years from 1881–4. Debates were recorded in each issue of *The Amoeba* but as this appeared only intermittently there are gaps in the story. Lord Petre as Speaker of the House and Sovereign as well, had both an advisory role and an ultimate veto – but that the boys had real power over many aspects of their communal life through their parliament is indicated by the nature of the bills presented to it.[18] It encountered the kind of problems one might be inclined to expect that it would: members had difficulty forming themselves into coherent 'political parties' founded on principles and tended instead to form shifting factions, with much crossing of the floor of the House! There were sudden falls of government and periods of chaos caused by divided cabinets, and attempts made by some to change the constitution in order to gain or hold on to power. The history of Woburn's Parliament as recorded in *The Amoeba* is fully as troubled as one might expect that of any 'fledgling democracy' to be. Complaints of inattention among some members, including chatting outside the lobbies and missing the vote, need to be balanced by the obvious fact that the sittings aroused much excitement. The biography of Gervase Elwes describes how he was pulled out of his bed in the middle of the night by his excited fellow pupils to take part in the division of the House.[19] The pages of the school journal reflect the immense pride the pupils took in their institutions of 'State' and the uniqueness of their school. 'Woburn without its Parliament would be like the play Hamlet without Hamlet,' wrote Chichester.[20]

A power struggle between the junior–seniors, the second of the three age-groups, and the seniors formed the dominant theme in the history of this parliament. For example, a bill introduced in the first session to give the junior–seniors certain duties in the library and on the cricket field was defeated due to the vigorous opposition of G.F.Stafford, who had attached to it the emotive term 'fagging' – a system well-known and feared in other public schools. Stafford however, soon became Prime Minister himself and immediately attempted to introduce similar measures, which he described by the euphemistic term 'mutual subjection, constitutionally defined' – a phrase greeted with much irony by the new opposition! By this time the defence of the 'liberties' of the junior–seniors had passed to the new opposition group among whom Jack Woodroffe began to scale the ladder of power, until 'Greenwich' (i.e. Woodroffe) became known as 'Birmingham's right-hand man. By the time Jack became Prime Minister himself, the junior–seniors bill had already passed into law and the opposition to it had crumbled – while the member for 'Birmingham' had suffered the fate of many another radical idealist and had been left in the political wilderness! This last gentleman, however, had clearly gone too far by challenging the position of the Sovereign (Petre) himself and attempting to form a Republic. His brief period in 'government', had been an era of chaos. Despite having been prominently associated with the revolutionary party, Jack claimed his position was one of moderation and compromise between 'extremes'.[21] (As we shall see in due course, this was rather typical of him.) In his inaugural speech as Prime Minister, he proclaimed his loyalty to the Crown and declared categorically that the experiment with democracy was over! In a long speech which already reflects his adult style, he announced a new era of stability and reconciliation. The story is told through the nine issues of *The Amoeba* with a great deal of adult seriousness, through leader columns discussing the political principles involved and articles by political correspondents analysing the state of the parties, all of it being written in a style which would not have been out of place in the columns of *The Times*.

Despite the evidence of machiavellian tactics displayed by some in parliament, it seems Woburn's junior–seniors were genuinely safe from the kind of 'fagging' their contemporaries endured in other public schools. Although the various 'governments' were always led by seniors, the second age group wielded enough influence through their representation to make any undue oppression of them difficult – so Woburn's 'constitutional safeguards' worked to that extent. Besides, Woburn had an articulated public opinion which was against the sort of abuses practised in other schools. The seniors in parliament made an ethical distinction between 'subjection' through purely public duties of an impersonal nature and a right to claim the kind of arbitrary power and command of personal services that the term 'fagging' usually implied. At the same time, there appeared a paragraph of explanation in *The Amoeba* reassuring the juniors in particular that they would be protected from bullying by older pupils.[22] The idea throughout was that Woburn was not going to follow the bad examples of other public schools. That the regime at Woburn was milder than these is affirmed by two sources. G.F.Stafford, the former 'Prime Minister' (later to be Governor General of Nigeria), wrote to the school's journal from Balliol College Oxford in 1883:

> It is no empty boast when we say that there are few if any schools in England where the members of the school enjoy so much real freedom and independence, where authority is so highly respected and reverenced, and punishment reduced to such a minimum as it is at Woburn School.[23]

The biographers of Gervase Elwes record that he first went to the Oratory School at Birmingham founded by Cardinal Newman, where he hated the 'tough' side of school life, by which he meant bullying. He was taken away when he fell ill and happily ended his schooldays at Woburn Park 'the like of which, so far as I know, has never before or since existed', he said.[24] Making a comparison with the Jesuit-run college of Stoneyhurst at the same period, Victor McClelland pointed out that the main complaint of aristocratic parents against Stoneyhurst was its harshness.[25]

The Constitutional Court

Bills were presented to parliament with meticulous attention to detail and were debated clause by clause through committees. Alongside the parliament, the court of constitutional justice interpreted disputed clauses. Members of government and opposition took on parallel identities as barristers, judges, crown solicitor and attorney general, and had to argue their points in legal language before Petre as chief justice. They seem to have taken to the procedure with the same ease with which they adapted to the forms and procedures of parliament. Here, too, Jack Woodroffe sometimes took a prominent role. The cases in court were argued with all the solemnity which attached to the parliament and were reported in *The Amoeba* in a similar vein. To a lay observer the reports, in fact, read just like the real thing and involve lengthy hair-splitting over precise meanings of words. In one issue, for example, several columns of the journal are devoted to reporting meticulous discussions around the exact meaning of a school term![26]

In both parliament and the court of justice it is evident that the headmaster played an important personal role, alternately arguing and arbitrating on contested issues. Raleigh Chichester was no doubt correct in saying that the system could not work without him. Nevertheless, it is remarkable how these sons of the upper classes took to the political and legal niceties of their institutional life without, apparently, much formal teaching beforehand in constitutional history or the law. It seemed to come to them like second nature.

The Amoeba

Why the school journal had this name is explained at the end of this chapter. The journal reflects the atmosphere of maturity which some critics of the school apparently considered precocious.[27] If it were not for the assurance, repeated in every issue, that the magazine was entirely the work of boys in their leisure time, one might be inclined to believe it was written by Petre or another adult. In fact the editor was either Petre or, more probably, G.F.Stafford. Jack Woodroffe was on the staff of writers.[28] The style is fairly uniform, but the content of the political articles (whether to do with Woburn or national politics) is not, and reflects opposing opinions. All the contributions in the earlier issues are written in a uniform very literary style and do not reveal much individuality in their authors. They are all either anonymous or signed by a pseudonym. The non-political articles read like English composition essays and cover a range of general topics such as 'The English and French Armies', 'Artifice in Art', 'A summer day in the country'. The most thoughtful essays were usually those to do with English history or politics: such as 'The Future of Whiggism' (by a Conservative) and 'Despotic and Democratic Governments' (by a Liberal). There was only one article about religion or philosophy. This was entitled 'The Growth of Thought, its Dangers and Safeguards'; it was about the challenge to Catholics of agnosticism and atheism, and it advocated a liberal, open attitude to religious doubt. (This article carried a note from the editor stating that its author had had no formal training in philosophy or logic, which shows these subjects were not taught at the school.)[29] Though this article possibly might be by Woodroffe, it could just as easily be by anyone else, for it is generally impossible to detect a personal style in the journal. Apart from showing that he obviously had a literary inclination, Jack's participation in *The Amoeba* does not bring us any nearer to his youthful outlook, and in particular does not tell us what his religious inclinations were while he was young. But as only one religious article appeared in the journal anyway, we can assume the ethos of the school was not a specially religious one. The aim of Woburn Park, whatever Petre's personal religious feelings were, was to turn out cultured gentlemen, well at home with the world, not to produce 'devotees' or 'renunciates'. In one of his pamphlets Petre said he was aiming at 'the abolition of asceticism, of mortification, of piety.'[30]

Jack Woodroffe's Personality

The high seriousness of the journal relaxes in some later issues: poetry makes its appearance (to protests from some critics) and gradually increases in volume, and there are a few lighter articles – it begins to look more recognisable as a school magazine. The sixth issue contains a satirical poem on the parliament entitled 'The Birds' Council' – with illustrations. The members were represented as various species of bird and their portraits were cleverly superimposed onto ornithological drawings; captions beneath each drawing described the habits of each 'species'. 'Greenwich' (Woodroffe) became 'the crested cockatoo' and the unkind caption read: 'This is an arrogant bird, and pecks other birds; but being weak, is often pecked badly in return.'[31] Many of the other captions were uncomplimentary but few were so cruel as this. Perhaps it was written by a personal enemy. Jack's younger brother Frank Woodroffe seems to have been more popular.

The seventh issue contains another political satire: a clever parody of *The Pirates of Penzance* with the members for 'Birmingham' and 'Greenwich' singing a duet. 'Birmingham' is made to sing: 'I am the very model of a modern rampant radical', while 'Greenwich' appears to support him while all the time having another agenda of his own.[32] In the ninth and last issue, a junior–senior writes light-heartedly about various characters at the school. Of the parliament he writes: 'Sometimes Woodroffe major makes a long speech, then you take an interest, but when he drums away on one subject all the time you wish you had never come.' Later on the same anonymous author remarks: 'There is a touch of the swag about Woodroffe major'.[33]

Woodroffe's Speech to 'Parliament'

This final issue of the journal also contains Jack's inaugural speech as 'Prime Minister'. Delivered in November 1883, when he was seventeen, it is already recognisably his style. Reviewing the history of the governments of the past three years he remarked that they had 'often taken up extreme positions and principles', while 'the truth generally lay between the extremes'. (As he was to do in later life, whatever his position he always tried to claim the middle ground). He went on:

> and the result of many stirring conflicts in the house is that we have come at last to a conclusion which I may take to be the truth – part of the truth at all events [he likes to modify his stronger statements]; and . . . there can be little doubt as to the main lines of action likely to be taken by the present Government . . . The policy will be one of sense and practicality.

Cries of "Hear! Hear!" suggested that he was in tune with a new spirit in the school, which seems to have grown battle weary. His government would, he promised:

> endeavour . . . to secure as quiet and tranquil a session in Parliament and in the nation generally [ie. the school] as possible. We shall endeavour to avoid unnecessary or heated discussion in the House.

Indeed, in promising everyone a quiet life he went even further:

> We shall attempt little that is original; we do not indeed propose to be original in anything that is of importance.

A most remarkable promise indeed for any government to make! He then went on to cover himself in case he did in fact need to do anything new:

> Our policy is based on the policy of those who have gone before us, but of course the form of our measures will vary on account of the change of circumstances which has been brought about by the growth of the nation.

So after denying that he was going to do anything at all innovatory, he then went on to announce several major changes. The first was a statement of principle: that the seniors must be recognised as the most important section of the school. This might seem uncontroversial enough – except that Woodroffe himself had just been involved in an opposition party that had challenged this idea all along. He was also going to introduce legislation to regulate the senior common room – this actually provoked gasps of surprise – and he proposed a big constitutional change: the introduction of some form of representation in the parliament for the juniors – something which does not appear to have been contemplated before. The only comment on his speech was made by an old boy who was visiting the school, who remarked that:

> Immediately the Prime Minister had stated that the Government were not going to . . . be original in anything they did, he said that the government intended bringing in a bill regulating the Senior Common Room – and what was that but a new idea?

Everyone laughed.[34]

It was very typical of Woodroffe. We shall see how in his defence of Tantrism he played down its differences from the rest of Hinduism. This was linked to his constant anxiety to appear to compromise – to have the 'middle' position, to be 'balanced', to hold the view with which all reasonable people would identify. Despite the fact that he did, in fact, take up quite controversial positions and strike out in new directions, he shows a strange timidity over conflict. This could reflect something of Lord Petre's conception of a gentleman, expressed in a letter to Gervase Elwes where he wrote: 'I hope you will settle down into a pattern English gentleman of no extreme opinions or violence of thought'.[35] It seems as if Woodroffe retained this ideal of mildness, tolerance and compromise, whatever strong views he actually possessed.

A situation to which he refers in this speech also points forward to his later outlook. At one point he spoke to loud cheers about the need 'to vindicate ourselves against those who wilfully and wantonly misrepresent or attack us.' This time he was speaking, not of himself or his government, but of the school. Victor McClelland shows us how Petre's educational theory and his experiment at Woburn provoked intense criticism in the catholic press, and that a particularly virulent attack on Petre appeared in an anonymous pamphlet about the school.[36] In one of his own pamphlets Petre intimated that he had been threatened with censure by the catholic hierarchy by having his name put on the Index, and he wrote: 'I have been made to drink deep of the hemlock-cup of unorthodoxy.'[37] Perhaps the abuse directed at Woburn and its headmaster prepared Woodroffe to take up the defence of a particularly despised and reviled brand of Hinduism. Once when explaining what first drew him to Tantra, he said: 'Following the track of unmeasured abuse I have always found something good' [SS:78]. Could it have been through his experience of Woburn Park School and its critics that he first learned this lesson?

Personality of Lord Petre

Petre stood in a tradition of charismatic and powerful nineteenth century pedagogues. As P.J. Rich points out:

> Not accidentally did Thomas Arnold serve Rugby as chaplain as well as headmaster. The Victorian headmaster was King, Prime Minister and Archbishop of Canterbury rolled into one.[38]

A portrait of Lord Petre[39] shows him to have been an extremely handsome man, and with his youthful spirit and obvious benevolence, one can well imagine the personal effect he had on the lives of his pupils. Already, when a young assistant master at the Benedictine school of Downside Abbey before he founded Woburn Park, Petre attracted a quite unusual degree of hero worship among the boys.[40] The biographers of Gervase Elwes noted 'the powerful and delightful influence of his exceptional head master':

> Petre took the most extraordinary trouble to understand the characters and difficulties of individual boys. The school was not large, and consequently he had far more opportunities for this than any ordinary schoolmaster. The complete success with which he gained Gervase's confidence, respect and deep affection had a profound effect on the boy's development . . .[41]

When Jack and Frank Woodroffe first joined the school at the beginning of 1879 they would both have been junior–seniors, aged between twelve to fifteen, and it was to them, according to Chichester that Petre devoted most of his attention. He liked to relax with them in their common room, where the atmosphere he created was like an aristocratic drawing room 'not indeed as to furniture. . .but as to the tone and manners of its inmates.' He had a favourite armchair where he would sit and read or chat to the boys and listen to their music. Raleigh Chichester said that he himself passed a pleasant evening in this room.[42]

The atmosphere of these sessions was described by a junior–senior in the rather 'flowery' literary style of *The Amoeba*:

> Our fire-side evenings have been rich in interest and amusement. Spell-bound we have listened to a 'sweet familiar voice' [Petre's] declaiming to us in tones full of sympathy Tennyson's Idylls of the King and we have thrilled and marvelled at the deeds of noble King Arthur, of Lancelot and the holy Sir Galahad.[43]

They also read from other poets and from Shakespeare, and there was music and songs. This was recorded in 1881, and by that time the elder Woodroffe was no longer a junior–senior.

One wonders if indeed Raleigh Chichester had been slightly shocked by the 'easy familiarity that existed between Petre and the junior–seniors'.[44]

Chichester recorded without comment that the headmaster's private sitting room opened off their dormitory with his bedroom adjoining, and that in the sitting room were 'a couple of beds for boys who happened to be a little more delicate than the rest.'[45] A modern observer might perhaps have been more suspicious about Petre's relationship with his pupils. In his pamphlets he echoed the same strictures against 'immorality' that were held by other catholic educators but he had a noticeably more relaxed attitude towards it, suggesting that some saw 'sin where no sin be.'[46]

Aesthetics and Ritual

A marked difference between Woburn Park and other catholic schools of the time lay in its rejection of austerity. Gervase Elwes had disliked the spartan surroundings of the Oratory School and found Woburn very different:

> So far as the refinements of life were concerned, conditions at Woburn formed a marked contrast with those at any public school of the day. In a very fine country house, the beautiful setting alone distinguished it; and one point of interest is that the pupils were allowed plenty of hot water to wash in – a dangerous innovation – and personal cleanliness and tidiness were at a premium.[47]

This was on a par with Petre's aesthetic love of beautiful surroundings and his sense of place and setting. Before opening Woburn Park, while he was still an assistant master at Downside Abbey school, he had benefitted that institution by donating a library, a cloister and a swimming pool, all of them exquisitely designed and furnished. There too his feeling for theatre had expressed itself when he produced plays and opera with great attention to their sets.[48] This is also very obvious in the external trappings of his parliament, which some critics ridiculed as mere ostentation. But there was a rather beautiful defence of the school ceremonial in *The Amoeba*:

> To meet such an attack we wish to confess and to confess with pride, the great value we set upon a sparing, though careful use of ceremonial. We envelop all our doings, even our driest and most practical business, in those formalities which have become historical throughout the system of the English nation ... Surely all these are but externals – in themselves mere nothings; yet who has not felt their influence? Every branch of life is green in its leafage of dramatic form, and if that leafage be removed the tree is bare and far from yielding fruit. To be real, our Parliament must be to us, even at first sight, really and indeed the House of Commons ...[49]

It is easy to see how such a sense of theatre in everyday life would appeal to schoolboys, but here Woburn Park was sharing in a characteristic of other public schools. P.J. Rich makes much of the connections between public school ritual and the pageantry of empire.[50] What he leaves out, is that before ritual could play a part in empire, it first had a crucial role to play in parliamentary democracy in England itself – something which Petre and his pupils had realised.

As for the religious rituals of Woburn school life, *The Amoeba* tells us that they were celebrated with great beauty and splendour[51] as one can well imagine they were, but little else is said about them, and it seems they did not arouse so much fascination as the 'secular' rituals focused on the parliament. One gets the impression, however, that the secular did not invade the religious realm as much as it did at the protestant schools where Rich suggests that school and imperial ritual took over the services in the chapels:

> In looking for religious influences in the Empire, the chapel buildings and the attitudes engendered suggest the possibility of an Imperial cult that was as much sustained by an ambitious public school, lodge and government ritualism as by Christian theology.[52]

Although it may be possible to see a connection between the elaborate ritual life of Woburn and Woodroffe's later interest in Tantra, it must be noted that the rituals belonged to very different spheres: the latter were private, personal and mystical or magical in intent; the former were entirely corporate and secular. It could be rather because he turned *away* from the secular imperial 'cult' – or, at Woburn, had been less exposed to it than others – that Woodroffe was less impressed with Empire than most other contemporary British people in India; but this did not apply to everyone else at Woburn. Generally its pupils served the empire in later life as much as those from protestant public schools.

CONCLUSION: WOBURN PARK'S INFLUENCE ON WOODROFFE

Woburn Park was considered by many to be a unique institution, and I think we can agree with them. Its pupils were spared the brutalities of life in both the protestant and the catholic major public schools. There can be no doubt that its regime was far milder, and Lord Petre seems to have been exceptionally humane and respectful of the dignity and autonomy of schoolboys.

Petre promoted values of manliness and vigour at Woburn, but in a mental and cultural rather than a physical, athletic sphere. There was an atmosphere of conscious aestheticism and refinement – which we shall see was to be reflected later on in Calcutta in the Woodroffes' beautiful homes, and their participation in the social circle around the Indian Society of

Oriental Art. Woodroffe's love of music, and his wide reading in several European languages in philosophy, religion and science, reflect Woburn's culture. So do his liberal, tolerant opinions on religious matters. Although we cannot guess what Lord Petre would have made of his former pupil embracing tantric Hinduism, it is likely that in every other respect, he would have seen in Sir John Woodroffe the epitome of the refined, urbane gentleman of wide culture he wanted to create.

Finally, although many of the links in the chain that led Woodroffe towards Tantrism are missing to us – and especially disappointing is the absence of any clue as to his personal religious feelings in youth – there can be no doubt that Lord Petre's liberal Catholicism was one important ingredient. Petre rejected the austerity and asceticism of nineteenth century English Catholicism; at the same time he recognized the value of ritual in a context that affirmed the senses. This was perhaps a unique combination which Woodroffe could quite likely have felt he rediscovered in Hindu Tantrism.

WOODROFFE AND PETRE ON EDUCATION: A COMPARISON

Tradition versus Vitality

Both Lord Petre and Sir John Woodroffe wrote on education, albeit in very different spheres. Woodroffe participated in the contemporary debate on Indian education when he was in Calcutta and his statements on the subject will be discussed in chapter 5. Although at first sight the problems of education in British India may seem a long way from those of the education of English Catholics in the nineteenth century, there are interesting similarities, sufficient for Woodroffe to have felt on familiar ground. Both his essays and those of Petre on catholic education deal with problems around modernization, in a context where the modernizing impetus came from what was perceived as an alien culture impinging upon a system of traditional values. In the pamphlets of Petre the challenging factor was defined as 'Protestantism'; in the writings of Woodroffe in the Bengali environment it was called 'the West' or 'the English'. To the Indians Woodroffe was addressing, the problem had apparently been framed quite simply by British colonial domination. For nineteenth century Catholics in England, it had arisen, paradoxically, through their gradual political and social emancipation during that century; and Petre implied that there were those who looked back nostalgically to the more secure world of the 'ghetto' created by isolation.[53]

Petre was a rebellious son of the Catholic Church, a reformer who sought change, but essentially an 'insider' appealing to other 'insiders'.

Woodroffe writing in relation to Hinduism was in a more ambiguous position. He wrote from the standpoint of a sympathetic outsider, yet seems to have been both personally involved and identified with Tantra. At the same time he was also a representative of the colonial culture which was perceived as both challenging and threatening to Hindu identity.

Petre insisted he was a reformer not a 'revolutionist'[54] but his emphasis was very much on change, for he was addressing the followers of a church which he saw as powerful. The situation reflected in Woodroffe's writings was more complicated, for Hinduism was perceived to be weak, under threat from the colonial culture, and needing to discover and cultivate its own innate strength: its *ātma śakti*, or its distinctive *Bhārata Śakti*. This was in the context of resisting the forces of westernization. In the background to Petre's writing there was no perceived threat to catholic identity as such. Nevertheless as a small minority just emerging from isolation there was a sense of inferiority in relation to Protestants: 'Among our Catholic aristocracy I should say there is a pretty universal sense of intellectual inferiority, by some acquiesced in, by some resented, by all deplored' he wrote, quoting a contemporary report into catholic education. He went on to reproduce twice a phrase from the same report about 'the terrible *vis inertia*' produced by 'comfortable, self-satisfied, mediocre unambitious traditions', while by contrast the protestant public schools were seen as producing 'expansion of mind, definiteness of aim, earnestness of purpose'.[55] This is reminiscent of the situation reflected in Woodroffe's writings, where the dominating culture was envied for possessing vigour while Hindus were perceived as enervated and weak. Swami Vivekananda had expressed the problem in gender terms: he described his mission as 'man-making' and urged Bengalis to emulate the vigorous manly qualities to be found in the West.[56] Petre rejected the Victorian cult of manliness in a physical sphere, but converted it into a quest for mental vigour.

Freedom: the amoeba's example

Both Petre and Woodroffe said that the most important pre-requisite for genuine education was freedom. Petre considered it essential for both intellectual and moral growth and his strongest criticisms of catholic education were on this point. While Petre thought in terms of liberty of the individual, Woodroffe wrote about collective, cultural freedom: that of the 'racial soul', or the 'seed of race' for which he adapted the tantric term *bīja* or 'seed'. As we shall see in chapter 5, he also made use of the same organic analogy that Petre had used when he named Woburn's school journal *The Amoeba*.

Petre used the amoeba as a metaphor for the schoolboy's natural process of growth. He was thinking of the creature's powers of assimilation of objects in its environment, the point being that these were driven from within, that is from the amoeba's own 'volition' in the form of its appetite, and were not imposed from without.[57] Woodroffe took over the analogy of assimilation by the amoeba and applied it not to the individual but to a culture which, like most people of his time, he confused with a race. A race, or a culture, if left free to develop on its own without being forced into a particular mould by external pressures, could assimilate foreign cultural elements in its environment and – most importantly – transform them into its own. Assimilation, he wrote, 'is an organic process, like an amoeba feeding'. The foreign substance ceases to be foreign and becomes part of the amoeba itself. In this way for example, Greek art derived from Egypt, yet its finished product was quite different from the Egyptian.[58] The point was that the amoeba was 'free', therefore it could safely assimilate. It was this freedom of a 'race' or culture, rather than political democracy as such, that Woodroffe wrote and spoke about in a style that identified him with Indian nationalism.

From his role as Woburn's Prime Minister, we next meet Sir John Woodroffe in Calcutta, and look at the five aspects to his life there. We begin in the High Court. In combining the roles of judge and orientalist, Woodroffe seemed to stand in the tradition of Sir William Jones in the eighteenth century, who had been a judge of the Supreme Court, the High Court's predecessor.[59] He inherited the image of great learning associated with the famous founder of the Asiatic Society, for like Jones he combined a reputation for scholarship on law with the apparently prodigious sanskrit learning of the pseudonymous Arthur Avalon. Overall we shall see that Woodroffe was a highly respected and popular judge. But we shall also see how the ambiguity of his position between colonialism and nationalism was highlighted by one very controversial case.

Chapter Three

THE HIGH COURT JUDGE

Popularity and unpopularity

All of Woodroffe's roles in Calcutta's life begin in the High Court: a group of senior judges supported the Tagore brothers in the promotion of the Indian Society of Oriental Art; it was in the High Court among the Indian barristers and vakils that Woodroffe's image as a nationalist was fostered; and it was among the Court's personnel that he may first have come in contact with the devotees of tantric gurus.[1] We shall see that according to Vasanta Kumar Pal's biography of Sivacandra Vidyarnava, it was the High Court Sanskrit interpreter, Haridev Sastri, who introduced Woodroffe to his guru. When gathering 'oral traditions' about Woodroffe at the High Court in 1991 I was told that his interest in Tantra had been aroused by his court clerk who had been healed of a long-standing ailment by a tantric guru. Another story ran that it was Woodroffe's wife who was healed of mental illness, again through an intermediary at the High Court. It was not possible to pursue these stories; but the fact that memories of Woodroffe lingered at the High Court at all was significant. Of one thing moreover everyone who knew of him there was quite certain: that he had been a Tantric. His name was linked to Atal Behari Ghose; and I was told of Ghose's house at Chaibassa in Bihar where the two men were believed to practise tantric *sādhanā* together in secret. The High Court was also significant as the source of the prestige which Woodroffe could lend to those aspects of Indian life with which he identified himself.

'An Exemplary Judge'

The Statesman of Calcutta of Friday 1 September 1922 described the scene in the High Court on the previous day, at the retirement of Mr Justice Woodroffe after eighteen years on the Bench. In a courtroom crowded with members of the public as well as the legal profession, Woodroffe was presented with an address written on silk-backed paper and enclosed in a silver scroll decorated with reliefs illustrating the arenas of Indian life in which he had been active. A miniature of the High Court building represented his judicial career; a cow being milked stood for his work for cow protection;[2] the *bīja* representing the 'seed of the Tantras' and a pandit reading the Śāstras represented the writings of 'Arthur Avalon'. The short address was headed 'An Exemplary judge'. It began with appreciation of his personality:

> . . . you have by your suavity of manners, your attainments, and above all your sympathy with the people of this country, earned the esteem and gratitude of all who came in contact with you.'

It referred to 'unfailing courtesy, strict impartiality . . .'. After briefly mentioning his contributions to legal scholarship the address moved on to the heart of this extraordinary tribute, to:

> . . . the good work done by you to our country in other spheres of action. The Indian Society of Oriental Art . . . will bear testimony to your solicitude in the cause of the neglected arts and crafts of the East and of Indian painting and sculpture. In the domain of religious philosophy, your labours have removed the ignorant obloquy from the Brahmanic Scriptures known under the name of the Tantras, and the erudition and scholarship you have brought to bear upon your exposition of this abstruse subject . . .
>
> . . . we cannot omit mentioning one other matter, viz.the fearless impartiality with which you repelled the aspersions cast on the civilization of India, with its historic past, and the thoroughness with which you have done it.[3]

Four of Woodroffe's public roles are brought together here, but at this time perhaps it was the last, defending the civilization of India, that was uppermost in people's minds. At the end of 1918 Woodroffe had published *Is India Civilized?*, a reply to a book called *India and the Future* by William Archer, whose attack on Hindu culture had outraged public opinion in the country. Woodroffe's book attacked westernization and what he believed was a political agenda behind views such as those of Archer.[4] He eulogised the Hindu spiritual heritage and believed that it gave India a special role in the modern world – essentially the same message as that of Swami Vivekananda. The strong statement in support of what was called the Hindu revival led some to compare him to the 'extremists' among the nationalist politicians.

The scroll had been presented to him by the Vakils' Association. To make such a tribute was quite unusual and had required special permission under the rules of the Home Department of Government. The only precedent was the retirement of a popular Indian judge some years previously.[5] The retirement ceremonies of most other prominent figures at the High Court, including judges, received only brief notices in the *Calcutta Weekly Notes*, whereas Woodroffe's covered three pages. His popularity with the vakils and with Indian members of the Bar was long established, and it was for much more besides his books on Tantra. The Address was far from mere flattery. Nares Candra Sengupta, a barrister and prominent writer who was contemporary with Woodroffe at the High Court, recorded that this British judge gathered around him a clique of enthusiastic admirers among the Indian members of the Bar who were impressed by his apparently deep learning in Sanskritic culture.[6] To them Woodroffe's defence of Tantra was an aspect of Indian nationalism. Nirad Chaudhuri, whose recollections cover the whole period of Woodroffe's career in Calcutta, made the same observation: Woodroffe was surrounded by admirers at the High Court, who were enthusiastic over his tantric studies because they contributed to nationalist self-esteem.[7] Woodroffe's talks and writings on cultural nationalist themes were collected by one of these admirers and published as *Bhārata Shakti*, a book which ran to three editions very quickly between 1917 and 1921.

The second edition of *Is India Civilized?* was published at an exceptionally sensitive time: April 1919, the month of General Dyer's atrocity, the Jallianwalla Bagh massacre of unarmed Indian demonstrators – an event which prompted Rabindranath Tagore to resign his knighthood.[8] The political atmosphere was specially tense, and would get more so. The Sedition Committee set up by the British Government had published its report at the end of the previous year and its recommendations had been implemented in the immensely unpopular Rowlatt Acts, which extended the provisions for detention without trial which had come into force during the 1914–18 war.[9] Woodroffe's book was very popular with the Indian press, a popularity no doubt enhanced by the hostile response it evoked in some sections of the British press in India.[10] If the publication of the book had anything to do with Woodroffe's retirement, then the vakils' gesture could also have been an act of defiance to the government of India, whose relations with the High Court were often strained.

Woodroffe was leaving three years before the normal retiring age of sixty, but the exact reason for this cannot be established as the relevant papers have not been preserved.[11] In his own speech of thanks to the address of the vakils he mentions 'circumstances which compel me to retire' but does not say what these were. A farewell address to Woodroffe by the Vivekananda Society of Calcutta refers to *Bhārata Shakti* and *Is India Civilized?* and the 'displeasure' they had incurred from his own countrymen.[12] I was told by several people in Calcutta that it was widely believed that Woodroffe was forced to retire early. There are, however, several indications that he had intended retiring even earlier. In 1915, one Indian newspaper commented that it was said that Woodroffe would retire in two years' time.[13] He wrote to Lama Kazi Dawasamdup in 1917 that he intended to leave India as soon as the European war would be over. A letter of Chief Justice Sir Lancelot Sanderson indicates that Woodroffe had said he might not return to India after his furlough of 1919–20;[14] and

Abanindranath Tagore wrote to Havell in England in 1919 that he did not think Woodroffe would return to India.[15] In the event, he did return and remained a judge for another two years. It seems probable that the immediate reason for his eventual retirement was the health of his son. Correspondence in the archives of Downside Abbey school reveals that James Woodroffe fell very ill at this time and his anxious parents took him away from the school in 1922. As we have seen, the health of other family members was also causing concern soon afterwards. These are most probably the 'circumstances' to which Woodroffe referred in his retirement speech. This tends to cast doubt on the story that he was actually forced to retire early, but we have no indication of what social or official pressures may have been on him as well.

WOODROFFE ON THE BENCH

The history of the Calcutta High Court does not seem to have attracted the scholarly attention it deserves. Its 125th Anniversary Souvenir contains reminiscences and a brief historical sketch.[16] Its day-to-day work is recorded in the *Calcutta Weekly Notes* (CWN), published by the High Court from 1895. The founder, and editor throughout Woodroffe's time, was a Bengali barrister named J.Chaudhury, who expresses the attitudes of Indian members of the Calcutta Bar, an institution which had a strong nationalist record.[17] The CWN consists of a weekly news sheet (the 'Notes') containing commentary on current affairs from a legal point of view and items of news concerning High Court personnel; this is accompanied by a selection of recent trial records and texts of judgments.

We have seen how in 1889 the young John Woodroffe, newly called to the Bar at the Middle Temple, came to join his father in Calcutta. He was not a member of the Indian Judicial Service and therefore not strictly speaking an 'official' of the Raj. Most British judges were either officers belonging to the judicial branch of the Indian Civil Service, or barristers promoted directly from the London Bar. The promotion of the younger Woodroffe to the Bench in 1904 from the local Calcutta Bar was greeted with enthusiasm by CWN – perhaps partly because it helped set a precedent for the appointment of more Indian judges.[18] We have seen that Woodroffe began his career with an established reputation for scholarship on law.

The High Court was divided into an 'original' and an 'appellate' side. The former tried criminal and civil cases originating in Calcutta, the appellate branch was the court of appeal for the whole province[19] (of Bengal until the partition of 1905 and of West Bengal and part of Bihar for a few years after that). Junior judges were usually assigned to the former, but Woodroffe almost right away was sitting on appeal benches as well.

These usually consisted of two or three senior judges and by far the greater portion of the cases were civil.

Woodroffe was immediately popular with Indian members of the legal profession, who were nearly all advocates, attorneys or traditional *vakīls*, Indian judges still being few in number. The editor of CWN mentions him warmly on several occasions and seems to have had a special liking for him. He noted the unusually large attendance at a dinner given for him by members of the Bar six months after his appointment as a judge. Describing how Woodroffe was admired for his 'unostentatious manners, uniform courtesy, patience, devotion to duty . . .' this appreciation at the beginning of his career is couched in language similar to that of the vakils at his retirement:

> The unusually large gathering of the members of the Bar signified to the popularity of the young judge . . . We must therefore congratulate the local Bar and Mr Justice Woodroffe that he has within so short a time made such an excellent impression on all sections of the profession. His popularity commenced on the Appellate Side of the Court where every Vakil who had occasion to appear before him, admires his unostentatious manners . . .' etc.[20]

A few years later in 1908, the elder Woodroffe died, and it was rumoured that the son might now retire, it being presumed that he had come into a fortune. CWN urged Woodroffe against this on the grounds of duty: perhaps such 'pro-Indian' judges were scarce.[21] But in 1912 as we shall see later on, there came a difficult political case which seriously dented his popularity for a time.

The Political Background: the 'swadeshi years'

The political temperature throughout Woodroffe's years on the Bench was high, and the first two decades of the twentieth century in Calcutta might seem to have been a specially difficult time for a British judge with Indian sympathies. The year after his appointment, in 1905, the viceroy Lord Curzon partitioned the province of Bengal – ostensibly a purely administrative measure, which nevertheless was seen as a political move. This was the spark which ignited a widespread protest in the province that was called 'the Indian unrest' or the period of 'swadeshi' agitation. It marked the beginning of the modern nationalist movement. *Svadeśi*, (meaning 'belonging to one's own country') was at first a generally pacifist movement to boycott foreign goods and government controlled education. Along with this went rejection of industrialism and westernization, manifesting first of all in the promotion of indigenous arts and crafts. This reflected a similar fashionable movement in England at the time and even some British officials supported it. Many of the more pacific swadeshi values were inherited in the following decade by Mahatma Gandhi, and became the centre of his ideology. But there was also a revolutionary side to the campaign, and these years saw the steady growth of more violent underground movements. There were assassinations and 'political' *dacoities* carried out by middle class English educated Bengali youth. They were accompanied in their turn by trials for 'sedition' in the courts, by executions and deportations which created 'revolutionary martyrs'.[22]

In common with the wider swadeshi movement, the revolutionaries appealed to religious ideology and sentiment, and adopted Hindu rituals and imagery. The *anuśīlan samitis* ('self-culture clubs') which were set up as part of the swadeshi movement, in some cases became covers for more violent revolutionary societies.[23] The later Sri Aurobindo was in 1905 a young man recently returned from England inspired with revolutionary ideals. He and his younger brother, Barindra Kumar Ghose, are now recognized to have been the main instigators and organisers of the earliest of the underground terrorist organizations in Bengal.[24] Aurobindo's inspiration for English educated young men is described by Nirad Chaudhuri.[25] Aurobindo already combined his European-inspired revolutionary ideas with Hindu spirituality. His brother Baren organised a revolutionary 'school' at Manicktolla, then a quiet suburb of Calcutta, where training in bomb manufacture was combined with yoga and study of the Upaniṣads and Vedas. After several unsuccessful attempts at assassination and *dacoity*, the Bengali revolutionary movement burst upon the public in April 1908 when Khudiram Bose and Prafulla Chaki, two young followers of Baren Ghosh, threw a bomb into what they believed was the carriage of Douglas Kingsford, a district magistrate. Instead they had killed two British women, Mrs Pringle Kennedy and her daughter.[26]

The two assassins were quickly arrested and soon Bengal acquired its first political 'martyrs'. Prafulla Chaki committed suicide on arrest, while Khudiram Bose went on trial at Muzafferpore in Bihar, and was subsequently hanged.[27] This early act of terrorism generated shock waves whose effects were later to engulf Woodroffe. The members of the secret society in Manicktolla were arrested and put on trial for conspiracy at Alipore district court. The case dragged on for many months, helping to fan the flames of revolutionary romanticism among sections of Bengali society, and causing panic among the British community, whose press reacted with verbal violence.[28] Further dramas accompanied the trial: an Indian detective involved in the case and the Indian public prosecutor were both gunned down in broad daylight, and an informer was murdered in Alipore jail itself.[29] Finally on 6 May 1909, Baren Ghose was sentenced to death and several of his followers received terms of transportation; but many others, and especially Aurobindo, regarded by police as the ringleader, escaped conviction. For the British authorities and the police, the case produced much frustration with the courts.[30]

Such political cases were usually decided by district judges or magistrates, and only reached the High Court on appeal. (Baren Ghose's appeal was heard there the following year, and his death sentence was reduced to transportation.)[31] At the end of 1908 the Criminal Law Amendment Bill set up Special Tribunals of three High Court judges to try some political cases;[32] but even after that and even when the political atmosphere was tense, the greater part of the day-to-day work of a senior High Court judge still seems to have been taken up with appeals on civil cases. When it came to political cases, however, the Bench was subject to pressure from the imperial government which often complained the judges were too lenient. Government criticism was echoed in both the British and the British–Indian press:

> The High Court prides itself on its popularity with the native press and the sedition-mongers . . . The result is that the trials of offenders on serious charges of murder or conspiracy against the Government more often than not are a pure farce . . . The necessity of a summary tribunal for dealing with such cases is most urgent.'[33]

For its part, the High Court – at least as far as its opinions were reflected in the CWN – saw itself as a bulwark defending a fragile constitutional liberty against the encroachments of a powerful bureaucracy.[34] Nevertheless it did not escape the insecurity created by 'revolutionary' or 'terrorist' acts. Among the papers of Asutosh Mukherji, the most senior Indian judge at the time, was a letter from the Home Department outlining the measures taken for his protection, which included four policemen to guard him day and night. Whether this was felt necessary for all High Court judges is not clear from the letter – Asutosh Mukherji may have been under special threat not only as an Indian judge, but especially because he was Chancellor of Calcutta University and had openly opposed the swadeshi education boycott.[35] It was the district judges and magistrates who were the most frequent targets of assassination.

After these initial events, revolutionary violence escalated and branched out through new and proliferating underground societies, culminating in a dramatic attempt on the life of the viceroy Lord Hardinge on his entry into the new capital at Delhi in December 1912.[36] The viceroyalty of Hardinge (1910–16) was continuously turbulent, and he complains of the stress in his memoirs. He described Bengal and Calcutta on his arrival in 1910 as 'seething with sedition': dacoities and assassinations were 'an almost daily occurrence' in the city and its neighbourhood.[37] The new viceroy was critical of Lord Carmichael, the Governor of Bengal from 1912, for being unable to control the situation. Lord Carmichael for his part noted the 'widespread distrust of the police and CID' amongst the public. He is quoted as saying that 'one of the gravest features, . . . of the situation here is the almost universal feeling of distrust – I may almost say hatred – of the

CID amongst ... Indians and Europeans alike.'[38] Nirad Chaudhuri describes the years 1910–16 as a time when life was lived between two shadows: those of the conspiratorial revolutionaries on the one hand, and along with them the 'unavowed watch of the (police) spies'.[39] In 1915 came the Defence of India Bill, allowing for internment by special tribunal without appeal to the High Court, a measure which had been passed in the belief that a general insurgency was planned on the outbreak of war. The First World War was indeed seen by many Indian revolutionaries as a great opportunity, and in September 1915 some Bengali insurgents armed by Japan were intercepted in Orissa.[40]

Meanwhile, however, the focus of nationalist agitation had shifted away from Bengal. These years, just prior to the emergence of Mahatma Gandhi on the national scene towards the end of the decade, were those of Annie Besant's ascendancy in India-wide politics, wielded from her position at the head of the Theosophical Society in Madras. Besant's ideal was self-government for India within a reformed and 'spiritualised' British Empire, something which put her at odds with many other nationalist leaders, especially Bal Gangadhar Tilak who was her main rival at the time. Nevertheless she was associated with 'extremism' in the eyes of the British administration. She too, like Gandhi and most other nationalists, combined political with religious goals, but in her case these were Theosophical.[41] In 1916 she and Tilak each formed their Home Rule Leagues and Annie Besant toured the country making speeches and rallying mass support. For a while she was extremely popular. The Calcutta newspaper *Amrita Bāzār Patrika* commented: 'Practically the whole of the educated Indian community has caught the cry of Home Rule in right earnest, first raised by this illustrious lady.'[42] Her ascendancy culminated in her election as President of the Indian National Congress for the year 1917–18. Both the Woodroffes, but especially Ellen, were personally acquainted with Annie Besant, and Ellen shared her faith in the young Krishnamurti who was then being educated as the future Theosophical messiah. The Woodroffes took her to the Ghose's house in Calcutta.[43]

This visit may have taken place in December 1917, when the Congress at which she was elected President took place in the city. Various measures taken against her by the government in Madras – culminating in a brief period of internment earlier in the year – had served immensely to enhance her popularity, and contributed to her election. As was usually the case each year, Congress coincided with the annual convention of the Theosophical Society which was also held in the same location. James Cousins, Annie Besant's close associate and editor of the Theosophical newspaper *New India*, describes the intensely excited atmosphere in his memoirs. The crowds sang the unofficial 'national anthem' *Bānde Mātāram* as they cheered Annie Besant from railway stations along her route. Calcutta was full of conferences, platforms and speakers. Alongside the meeting of Congress and the Theosophical Society Convention, there were numerous smaller conventions as well, including that of the All India Cow Conferences Association, at which Woodroffe himself presided that year. James Cousins had come to know the Woodroffes through exhibitions organised by the Indian Society of Oriental Art, and he stayed with them when he came to Calcutta for the 1917 Congress.[44] Woodroffe's friendship with Cousins and Annie Besant places him among radical British[45] critics of empire in India, of whom there were several other examples; among the better known being the clergyman C.F. Andrews, the friend of Gandhi and Tagore.[46] It was not altogether unusual for a British person in India openly to support the nationalist cause: what was less usual was to be outspoken while at the same time holding a high position in the judiciary.

Annie Besant had reached her apogee in 1917. By the following year she had lost her influence in the Indian National Congress. In July 1918 the Montagu–Chelmsford Report granted important concessions on Indian self-government, but was followed almost immediately by the Sedition Committee report which led to the unpopular Rowlatt Acts. Congress was divided by the proposed reforms, but those who rejected them won the day and Annie Besant, who had supported them, was isolated.[47]

Besant's 'star fell' on the national scene as that of Mahatma Gandhi rose. 1917 saw the first of his *satyāgraha* campaigns in India, in support of the indigo workers against the planters at Champaran.[48] The campaign against the Rowlatt Acts followed in 1919, and in the following years his non-cooperation movement gained ground throughout India growing into a mass movement which swept aside Annie Besant and her Theosophist followers, as well as the other leaders of Congress whether 'moderate' or 'extremist'.[49] Neither the swadeshi agitation of the previous decade in Bengal, nor its revolutionary 'shadow' became an India-wide movement.[50]

Woodroffe's time in India was the pre-Gandhian era in Bengal. Gandhi's influence on him is conspicuous only by its absence, for the only impression recorded is a negative one. In one of his speeches Woodroffe rejects the asceticism and passivity which is associated with Gandhian ideology – Gandhi did not appeal to *śakti*. The language of Woodroffe's speeches and of parts of *Shakti and Shākta* has echoes of Vivekananda and of the political 'extremists' of the swadeshi period in Bengal who were inspired by him.

'Śakti' and Politics

Some tantric symbolism, and especially the notion of *śakti* – (energy or power) which had a theological meaning in Tantra[51] – as well as the various images of the Goddess, were appropriated by the Bengal revolutionaries. During the period of swadeshi agitation many British supporters of imperialism saw Tantra in a particularly sinister political light as a branch of the Hindu religion which encouraged, or even worshipped, violence. The journalist Valentine Chirol's views expressed what was probably the normal British official attitude, in a widely read book:

> Nowhere is the cult of the "terrible goddess" worshipped under many forms ... more closely associated with Indian unrest than in Bengal. Hence the frequency of the appeals to her in the Bengal press.[52]

What is more this political violence is specifically linked in Chirol's mind with the erotic aspects of Śāktism:

> In some quarters there has been some recrudescence of the Śakti cultus, with its often obscene and horrible rites and the unnatural depravity which was so marked a feature [in the murder of Mr Jackson] represents a form of erotomania which is certainly more common among Hindu political fanatics than among Hindus in general.[53]

He has just referred to 'secret societies' which placed their 'murderous activities under the special patronage of one or other of the ... popular deities.' This seems to refer to the *anuśīlan samitis*, the 'self-culture clubs' which were part of the swadeshi movement and in a few cases developed into underground revolutionary societies. Their initiation ceremonies sometimes included taking vows before an image of the ferocious goddess Kālī,[54] and in her form as Durga the Goddess took on new significance as a symbol of the Motherland.[55]

This nationalist 'Śakti' had been born much earlier, in Bamkim Chandra Chatterji's nineteenth century novel *Ānandamath* which was a tale about a band of politically militant *sañnyāsis.* The song *Bānde Mātāram* from that novel became the unofficial 'national anthem' of Bengal after being set to music by Rabindranath Tagore during the period when he was caught up in the early swadeshi fervour.[56] During the 'swadeshi years' the song was banned and the concept of *śakti* and the Goddess viewed with suspicion. Nirad Chaudhuri describes the angry reaction of a local magistrate in East Bengal when taunted with the song by small boys in his neighbourhood.[57] Bamkim Chandra's imagery was taken up by Aurobindo in his 1905 pamphlet entitled *Bhawāni Mandir* promoting the cultivation of 'Shakti' as political strength, the strength of Mother India.

> What is our Mother country? ... It is a mighty Śakti composed of all the śaktis of all the millions of units that make up the nation. Just as Bhawani Mahisha Mardini sprang into being from the śakti of all the millions of gods assembled in one force ...
>
> It is not till she [the Motherland] ... takes shape as a great Divine and Maternal Power in a form of beauty that can dominate the mind

> and seize the heart . . . that . . . the patriotism that works miracles and saves a doomed nation is born.[58]

The reading of violence into this Puranic imagery could be quite explicit and alarming, as in a famous editorial in the revolutionary newspaper *Yugāntar*, which was quoted by Valentine Chirol:

> Will the Bengali worshippers of Shakti shrink from the shedding of blood? . . . If you are firm in your resolution you can bring English rule to an end in a single day. Lay down your life but first take a life. The worship of the goddess will not be consummated if you sacrifice your lives at the shrine of independence without shedding blood.[59]

The term had a less violent meaning in swadeshi vocabulary: *ātma śakti* meaning self-reliance or self-help was integral to the movement, and was associated with passive resistance rather than with violence. But the association of *śakti* with national self assertion and forceful action, was a consistent theme.

Woodroffe also used the concept of *śakti* in a non-tantric context in the speeches and articles collected in his *Bhārata Shakti*, first published in 1917. What he meant by the term was closer to an immanentist interpretation of Śākta metaphysics than to any political terminology.[60] Nevertheless, he used it of India as a nation:

> India is not a mere geographical Expression . . . India is an Idea. It is a particular Shakti, the Bhārata Shakti, distinguished from all others by Her own peculiar nature and qualities.[61]

This was reminiscent of Aurobindo's language, and Woodroffe was joining himself to the 'extremist' campaign against westernization in culture.[62] Although his book was a long way from Aurobindo's revolutionary politics, he was using the word *śakti* in the context of resistance to British influence and the book had a nationalist ring to contemporaries, attested to by its reception in the Indian press.

So what was a British High Court judge doing, apparently using the language of the 'extremists' of the nationalist cause and plunging into the defence of Tantra, the most 'extreme' form of the Hindu religion on an imagined scale of degradation and violence?

By around 1915 when Woodroffe began delivering the speeches which went to make up *Bhārata Shakti,* although the situation remained tense, the political climate was different from the 'heady' swadeshi days of the previous decade. The nationalist movement had become more India-wide with Annie Besant's influence, and after the Morley–Minto reforms of 1909 the British had conceded some ground to Indian opinion. The language of the 'extremists' had perhaps become less threatening in the British 'official' world,[63] which had for some time anyway felt able to appropriate the pacific, cultural side of swadeshi, as we shall see in the next chapter. In 1914 the Governor of Bengal Lord Carmichael, who was a keen supporter of swadeshi industries, addressed the Sanskrit Convocation at Calcutta University in Bengali ('a lesson to anglicised Indians who hate to speak their mother tongue', commented one Indian paper.)[64] At the end of 1917 when the Secretary of State, Sir Edwin Montagu, was touring India prior to drawing up his reform programme, he was invited to stand up at a dinner while *Bānde Mātaram* was sung: something which he readily did, describing it as 'that harmless wailing song'.[65] University education had been one of the most important swadeshi issues and in 1917–18 a special commission under a visiting British expert, Sir Michael Sadler, was called in to investigate the problem and to address the grievances of the students.[66] Lord Ronaldshay, Governor of Bengal in 1919, specifically stated that by giving a government grant to the Indian Society of Oriental Art he was encouraging the 'positive' (ie the cultural) aspects of nationalism.[67]

So when Woodroffe as a High Court judge talked on public platforms about the need for Indians to identify with their cultural heritage and did so in the name of 'Śakti', this was not as controversial in 1916–17 as it might perhaps have been a decade earlier. Nevertheless, his opinions were recognised by both admirers and critics, and by both Indians and Europeans as sympathetic to nationalism.[68] In 1918 *Is India Civilized?* was a stronger statement than he had yet made. As one British reviewer commented: 'It is rather unusual to find among the British members of the Indian Judiciary an apologist for the claims of the Neo-Hindu revivalists and their allies, the Extreme Nationalists.'[69] But that is what Woodroffe could sound like, if by 'extreme' support for violence is excluded. Although in the mind of Valentine Chirol, the two might be equated and bracketed with religious fervour, this was not universally the case. As Sumit Sarkar points out, 'extremist' referred to a certain political programme, ie. out and out independence as opposed to colonial self-government, which was the aim of the 'moderates'.[70]

Where the latter were concerned, there were other prominent British supporters, some of whom also held high ranks under the colonial administration. The most obvious comparisons would be to a previous generation: to people like Sir Henry Cotton,[71] and Woodroffe's own second cousin Alan Octavian Hume. What these men had fought for was Indian representation and participation in government on democratic principles, but with India remaining within the British empire. Colonial self-government not complete independence was their goal.[72] By the end of the second decade of the twentieth century, the political situation had by-passed this issue. Some limited self-government had been granted through the Morley–Minto Reforms of 1909 and this was extended in 1919 by the Montagu–Chelmsford Reforms, but they had not satisfied Indian demands and the situation was more polarised. Woodroffe was quite different from Hume and others of his generation. Torick Ameer Ali was probably right in his observation that he had no real interest in politics as such, for he expresses no interest in constitutional matters. Like Nivedita, Vivekananda's famous British disciple, his passion for cultural and religious nationalism stemmed from his strong personal identification with Hinduism.

Unlike Nivedita, however, there is no suggestion of Woodroffe having sympathies with the revolutionaries. In fact the evidence points the other way and Woodroffe's publicly expressed nationalism does not seem to have made him stand out as more lenient than other British judges in the specifically 'political' cases that came before him. On the contrary, in what might appear like a contradiction, the exact opposite seems to have been more often the case, as we shall see.

THREE CASES TWO *CAUSES CELEBRES*

In the course of his years on the Bench Woodroffe was involved in two cases which, for different reasons, each attracted a lot of attention in the press. The first occurred at the beginning of his career in 1905 and was not a 'political' case, the second was so, and came in the middle, in 1912. A third, otherwise entirely obscure case, shows how Woodroffe passed into local legend.

A Popular Judge: the case of the *Kālki Avatār*

The case of the *Kālki Avatār* of 1905 has found its way into contemporary historiography in an essay by Sumit Sarkar.[73] It was not the judgement so much as the details of the case itself which aroused interest. It concerned a ritual murder; such things had occurred in tantric contexts, but this case concerned a Vaiṣṇava guru, and was not specifically associated with Tantrism. The *Kālki Avatār* is held to be the future and final incarnation of Viṣṇu, whose appearance will herald the end of the *kāli yuga*. The guru, who claimed to be this *avatār*, had instigated the ritual sacrifice of one of his two 'untouchable' disciples by the other. The guru was a Brahmin, who had been treated leniently by the district court in contrast to the disciple. Woodroffe and his colleague in the appeal court redressed the balance by giving them equal life sentences.[74] The verdict was widely approved in the press. Commenting on the judgement, Sumit Sarkar remarks on its sympathy with Hinduism:

> There was no attempt ... Christian missionary style, to classify the case as an instance of rank Hindu superstition, nor were there efforts to use the affair to discredit the bhadralok ...

He puts this down to the political climate at the beginning of the swadeshi years: 'Perhaps the judges wanted to avoid giving any impression of interference with religion.'[75] In this instance Sarkar did not note that he was writing about an individual British judge who, to all intents and purposes, was or soon would be a convert to Hinduism.

Whether or not it was this case which helped to promote his popularity, Woodroffe had a reputation as a judge who was sympathetic to Indian tradition. His reputation may also have been based on more general qualities of humanity and common sense. He seems to appear at his best in cases which involved day-to-day conflicts between ordinary people where he attempted to bring reconciliation. One example concerned the custody of the two sons of a woman who wanted to convert to Christianity. Woodroffe's decision, which aimed at keeping the children with their mother while preserving the influence of their Hindu relatives, won approval in the Indian press.[76]

Debottarer Tān

There is an interesting example of Woodroffe turning into legend as a judge who was given divine aid in arriving at a miraculously just decision. The story is told by a poet called Kumud Ranjan Mallik, who learned it from a court journalist who used to visit him. *Debottarer tān* means 'the attraction of the devotee', that is, the attractive power of a *bhakta's* devotion which can compel the divinity to come to his aid. But the word is a pun, for it was also a legal term designating property which had been donated to a divinity, usually land on which a temple was built. In these cases the divinity, the *devatā*, was technically the owner of the property, but there was need for a person to stand as surrogate legal owner on the divinity's behalf. This person was usually the priest at the temple, known as the *śebait*, who thereby enjoyed tenancy for life. The two terms were anglicised in legal terminology into 'debutter' and 'shebait'. This was an example of Hindu law which had been adopted by the British legal system, and features prominently in CWN. 'Debutter' cases were extremely frequent in the civil litigation before the Calcutta High Court, which protected the rights of the shebaits. The poem was about a shebait who had been cheated by a local zamindar who had lodged a case against him, bringing many witnesses on his side while the shebait had no-one to speak for him. The poem was given to Samarendranath Bagchi, retired judge of the High Court, by the poet's son, who told Mr Bagchi that although Woodroffe is not named in the poem, his father had originally entitled it *judge Woodroffe*. The following is a translation of an extract from the Bengali:

> The judge getting up at dawn hurriedly summoned the peśkār[77] by sending his chaprassi with a message about very urgent business (*zaruri darkāre*)

He said secretly: 'Which Devatā has a beautiful figure and whose complexion is brightly white?'

Saluting him, the Peśkār said 'He must be Śiva Maheśvara'.

The judge in reply asked: 'I know that but what other name has he? Whose complexion is all-white and on whose shoulder hangs the plough?'

The peśkār said: 'Now I understand, we call him Balarām'. The judge said: 'Do you think he is called a man of anger?' (*rāgi*)

The Peśkār said: 'He is angry at injustice (*anyāya*) and very much on the side of justice (*nyāya*)'.

After the vacation the judgement was published, and the shebait was astonished. The zamindar had lost the case and he had won it.

The leading lawyers of the court were all charmed on reading the verdict and all said in chorus: 'How great was the judge! How great was the judge!. The judgement reads as if the judge himself has witnessed everything with his own eyes!'

The Peśkār rushed to the judge and informed him of the happiness and appreciation of the people and the blessing of all.

Finding the Peśkār so delighted, the Sahib said with a smile: 'For the sake of the *Bhakta*, do you know that the *Devatā* himself came to give witness?

The *Devatā* is true, I am only a humble copier. He is the true Mallick giving the order and it is he alone who is imperishable.

Now it is confirmed that the *devatā* is attracted [has an attraction (*tān*)] to the devotee (*devottar*) And blessed are we both, the judge and the Peśkār'.[78]

Although it was the devotion of the temple priest which brought about the deity's intervention, the judge himself is portrayed as a devout and wise person, knowledgeable about Hindu iconographic tradition. In contrast to the stories recounted by Vasanta Kumar Pal which we shall look at in chapter 6, Woodroffe is the centre of this story, whereas Pal portrays him only as the humble disciple of the guru. The incident shows Woodroffe living on in folk memory, independently of Arthur Avalon's books.

An Unpopular Judge: the Midnapore appeal case

We now turn to a very different case, whose context brings us back to the atmosphere of the swadeshi years, from 1905 onwards. During this time the High Court frequently appears in an embattled position in relation to the imperial administration in India. In the pages of CWN the court stands as a bastion of defence of the rights of the individual and of its own independence, against the powerful encroachments of government. This becomes the dominant theme of the journal from the time of the partition of Bengal and the subsequent unrest.[79]

Matters seemed to come to a head with the Midnapore Appeal Case of 1912, which was a civil case that had grown out of a criminal prosecution three years previously. It placed Woodroffe and his colleagues on the appeal bench at the focal point of the conflict between the judiciary and the government. Tension was particularly high because the case was one of a series where the High Court had been accused of letting political 'terrorists' go free, while some judges had made accusations against police and magistrates of planting evidence and extracting forced confessions.[80]

The story began four years previously, when in the wake of the Muzafferpore bomb case and the arrest of Khudiram Bose and Prafulla Chaki, the members of the secret revolutionary society in Calcutta were rounded up by police and put on trial. A branch of the society also existed at the town of Midnapore, run by Satyendranath Bose, Hem Chandra Das and others, who were also arrested. The District Magistrate of Midnapore, a Mr Douglas Weston, believed that he was also, like his colleague Kingsford, the object of an assassination conspiracy. Weston's deputy Superintendent of Police, *maulvi* Mazharul Haq (called 'the *maulvi*' in all accounts of the case), was the first to penetrate the revolutionary societies in Calcutta and Midnapore through two informers in his pay.[81] The informers' reports resulted in the arrest of over 150 people in Midnapore. No arms or explosives were discovered, however – except for a single home-made bomb which was found in the house of a young man called Santosh Das, who had belonged to an *ākhāra* (gymnasium) believed to be run as a cover for the Midnapore revolutionary society.[82]

The list of those arrested in Midnapore included many prominent citizens of the town who were claimed in the informers' reports to be secretly allied to the revolutionaries. No doubt Weston and the *maulvi* were attempting to catch in their net the kind of wealthy, middle class sponsors of the young activists, who in Calcutta had so far escaped detection. Perhaps also their early success in penetrating the secret societies had led to an excess of enthusiasm, though accusations of blackmail made in court against the *maulvi* suggest another possibility as well.[83] At any rate a miscarriage of justice in the case of Santosh Das is patently obvious from reading the judicial accounts of the case.

Most of those arrested were later released and eventually only three young men were brought to trial: Santosh Dass and two of his young friends. The three were convicted by the sessions judge of Midnapore in February 1909 on the basis of a confession made by Santosh while under arrest by Weston. The three were sentenced to terms of transportation. However, in June of the same year these convictions were overturned on appeal at the High Court by Chief Justice Sir Lawrence Jenkins and Asutosh Mukherji (The Midnapore Bomb case appeal of 1 June 1909). In the High Court Santosh Das had retracted his confession, claiming he had been put under pressure by Weston through the latter's arrest of his elderly father, Peary Mohan Das. The two High Court judges declared Santosh Das's confession invalid for two reasons: because he had withdrawn it protesting undue influence (the arrest of his father) and secondly because of suspicions that it had been influenced by the police as it followed too closely the testimony an informer. The Chief Justice criticised the behaviour of the police in the case and strongly implied that the bomb had been planted on Santosh Das and that his father had been arrested with the intention to put pressure on his son.[84] This was merely an allegation however which remained unproved, though Santosh was freed. The decision of the court caused consternation among official circles and led to an inquiry being instituted into the whole situation in Midnapore.[85]

There matters might have rested until the result of the government inquiry was published, but this was forestalled by Peary Mohan Das, who subsequent to his son's acquittal on appeal brought a civil suit for damages on account of his own arrest against Weston, the *maulvi,* and the latter's police subordinate. As this meant that the matter was once again *subjudice*, the publication of the inquiry was postponed.[86] This civil case (The Midnapore Damage Suit of 1911) was tried by Justice Fletcher.

Now Justice Fletcher already had a history in the eyes of the government in India. It was almost certainly he (and definitely not the later 'nationalist' Woodroffe) to whom Lord Hardinge referred in his memoirs as being a particular nuisance at the High Court.[87] Fletcher had been appointed to the Calcutta Bench from the London Bar in 1907 and almost immediately made himself unpopular with the authorities. In 1908 he imposed a fine on the district magistrate L.O.Clarke for exceeding his powers of search in a 'political' case.[88] Although his judgement was upheld by other judges on appeal in 1909,[89] Clarke pursued it as far as the Privy Council, who finally overturned Fletcher's decision.[90] Meanwhile in July 1909 (the very month after the Chief Justice and Asutosh Mukherji overturned the conviction of Santosh Das and his co-defendants), Fletcher won great praise in the Indian press for awarding libel damages to the deported activist Lala Lajput Rai against the *Englishman* newspaper. This was another *cause célèbre.* The damages awarded were 1500 rupees, a large sum in those days, and opinion in 'official' circles and the British press was very angry against Fletcher.[91] In this case, too, Fletcher's decision was upheld on appeal a year later, but this time the large sum he awarded in damages was very substantially reduced to 100 rupees, thereby also reducing the political impact. Of the two judges on the appeal bench, one was Woodroffe.[92]

On 7 August 1911 Fletcher's judgement on the Midnapore damage suit was published: he awarded 1000 rupees in damages against Weston and his two Indian subordinates. In his judgement he outlined the suspicious circumstances in which the bomb had been found in the Das family's house; and the suspicious timing of Peary Mohan Das's arrest – not when the bomb was found, but two weeks later at a time when his son was under interrogation by Weston, but had so far refused to confess.[93] The judgement was praised by CWN and in the Indian press generally, but it caused much embarrassment to the British authorities, especially as the two Indian policemen – the *maulvi* and his subordinate – had meanwhile been promoted and decorated in the Honours List the previous year, something which had caused questions to be raised in the Commons.[94] An appeal against Fletcher's decision was immediately set in motion and funded by the Indian government.[95] It was this, the Midnapore Appeal case, which opened before Woodroffe and two other judges in April 1912.

The appeal hearing lasted until August that year. In the meanwhile, on 24 June 1912, the Privy Council published its findings on what was called 'Clarke's case' and overturned Fletcher's decision of 1908 against the district magistrate. This was greeted with great enthusiasm in Britain and the British-owned press in India. It provided a pretext for further criticism of the High Court of Calcutta, but especially of Justice Fletcher. Although his original decision in Clarke's case had been upheld by the appeal judges, he was singled out as incompetent in reports of the Privy Council's decision.[96]

Then, on 17 August came the judgement on the Midnapore Appeal case. Three judges sat on the Appeal Bench: Woodroffe, another English judge, and an Indian judge, Justice Digambar Chatterji. As was usual, however, only the senior judge, in this case Woodroffe, delivered the judgement, the others only contributing on minor points, or where they disagreed. Woodroffe's judgement was so long that it took three days to read out in court. Reduced to its barest essentials, it overturned Fletcher's decision to award damages for wrongful arrest to Peary Mohan Das on the grounds that, since a bomb had been found in his house it was legally correct for the police to arrest the owner. The alleged motive for the arrest – to put pressure on his son to confess – was dismissed as irrelevant.[97] From a strictly legal point of view, Woodroffe's judgement was probably correct and Justice Fletcher had indeed made mistakes. He had not declared it proven that the bomb had been planted by the police in the Das's house, he merely said: 'I do not know who planted the bomb but I am certain of one thing, that Santosh did not.' This central fact being unproven meant that the rest of the case fell apart, and Woodroffe was able to pass over the extremely suspicious circumstances which had been outlined in Fletcher's judgement. Fletcher had been too timid: he granted Peary Mohan Das his suit but wanted nonetheless to exonerate the magistrate. Consequently his judgement was inconsistent.

Peary Mohan Das's legal advisers had also made a tactical mistake: it would probably have been more sensible to wait for the publication of the government inquiry before taking out their civil suit for damages. As it was, the report of the inquiry had been completed but remained unpublished. Because of the legal proceedings it was declared 'privileged' by government: that meant it could not officially be used in the case, and hence could not be challenged in court. Woodroffe ruled that 'no adverse inference can be drawn from its non-production.' Nevertheless he and the other judges had seen and read it.[98] With the report remaining unpublished, in effect Woodroffe's judgement in the appeal on the civil case could be taken as a verdict on the guilt or innocence of the magistrate and police in their conduct in the original criminal case – and was so taken.

Woodroffe's judgement went much further than merely overturning Fletcher's decision. He not only criticised his colleague in strong terms, but produced an account of all the events surrounding the case that was entirely favourable to the defendants' interpretation of them. That was certainly how it was taken: as a full vindication of the behaviour of the magistrate and police. Consequently the findings of the official inquiry never came to be published.[99] Woodroffe had given the British administration everything they wanted: Douglas Weston was vindicated, and the slur on an ICS official and the police repudiated in the very court from which it had originated. Even better from the government's point of view: Justice Fletcher's judgement had been torn apart by one of his colleagues and his 'incompetence' exposed once again. The fact that it was the Chief Justice who on several occasions expressed concern at the conduct of the police in the affair could be passed over. Fletcher was a much easier target.

'The Midnapore Case: Vindication of Mr Weston' declared the headline in *The Englishman* on 19 August 1912. Other British-owned papers in India were similarly enthusiastic, even the more moderate *Statesman* of Calcutta expressed approval.[100] The response from the Indian press was a long and sustained howl of outrage. Overnight Woodroffe became the most unpopular judge in Bengal. The India Office's selection of items from Indian newspaper reports was dominated by the case for several weeks.[101] The CWN was severely critical not only of the decision but of the language and tone of Woodroffe's judgement which it considered to be flagrantly biassed.

> The appellate judgement of Mr Justice Woodroffe in the Midnapore conspiracy case, for its inordinate length, its tone and temper, its wholesale condemnation of the Plaintiff's case and his counsel and witness, its almost unqualified acceptance of the plea advanced by the Defendants' counsel at the Bar, its unseemly observation concerning the judgment of a colleague on the Bench ... is unsurpassed in the history of judicial pronouncements in this country.

It concludes with an expression of disappointment:

> We have for many years entertained a very high opinion of Mr Justice Woodroffe as a judge and this judgment has, therefore, come upon us as a most painful surprise.[102]

It certainly was that, and other papers also expressed the same disappointment and surprise. The *Amrita Bāzār Patrika* commented:

> We are sincerely sorry to be constrained to criticise in this manner the judgement of a learned judge who has the reputation of being pro-Indian in his feelings and tendencies. No wonder such a judgement should have produced an effect upon the Indian public which it is simply impossible to describe.[103]

Reading the judgement with a lay person's eye, the accusation of bias seems to be justified. Woodroffe's tone throughout is one of irritation at the case of the plaintiff, Peary Mohan Das, which is declared to be 'malicious', and to have been instigated with political motives:

> For I have no doubt that this suit is not the Plaintiff's suit only (if it is his suit at all), but that he is the mouthpiece of others whose implication, and possibly in some cases false implication, in the alleged 'Bomb Conspiracy' or other personal reasons have caused them to promote or support this suit with its extraordinary and as I find malicious charges. Mr Weston seems not to have been a popular man at Midnapore with the Nationalist Party, whether of the right wing or soft (*naram*) or Moderate Party . . . or, the left or 'hot (*garam*), or as it is called Extremist Party.'[104]

Woodroffe criticised Fletcher's judgement for bringing in matters he, Woodroffe, considered irrelevant to the immediate charges; but he himself not only brings in many extraneous matters, but goes much further. He appears well informed of the political background in Midnapore, perhaps because of what he had read in the unpublished government report:

> The conspiracy was fomented by older heads whose writings and outside support induced and upheld it. Amongst many of the educated and wealthier class there was a sympathy with extreme doctrine . . . There is no doubt that some of these persons . . . were not loyal or law-abiding . . . men who, like the Raja of Narajole . . . were without doubt fomenters of the agitation which produced the overt sedition . . . [people who were] deeply implicated in the swadeshi boycott and kindred movements . . .[105]

This sounds like the government and police reading of the situation, and seems to have been true of certain persons in the light of later knowledge.[106] But these political considerations were irrelevant to the question of whether or not the police had been guilty of malpractice in this particular case. Woodroffe considered Peary Mohan Das's allegations unproven, but then seems to go out of his way to declare the charges against the police, not merely unproven but, in his own words, 'malicious' 'extraordinary', and biassed by political motives. The language of the judgement is especially strange considering that it comes from someone who would soon be regarded as a nationalist supporter. Strange, too, are Woodroffe's very obvious sympathies in this case.

Woodroffe's allegations of political motivation centre upon the fact that Peary Mohan Das's advocate, Mr K.B. Dutt, had himself been briefly implicated by the informers' reports, though no charges were made against him. He was a leading 'moderate' nationalist, and had been their leader at the recent Midnapore District Conference of the Indian National Congress, where he had endured a showdown with the 'extremists', a situation that must have been extremely unpleasant for him.[107] This might in itself tend to suggest that he would not defend, for political motives, someone he believed to be associated with 'extremism'. But Woodroffe's suspicion of his motives contrasts with what seems like a striking naivety towards the motives of Weston and the police.[108]

Some strong emotion underlies Woodroffe's judgement, where the irritable tone betrays his bias throughout. He placed almost all reliance for his decision on the single fact that in Fletcher's judgement the planting of the bomb by police remained unproven. But having stated this, Woodroffe then went further to declare it *false.*

> A bomb was found. The Plaintiff's attempt to explain its presence by the allegation that the Defendants put it there ... has been found to be false.[109]

Later he declares it not only false but malicious:

> Every one of these charges goes by the board in Justice Fletcher's judgement. All of them are not only in my opinion false but very malicious and wicked charges for which there is no foundation, of which fact the Plaintiff or others ... must have been well aware.'[110]

From reading all the judgments in this long, complicated case, it is clear that at the very least there was some foundation for Peary Mohan Das's case, and genuine reasons for suspicion of the police actions. Apart from anything else, no-one disputed that the very crude bomb that had been found in the Das's home was lying on the floor among some other objects behind the living-room door, and the informers' reports claimed that Santosh had taken it to the house some days previously. That it is extremely unlikely that a young man whom no-one considered mentally disturbed, would place himself and his own family at such risk was something to which the Chief Justice drew attention in his judgement on his appeal.[111]

Woodroffe's Indian colleague on the Appeal Bench, Justice Digambar Chatterji, did not go so far as to reject the senior judge's decision, but he cautiously put forward his own reading of the case which, he regretted to say, differed from that of Woodroffe. It differed in fact very significantly, and in most respects, agreed with Fletcher's.[112]

We are forced to the conclusion that in his judgement in the Midnapore appeal case Woodroffe allowed himself to be used in an official cover-up of a case of police malpractice. Why did he do it?

Sympathy with Weston and the two Indian policemen may certainly have been a factor. The lives of all of them were in danger, as events surrounding and subsequent to the Muzzaferpore and Alipore cases showed. The *maulvi* and his informers had brought the police their first break in penetrating the revolutionary cells, which would have made him extremely unpopular.[113] This however did not mean that Weston and his police had no case to answer in their treatment of Santosh Das and his father. Instead of being impartial, Woodroffe simply closed ranks with the British establishment.

Woodroffe no doubt was under great pressure. The political atmosphere was extremely tense with strong feelings being expressed both by the British community and the nationalists. Woodroffe was allowed six months' emergency leave on 'urgent private affairs' immediately after the case.[114] There is no record of the reason for this, but perhaps it was felt necessary to get him away from the heat of the situation, or perhaps the strain had affected him. That he was under stress is revealed in a comment in the CWN that he had in fact broken down on the third day of reading his judgement in court.[115] Justice Fletcher had been under immense pressure two years previously. The Chief Justice, Sir Lawrence Jenkins, in a letter to the viceroy expressed fears for Fletcher's mental health and wrote of 'the discreditable ill-feeling to which he had been exposed'.[116] In another letter on the occasion of the Lala Lajput Rai case, he wrote to Morley, the Secretary of State, that Fletcher had received a threatening letter 'and is anathema to the white man'. Jenkins himself at that time was regarded as being 'in league with the agitators' because of his friendly relations with Indian people.[117] But these two British judges steadfastly resisted the pressure of their compatriots.

What pressures were acting upon Woodroffe we can only speculate. August of 1912 was six months before the first 'Arthur Avalon' books appeared, but Woodroffe's interest in Tantra was public knowledge, if we take account of an ironical reference in an Indian newspaper to his work on the *mahānirvāṇa tantra*.[118] 1912 was also the year in which he may have allowed himself to be photographed in Indian dress at the Konarak temple.[119] But if his tantric associations had made him feel especially vulnerable to official censure, it was not the first time that Woodroffe had strongly upheld the 'official line'. His attitude in the Lajpat Rai case was also strongly supportive of government.[120] Yet he too had in 1907 rejected a confession made under suspicious circumstances: on that occasion he had ordered the police officers concerned to appear in court for cross-examination. That case however had not involved a British magistrate and had not aroused controversy.[121]

I believe that what chiefly underlay Woodroffe's Midnapore appeal judgement was the unpublished government report, which only he and his fellow judges had read, which was not permitted to be challenged in court, and which was not subsequently published. The report's terms of reference did not only cover the accusations against the police but chiefly it was an investigation into the existence of a 'conspiracy' in Midnapore.[122] Woodroffe's conviction that there was such a conspiracy – which contrasted with the view of the Chief Justice in the original appeal by Santosh Das – was correct in the light of later knowledge, but one wonders how Woodroffe had access to it, if not through the government report. His language suggests the influence of government or police assessments of the situation, which seem to have coloured his view of the case and of all the participants in it.

His language and sympathies at any rate do not sound like those of someone who ten years later was to be acclaimed for writings in support of nationalism. Perhaps this indicates that his self-identification and his sympathies changed during the following decade, but perhaps it is more likely that he always maintained a split within himself.[123]

If Woodroffe's Midnapore judgement was surprising, what is even more remarkable is how short-lived was his unpopularity. By 1915 the CWN was calling for his promotion to Chief Justice on the retirement of Sir Lawrence Jenkins. The call was echoed in a few Indian papers, although support for Asutosh Mukherji was stronger.[124] Woodroffe was not made Chief Justice except for a brief inter-regnum lasting one week in 1915, but in that year he also received his knighthood and on approving this the CWN described his reputation as standing 'incontestably high'.[125] It seems that the Midnapore affair was quickly forgiven and forgotten, or accepted (in the words of one paper) as an 'aberration'. There is however an allusion to it in the CWN account of Woodroffe's retirement, which seems to give him rather faint praise for his independence.[126] There is a marked contrast here with the fulsome praise for this quality bestowed upon the Chief Justice Sir Lawrence Jenkins.[127] Otherwise by the time of his retirement, a decade after the Midnapore appeal case, Woodroffe's popularity at the High Court appears unchallenged. The whole of the writings of 'Arthur Avalon' and *Is India Civilized?* came in between. However, the importance of the Midnapore case for the government is underlined by the fact that Woodroffe received a personal telegram of congratulation from Lord Hardinge for the courage and 'independence' of his judgement.[128]

Had Woodroffe's support for Indian nationalism been the result of liberal *political* thinking he might perhaps have been better able to perceive the political situation in which he had been caught. As it was, he appeared to show little sensitivity to questions of constitutional and individual liberties, concerns voiced by the Chief Justice and others involved in the case. Despite his legal scholarship which produced his books on British Indian law, the tone of his Midnapore judgement suggests Woodroffe was driven by emotion, and by a bias towards authority that appears naive.

Indian cultural and religious nationalism, however – India as an *idea*, the symbol of values lost in Western European modernity – was what really stirred him, for this affected his own religious and emotional identity. Here too, though, there were ambiguities, as we shall see in the following chapters.

If Woodroffe was seen as standing in the orientalist tradition of Sir William Jones, it was not only for the combination of legal and sanskritic studies, it was also because his knowledge or 'expertise' was seen to extend widely through Indian culture. Before he became known as a tantric scholar, he was among a small group of Europeans and Indians who 'discovered' Indian art. By Woodroffe's time the roles of orientalist and nationalist sometimes 'veered closely together', as Tapati Guha Thakurta puts it, in the artistic sphere.

Chapter Four

THE ART CONNOISSEUR

Romantic orientalists

In India, as in other countries, nationalism was closely connected both with religion and with a revival of the arts; together they comprised the 'Indian Renaissance'.[1] But paradoxically perhaps it was among Europeans and in the heart of the British establishment in Calcutta, that Indian art first became fashionable. Appreciation of 'oriental' art became an arena where members of the European and Indian élites in the city came together with a common programme. This movement has been analysed by Partha Mitter[2] and by Tapati Guha-Thakurta. In her study of art and aesthetics in Bengal, Guha-Thakurta identifies what she calls a 'new orientalism' among European art critics at the beginning of the twentieth century, which became allied to Indian nationalist attempts to define an authentic national art.[3] The Indian Society of Oriental Art (ISOA) was the pivot of this movement, and Woodroffe was regarded as one of its leading spirits from its foundation in 1907.[4] He was one of a group of European connoisseurs who supported Abanindranath Tagore's New Bengal School of painting which was at the heart of ISOA's ideology and activities.

O.C. Ganguly

A pen-portrait of Woodroffe sets him in this cultural role. It comes from the memoirs of the art historian Ordhendu Kumar Ganguly (1881–1974) who in 1914–15 came to know Woodroffe well, when they were respectively secretary and president of the art society.[5] Ganguly also records a time when as a young solicitor he knew the older man as a figure at the High Court.[6] Although he says that they came in close contact (*ghaniṣṭh saṁsparṣa*) with each other Ganguly's picture lacks the vivid personal touch that Torick Ameer Ali gives. Though writing many years afterwards, there is perhaps flattery and certainly circumspection in his account of Woodroffe. If he thought his older British friend eccentric in some ways he does not say so openly. He depicts him in the style of Sir William Jones and the early orientalists, a humanist scholar with well-rounded knowledge in many spheres. After detailing his scholarship in Law, and his Sanskrit learning, Ganguly describes Woodroffe as a perceptive art connoisseur (*vicakṣaṇa kalārasika*) with a profound knowledge of the history of oriental art, and a patron of the New Bengal School who bought many of their paintings at the society's annual exhibitions. As a collector he was also interested in ancient Indian art and he thus gradually amassed an 'enormous' (*virāt*) collection, which Ganguly believed he took back to his home in 'Paris'.[7]

Also regarded as part of Woodroffe's expertise was an understanding of Japanese and Chinese art: it was high praise for him to compare the style of a painting by Ganguly's cousin Surendranath (a pupil of Abanindranath) with that of a Japanese artist.[8] Japanese ideology about a unified 'orient' formed a significant element in the inspiration for the Indian Society of Oriental Art, through the visits to India of the Japanese art historian Kakuzo Okakura (see below). Okakura's art periodical *Kokka* reproduced two paintings by members of the New Bengal school, with a short introduction by Woodroffe.[9]

New Attitudes to Indian Art: Havell and Coomaraswamy

Partha Mitter, in his comprehensive history of European attitudes to Indian art, reveals an ambivalent relationship in this period, affected by racial attitudes and Euro-centric schools of art criticism. Accurate realism was seen as a universally applicable norm and consequently European classical and renaissance art was held to be the exemplar of taste against which all Indian art was deemed inferior, even when admired.[10] A new vision was born at the beginning of the twentieth century with the writings of two prominent historians of Indian art, Ernest Binfield Havell and Ananda Coomaraswamy. Indian, along with European Gothic, art was held to represent a more spiritual and imaginative ideal than the 'mere' imitation of nature of classical Greece or the European renaissance, and Indian aesthetic ideals became acceptable on their own terms.[11] It is to the schools of thought of Havell and Coomaraswamy and their circle, that Guha-Thakurta refers by the term 'new orientalism'.[12] It was not, however, all that new when set in the wider context of idealistic or romantic orientalism that first found its expression in Sir William Jones and his circle; for here we find ourselves back again in the 'spiritual East'.

It was not that nineteenth century European writers never admired Indian art; but as Guha-Thakurta shows, orientalist admiration had been confined hitherto to the 'applied' arts – to decorative design and handicrafts. This was art with a functional or religious purpose which was not placed in the same category as 'fine art'. It was held as a maxim that India had produced no tradition of fine art.[13] Hence enthusiasm for a revival of an Indian artistic tradition was at first associated with a late nineteenth century 'arts and crafts' ideology of anti-industrialism. This was also the milieu in which the swadeshi movement arose: the Dawn Society, one of the earliest and most active of the swadeshi organizations, had a strong crafts ideology. Founded in 1902 by Satis Mukherji it was under this society's auspices that swadeshi stores were first opened selling local handmade products. Several Europeans, including Havell, had connections with it, and Havell was active in promoting the hand spinning wheel, later adopted by Mahatma Gandhi.[14]

Ernest Binfield Havell (1864–1937) was a close friend of Woodroffe. A member of the Indian Education Service, he was superintendent of the Madras School of Arts from 1884 and of the Calcutta Government Art School for ten years from 1896. His interest in preserving Indian handicrafts against the threat posed by European manufactured goods was eventually transformed into a 'crusade' aimed at the restoration of an Indian fine art tradition. Rejecting the notion that Indians needed to look to European models for an artistic style that was 'higher' than the merely decorative, Havell made a revolutionary move with his decision in 1904 to start selling off the Government Art School's collection of European paintings and to purchase in their place examples of Indian art.[15] Woodroffe as a member of the Art Gallery committee of the Indian Museum, lent sympathetic support to Havell's policy, and helped with the selection of the new purchases. The action initially caused a storm of protest among the Western educated classes of Calcutta who saw it as an attempt to deprive them of access to 'fine art'.[16] But Havell was fully supported by Lord Curzon. The Viceroy who above all others embodies the image of imperialism at its most dominating and self-assured, was also an enthusiast for the revival of Indian artistic traditions, a factor which perhaps augmented the suspicions of some citizens of Calcutta.[17] Havell's articles criticising the 'philistinism' of the more prevalent British attitudes started appearing at the turn of the century.[18] His two major books, *Indian Sculpture and Painting* (1908) and *The Ideals of Indian Art* (1911) were published after his return to England. A severe mental breakdown caused him to be permanently retired from India in 1906.

Ananda Kentish Coomaraswamy (1877–1947), born of a Ceylonese Brahmin father and an English mother, spent his childhood and early adult life in England.[19] His first visit to the Indian subcontinent took him to Sri Lanka in 1902 as a geologist, but he was immediately conscious of the inroads into Sinhalese culture made by Western industrialism. A disciple of William Morris in England,[20] Coomaraswamy's first major book, *Medieval Sinhalese Art* (1908), set opposite to the modern industrial world an idealised 'traditional' society located in the Kandyan kingdom of Sri Lanka prior to British colonisation. In *The Indian Craftsman* in 1909 he turned his attention to India, which for Coomaraswamy had 'emerged from a craftsman's paradise to an ancient homeland of a most sublime and independent tradition of fine arts'.[21] Nostalgia for the European Middle Ages was linked in Coomaraswamy's world view with his vision of 'traditional' Indian society, where religion cemented the social framework and was the major inspiration for art. India and Sri Lanka were living examples of such a society, the antithesis of Victorian industrialism.[22]

Coomaraswamy's first visit to India was in 1907, and from 1909–13 he travelled frequently between that country and England. He joined the circle around the Tagores and the Indian Society of Oriental Art. He collaborated with Nivedita on a book of hindu and buddhist mythology, illustrated with paintings by the artists of the New Bengal School.[23] Encountering the swadeshi fervour at its peak, he wrote essays on art and nationalism.[24] In 1910 he lectured in Woodroffe's house on Rajput painting – later to be the subject of his book of 1916 – where he detached Rajput (Hindu) painting from the Islamic Moghul tradition to which it had links. He celebrated the former as the more genuinely folk art, as well as the more religious in inspiration, opposing it to the aristocratic 'secular' court art of the Moghuls.[25] Nandalal Bose's famous painting 'Satī', where the act of *satī* was idealised, gave expression to ideals of Indian womanhood put forward in essays by Coomaraswamy. Here Woman represented the refined spiritual essence of Hindu culture; this metaphorical use of the act flew in the face of reformist emphasis on its barbarity.[26]

Conflict between old and new

In England, the clash between the old and the new attitudes to Indian art came to a head in 1910, a year which Mitter regards as a watershed.[27] It was initially due to Havell – now in England – who in February of that year delivered a lecture to the Royal Society of Arts in which he put forward his ideas about a 'fine art' tradition in India. In the chair at the meeting was Sir George Birdwood, at that time the leading British writer on Indian handicrafts.[28] For him, however, 'fine art' was a different matter, and Havell's remarks provoked a reaction from Birdwood whose strong language deprecating Indian art caused the meeting to break up in disarray. It also provoked a letter to *The Times* of London, in which a number of prominent people publicly dissociated themselves from his views. Birdwood's 'infamous' statement that had caused the furore was a description of an image of the Buddha which ran:

> The senseless similitude, by its immemorial fixed pose, is nothing more than an uninspired brazen image, vacuously squinting down its nose to its thumbs, knees and toes. A boiled suet pudding would serve equally well as a symbol of passionate purity and serenity of soul.[29]

This would have been all-too-familiar territory for some. The language of contempt directed at Indian art was akin to that bestowed upon Tantra.

Like Arthur Avalon on Tantra, Coomaraswamy had opened his work with a review of denigratory statements made by other authors which he used as a point of departure for his re-evaluation.[30] So did Havell in 1908, though by the second edition of his *Indian Sculpture and Painting* these passages were omitted as he considered changed attitudes had made them less relevant.[31]

A famous statement by Ruskin on the corrupting qualities of Hindu art due to its 'distortion' of nature, was seen as the prototype of the attitudes which thinkers like Havell and Coomaraswamy challenged:

> It either forms its compositions out of meaningless fragments of colour and flowings of line; or if it represents any living creature it represents that creature under some distorted and monstrous form. To all the facts and forms of nature it wilfully and resolutely opposes itself; it will not draw a man but an eight-armed monster; ...[32]

Ruskin's statement was made in 1859, soon after what is called the Indian Mutiny. James Cousins, recalling it in 1918, commented: 'According to him [Ruskin], the whole Indian race was guilty of the crimes of the mutineers and those crimes were the outcome of the nature of Indian Art.'[33] Alongside such prejudices, Cousins considered, there ran distrust of the imagination, of mysticism and symbolism. The 'facts of nature' which Ruskin insisted on, Cousins acerbically commented 'were actually emotions that he could understand ... the little truth that he himself was capable of apprehending.'[34]

Birdwood, who wrote in the 1880s, differed from Ruskin, not only in that he admired Indian handicrafts but, like Havell and Coomaraswamy he appreciated their religious inspiration, and saw spirituality as of their essence. He wrote that Hindu life was 'absorbed ... in the unseen realities of man's spiritual consciousness'.[35] However, like other Europeans who tried to appreciate the foreign culture but could not overcome innate prejudices, he was ambivalent, and shared Ruskin's distrust of the popular expressions of Hinduism, writing of the 'evil influence' of the *purāṇas* on Indian art:

> The monstrous shapes of the Puranic deities are unsuitable for the higher forms of artistic representation; and this is possibly why sculpture and painting are unknown as fine arts in India.'[36]

Alongside the aesthetic fashions and racial theories in Europe which Mitter traces, therefore, what marked out 'new' from 'old' or nineteenth century orientalist attitudes was a different reaction to India itself, and especially to Hinduism. It is interesting that behind Ruskin's condemnations quoted by Cousins, can be traced a reluctant admiration allied to fear: Ruskin actually acknowledged the superiority of Indian decorative skill but specifically linked it to vicious moral qualities.[37] Cousins, writing sixty years later, by contrast glosses over a possible aesthetic disappointment with the New

Bengal School by appealing to its lofty philosophy. For example, what he obviously felt was a degree of imitativeness among the pupils of Abanindranath, he put down to the 'eastern' sense of unity.[38] When commenting on the socially satirical sketches of Gaganendranath Tagore – which clearly disturbed his rather anodyne image of the new 'Indian' art – Cousins claimed that the subject of all the Indian painters was an abstraction called 'life'; they did not enter its 'dark places' as 'fault finders' but expressed the 'deep compassion of the sense of unity which is India's contribution to the thought of the world'.[39] Cousins followed Havell in finding the true location of 'Indian' art in the realm of the spiritual. Generalising on the difference between the new Bengal School and the art of the West, he declares of the Indian works that 'every one of them expresses soul', whereas Western art expresses 'muscularity, vigour, emotion'.[40] This indicates how far in the years since Ruskin and the 'Mutiny', Hinduism had ceased to seem threatening in Britain, and was becoming for some an ally, or a refuge, in the conflict with Western modernity and empiricism.

For when Havell rejected the established norms of Western art criticism it was because he considered them narrowly realist. The emphasis on 'naturalism' denied the imagination as well as 'the Spirit'. He urged that Indian art should be understood in relation to Indian ideas and goals. Identifying these as 'spiritual', he placed them above and beyond the material world in a realm where accurate representation of outer reality was irrelevant. He did not deny that Indian art could be 'realistic', but pointed to the philosophy of Vedānta, with its doctrine of *māyā* as more significant:

> Indian art *can* be realistic in the European sense, but his philosophy regards all that we see in Nature as transitory, illusive phenomena and declares that the only Reality is the Divine Essence or Spirit'.[41]

Beyond the sphere of *māyā* stood the yogic ideal of the 'divine form' which underlay the images of deities, and especially the Buddha image, rather than the strict adherence to anatomy of Western art. In the *yantras* of tantric ritual Havell saw, not the magic diagrams perceived by most other Western writers, but abstractions expressing what was beyond imagery. No longer consigned to the 'primitive' and 'superstitious', Havell had placed these instruments of tantric ritual in the vanguard of European thought. Hindu iconographic art, he declared, 'like modern criticism joins mathematics with aesthetics'.[42]

In this 'new orientalist' dichotomy of 'East' versus 'West', to the former was assigned the 'higher' values of intuition and idealism, over against the 'muscular realism' of the latter. While newly applied to art criticism, this was an adaptation of the nineteenth century Indian idea of complementarity between the supposed practical or empirical values of the West and those of the 'spiritual East'. Instigated by Keshub Chandra Sen and P.C. Mazoomdar, and widely popularised in India and the West by Vivekananda and later by Rabindranath Tagore, it has been seen as a response by Indian thinkers to the Western projection of a unified 'Asia' as a counterweight to European civilization, or as Europe's 'Other'.[43] Whereas for the most part the prevailing orientalist theories assigned higher value to Europe, the 'new' or romantic orientalists accompanied some nationalists into a 'reversal of hierarchies between East and West'.[44]

Most European commentators on Indian history viewed it through a theory of continuous decline from an idealized past. This was linked to the prevailing racial theories around the Indo-Aryans and their 'degeneration' in subsequent Indian history through racial intermixture.[45] The effect was to make it possible to devalue the living Hinduism they encountered, while continuing to idealise the 'Aryan' civilization associated with the Vedas, and the equally remote early Buddhist period.[46] The shift of emphasis in Havell's writings was subtle but significant. Like other European orientalists, Havell sought a 'golden age' in India's past, but he located it in the Mauryan and Gupta periods. The latter was a quintessential Hindu one when Hinduism's 'glory' spread through South East Asia. It is true that Havell also idealised the Aryans, but in a sense that was closer to the way in which Hindus themselves did. He did indeed see them in mythical terms, as Mitter suggests, but as a 'mythical' race whose qualities underlay and blossomed in subsequent Indian history. He believed the vedic age contained the essence of later Hinduism and believed in the 'great synthesis' whereby Buddhism (and all else that was considered of value in Indian history or culture) was absorbed within Brahmanism, the carrier of 'Aryan' tradition. This was in contrast to theories which saw later Hinduism as the result of the decline of the 'Aryan' race into 'barbarism' and 'superstition', and was closer to the concepts of Indian history held by higher caste Hindus.[47]

Coomaraswamy, like Havell, also linked art to yoga, and expounded upon the connection between iconographic art and *dhyāna*, the mental construction of divine images in meditative practice.[48] This was something also commented on by Heinrich Zimmer, who had read Arthur Avalon's translation of Sivacandra Vidyarnava's *Tantratattva* and drew from it an argument for a separate aesthetics for Indian art.[49] Vasanta Kumar Pal reports a rumour that Woodroffe's guru instructed both Coomaraswamy and Havell. Although this is problematical, Coomaraswamy is said to have asked Sivacandra to ritually 'receive' him into Hinduism.[50] Both men moved in the same social circles as Woodroffe, and Havell's name, as we shall see, was linked with his in their common pursuit of 'gurus' and 'pandits'. Havell could well have learned from Sivacandra the meaning of the *yantra* in tantric ritual, which we have just referred to. A 1905 reference to Kālī symbolism and to the *mahānirvāṇa tantra* sounds as if he could have consulted Woodroffe or Ghose if not their guru.[51] But in any case, whether Sivacandra's influence is present or not, Havell at least can be located as close to Hinduism as to neo-Platonism or Theosophy where Mitter and Guha-Thakurta situate him. Coomaraswamy, too, Mitter calls 'the last of the neo-Platonists' and explains him entirely as a Western thinker.[52] No doubt this is correct, but Mitter and Guha-Thakurta tend to treat both these foreign art historians as if their theorizing was entirely sealed off from Indian influence.

Havell on art and Woodroffe on Tantra bear many resemblances to each other. They both stressed the remoteness of European consciousness from the inner world of Indian ideas and the consequent need for a European scholar to 'place himself at the Indian point of view'.[53] Both considered they had a mission to woo the Indian *bhadralok* away from prejudices against their own culture implanted by Europeans; they both ardently espoused the despised and rejected in Indian culture; both were also personally involved in the practice of *sādhanā* and believed in *advaita vedānta.* Woodroffe however did not share Havell's enthusiasm for imperialism.[54]

Since, according to the 'new orientalism' what was 'eastern' was the more 'spiritual', it was by expressing the higher and purer realms of the spirit that Indian artists could be true to their own racial inheritance and produce 'nationalist' art. This was in the context of what Mitter calls the 'racial romanticism' which was fashionable in Europe at the time.[55] The resurgence of a truly 'Indian' art was believed essential for the regeneration of the nation and (what was synonymous with 'nation'), the race.

Abanindranath and the New Bengal School

The new art movement in Calcutta grew out of the relationship between Havell the art critic and the painter Abanindranath Tagore (younger cousin to the poet Rabindranath). When they met in the late 1890s, the latter had already started experimenting with styles drawn from medieval Indian miniatures and the art of Ajanta. Havell publicized his work in articles from 1902 onwards, and invited him to teach at the Government Art School, where Tagore gathered around him a circle of pupils.[56] They produced self-consciously 'oriental' art by blending traditional Indian themes and styles, with some Japanese and Chinese influence, but with a strong residue, nevertheless, of European naturalism.[57] Abanindranath and his followers were soon involved in an ideological battle with Bengali artists and critics who preferred the European style of 'academic' art with its techniques of naturalism and opposed the new school's claim to be exclusively Indian.[58] The work of Abanindranath and his followers appealed to the British establishment however in their endeavour to encourage 'Indian-ness' in art, at the same time as it reflected the nationalism of the swadeshi movement in its early years. Guha-Thakurta illustrates this convergence by pointing out that in 1903 Abanindranath's *The Passing of Shah Jahan* won a silver medal at Curzon's Delhi Durbar exhibition; while in 1904–5 his *Bhārat Mātā* 'more than any other, fixed the epithet nationalist to his recreation of an Indian style'.[59]

The Indian Society of Oriental Art

An oriental art exhibition was first held in 1902 on the premises of the Landholders' Association, an organisation of Bengali zemindars to which not only the Tagores but also, for some reason, Woodroffe and his friend, the businessman Norman Blount, belonged. Kakuzo Okakura was in Calcutta at the time and lent some Japanese prints for the occasion, which were displayed alongside paintings by Abanindranath. Abanindranath organized the first formal meeting of the Indian Society of Oriental Art in 1907, after Havell had left India, but the inspiration for the society had grown out of the circle around him at the Government Art School.[60]

The majority of those listed as attending the first meeting were European, three of them High Court judges, including of course Woodroffe himself. Among the Indians, four were members of the Tagore family. This art society, whatever its emphasis on Indian national expression, was closely entwined with the British establishment. Lord Kitchener (chief of staff of the armed forces in India) was its surprising choice as first president. Woodroffe succeeded him, to be succeeded in his turn by another High Court judge (Holmwood) and after that by Lord Carmichael, Governor of Bengal. Woodroffe served on the first committee of the society and was one of the most active and influential members in the early years.[61] Although it remained an élite organisation – according to one account it only had 120 members by 1916 and only 47 of them were Indian[62] – it quickly became influential in its attempts to propagate the new nationalist art. Over many years a colour plate reproduction of a painting by a member of the New Bengal School was the frontispiece of every edition of Ramananda Chatterji's influential Calcutta journals *Modern Review* and *Pravaśi*.[63]

The society rented a house in Park Street where annual exhibitions were held, and Woodroffe's enthusiasm seems to have been their driving force from the beginning. The paintings of the Tagore brothers, Abanindranath and his brother Gaganendranath, and their followers took central place, alongside examples of ancient and medieval Indian, Tibetan, Chinese and Japanese art.[64] The first on a large scale was held at Allahabad in February 1911 as part of the United Provinces Exhibition and was organised by Coomaraswamy, though Woodroffe seems to have felt himself responsible for ISOA'S pavilion there.[65]

Meanwhile 1910 saw the formation of the India Society in London, by the artist William Rothenstein and a group of people who had supported

Havell in his controversy with Birdwood. Links were immediately established with the art society in Calcutta. The highly enthusiastic William Rothenstein toured India in the winter of 1910–11, setting off with letters of introduction from Havell to Woodroffe and Abanindranath. This momentous visit was to result in a friendship with Rabindranath Tagore which led to the poet's 'discovery' by the West, his 1913 Nobel prize and his elevation as an international figure and icon of 'oriental' spirituality.[66] In 1914, the year following Rabindranath's first European tour, the Indian Society of Oriental Art held exhibitions in Paris and London, the former being organized by the two Karpélès sisters, daughters of a French businessman in Calcutta and admirers of the poet.[67]

Meanwhile the society's exhibitions in Calcutta became a major feature of the winter social scene and attracted crowds from all over the country.[68] Reviews in the Indian and foreign press helped to educate the public on 'oriental' art. Before long they attracted the attention of James Cousins in Madras. Annie Besant's close friend and colleague, who was editor of the Theosophical Society's paper *New India*, thereafter became an enthusiastic and influential supporter of the movement. After accepting a personal invitation from Woodroffe to visit Calcutta to view the exhibition held there in January 1916, Cousins arranged for it to be transferred to Madras, where it was displayed at the premises of the Young Men's Indian Association, a Theosophical organisation. Cousins implies that it was through the influence of ISOA that Annie Besant and the Theosophical Society were first won over to wholehearted encouragement of a nationalist style of Indian art.[69]

Cousins – always enthusiastic – covered up what was perhaps a slight disappointment at the physical environment of the exhibition rooms in Calcutta in 'what ordinarily would have been a large shop or office on a main thoroughfare of the city'. But: 'good taste had turned bareness into an exquisite attractiveness that, on a first glance, had a curious delicacy and reserve . . .' Being an Irish nationalist, he perceived affinities with the situation at home. He considered he was . . .

> witnessing that exciting and incalculable thing such as I had experienced in the Irish literary and dramatic revival, the reawakening of a gifted nation to recognition of its artistic past in one of the arts, and to realisation of its ability, in the persons of some of its nationals, to emulate, and in some phases to equal, ancestral achievement . . .[70]

'Ancestral achievement' was the *leitmotif* to this 'new orientalist' or nationalist art movement. Racial theories that the 'spirit' of a nation or race could alone be expressed through its own culture and through no other are strongly reflected in Woodroffe's *Seed of Race* and *Bhārata Shakti*, to be discussed in the next chapter. Applied to art, this meant that imitation of the style of another 'race' led to work that was not authentically one's own, as Woodroffe wrote in the Japanese journal *Kokka*.[71]

Along with Woodroffe's, several other European names were connected with the Indian Society of Oriental Art, as prominent members and influential connoisseurs. Norman Blount, an English jute broker, seems to have been a close friend of Woodroffe, for their names are linked continually by Abanindranath and others. Blount was the Society's first joint secretary along with Abanindranath. He and Woodroffe were frequent visitors to the Tagores' famous 'southern verandeh'; and the artist is said to have asked Blount's advice on his paintings.[72] Another founder member was Hjalmar Ponten Moeller, one of two Swedish businessmen who were described as very active in the early years.[73] Also a diplomat, he looked after his country's embassy in Calcutta and lived in the city until his death in 1944.[74] Moeller, like Blount, was a friend of both Woodroffe and Atal Behari Ghose (see chapter 6 below). Another early member whose name crops up several times is that of Edward Thornton, an architect whom Abanindranath describes as one of his best friends.[75]

European women took lessons in Indian art at an informal club run by Thornton after hours at the Government Art School, and one of them contributed some flower paintings done in the style of Indian miniatures to the first ISOA exhibition.[76] Interestingly, this possibly reflects the invisibility of women's art, for the role of the European *men* in this art movement was firmly restricted to that of support for Indian artists: as connoisseurs, financial sponsors – 'consumers' not producers or rivals – and sources of approbation. Many of them, most notably Woodroffe and Blount, were holders of prestige and 'expert' knowledge by which the new school could be assessed – always, of course, positively.[77]

Set somewhat apart from the other Europeans was Nivedita, Swami Vivekananda's famous disciple. Although not among the founder members of the art society her championship of Indian art as an aspect of nationalism is well known and was a powerful influence. Her articles and book reviews in the first decade of the century popularized the ideas of Coomaraswamy and made art into a 'highly conscious vehicle of nationalism'.[78] Nivedita exerted an influence over Abanindranath's young pupils, as well as casting something of a spell over the master himself. Abanindranath describes how he met Nivedita for the first time at a reception in Calcutta for Kakuzo Okakura. Some time afterwards he invited her to a party where she made a dramatic impression, and where he introduced her to Woodroffe and Blount, who seem not to have known her by sight before that.[79] This indicates that, despite sharing beliefs in nationalism and neo-Vedanta, Woodroffe and Nivedita did not meet within the circle of Vivekananda's disciples. Woodroffe however had contacts with other disciples of the Swami later on, and he was for a time President of the Vivekananda Society in Calcutta. Nivedita died in 1911 before any of the books of Arthur Avalon were published.[80]

A Japanese Visitor

Kakuzo Okakura in Japan, like Abanindranath Tagore in Bengal, had founded an alternative art school which aimed to be independent of European academic structures: the *Nippon Bijutsuin* school outside Tokyo. Like Abanindranath, he too had been influenced by a foreign orientalist in seeking a revival of his country's artistic traditions.[81] He first came to India with Mrs Josephine Macleod at the end of 1901 to meet her guru Vivekananda, whom he regarded as the 'very personification of Asian or Oriental ideals'. Another purpose was to visit Bodh Gaya which he wished to restore as a buddhist pilgrimage site. This first visit lasted until 1903. There is a suggestion that he might possibly have been an agent for the Japanese empire.[82] Whether this was true or not there, was a strong current of Japanese nationalism underlying his pan-Asian philosophy. During this visit he completed his book *Ideals of the East*, which put forward the picture of a unified civilization of the Orient that was superior to the materialistic culture of modern Europe. 'Asia is one' he wrote, opening his book: 'The Himalayas divide, only to accentuate, two mighty civilizations . . . But not even the snowy barriers can interrupt for one moment that broad expanse of love for the Ultimate and Universal which is the common thought inheritance of every Asiatic race'.[83] Okakura's ideas and personality inspired the nationalism of the young Bengalis he met, as recounted by Surendranath Tagore,[84] as much as they fed the romantic orientalism of the Indian art movement with its dichotomy of 'spiritual east' and 'materialist West'. While paying tribute to India as the matrix of Asian culture and the homeland of Buddhism, Okakura nevertheless considered that Japan alone had preserved the greatness of Asia, whereas India and China had succumbed to foreign invasion. Nivedita wrote an introduction to his book in which she shifted the bias towards India.[85] Underlying both was a new vision of the 'orient', no longer as a lost civilization of antiquity, but a living culture whose superiority could resist colonisation by the West. Japan's status as a symbol of Asian resurgence rose dramatically in 1905 with its victory in the Russian–Japanese war. That year Okakura published his second major book *The Awakening of Japan* where he proclaimed the secret of Japan to lie in its ability to assimilate Western knowledge without sacrificing its spiritual and cultural independence.[86] We shall see how this was echoed in Woodroffe's writings as a pattern for India to follow.

A Charmed Circle

The Indian Society of Oriental Art was part of an élite and privileged world, inhabited by the 'cream' of both Indian and European society and one of highly self-conscious aestheticism. Abanindranath describes a glittering social scene, with sumptuous parties where *pāñ* was served to

Indian guests in European homes. Lectures were held in private houses, including that of the Woodroffes whose aesthetic sensibility was reflected in their Calcutta homes. We have seen that Torick Ameer Ali described his stay with them at Camac Street as 'a week of gracious living'. Others had similar reactions. In 1910 Ananda Coomaraswamy wrote to William Rothenstein on the eve of his Indian tour: 'You will find Woodroffe a splendid person, a real student and thinker, and one who knows how to make his immediate environment beautiful.'[87] James Cousins and his wife Margaret found their visit to the Woodroffes' a memorable experience when they returned to Calcutta in 1917 for the Indian National Congress convention. The couple described how they were motored by Woodroffe 'to his commodious and artistic home', where 'the day ended with intuitive fitness' at dinner with the Tagore brothers after which they 'retired with the atmosphere of art and beauty and high philosophy'.[88] A decade earlier another Woodroffe home was mentioned by Cornelia Sorabji, the only female lawyer at the High Court. She was not a member of ISOA but had been given entry to the social circle of the 'memsahibs' of Calcutta. She mentioned the 'lovely house' of the Woodroffes in a letter to a British friend in 1906.[89]

The Woodroffes in 1912 were able to introduce the French buddhist traveller Alexandra David-Neel to an enchanted 'oriental' world such as she felt most tourists would never be able to penetrate. Good fortune, she wrote in her letters to her husband, had introduced her to the Woodroffes who were '*charmants*'. They had brought her to 'some very rich Hindus' for an evening of Indian music. She was impressed by the atmosphere which was 'like The Thousand and One Nights' with the musicians seated, Indian-fashion, on a great mattress on the floor decorated with brocades and cushions and surrounded by works of art. Among them 'the masters of the house moved about in white robes with borders of Kashmir silk'[90] A couple of months later she was invited to a musical 'afternoon' by the Woodroffes themselves. Tea served in the garden was followed by music in the salon. David-Neel fell into a rapturous philosophical reverie over the dream-like strains of the *vīna*. Once again, it was not the sort of music that the mass of tourists in the city heard (even though she felt the company did not compare with those who visited the Tagores!) It was a mixed gathering of Europeans and Indians, with '*ranis* dressed in golden muslin' among the women guests. She was seated next to a Bengali poetess. After the *vīna* came Western music, played by the Director of the Calcutta Conservatory accompanied by Mrs Woodroffe on the piano. Then, after most of the guests had departed, a select few were invited to remain while the *vīna* player returned and enchanted them for the rest of the evening. '*La musique hallucinée recommence . . .*' provoking much philosophical and generalising comparison with the Western music which had preceded it. Among other things, not only was the 'Eastern' more dream-like, it was also more sensual.[91]

Evenings with a *vīna* player are recaptured by Abanindranath in his memoirs, this time at the Tagores' famous mansion: 'And once again Blount Sahib, Woodroffe Sahib and some of our own enthusiasts for national music having met together, I brought a vina player from Madras.' Orange, sherbet and *pāñ* were kept in ready supply. At night 'when the roar of the city stopped, the children of the house had gone to sleep, the work of all the servants was done and there was peace on all sides, then the vina would arise . . .' Count Herman Keyserling, the Austrian philosopher, was there on one occasion, we are informed.[92] Keyserling himself recorded the scene in his travel diary of 1911, where the 'oriental' music gave rise to much the same sort of dreamy mystic reverie as it had done for David-Neel.[93]

Joṛāsānko

The magic of this élite world of 'oriental' culture had its heart in the mansion of the Tagore family at Joṛāsānko in north Calcutta at number 6 Dwarkarnath Tagore Lane, home of the poet Rabindranath, while his cousins Abanindranath and Gaganendranath lived opposite at number 5. Coomaraswamy's biographer says that he 'entered a charmed circle early in 1909 when he joined the Tagores at . . . Jorasanko'.[94] Whether or not they were the '*très riches hindous*' to whom the Woodroffes had taken Alexandra David-Neel on her arrival – and they most probably were – we have just seen that two months into her time in Calcutta she was comparing the Woodroffes' circle unfavourably with that of the Tagores. A visit to the Tagores seems to have been essential for any distinguished foreigner who wanted to encounter 'Eastern' culture, whether in the field of art, music or literature. Lord Zetland, newly appointed Governor of Bengal in 1917, was entertained to a production of Rabindranath's *The Post Office* at Joṛāsānko performed by members of the family;[95] and in the same year his private secretary took the visiting Secretary of State Sir Edwin Montagu, 'to see the three Tagore brothers and their paintings'.[96]

Rabindranath's son, Rathindranath Tagore, describes in his memoirs the famous 'southern verandeh' where his artist cousins held court 'like Oriental monarchs' receiving visitors and students while they worked at their painting. He also recalls 'many an unforgettable evening' in the drawing room, no doubt the same ones Abanindranath describes: 'There would be a few lovers of art and music reclining in meditative poses on spacious divans with lights dimmed listening to the melodious strains of the Veena.' He would watch silently from an 'obscure corner' the 'distinguished foreigners' who formed the company.[97]

William Rothenstein wrote of Joṛāsānko that he used to leave 'as though there were an inch of air between my feet and the ground. Where indeed could I find such company as I met there? . . . These are the precious hours of life, the hours spent with exciting minds, when one's best self, too, is evoked.'[98]

Before meeting the Tagores, Rothenstein had met Woodroffe (who at the time was President of ISOA) at Christmas in Benares. 'He is one in ten thousand' Havell had written in his letter of introduction, 'a born artist – and one of the few strong men at present belonging to the Anglo-Indian administration – with none whatever of the usual Anglo-Indian prejudices.'[99] 'Sir John Woodroffe' recorded Rothenstein in his memoirs 'of all the Englishmen I met in India, showed most desire to plumb the depths of the Indian spirit. With a pandit he was studying the Tantric writings on which he became a learned authority.'[100] The visitor thus saw Woodroffe, within a social setting that sought to penetrate and capture 'Indian-ness', as someone who had travelled further along that path than any of the other Europeans in his circle. Woodroffe accompanied by a 'pandit' friend offered to show him round Benares, and made arrangements for him to visit the exhibition being organized at Allahabad.[101] But, Rothenstein complained, Woodroffe who 'knew the Tagores well' had spoken only of the artists Abanindranath and Gaganendranath and had not told him of their wonderful 'uncle', the poet Rabindranath.[102] Woodroffe indeed was such a frequent visitor to Joṛāsānko that a special room was kept there for him to use as he pleased.[103] Whenever he appeared people in the family would say 'Sahib has come!' – which always meant Woodroffe not anyone else.[104]

The Tagore home had not always seemed 'oriental'. Dora Ross (wife of Sir E. Denison Ross) visited it at the very beginning of the swadeshi era:

> 21st Aug 1905: Today we paid a visit to a typical Bengali family, the well-known Tagores of Calcutta.' [We were] 'received with great kindness and old-world courtesy... One felt that the charm of Hindu family life was here seen at its best'. All the men wore Indian dress, but the drawing room had 'every form of Victorian horror rampant'.[105]

Even then, it seems, the Tagores were already on display as a 'typical' Bengali Hindu family. But this was before the influence of the swadeshi movement had led them to redecorate and refurnish their home. The poet's son Rathindranath confirms that the family house had originally been furnished in the conventional Victorian style, until Abanindranath and Gaganendranath applied their talents to it. Their greatest success was with the drawing room which was transformed into 'a magnificent example of semi-oriental treatment – decorated with the choicest collection of paintings and Indian art-ware, a room that has been the envy of connoisseurs from the world over'.[106]

A Bengali novelist, Pavitra Gangopadhyay, in his memoirs recalled a party he had shyly attended in his youth where among the distinguished guests he had seen Sir John Woodroffe wearing Indian dress.[107] His host was an Indian High Court judge, and was almost certainly Justice Asutosh Chaudhury, who was related by marriage to the Tagores. He was a member of both the Landholders Association and of the Indian Society of Oriental Art. The self-consciously Indian ambience of the party which Gangopadhyay describes is striking when it is recalled that Asutosh Chaudhury was a member of a class of Bengalis caricatured as the *Inga Bhanga Samāj* – people who were entirely anglicised in their manners and customs.[108] As Rathindranath Tagore pointed out, however, this did not mean they were 'anti-national': on the contrary they formed the backbone of what was known as the 'Old Congress' – that is, the political 'moderates'. Asutosh Chaudhury took an active role in the swadeshi era when he was one of the leaders of the National Education Movement, but like Rabindranath, he was alienated by the violence of the revolutionaries.[109] As a representative of an older wave of nationalism, Chaudhury, like Rabindranath himself, was a critic of Gandhi and he actively opposed his visit to Calcutta in 1918.[110] Woodroffe appears to have assimilated himself to the world of the élite Bengali western educated nationalists. He seems to have fitted himself into the pacific, cultural nationalism of the swadeshi era with its extension into political 'extremism' but without overt support, at least, for violence. We have to pause for thought only over his friendship with Gaganendranath Tagore who, I was informed, was particularly close to Woodroffe and was also believed to be secretly in league with the revolutionaries.[111] If this was so, Woodroffe the High Court judge is unlikely to have been aware of it, but the suggestion hints at the complexities that may have lurked beneath the surface of this social world of friendships between members of the Indian and European (especially British) élites.

The Marquis of Zetland

Lord Ronaldshay, Marquis of Zetland, who became Governor of Bengal in 1917 followed his predecessor Lord Carmichael in giving keen patronage to the Indian Society of Oriental Art. He was also genuinely fascinated by Indian philosophy, holding discussions with pandits and other scholars[112] and himself writing on Indian culture. He acknowledged Woodroffe as 'the greatest living European authority' upon Tantra, but remained unconvinced by his defence of it.[113] In 1919 he offered ISOA a government grant which they cautiously accepted. In this as we have noted he believed he was encouraging the 'positive' as opposed to the 'negative' aspects of nationalism. It was accepted with reservations.[114] According to Lord Ronaldshay the society was languishing by this time – possibly because of the war[115] – but there was also said to be a 'slackening of the ties between the Indian and European members' after 1915, when Abanindranath left the Government art school following disagreements with Havell's successor. From then on the Tagores devoted themselves to their own newly formed cultural club based in the family home.[116] The decline might also have reflected the fact that 1916 was the last year in which Woodroffe was recorded as President of the Society. He was not on the committee which consulted with Lord Ronaldshay about the government grant,[117] though this may have been because he was out of the country on furlough. According to his correspondence with Dawasamdup, he was very busy with the *Tantrik Texts* by 1916, and most of his writing on Tantra was produced in the second half of the decade.

Whether or not his appreciation for Indian art helped to lead Woodroffe towards Tantra as some believed,[118] we shall see in a later chapter that the two worlds were closely linked for him and for other Europeans in the art society. His 'romantic orientalism' or his nationalism – depending on how one views it – also led him to voice opinions on wider aspects of Indian society, culture and education and were published in three books which appeared in the second half of the decade. These books are strongly imbued with contemporary ideology about the essence of a race being expressed in its culture. Woodroffe sometimes points to Japan as an example of an Asian nation which had been able to assimilate Western influence without losing its distinct identity or its 'soul'. In *Is India Civilized?* he presents the reader with a 'spiritual' orient set over against a 'materialist' Europe, with its matrix in India. Westernization and modernism are to be resisted as the twin enemies of 'true culture', which is always 'spiritual'. We turn to these writings on culture in the next chapter.

Chapter Five

THE DEFENDER OF HINDUISM

'India is an Idea'

In the three books discussed in this chapter Woodroffe attacked what he called the 'de-nationalizing' effect of the British education system in India, a theme of widespread concern at the time. Education is the main theme of *Bhārata Shakti* and *Seed of Race. Is India Civilized?* is a more general book in defence of Hindu tradition.

Bhārata Shakti: Woodroffe on public platforms

'India is not a mere geographical expression ... India is an Idea' wrote Woodroffe and he called it 'a particular Shakti, the *Bhārata Shakti*'.[1] The title was given to a collection of short writings, talks and speeches by Woodroffe compiled and edited by Nolini Mohun Chatterji, who wrote that the addresses were of great value 'at a time of mental and political unrest'.[2] Their popularity is shown by the fact that the book ran to three editions between 1917 and 1921, by appreciative reviews in the Indian press and by the fact that several of the addresses had been published or summarised previously in the *Bengalee*, the daily paper edited by Surendranath Bannerjee, the nationalist politician.

The second edition included Woodroffe's reply to questions put to him by the Sadler Commission which visited India in 1917–18 to inquire into the system of higher education. There was much talk at the time of Indian youth being 'deracinated' – alienated from their cultural heritage because of Western education. This was a debate which had started over a decade previously during the swadeshi era, when the Indian National Education Movement first organized its boycott of government controlled schools and colleges.[3] The question was now no longer associated with political extremism and it was becoming official government policy that Indian culture needed to be represented in the education system. No longer self-confident about the value of bestowing Western culture on India, as the 'Anglicists' of the previous century had been,[4] the British authorities sought a range of opinions from representative figures both Indian and

British. The notions about race discussed in the last chapter had a wider influence than the sphere of art: to be authentic, each must be 'true to his own' in every sphere. Woodroffe constantly expressed this theme, and in his reply to the questions put by the Commission, he declared government control of education to be 'deracializing, devitalizing and deforming'.[5] But with his instinct for compromise or 'balance' he did not like to play the radical and claimed he did not altogether deny the value of Western education; he sought, as he always claimed to do, a 'middle path'.[6]

Woodroffe's attack on westernization recalls that of some modern writers: he condemns imperialism for colonising the mind of the colonised, and opposes what more recently has been called 'the Europeanization of the globe'.[7] But he does this in the name of a racial ethics in which each must be true to his 'type' and perfect it for the benefit of humanity as a whole. Indians therefore must: 'be Indian, and shape themselves as such by the study of the literature, art, philosophy and religion of their ancestors.'[8] The same theme runs through all the addresses in *Bhārata Shakti*.

The earliest of them to be delivered was Woodroffe's presidential address to the annual general meeting of the Ram Mohun Roy Library in Calcutta, on 20 March 1915, a summary of which appeared in *The Bengalee*.[9] The thought of Raja Ram Mohun Roy (1772–1833), the social and religious reformer, inspired the foundation of the Brahmo Samaj in 1843.[10] Addressing a gathering which must have included many members of the Samāj – the philosopher Dr Brajendranath Seal introduced the speaker[11] – Woodroffe's talk nevertheless reflected some reservations about the man regarded as 'the founder of Hindu modernism'. Perhaps it was a paradoxical position for the pseudonymous Arthur Avalon to be in, since he had only recently published *Principles of Tantra*, the translation of Sivacandra Vidyarnava's book which was largely aimed against the Brahmo Samāj and other modernisers. On the other hand, Avalon had also recently translated the *mahānirvāṇa tantra* which was a favourite text of Ram Mohun Roy himself as well as being popular with his followers.[12] Woodroffe said little about the Raja's religious beliefs and probably felt confused by them. He concentrated instead on his greatness as a 'patriot and social worker'.[13]

Woodroffe expressed reservations about Ram Mohun's legacy as the first Indian to further the cause of Western education, but he defended his universalism, noting that this was unfashionable among contemporary nationalists.[14] He also felt himself on firm ground when praising the Raja's opposition to *satī* and his championship of women, but then this was something uncontroversial. He praised him for his 'tenderness to the poor' – but then sounded generally cautious himself about social reform. He tells three stories in this short address, two of them to illustrate the ambivalence of reform. One of these was the Taoist allegory of the 'Rulers of the Southern and Northern Oceans', who attempted to assist Chaos by giving him seven orifices for seeing, hearing etc like men have. 'But when they dug them for him he died'.[15] Reform involved dangers of turning people away from their 'type' or *svabhāva* – the Sanskrit term which Woodroffe uses elsewhere which probably corresponds to what he means by 'type'. He ended his address diplomatically by praising Ram Mohun as a 'true Muni' in the sense of an independent thinker.[16]

The address reflects the contradiction in Woodroffe himself, who seems to have been regarded as an ally on occasion by modernisers and secular reformers as well as by more conservative supporters of the Hindu revival. Yet here his instincts seem to lead him to come down on the conservative side. He felt akin to Ram Mohun in his humanism and universalism, but distrusted him for his 'protestant'[17] rejection of aspects of Hindu tradition. In his introduction to Sivacandra's book Arthur Avalon had made a specific comparison between Sivacandra's defence of Hindu orthodoxy against the Brahmo Samāj, and 'a Catholic protest against "modernism"' [PT/1 p. 31]. It seems that Woodroffe's Roman Catholic background may have encouraged him to identify instinctively with Sivacandra's attack on the Brahmo Samāj, and extended this to the man who was its inspiration.

A year later Woodroffe addressed the Friends Union Club, a student organisation. This was on 30 May 1916. At a time of ferment in the colleges of Calcutta, Woodroffe introduced his address by saying that 'students had lately been severely spoken of'. This was not surprising as only a little while before, in February of 1916, an unpopular British teacher had been physically attacked in Presidency College.[18] Students were suspected of having revolutionary sympathizers amongst their number and indiscipline was a problem. Far from criticising them for this, Woodroffe declared he was 'not alarmed at their condition' and though they had faults, these were connected with qualities of energy and self respect.[19] The teacher, Mr Oaten, had been attacked, among other things, for making racially insulting remarks.

Bhārata Shakti reprints the summary of Woodroffe's address that had been published in *The Bengalee.*[20] Woodroffe urged the students to be true to their religious and racial 'type' and criticised Indians who had become 'so anglicised that they had almost lost their Indian soul'. India was a living survival of the great civilizations of the past; but that was not all – it was also a powerful force to influence the future:

> India is not the mere subject of academic talk, but is a living force. India is still feared where she is not loved. Why again? Precisely because she lives. Because she is potentially powerful to impose her ideas upon the world.[21]

India's culture had been preserved because of her 'world purpose'. This was the 'new orientalism' of the art movement and of Okakura. It was also the message of Vivekananda and Nivedita, and quite distinct from the kind of orientalism which saw Indian greatness only in an idealized past. It was the belief that India could be effective, could influence the present and the future, that linked this approach to nationalism.

In this speech Woodroffe applied the term *śakti* in an incarnational sense, both individuals and nations being fragments (*aṁśa*) of that divine Power. What India needed at present was a 'Religion of Power' where each recognised this and consequently asserted himself for 'his own good and that of the country'. He set this against the 'other side of the Spirit' – that is, ascetic withdrawal from the world. In the manner of Vivekananda, who urged the virtues of 'manliness' upon Indians, he called on them to 'dispel all present weakness and sloth' and assert their will vigorously. 'We are what we have made ourselves in the past. We shall be what we *will* to be'. The emphasis on vigour, on power and on will in Woodroffe's speech echoed contemporary Bengali concerns. It was part of the appeal to *śakti*. Vivekananda had preached an ethic of 'manly virtues' which was a reaction to British stereotyping of Bengalis as weaklings both physically and mentally. The revolutionary movement was another aspect of the same reaction.[22]

Despite the similarities to Gandhi in his rejection of westernization, it is interesting to note how "un-Gandhian" Woodroffe's 'Religion of Power' is. Writing in 1916, just before the Mahatma became a major figure on the Indian scene, Woodroffe urged the virtues of active social commitment, but he called this the *pravritti* path ('turned towards' the world) and contrasted it with the religion of Jesus which he equated with that of the 'world-renouncer' and which he called *nivritti dharma* ('turned away' from the world).[23] The former was the path for ordinary people; it was the way of 'Power', while Jesus's way was only for the few. 'On the Pravritti path we are power and develop power', he said.[24] There is here no Gandhian admiration for the Sermon on the Mount and non-resistance to evil. On the contrary, Woodroffe quotes with approval a Christian bishop who is reputed to have said that a state founded on these principles 'would not last a fortnight'.[25]

The other writings in *Bhārata Shakti* reiterate the call to Indians not to abandon their 'Indian soul'. A speech delivered to the annual meeting of the Calcutta Mudrassa is the only instance where Woodroffe's attitude to the Muslim strand of Indian culture is recorded. The Mudrassa, of which Denison Ross had been the Principal earlier on, provided Islamic education alongside Western learning, on a similar pattern to the Sanskrit College for Hindus.[26] Woodroffe's message to Indian Muslims was the same as that to Hindus: that they must be true to their 'type' and perfect it for the ultimate good of the whole; but in this speech there is distinctly more emphasis on the value of Western learning and rather less on the dangers of too much 'imitation' of the West. He urged them to recognize their 'Indian-ness' which distinguished them from 'brother Muslims of other races' and to accept their common interests with other Indian communities.[27] He was speaking in a similar vein to the Hindu-led Congress, where Muslims and Hindus had recently made common cause at the 1916 convention, partly mediated by Annie Besant.[28] Like many other nationalists, Woodroffe believed that non-Hindu communities could be assimilated into the Indian national identity, but tended to define that identity primarily in relation to Hinduism.

In July 1917 Woodroffe addressed the annual prize-giving of the Mahākālī Pathśāla, a Hindu school for girls conducted on strict orthodox lines. It was founded by an interesting woman known as Tapasvini Mataji. Born in 1835, the daughter of a Mahratta prince, she had fought alongside the famous Rani of Jhansi in the Mutiny before fleeing to Nepal where she performed strict *sādhanā* for thirty years, thereby earning her title *Tapasvinī*. She came to Calcutta in 1890 and founded her school in 1893.[29] According to one of his obituaries, Woodroffe gave her school a lot of support,[30] which might be why he felt free to speak his mind to them. His speech began by affirming the education of girls in their own cultural tradition, but he soon delivered some strong criticism of the school for allowing the pupils to abandon their education for the sake of early marriage. Once again he invoked the notion of *śakti*, this time in the cause of women's emancipation, as Annie Besant had also done. Citing the Śākta doctrine that all women are the earthly embodiments of the Goddess, he urged them to 'Honour woman', and 'remove all customs which stand in the way of her true freedom and advancement. If you do not your race will pass away by the will of that great Shakti ...' He quoted from a tantric hymn: 'Woman is God, Woman is life',[31] and ended with what sounds like a note of passion, emphasising the words 'Life itself'.[32] It is the only occasion on which Woodroffe is recorded as making an unequivocal public criticism of any Hindu institution, custom or practice. He usually hedged any reference to 'abuses' of Hinduism with generalising remarks about similar problems in the West, or 'elsewhere'. Here he does not. This shows how questions affecting the position of women were of great significance to Woodroffe. His championship of Hinduism itself often has a kind of 'chivalrous' appearance, as in his defence against William Archer's attack, which we shall examine later in this chapter. Woodroffe could be seen as subliminally defending the Mother, and this perhaps reflects the feminine role of India in colonial consciousness.[33] One of the factors which attracted him to Śākta Tantra, he always claimed, was the high status he believed it accorded to women, and we have seen in chapter 1 above, how the bond with his own mother could have played a part in his attraction to Śāktism.[34]

Woodroffe's speech was reported appreciatively by Ramananda Chatterji in *Modern Review*, a periodical which supported social reform. Sir John Woodroffe 'whose sympathy with and knowledge of Indian thought and life are deep and real' was here welcomed as an influential voice endorsing the cause of reform to a conservative section of Hindu society.[35]

The second edition of *Bhārata Shakti* included Woodroffe's first presidential speech to the All India Cows Conferences Association, one of the smaller conferences which took place during the 1917 Congress Convention in Calcutta. Despite Torick Ameer Ali's amused reference to it (above p. 16) this society was not an extremist Hindu movement against cow slaughter. Its motivation was proclaimed as economic and humanitarian, its aim to promote humane treatment of cattle and to reduce the slaughter of milch cows – something which had disastrous economic consequences. Woodroffe's address was entitled 'Food is Power – Agriculture'.[36] 'Power' carried philosophical connotations, being *śakti*, but this is the only place in his writings where it was translated into economic and practical terms – although he said: 'Personally I believe that there is no question which does not ultimately touch religion'. Woodroffe announced a six-point reform programme and underlined the non-sectarian character of the organisation.

Woodroffe had been invited to be president by a group of founding members, many of whom were connected with the High Court, and he was succeeded in the position by another British judge (Justice Greaves) a few years later. But the leading spirit of the organization was Nilananda Chatterji, a member of the Bengal Humanitarian Association, who had a long-held commitment to the cause.[37] In 1926 he published a report based on a nationwide survey of the condition of cattle organized by Woodroffe while President.[38] In 1920 the association succeeded in persuading the Corporation of Calcutta to ban the slaughter of milch cows, a measure which unfortunately however was overturned in 1923 by the Bengal Legislative Council, after Woodroffe had left India.[39] Woodroffe's contribution to the welfare of cattle was represented on his retirement scroll by engravings of a cow being milked and of a farmer and his plough, to indicate its bearing on agriculture. The Cow Conferences Association also presented him with a second silver scroll on their own behalf.[40]

Another organisation which invited Woodroffe to be its patron on its formation in June 1919 was at first sight a surprising one: the Indian Rationalistic Society would not seem to be a likely group of people to approach a well-known writer on religion. The first issue of its Bulletin declared:

> We, the members of this society feel convinced that science supplies us with the most reliable knowledge attainable about nature ... we believe it is our duty to stand by the practical conclusions to which it inevitably leads ... that ideas and institutions which are concerned with problems which come within the range of science should be judged by the data which it furnishes ...[41]

Yet six months after the first publication of *Is India Civilized?*, the society considered itself extremely fortunate to secure Woodroffe as their patron. 'His name will give the undertaking an importance in the public eye which it would otherwise secure only by years of patient work.' Language familiar from Woodroffe's writings recurs in the Bulletin: references to the 'fight' against 'mental lassitude and physical languor'; belief in the 'great principle of evolution' being 'activity . . . not passivity'; 'An active mind should be creative. . .it should create new powers . . .' Looking more closely, we see the name of Nolini Mohun Chatterji again – Woodroffe's admirer and editor of *Bhārata Shakti* was President of the society. He hosted a farewell dinner for him on his departure for England on furlough in August 1919. Among the long list of those attending were several Muslim names, including Torick Ameer Ali. A few days later, on 28 August, they all saw him off with flowers from Howrah station.[42]

A lecture Woodroffe delivered to the society before his departure, entitled 'The Gayatri as an Exercise of Reasoning' was published in the September edition of the bulletin and showed clearly that, to him at least, 'rationalist' in the Indian context meant something rather different from the 'rationalism' of European philosophy.[43] The first section of the article defined the limits of reason as a means of knowledge for supersensual realities or ultimate truth: the Self (*Ātman* or *Brahman*) can never be an object of ordinary knowledge. The lecture is a straightforward one on neo-Vedanta philosophy, with an emphasis on spiritual and psychical experience as the proof of realities beyond the senses. The second part of the lecture is a meditation on the *Gāyatrī* mantra and seven ascending states of consciousness. The lecture was reprinted in *Garland of Letters*.[44] It is interesting that Woodroffe claims he was at first at a loss over a subject for his lecture, until he came upon a 'note' provided for him some time ago on the *Gāyatrī*.[45] I discuss in chapter 11 such instances of Woodroffe's use of material supplied to him by others.

Nolini Mohun Chatterji seems to have been a gifted speaker himself who could fill a lecture hall every week on subjects such as 'The economic independence of women', 'Science and Morality', 'Science and Vedanta'.[46] The son of a Western educated father who nevertheless remained a devout Brahmin, he was said to have made 'vehement denunciations' of his ancestral religion. A critic in the society's bulletin pointed to him as representing a 'type' of those overcome by excessive admiration of Western science and culture.[47] He thus sounds exactly the sort of person against whom Woodroffe directed his exhortations not to lose their 'Indian soul'.

Despite the commitment with which he defended Hindu tradition and especially Tantra, Woodroffe also proclaimed humanist values of tolerance and universalism, reflected in his ever present desire to compromise, not to be seen as 'extremist' in any sense. A notice in *Modern Review* detected a likeness in *Bhārata Shakti* to Herbert Spencer and the Positivists of the last century – a surprising comparison for a book by an author so much more immediately identified with the revival of Hinduism.[48] Woodroffe's admirers in Bengal are perhaps exemplified by Nolini Mohun Chatterji. In the report of the Sadler Commission, Woodroffe is quoted as saying that

Indian students suffered 'a paralysing inner conflict'.[49] Young Indian men who were deeply imbued through their education with Western ideas which they admired, and yet who also felt deeply rooted (perhaps more than they knew consciously) in their own culture, seem to have responded to Woodroffe as a mediator between their two worlds. Whether he could do so more than superficially remains an open question, but it seems his language at least could embrace both 'tradition' on the one hand, and popular Western ideas. Lectures in which he reinvented śākta-tantric metaphysics in terms of contemporary science, would certainly have made a strong appeal to Nolini Mohun Chatterji and his friends in the Indian Rationalistic Society. As we shall see in chapter 10, Woodroffe sought to present Tantra as 'scientific' as well as transcending the limits of science.

Bhārata Shakti reflects not only the concern to preserve the Hindu cultural heritage, but also the reassuring message that this culture could be fluid enough to grow and change. The image, as Woodroffe put it, 'is an organic one, like an amoeba feeding'.[50] This as we have seen was an evocation of an image provided long ago by his headmaster Lord Petre, who had applied it in a psychological sense to the education of the individual child.[51] Woodroffe applied it to a collective entity, the race or culture. The 'amoeba' was translated by Woodroffe into the *bīja*, what he called 'the seed of race' in his book of that title published in 1919, in which he attempted to express the idea of a racial soul.

The Seed of Race

This book may have come about through the influence of P.N, Mukhopadhyay, Woodroffe's friend and mentor who later became Swami Pratyagātmanand Saraswati. Mukhopadhyay himself gave addresses on education. He was Professor of Philosophy at Ripon college in Calcutta in 1916. It is possible they came to know each other through Woodroffe's address to the students of the Friends Union Club, for the summary of that talk published in *The Bengalee* prompted Mukhopadhyay to write to Woodroffe, attracted by his idea of a 'Religion of Power'. Woodroffe's letter in reply was then forwarded by Mukhopadhyay to the paper, and this too subsequently also found a place in *Bhārata Shakti*.[52] In the letter he addresses Mukhopadhyay 'Dear Sir', implying they may not have known each other before.[53]

Both in the letter and in the book Woodroffe attempts to define what he calls the 'collective *saṁskāras* of the race'. 'There is a Bīja but it is difficult to seize and define though one can feel it without difficulty,' he wrote to Mukhopadhyay. The word *bīja* meaning 'seed' has a special meaning in Tantra, but here Woodroffe adapted it to a different context. He wanted to express something like the essence of a race and its connection to its culture, which he believed could be distinguished from what he saw as 'foreign accretions'. By this he meant primarily what he regarded as excessive westernization in the Indian context. A race/culture should be able to assimilate foreign elements without losing its essential identity. Its *bīja* – 'seed' – should be 'like an amoeba feeding': the foreign substance ceases to be foreign and becomes part of the amoeba itself.[54] Woodroffe also used *bīja* here in its philosophical context: the 'drop' – *bindu* which divides into *bindu* and *bīja* [GOL:136],[55] – is the first condensation of the cosmos out of the divine mind, and it contains, or is identical with, the *saṁskāras* which are the latent impressions, or memories, of past universes. Consequently 'a particular racial consciousness' is a defined stream in the cosmic manifestation: 'A particular part of the general Cosmic Memory realises itself as a Race with its beliefs, practices and social institutions.'[56] If this appeared to concretize these practices and institutions, Woodroffe wanted to assert that 'what is important' is the *saṁskāra* itself, the essence, not the particular forms in which it is invested at any time: ie. what mattered was the 'General Memory or Spirit of the race', not necessarily any particular social institutions or beliefs.

According to one reviewer *Seed of Race* despite its Hindu terminology was merely about 'recognition of the forces of racial heredity'.[57] Yet the concept of 'race' in this book does not suggest the idea of biological inheritance. Woodroffe does not distinguish between a race and a culture; but what he really means by it, as he reveals eventually, is closer to culture – ie 'Aryan' culture, of which Hinduism or Brahmanism is the developed product. This subsumed the body: 'The Seed of Race today is thus the Indian Saṁskāra which has produced the minds and bodies of the Indian people of our time.'[58] But Woodroffe has equated 'Aryan culture' or, as he prefers to call it, 'Brahmanism'[59] with the Indian race as a whole, excluding implicitly the non-Hindu communities in India. Whether intending to or not what he ended by defining as a 'race' was what shortly afterwards came to be called *Hindutva*, the 'Hindu nation'.[60]

Racial theories were widely held and discussed at this time. The idea of the existence of a 'racial soul' found its way into the psychology of C.G.Jung as the 'racial Unconscious'. The racial ethics to which Woodroffe gave expression, concerned with each race perfecting its 'type' for the benefit of humanity, was the theme of Brajendranath Seal's speech to the Universal Races Congress of 1911 in London. Both Annie Besant and Nivedita also spoke there.[61] The event was closely covered in *Modern Review*, where it was strongly criticised by E. Willis, who considered its theme of racial harmony concealed the motive to promote the cultural hegemony of the 'dominant races'. Willis, rejecting such European 'conceit' believed (like Seal) not only in the variety but the '*permanence of the* (racial) *types*'.[62] This too was Woodroffe's position, as we shall see below.

In *The Seed of Race* Woodroffe expressed views which would be characterised as 'racist' today. He wrote of different racial 'stocks', some 'high' and some 'extremely low' which went to make up the Indian nation and regarded this racial mixture as 'probably' – for Woodroffe as usual tries not to be dogmatic – the cause of its present 'degeneracy'. What is more, he looked on the alleged dangers of racial mixture as a justification for the caste system, saying this was something 'overlooked by European critics' of the system.[63] In *Is India Civilized?* he praised several times the 'wonderful system of Varnāshrama Dharma'.[64] This appears inconsistent with Woodroffe's praise of Tantra for supposedly transcending caste and his acceptance here of the general view of India's 'degeneracy', is also inconsistent with the affirmation of 'Hinduism as it exists today' in his writings on Tantra.[65] But the alliance between the prevailing racial doctrines of Europe with those of Hindu caste ideology was not at all unusual at the time.[66]

Woodroffe does Battle with Archer: Is India Civilized?

In chapter 2, I mentioned a lecture reproduced in *Shakti and Shākta*, where Woodroffe answered the question of what had initially attracted him to Tantra.[67] He replied that it was the very attacks upon it which had produced a reaction in him: 'Following the track of unmeasured abuse I have always found something good' [SS:78]. We shall see later how Arthur Avalon confronted the kind of verbal abuse which Western commentators of the worst kind often poured out both upon Tantra and upon the Indian people as a whole. One of the very worst was William Archer,[68] an English theatre critic, who wrote his book *India and the Future* on the basis of a three-week visit to the country just before the First World War.[69] Its flavour can be indicated by the passage which Woodroffe quoted at the opening of his own first chapter:

> Barbarian, barbarism, barbarous – I am sorry to harp so much on these words. But they express the essence of the situation . . . There are of course many thousands of individuals who have risen and are arising above it (barbarism), but the plain truth concerning the mass of the (Indian) population – and not the poorer classes alone – is that they are not civilized people.[70]

Woodroffe's title *Is India Civilized?* was a direct response to the term 'barbarism'. It had a technical meaning in eighteenth century Enlightenment thought and designated a society which was developing towards 'civilization' but had not yet arrived at it.[71] *India and the Future* was certainly a bad book and a strange one which seems deliberately designed to cause offence while at the same time proclaiming its author a 'friend' of India. It provoked outrage similar to the furore caused later on in the 1930s by Katherine Mayo's *Mother India*. The book is merely abuse. 'Abuse' is the right word because in Archer's mind India is a victim who can get nothing right, who is always inferior from every aspect, and who is subjected over-and-again to what can best be described in psychological terms as 'verbal sadism'. Its author counted himself a liberal politically, who saw the modernisation of India as an essential aspect of the independence process. In itself this was far from being an unpopular or unusual position, for the Congress movement, especially in the times of the 'Old Congress' or 'Moderates', always had strong links with English Liberals. In later chapters (for example, one on education) when the abuse has spent itself Archer is even able to make a few genuinely perceptive remarks.[72] But the tone of most of the book is so offensive that it is very difficult to carry away from it an impression of anything else the author may have wanted to say.

Archer was neither an orientalist nor a Christian missionary (Avalon/Woodroffe's more usual targets) but a rationalist who regarded even the wearing of the cross by Christians as superstition, so his reaction to the richly symbolic culture of Hinduism can be imagined. His main target was Hindu art which – strangely in view of his prejudices – he claimed once to have liked; indeed, he said, it had even 'cast a spell' on him until he reacted against it. It is interesting to see that Archer blamed his reaction on what he called the excessive adulation of Indian art and culture promulgated by Havell 'and the sturdy little phalanx of India-worshippers'.[73]

Woodroffe leapt to the defence of India, here the abused victim, replying point-by-point to his opponent, sometimes with a fine irony, but putting forward also Woodroffe's own vision of India. *Is India Civilized?* greatly increased his popularity with the Indian public, and on a wider stage than Bengal. It won appreciative reviews in the Indian press, where 'fairness', 'lucidity', 'insight' are frequent adjectives. There is a contrast with the more adverse comment that appeared in some English papers in India.[74] A.G. Widgery, reviewing both books in *Indian Philosophical Review*, condemned them equally, implying that the battle created more heat than light: 'Let us say frankly that we consider both Mr Archer and Sir John Woodroffe in this episode a nuisance ...'[75] But it was unjust to put Woodroffe's book on the same level as Archer's.

Widgery's review objected among other things to Woodroffe's generalisations about 'East' and 'West'. Woodroffe does generalise in this way and from one point of view the 'gladiatorial' contest between the two English writers, Archer and Woodroffe, epitomises the conflict between the two kinds of orientalism: 'negative' (ie 'the West has a civilizing mission to the orient') and 'positive' or 'romantic' ('the East preserves spirituality that is lost to the West'). Interestingly, *both* of the British protagonists assume that Indian independence is inevitable. What was at issue was westernization and the future of Hinduism. Woodroffe contended that Archer had a political motive behind the attacks he made: that he was driven by fear that an independent India, which would be equal and yet 'other', would exert an influence over Europe. Woodroffe saw westernization as an alternative means of control when political power over Asia had been relinquished by the European nations.[76] This particular perception was more than orientalism, romantic or otherwise, and finds echoes in some modern Asian thinkers.[77]

With whatever political overtones, this book is primarily an attack on westernization and its associated secularism. It aims at the preservation of an essentialised 'religious' culture of (Hindu) India in the face of what its author sees as the aggressive materialism which he places opposite it, writing of 'the dark, terrible and efficient West'.[78] Tantra is barely mentioned. Instead he writes of 'Brahmanism', which he calls a branch of 'Bhārata Dharma' – eschewing the word 'Hinduism' – of which Buddhism and Jainism are other branches, and of which the Śākta teaching is one expression.[79] This statement tends to exclude the Indian Muslim and Christian elements from *Bhārata Dharma*, or 'Indian' religion, though elsewhere we see that this was not his purpose. Woodroffe's main use of the theme was to define a position for the Śiva–Śakti doctrines within the broader framework provided by 'Brahmanism'.[80] Indian non-Hindus are mostly ignored or subsumed under the category of 'the East'.

The history of contact and conflict between 'East' and 'West', between Europe and Asia in global terms, is the starting point of the book. Such conflict is a necessary part of the process of evolution, which is interpreted as a spiritual process: the increasing manifestation of Spirit in humanity.[81] There is no doubt on which side of the struggle 'Indian' culture stands. 'India has taught that the Universe is in its ultimate ground Spirit.'[82] The visible and material world – the world of 'forms' – is a projection of the divine in greater or lesser degree. At the level of 'brute force' the West, with its stronger grasp of material reality, has won a temporary ascendancy, but this is relegated to the lower levels of the cosmic manifestation. The tantric doctrines of three 'bodies' or 'levels' of existence of all phenomena – the 'gross' (outward or material), the 'subtle' (mental) and the 'causal' (absolute or 'spiritual') – are applied to nations and cultures. With the increasing 'spiritualisation' of humanity, the gross (*sthūla*) forms of conflict in terms of warfare and colonial domination will pass away, but then the focus of conflict will pass to the cultural or 'subtle' level. By a process of cultural Darwinism, what is of most value in the different cultures of the world will triumph while the less valuable will be eliminated. In this struggle it is the duty of each race collectively, to 'maintain its own'. 'Failure to do so is the biological sin,' he writes.[83] The aim of evolution is 'complete Humanity' which is the same as Divinity, of which 'perfected man is the highest earthly form.'[84] The process has barely begun, except for certain 'Illuminate Masters of Humanity' who have appeared in every race.[85] This reference to 'Masters' does not suggest Theosophy, so much as connotations of Comte's 'Religion of Humanity' which was so popular with Western educated Indians of the nineteenth century. The book asserts love and altruism as the motive forces through which Humanity will raise itself to the higher levels of the Spirit, where conflict will no longer be a biological necessity. This does not sound occultist and is a contrast to the books on Tantra where Avalon/Woodroffe rarely refers to altruistic love as a virtue in the individual. Nevertheless the emphasis of *Is India Civilized* remains strongly on collectivities like race, to which the individual is subordinated, or on abstractions like 'the Spirit'.[86]

The theme of conflict – on the physical plane of warfare and on the spiritual plane of culture – no doubt reflects the book's time of publication: just after the end of the First World War. Its attitude to conflict reflects that of the *Gītā*: warfare is inevitable, part of the destiny of the cosmos fixed by the impersonal forces of the *saṁskāras* and of *karma*. Whereas the *Gītā* taught that the individual could free himself from this process through the spiritual detachment of *niṣkāma karma*,[87] Woodroffe is less interested in the individual than in the destiny of the race – whether the Indian race, or the wider human race. Humanity can be freed from its past through individuals exercising their wills to live sincerely by whatever light of truth has been given them through their racial/cultural inheritance, and by developing love, altruism and tolerance. He sums up the teaching of 'the East' as that of India:

> India has taught that the Universe is in its ultimate ground Spirit; that what is material is the expression of the Eternal Spirit in time and space; that Man is essentially either that self-same Spirit, or a part of, or akin to it; that the Universe is governed by a Just Law which is the very nature of its true expression; that all Life is sacred; that Morality is the law of humanity, which is the master of its destiny and reaps only what it has sown; that the universe has a moral purpose, and that the Social Structure must be so ordered as to subserve it; and many another sublime truth which is the warrant of Her high civilization, which may yet bear fruit not only in India, but throughout the world, thus justifying her claim to be the Karmabhumi.[88]

In the wider cultural sphere as well as with the specific issue of Tantra, Woodroffe tended to write as if power and agency resided with the West. A threat was presented by the Western politician, missionary or orientalist, by whom Indians could be seduced into losing their 'racial soul'. He refuses to concede the opposite side of the matter: that the trends towards 'reform', or modernisation of Indian culture were often driven by Indians themselves, from the time of Ram Mohun Roy onwards into his own time. Yet the language he uses in these three books reflects that used by Bengalis of his time, especially the constant calls for 'vigour', 'awakening' and the need for 'power' or *śakti*. It is paradoxical that Woodroffe, who mostly declared himself opposed to the Brahmo Samaj, nevertheless expressed many ideas which stemmed from them. The universalism and tolerance he claims as his most important values were also the stated ideal of most Brahmos, as were the Positivist ideals of human spiritual progress. The theme of Woodroffe's book echoes Brajendranath Seal's speech to the Universal Races Congress, mentioned above, who also spoke of India's role being 'bearing witness to the life of the Spirit'. For both Woodroffe and Seal this is in the context of preserving Indian *distinctness* in the face of European hegemony.

The duty of being 'true to type' was also not new. Dvijendranath Tagore, leader of the Adi Brahmo Samaj, had criticised 'imitation' (of the English) and declared that each should hold to his own, in language very similar to that later used by Woodroffe.[89] There are some striking similarities to the nineteenth century writer Bhudev Mukhopadhyay who also condemned 'imitation' and loss of cultural identity leading to lack of self-respect, but who also said that a tradition could change 'within the laws of its own being'. (Woodroffe knew of Bhudev, whom he refers to in *World as Power*, saying he should be better known.)[90]

As we shall see was the case with his tantric writings, here too Woodroffe wrote and talked like a Bengali intellectual. Many of his ideas could be characterised as 'orientalist' in the positive or romantic sense, but these could also be called nationalist. It depends on how he is to be situated. Woodroffe studied from Indians, and if many of them also seemed ready to learn from him it was mainly because he echoed and reinforced them. Perhaps this is why even some of those who criticised Annie Besant and the Theosophists for presuming as Europeans to lead them in their own nationalism, seem to have accepted Woodroffe.[91]

The editor of CWN noted that he had gathered around him a very wide circle of friends from every community in the country, and 'notably from amongst the intellectuals of Bengal'. He added, however, that he did not personally always agree with Woodroffe as an exponent of Hindu culture.[92] There were other Indians who were cautious about him too. Nares Candra Sengupta, who knew Woodroffe at the High Court (see above p. 39) believed him socially conservative and considered his support for tradition had a reactionary influence. He took issue with him in one of his own essays, where he protested at his superficial criticism and misunderstanding of Ram Mohun Roy.[93] Ramananda Chatterji's *Modern Review* strongly praised *Bhārata Shakti* but was more cautious about *Is India Civilized?*, fearing it could encourage a 'blind racial vanity'.[94] The historian Jadunath Sarkar, who wrote of 'the seductive cry for going back to the undiluted wisdom of our ancestors' and believed that India 'must embrace the spirit of progress', strongly attacked Woodroffe's influence in a Bengali essay.[95]

Woodroffe's enthusiasm for Indian nationalism was for him all of a piece with his rigid racial theories, and his identification of race with culture and nation. Nowadays his views might be associated with modern Hindu political extremism; but Woodroffe would not have welcomed that. He was not a political thinker, and to the extent that he identified with India it was because it represented for him a spirituality that was beyond politics. In today's context he would have modified his statements with more universalism – for he always wanted to be 'balanced'. Nevertheless his persistent tendency to see India in collective terms combined with his anxiety to preserve the Indian 'self' could be experienced as subtly seductive by those among Indian people who sought to welcome social change and to modernize and diversify their society.

Woodroffe did not, however, like Annie Besant or Havell, believe in a 'spiritual' India within a reformed British empire. He never made direct political statements, but writing in 1922 in reply to a British reviewer of *Is India Civilized?*, he described the reaction against westernization as: 'the so-called "unrest" which alarms some and is as refreshing as the Dew of Dawn to others.'[96] Very few other British people in India at that period would have made such a statement. In the same preface he wrote: 'Resistance is the characteristic of a Self'[97]

What, however, of his own 'self'? His 'chivalrous' defence of India when under attack, suggests India's feminine role in European consciousness. His strong and repeated anxiety that Indian people should on no account 'lose their Indian soul', or that India itself should not lose its soul, suggests that he identified his own inner self and vulnerability with this femininized India. He defended it against a 'masculine' penetrating verbal aggressiveness that was all too common at the time.

In his quest to preserve the Indian 'Self' one wonders how Woodroffe identified his own British one. Did the 'paralysing inner conflict' which he noted in the Indian student not affect him? Woodroffe told Indians not to imitate European manners or ways of thought, while he himself seemed to feel free to adopt Indian ones. Woodroffe as we shall see did not always act in a way that was 'true' to his racial 'type'. Was he aware of this inconsistency, or was he influenced by some unconscious racial superiority, that made him believe it was in order for an Englishman to imitate another, because his identity was secure: he could never cease to be English?

Woodroffe seems to have had a chameleon-like quality that led him to take on the colours of his environment; sometimes he spoke with the tones of the British–Indian establishment as we heard him do in chapter 3, but also with those of his intellectual Bengali friends and mentors. This seems to suggest there was indeed a split within him.

To wear Indian dress at a party might be seen as a political act, deliberately and publicly identifying with India, or it could simply be 'dressing up'.[98] But the occasion remembered by Pavitra Gangopadhyay (above p.75–6) was not the only one on which Woodroffe did this, as we shall see in the next chapter. We begin to see Sir John Woodroffe leading what looks like a double life. One identity is public, British and official: the judge, the scholarly orientalist, the patron of Indian art. The other is secret, tantric, and Indian.

Chapter Six

THE SECRET TANTRIC

'An Indian soul in a European body'?

Photographs and Rumours

Most of the recent editions of the Avalon/Woodroffe books have as a frontispiece a photograph of Woodroffe dressed in a white *dhoti* standing beside the wall of a temple [plate 5]. It was not just any temple – he was at Konarak, the thirteenth century Sun temple, an archaeological site rediscovered in the nineteenth century. Well-known for its erotic sculpture which is displayed prominently along its outer walls, the Konarak temple was most probably the site of an ancient tantric cult devoted to Surya, the vedic sun god.[1] The temple represents one of the high points of Hindu architectural and artistic achievement. There was a link here between Woodroffe's two worlds of art and Tantra. In his preface to *Garland of Letters* he wrote about the landscape around Konarak, then a quiet isolated place filled with the sound of the sea's breakers, which seemed to be chanting the holy syllable *Oṃ*. This was the scene 'which I have known and enjoyed for many years', he wrote, and he was taking a sad farewell to it in 1922 [GOL:xiii–xiv].

Woodroffe showed the photograph to O.C. Ganguly. 'At that time' comments Ganguly in his memoirs 'no other highly educated Englishman was seen wearing our *dhoti*.'[2] Ganguly thought it was Woodroffe's habit to go to Konarak nearly every weekend. He would take the train to Puri immediately upon leaving the High Court on a Friday and travel from there to Konarak by *palki*. Ganguly presents this information in the context of Woodroffe's regular practice of visiting historical and religious sites,[3] something which was perfectly 'respectable' for a Sahib to do, if the motive was scholarly curiosity. Others as we shall see claimed that Woodroffe and his friends went there to perform tantric *sādhanā*. Abanindranath Tagore also mentions the 'fascination' (*jhok*) that Konarak held for Woodroffe and his friend Blount, something which inspired his own first visit there.[4] Just what went on at Konarak we cannot know for certain; it was an archaeological site, not a living temple, and a secluded place. Whatever else these visits meant to Woodroffe, his dress proclaimed that while there he could escape from his British identity and assume the outward forms of the Indian identity he urged upon others.

Although as we shall see, he describes himself as a disinterested scholar in his books, there is evidence that Woodroffe was more personally involved in Tantra than that, according to the testimony of many people. He does not seem to have talked about Tantra to O.C. Ganguly for the younger man discusses this aspect of Woodroffe's life by drawing on rumours and on other people's writings.[5] Ganguly tells us that shortly after becoming a judge, Sir John studied Sanskrit with Haridev Sastri, the High Court interpreter. Soon he became immersed (*nimagna*) in the study of an abstruse and neglected branch of Indian knowledge and esoteric practice (*gabhīr sādhanā*), namely Tantra Śāstra. He tells us that according to what some people thought, (*kār o kār o mate*) Woodroffe and his wife were initiated, and that their guru was 'the famous *sādhak*, Sri Srijagadambikā Ambā Saraswati'. 'But recently it has become known,' he adds that they were initiated into Tantra by Sivacandra Vidyarnava, whom Woodroffe first met through Haridev Sastri.[6] It seems that Ganguly, who published his memoirs in 1969, had just come across Vasanta Kumar Pal's story of Woodroffe's initiation by Sivacandra which was serialised in a Bengali magazine from 1965–6, for some of the other information he gives has been taken from Pal's account.[7] Ganguly however gives slightly more importance than Pal does to Atal Behari Ghose – 'a vakil who was expert in Tantraśāstra' with whose help Sir John read widely in the Tantras. But he credits Woodroffe with translating and editing ten books on Tantraśāstra, through which he earned a permanent place among the best orientalist scholars (*prācyavidyār panditamahale*); and says that no judge since Sir William Jones had attained such a level of Sanskrit learning.[8] Woodroffe's enthusiasm for Tantra is assigned a place within 'respectable' orientalism and is described here almost as a natural progression from his Sanskrit studies. Sanskrit scholarship serves as a cover: the 'profound' (*gabhīr*) subject of Tantra is associated with study (*adhyāyan*) and 'research' (*gabeṣaṇā*); Woodroffe's enthusiasm is indicated by the word *nimagna*, immersed or 'drowned'.

Another photograph, of which I obtained a copy in Calcutta, was also taken at Konarak. It shows three men seated on the steps of the temple, all in Indian dress: one is Woodroffe, another is Atal Behari Ghose, and the third a European identified by the Ghose family as H. P. Moeller, whom we have already encountered as a prominent member of the Indian Society of Oriental Art. He had been initiated into Vaisnavism, and he also studied tantric texts with Atal Bihari Ghose. There were signed portrait photographs of Moeller and his wife in the Ghose family house and he seemed to have been a close friend. The three men are wearing the white *dhoti* and upper garment (*kṣaumvastra*) which is the dress of a *brahmacārī*, a disciple [see plate 6].[9]

It is possible that this photo was taken during a visit to Konarak by the three men and perhaps their wives (or at least Mrs Ghose) which was the subject of a letter from Woodroffe to Ghose [Appendix I: letter 2]. The visit seems to have been undertaken in connection with Johnson Hoffman, the Calcutta photographers. Woodroffe wrote the letter shortly after their journey, carefully dividing up the money each person owed to each on account of it. He mentions a Mr Wurthle and his carts, for which they could obtain reimbursement from Hoffman's. (The carts, presumably, were used to take the group from Puri station instead of *palkis*.) Mr Wurthle is recorded by Thackers Directory as being in the employ of Johnson Hoffman only in the year 1912. The reference at the end of the undated letter to the printing of *ṣaṭ-cakra-nirūpaṇa*, which was published early in 1913, as well as the address at the top also point to this year, the same year in which Woodroffe gave his unpopular Midnapore judgement.[10] Johnson Hoffman had by 1915 published a collection of albums of Indian architecture,[11] and it is possible that Woodroffe and his friends had been commissioned by the firm to photograph the temple on their behalf. At some time the photo of the three men came to be published in a Bengali magazine and is said to have caused a furore among the British in Calcutta.[12] It was certainly published in 1936 in both *Bhārat Varṣa* and *Baśumati* in their obituaries of Woodroffe,[13] in which the former records that Woodroffe was still remembered walking barefoot on the beach at Puri, deep in thought.[14]

Besides Moeller, the other European whose name we have seen frequently in association with Woodroffe, and with Konarak, was Norman Blount. According to a rumour repeated by the artist Nandalal Bose, one of Abanindranath's former pupils, it was Blount who practised tantric *sādhanā* at Konarak with Woodroffe and Havell, with Ghose as their guru:

> There were three people, perhaps, Havell, Woodroffe and their friend Blount. They went to Konarak and did sādhanā, tantrik sādhanā. From what they saw in Tibetan thankas they carried on with the joining of Puruṣa and Prakṛti and other such secret practices. They wrote bij mantras and their explanations on the backs of dharma thankars. Possibly it was through their Guru Atal Babu that they tried to practise bij and bhed. Day and night their only thought was ṣaṭ-cakra-bhed.'

Ṣaṭ-cakra-bhed means *kuṇḍalinī* yoga – something Woodroffe himself denied having practised [SS:679]. The reference to secrecy, to what was seen in Tibetan *thankas* and the 'joining of Puruṣa and Prakṛti' might perhaps be intended to imply sexual rituals.[15] The intensity of their enthusiasm is also once again indicated.

It is possible that here rumour may have confused Blount with Moeller. However that may be, both these men were friends of Ghose and visited his house at Chaibassa near Ranchi in Bihar, where High Court rumour said that Woodroffe practised *sādhanā* (see above p. 37). The Ghose family told me that Woodroffe, Moeller and Ghose used to go there to study tantric texts. Blount and his wife appeared on a photograph taken at Chaibassa before a tour of Kashmir in 1914, in which the Ghoses, the Woodroffes and Blounts, along with some other Europeans, made up a party. Ranchi featured in James Woodroffe's memories too, but simply as a place where his parents and Mr and Mrs Ghose took holidays together on which he was taken along.

Nandalal Bose's reminiscences, however, mainly concern Havell and lead up to the story of his madness, which caused his retirement from India in 1906. It was believed by some that this was the result of unwise dabbling in Tantra:

> On the staircase of the art school there was a Tibetan Buddha image kept in a glass case. Seeing this image as he went to and fro on the staircase, Havell would become plunged in trance, sitting in a meditation posture. After a while he became even more beside himself and uncontrollable. In the end, not seeing any alternative, Abanibabu [Abananindranath] wrote a letter to the Fort. Three Sikh soldiers came and took Havell Sahib away. This was the fatal fruit of the unsuccessful Tantrik sādhanā of Havell, the lover of Indian art.

Abanindranath tells the same story but does not mention Tantra. Although a great friend of Havell he considered him gullible and easily influenced by 'worthless' (*bāje*) *sañnyāsis*. Havell's wife complained to him that her husband was very deeply involved in yoga and was ready to learn meditation from 'any sadhu he meets'. Eventually a *sādhu* turned up at the art school and became a frequent visitor to Havell's flat. He offered the Englishman a myroloban fruit with the promise that it would bring him eternal youth, and Havell, according to Abanindranath, was gullible enough to accept it and believe in it. Abanindranath implies this was the cause of his madness.[16] Havell was also said to be devoted to the more orthodox and deeply respected Swami Bhāskarānanda of Benares.[17]

Some other information passed on by Nandalal Bose concerned Woodroffe and his wife, and found its way into Bhupendranath Datta's biography of his brother Swami Vivekananda:

> Sir John Woodroffe and Lady Woodroffe were the disciples of Śri Jagadambāmba, a Deccanese Bhairavī. By taking initiation (*dīkṣā*) from her, Woodroffe and others used to practise Tantric sadhana. Besides these persons, Śri Atalananda Saraswati and Śrimati Gouramba Garu were their fellow disciples.[18]

We can see that O.C. Ganguly had heard the same story. According to Vasanta Kumar Pal (and this was confirmed by the Ghose family)

Woodroffe received two initiations, one from Sivacandra Vidyarnava and another from a *bhairavī* (a female Tantric) called Jayakali Devi. This Jayakali Devi was also Ghose's guru.[19] Whether or not rumour has mistaken the name of the *bhairavī*, the names Atalananda Saraswati and Śrimati Gouramba Garu refer to Atal Behari Ghose and his second wife, whom the Woodroffes knew, and who was called Gaurammā. Atalananda Saraswati is the name used by Ghose on the Sanskrit title pages of some of his later editions in the *Tantrik Texts* series.[20]

We have seen Nandalal Bose refer to 'Atal Babu' as the guru of Havell, Woodroffe and Blount. He said the same in a letter to Barendranath Ghose:[21] 'To understand the fundamentals of Tantras Mr Havell accepted the guidance from a tantric Guru (Atal Ghose)'.[22] But possibly he meant here the *śikṣā guru* – the teacher of textual knowledge – not the *dīkṣā guru* who gives initiation and is a spiritual guide, because there is no suggestion anywhere in the correspondence of Woodroffe and Ghose that the latter took the role of a guru. Nor did the Ghose family claim that he was a guru. What does emerge is that Atal Behari Ghose besides being Woodroffe's teacher, also had a small circle of European friends and students whom he instructed about Tantra; and we shall see that in later life this extended to a much wider sphere.[23] He appears to have been an extremely influential mediator of the tantric tradition.

There is no evidence that Ghose himself was a member of the Indian Society of Oriental Art, but it is interesting to see that at least three, possibly four Europeans prominent in the art movement were his pupils. It begins to look as if the art society had a secret tantric side to it, at least as far as some of the Europeans involved were concerned. Even if it was Ghose, and not Sivacandra as Pal claimed, who instructed Havell – there is still a perceived connection between the Indian art movement and Tantra, and the link in the chain is Woodroffe. Bhupendranath Datta on the other hand, in his biography of his brother Vivekananda, is trying to argue for the Swami's and Nivedita's influence on Havell and the art movement. But in order to do this he has to counteract another 'tradition': namely the influence of Tantra and of various 'pandits' over both Havell and Woodroffe.[24] It seems to be accepted that some of the Europeans who were interested in Indian art were also involved in Tantra. It was a different matter, however, with the Indians who were prominent in the movement. Both Abanindranath and Nandalal Bose express disapproval of Havell's dabbling in such areas. In Santi Niketan I spoke with Dhiren Krishnadeb Burma, a former pupil of Nandalal. He firmly believed that Woodroffe and Havell were Tantrics and expressed very strong disapproval. He said that Woodroffe had become unstable and 'unable to continue his duties' as a result of his practices; but it is possible that here he had confused Woodroffe's story with Havell's for I have come across no other reference to madness in connection with Woodroffe himself.

These stories of Woodroffe and his European tantric friends circulated among people connected with the art movement. But the main source of 'oral tradition' concerning Woodroffe are the stories of his initiation by the charismatic guru Sivacandra Vidyarnava which circulated among the saint's disciples. These stories were collected by Vasanta Kumar Pal in his biography of Sivacandra. Pal however assigns a minor role to Atal Behari Ghose. By contrast, the other 'tradition' seems to place more importance on Ghose's role, and does not mention Sivacandra. O.C. Ganguly has clearly been influenced by both. As Ghose was also a disciple of Sivacandra, these two currents of 'oral tradition' do not conflict. What is interesting is that there are two, relatively independent ones, adding to the authenticity of the picture of Woodroffe as a practising Tantric.

VASANTA KUMAR PAL

Vasanta Kumar Pal was a railway Guard and a humble disciple of Sivacandra. Although his account has been embellished and romanticised, Pal gives specific sources either written or oral for his most basic information. Many of his stories probably emanate indirectly from Haridev Sastri, the High Court's Sanskrit interpreter who claimed to have first introduced Woodroffe to Sivacandra. Haridev Sastri may have embellished his tales somewhat, but that he acted as a link between Woodroffe and his guru is borne out by a brief notice in *The Bengalee* newspaper a few days after its report of the saint's death, where it states that Justice Woodroffe had sent Haridev Sastri to Sivacandra's family with a generous gift of money.[25]

Vasanta Kumar Pal's book was the source for two other accounts of Woodroffe and his guru. A chapter on Sivacandra in S.N. Ray's *Bhārater Śādhak*,[26] a collection of lives of modern saints, relies mostly on Pal. So does a series of articles, published in a Bengali religious magazine, by a retired judge of the High Court, Mr Samarendranath Bagchi. S.N.Bagchi was also a tantric practitioner whose own guru had been a disciple of Sivacandra. Despite being so favourably placed, however, his articles are essentially a religious and philosophical commentary on Pal's information, with only a little variation in detail.[27] I met the late Mr Bagchi in 1991 and was very grateful for his generous help and interpretation of Woodroffe's story as told by Pal.

Pal was no longer alive in 1991, but Mr Bagchi had met him. Pal told him that he had first encountered Woodroffe and his wife Ellen when they were travelling on the Chittagong Mail. To the Mail Guard's immense surprise, a Sahib, barefoot, wearing an ochre robe[28] and a necklace of *rudrākṣa* beads, got out of a first class compartment and wanted to buy a copy of *The Statesman* newspaper. Woodroffe told him that he and his wife were on their way to Kumarkhali – Sivacandra's birthplace where he had one of his ashrams – to pay their respects to 'our most revered gurudev', and he responded warmly when Pal introduced himself as a fellow disciple. According to Mr Bagchi, a close friendship developed between the two men but Pal does not claim this in his book, nor does he claim to have received any of his information directly from Woodroffe himself.

The Guru, Sivacandra Vidyarnava

Kumarkhali, Sivacandra's birthplace, was then a village in East Bengal; now it is a town in Bangladesh. He was born into a family of Brahmin Tantrics and was educated in the traditional fashion as a pandit at the nearby Bhatpāra *Tol.* Later he had ashrams at Kumarkhali and at other places, including Calcutta and Benares. His greatness was acknowledged in his lifetime. He was a well-known charismatic saint rather like his contemporary Ramakrishna, and like him attracted the English-educated urban *bhadralok* to his re-statement of the traditional forms of religion.[29] The obituary of Woodroffe in *Bhārat Varṣa* declares that authentic Tantrics such as Sivacandra were rare at this time.[30] Like Ramakrishna, he was an ardent devotee (*bhakta*) of the Mother, whom he called, however, not *Kālī* as Ramakrishna did, but *Tārā* and *Sarvamangalā*. Unlike Ramakrishna, he had literary skills: he was a poet, and a fine orator who drew large crowds.[31] He was also famous for the elaborate rituals he conducted. He practised his own *sādhanā* in the cremation grounds. Along with other prominent traditionalist figures including the 'reactionary' Hindu revivalist Sasadhar Tarkacudamani, and Gopal Krishna Goswami (who departed from the Brahmo Samāj in favour of a passionate *vaiṣṇava* devotionalism),[32] Sivacandra founded the *Sarvamangalā Sabhā.* This organization attempted to unite Śākta Tantrics in Bengal and elsewhere but also aimed to build bridges between *śāktas* and *vaiṣṇavas*, the other main sect of Bengal. Sivacandra also had connections with the *bauls* who were on the fringes of society, and invited the famous *baul* saint, Lalan Faquir to sing at his ashrams.[33]

Arthur Avalon's translation of the guru's *Tantratattva* gives an insight into his religious outlook, which was equally devotional as it was ritual [*Principles of Tantra* vols 1 & 2]. Sivacandra's book defends traditional Śākta Tantrism against its detractors from whatever direction: orthodox ('Vedic') *advaitins* who renounced the senses, *vaiṣṇava* sectarians who condemned Śāktism, and modernist reformers such as the Brahmo Samāj. Against the latter he argued passionately and cogently in defence of ritual and the worship of images in the face of their 'protestant' rejection of both. He defends the multiplicity of divine forms ('polytheism') arguing that this accorded with the notion of ultimate unity better than what he calls the 'ephemeral and modern monism' of the Brahmo Samāj who claimed to worship only the 'formless Brahman'. In a passage where his powerful oratory and poetic skill come through strongly in translation he shows how 'magic powers' (*siddhi*) and liberation are seen as one and the same goal and gives a vivid, dramatic picture of what a traditional *kaula* tantric's faith was:

> In every Indian cremation ground the refulgent and divine halo of Bhairavas and Bhairavis is yet to be seen mingling with the light of the flames of funeral pyres rending apart the waves of nocturnal darkness and illuminating the wide expanse of Heaven. Dead and putrefying corpses submerged near cremation grounds are still brought to life by the force of the Sādhakas' Mantras, and made to render aid to Sādhanā and Siddhi. Tantrik Yogis even now and in this world obtain, through the potency of Mantras, direct vision of the world of Devas, which lies beyond our senses. She, with dishevelled hair [Kālī] the Dispeller of fear from the hearts of those who worship Her, still appears in great cremation grounds to give liberation to Her devoted Sādhakas who, fearful of this existence, make obeisance . . . to Her . . . The throne of the Daughter of the Mountain is still moved by the wondrous, attractive force of Mantras. This, in the eyes of Sādhakas, is the ever broad and royal road upon which they travel untiring to the city of liberation. Maybe there is nothing but darkness for the bedridden and dying blind man. Yet know that of a surety, oh blind man, that the darkness exists only in your eyes.[PT/1 p. 204–5]

Although traditionalist, Sivacandra was not simply 'reactionary'. His reaching out to *vaiṣṇavas* and, more controversially, to the *bauls,* many of whom were Muslim, was a bold innovation. S.N. Bagchi commends Sivacandra especially for his openness to the foreigner Woodroffe and the half-foreign Coomaraswamy and this is one of the themes of his articles.

A Religious Legend: the Guru and the British Judge

The story, in all three accounts of Sivacandra, begins in the High Court shortly after Woodroffe became a judge. Woodroffe's status as a High Court judge is mentioned many times, emphasising the importance of his social position for the prestige it conferred on his guru in the eyes of humbler disciples.

According to Pal, Woodroffe first heard of Sivacandra when a case at the High Court required an expert interpretation of a particular point of Hindu law, and Haridev Sastri recommended his own guru, who was consequently summoned to Calcutta from Benares, his main place of residence. Thus the first meeting between the renowned guru and the famous judge–disciple took place in Court, where Woodroffe was immediately impressed by the saint's sastric learning.[34] We need not take this too literally, for where else, in the devotees' imagination, *could* such a meeting take place? Pal gives no date for the encounter but if his claim that Woodroffe subsequently introduced Havell to Sivacandra is true, then he would have had to meet his guru before 1906 when Havell left India. Mr Bagchi gives dates between 1906–7 in his version but without providing any basis for his chronology.

Pal says that it was after meeting Sivacandra that Woodroffe started to study Tantraśāstra and to collect manuscripts from all over India and Tibet.[35] He does not mention Atal Behari Ghose at this point but in an epilogue to this section, he adds that Woodroffe's interest in Tantra *might* first have arisen through joining Ghose's *Āgamānusandhana Samiti* (Āgamas Research Society).[36] According to S.N. Ray's account, Woodroffe was already studying tantric texts before his encounter with Sivacandra, as a result of having met Atal Behari Ghose and other scholars through the Samiti. Woodroffe recognized the need of an expert *kaula* practitioner to provide him with a deeper understanding, and grasped the opportunity when Sivacandra attended the High Court as a witness.[37] According to S.N. Ray, Woodroffe did not question him in court, but invited him to his private house in Calcutta, where immediately the English judge was powerfully impressed both with the guru's learning and with his appearance:

> He seemed the living image of Tantrik learning and Śakti sadhana, his eyes like very sharp knives, his hair very long. He had a bright red tilak on his forehead and red sandalpaste smeared there. Around his neck were rudrākṣa beads and other stones. And (he wore) a saffron robe. So Woodroffe kept looking at this figure almost as if in a trance. Long discussions on the Tantra began. Whatever question Woodroffe put to him, Sivacandra seemed to solve with lots of examples from the Sastras and Woodroffe was amazed. He thought that this kind of mind does not occur from just scholarly engagement in texts. There was something supernatural in the power he had as he interpreted and dispelled doubts from Woodroffe's mind.[38]

S.N. Bagchi's account focuses on Woodroffe as the elected disciple, someone already prepared by his previous incarnations, whose guru recognized him at the propitious time. He opens with a discourse upon the relationship between Guru and Disciple, with reference to the writings of Gopinath Kaviraj and Aurobindo. Like S.N. Ray he too thought that Woodroffe had already acquired textual knowledge of Tantra through meetings with scholars at the *Āgamānusandhana Samiti*, among whom the name of Atal Behari Ghose is only one of several. All three authors have probably confused the Āgamas Research Society (which was actually a publishing company) with the Varendra Research Society (*Varendrānu-sandhana Samiti*), a historical association to which Ghose belonged, for they also refer in this context to the historian Akshay Kumar Maitra, who was its

Director.[39] Bagchi claims Woodroffe was inspired by A.K. Maitra to learn Sanskrit and Tibetan.[40]

S.N. Bagchi emphasises the inferiority of mere scholarly knowledge to spiritual intuition which comes through initiation by a True Guru (*sadguru*). His section on the disciple's first encounter with the guru is headed 'An Unexpected Revolutionary Event in the Environment of the Court'.[41] The 'revolutionary' (*vaiplavik*) event is the powerful influence Sivacandra exerted on Woodroffe's mind: this is the real moment of initiation, known as *śaktipāt*, the descent of *śakti* (or 'grace'), and not the outward ritual which followed it some time later. Bagchi has Woodroffe say to Haridev Sastri after Sivacandra has gone away: '. . . can you tell me why all of a sudden Sivacandra's image appears again and again before my mental eyes and strangely enough at that very time some invisible power overwhelms me . . .'[42] Mr Bagchi's account here is the most elaborate of the three. Being a retired judge himself, he could enhance the scene in court: he knew that the judges sat on the appeal bench in pairs, and he has Woodroffe discussing with his co-judge and with counsel the necessity of calling Sivacandra as an 'expert witness' (*viśeṣajña sākṣi*); he has the saint giving evidence in court for three full days, in Sanskrit, answering Woodroffe's questions through Haridev as interpreter.

The Initiation – *śaktipāt*

The three stories continue with Woodroffe's first visit to Sivacandra's ashram at Benares accompanied by the ever-present Haridev Sastri. The guru was in the middle of a long *pūjā* to the Mother when his distinguished visitors arrived and so they were made to wait in an adjoining room for three hours.[43] (Mr Bagchi specifies that it was the night of *kālīpūjā*, probably because this is an auspicious time. He gives the year as 1906). This is how Pal describes the dramatic experience that happened to Woodroffe:

> Woodroffe said: just as I entered the house of Sivacandra I felt something like an electric shock through my body. I felt as if the world was spinning and receding from me. My mind stopped and I lost all the senses of the outer world. A little while later a white Omkāra in the form of lightening and decorated with Maya-bija and Matri–bija mantras was floating in front of my eyes. I stood there speechless in wonder and was made to sit down by Haridev perhaps at a sign from Sivacandra.

After that a change came over him. 'I felt a mental magnetic attraction towards Sivacandra and his face full of *tejas* is ever illuminated in my mind since then.'[44] (Pal says the story was told by Haridev Sastri to Danbari Gangopadhyay, secretary of Sivacandra's *Sarvamangala Sabhā*.)

The ability to induce a change of consciousness by look or touch is a recognized power of a *sadguru*. The ability to make a disciple swoon is referred to as *vedhadīkṣā* in the *kulārṇava tantra*.[45] Woodroffe's experience is like a tantric variation on Vivekananda's experience of being touched by Ramakrishna's foot.[46] Whether it happened like that or not, the point of the story is to show that Woodroffe received the highest form of initiation – the direct transmission of a state of mystical awareness from guru to disciple. Bagchi cites Gopinath Kaviraj and other sources to make his point that this was Woodroffe's *real* initiation: the moment when the disciple's *kuṇḍalinī* was awakened and his 'animal state' – *paśubhāva* – was transformed, removing the obstacles to clear vision.[47] It shows that Sivacandra was the *sadguru*.

After this dramatic occurrence, Sivacandra and Woodroffe discourse on Tantra for four hours. But strange to say, Woodroffe still has doubts whether Sivacandra really is the right choice of guru. Therefore Sivacandra orders him to seek out other *sadhus* all over India. Woodroffe accordingly gathers a team of informants around him and sets off for the Himalayas, accompanied still by the faithful Haridev Sastri. His meetings with three cave dwelling *yogis* are recorded at Rishikesh, Hardwar and Guptakashi, and then with a fourth in Darjeeling. Very ancient and living in continuous *samādhī*, these holy men come out of their trance state to discourse with Woodroffe and to tell him, one and all, that his true guru is Sivacandra.[48] For the fourth story – that of a Bengali sadhu who lived at Darjeeling – Pal quotes a source: a magistrate called Jagdish Chandra Sanyal had told him of it.[49] Perhaps in part Pal's imagination was caught by hearing of photographs of Himalayan holy men seen in Woodroffe's home in England (see below). Perhaps, too, Woodroffe was well-known for visiting many *sādhus*. Pal interprets the story by casting Woodroffe in the role of the 'scientific' modern doubter who cannot accept Sivacandra's word until it is tested out and miraculously confirmed.

With all his doubts finally resolved, Woodroffe at last asks Haridev to arrange for Sivacandra to come from Benares to Calcutta formally to initiate himself and his wife Ellen. The saint was received at the Woodroffes' home and taken into their bedroom (*śayankakṣa*) where the married couple were instructed in the tantric rites.[50] This was the first stage of the 'gradual' (*krama*) form of initiation; the full initiation (*mahāsamrāj abhiśekha*) was to come later – this was called *siñchan* ('sprinkling') and was performed by Jayakali Devi, since for this the initiation had to come from a woman.[51] According to Ray and Bagchi, Sivacandra lived with the Woodroffes for some time, giving them instructions in yet more rituals and *dhyānas* (visualizations), but Pal simply says the guru was a frequent visitor whenever he came to Calcutta. He informs us that Woodroffe's tantric worship was performed to a golden image of Durga *dasabhujā siṁhavāhinī*;[52] that whenever he was at home he would wear ochre clothes (*gairik basan*);

that in Sivacandra's presence he would wear a garland of *rudrākṣa* beads and go barefoot; and that he used to touch the feet of Sivacandra and his wife like a Hindu.[53] Pal cites a witness – Pandit Radhavinod Vidyavinod, who in an article giving his personal reminiscences of Sivacandra wrote: 'Justice Woodroffe heard from his Sanskrit tutor Haridev Sastri that Sivacandra Vidyarnava was the greatest living Sādhaka . . . and became a disciple of him with great faith (*parama śraddhā*).[54] Pal also quotes this pandit's childhood reminiscences of Sivacandra's gatherings, when he felt overwhelmed not only by the great saint's charisma but also because of his prestige as 'the Guru of the Chief Justice [sic] of the High Court, Sir John Woodroffe'.[55]

The Disciple Spreads the Guru's Message

To the circle of Sivacandra's disciples the most important feature of Woodroffe's tantric initiation is not his ritual practice so much as his devotion to his guru. He is portrayed as a humble and devoted disciple, whose writings as 'Arthur Avalon' were his initiation gift to the guru (*gurudakṣinā*) undertaken at the bidding of Sivacandra, who requested that instead of giving him riches he wanted Woodroffe to spread knowledge of the *tattva* (religious principles) of the Mother. Again: Woodroffe wanted to write a biography of his guru, but instead Sivacandra told him to write a biography of the Mother, and so he started to translate his guru's book *tantratattva.* Pal seems to be quoting when he casts Woodroffe in the role of Vivekananda to Sivacandra's Ramakrishna in spreading his guru's message to the West.[56]

Havell and Coomaraswamy

Pal's story appropriates every aspect of the prestigious disciple's fame in the name of his guru. Not only was his writing on Tantra the propagation of the guru's teaching, carried out in response to his command, but the art movement in which Woodroffe was prominent and his famous friends involved in it, are also seen as extensions of the field of Sivacandra's influence. According to Pal, Woodroffe introduced both Havell and Coomaraswamy to Sivacandra, and they learned from him the Hindu theories of art and crafts (*cārukalā, śilpavidyā*) which they passed on in their books. He paints a picture of Sivacandra lecturing in Sanskrit to them both in Woodroffe's home, with Woodroffe and Haridev as interpreters. Pal says here, 'I have heard . . .' suggesting that he is repeating rumours. The scene was not possible chronologically, as the two art historians were not present in Calcutta at the same time. Nevertheless, Sivacandra's influence cannot be entirely ruled out. That Hindu art related to forms above ordinary perception is probably the kind of thing Sivacandra would have said to them, if they discussed the matter with him.[57] It is more than likely that Woodroffe would have introduced both these friends to his guru, and we have seen how Havell's wife was concerned about the influence of 'yogis' upon her husband. Also interesting is the story that Coomaraswamy wanted, as a foreigner, to be formally received into Hinduism. Against the opposition of the more rigid pandits of Bhattapara *Tol* to which he belonged, Sivacandra 'discovered' a suitable rite in the Śāstras.[58]

Mourning

From all this we can only accept as established fact the broad basis of the story of Woodroffe and Sivacandra: that Woodroffe was perceived as an initiated disciple by many people, both within and outside the circles around Sivacandra. Some details of the story – the meeting at the High Court, the initiation experience, the travels to Himalayan hermits, the lectures to Havell and Coomaraswamy – could be legendary. But with the death of Sivacandra at the end of March 1914 we encounter a public event witnessed by prominent people still alive or only recently deceased at the time when Pal was writing. A condolence meeting (*śoksabhā*) was organized by the people of Calcutta and was presided over, according to Pal, by the dramatist Amritalal Basu. Woodroffe and Atal Behari Ghose were among the prominent speakers invited there; and so was Hemendraprasad Ghose, a leading nationalist of the 'extremist' faction,[59] and editor of the journal *Baśumati*. The latter described what happened when Woodroffe stood up to speak, and Pal reports his words:

> When Sir John Woodroffe stood up at the meeting to speak about Pandit Sivacandra, he was so overcome with grief at the death of his Guru that he was speechless; he could not utter a single word and tears were streaming from his eyes all the time. Sunk in grief just like a helpless orphan child no word about Sivacandra or any sound except weeping could be heard from him. Seeing him in such a pathetic and tragic state nobody in the meeting that day could restrain their tears as well. Finally the assembled speakers and other gentlemen there consoled the judge and made him sit on a chair.[60]

Pal places this passage in quotation marks, but does not make clear its source: whether it was reported to him verbally by Hemendraprasad at a meeting he had had with him (see below); or whether it is taken from an old issue of *Baśumati*.[61]

Eventually Woodroffe managed just to scribble a note on a piece of paper and handed it to the president of the meeting. Pal quotes the note in Bengali:

> At one time I was searching for the path of life with a restless mind, wandering hither and thither without direction. I thought desperately: in my search for the true path, who will place me on the ladder

> to the highest sādhanā? I felt deep in my heart that there was no guru to be found in this life and with that thought I could find no rest. At that very moment the man who first showed me the path and whose company – the company which was blessed by the gods – calmed my mind and directed it to the path of self realization (*ātmacaitanya*), saved me from utter destruction. To that man, the great man amongst all men, the king among all the kings, my guru, God's gift to humanity, Sivacandra, to the feet of that person I offer all my humble prayers and humble offerings. Blessed be the guru.[62]

Again, Pal does not say how this note was preserved, or how he came by it. There is no mention in *The Bengalee* or *Amrita Bāzār Patrika* – two major English language dailies in Indian ownership – of a high British official making such a public display of himself. However they do mention a crowded condolence meeting held at Kumarkhali, not Calcutta, organized by Jaladhar Sen, editor of *Bhārat Varṣa*, where people made speeches about the deceased saint. *Amrita Bāzār Patrika* adds that some speakers were visibly moved and that this 'struck a responsive chord in the audience'.[63] Nevertheless, I believe there is little reason to doubt Pal's story of Woodroffe's public grief, even if he has got the place, and the name of the president of the meeting wrong.[64] His witness, Hemendraprasad Ghose, was a well-known personality who had died shortly before Pal wrote; and other prominent citizens would have been at the gathering.

Funeral Rites

Pal claims that Woodroffe organized a *śrāddha* rite for Sivacandra at the required time after his death. He held a feast for brahmins and some famous tantric *sādhakas*, carefully prepared by brahmin cooks. He gave to each of them the prescribed gifts: of money, ritual cloths with the inscribed names of divinities, and copies of the scriptures. All this was said to be organised with the help of the ever-willing Haridev Sastri. Pal lists some of those invited, who include several well-known names of the contemporary tantric world, among them Jyotindranath Panda, leading disciple of the famous deceased saint Vāmakhappa and *śebait* (temple priest) at Tārapith (the scene of Vamakhappa's *sādhanā* and a pilgrimage site in West Bengal). Another well-known disciple of Vamakhappa who was reported to be present was Tarakhappa of Basighat. After feeding his guests, Woodroffe holds discussions with them and wins their admiration for the depth of his knowledge of *mātritattva* (the philosophy of the Mother) and his ability to discourse on it at length. How could he, a foreigner and a 'Christian' acquire such insight? Modestly, Woodroffe gives all the credit to his guru Sivacandra.[65] A few pages later Pal reports another meeting organized by Woodroffe in memory of Sivacandra, this time an intimate gathering of close disciples of the deceased saint. The list of those attending has many of the same names as the *śrāddha* guests but this time includes Hemendraprasad Ghose again, and also Pañckori Bāndyopādhyay, a prominent contemporary journalist and writer on Tantra in Bengali.[66]

THE DISCIPLE IN LATER LIFE: AN INTERVIEW WITH WOODROFFE[67]

Another prominent person who was one of Pal's sources was Rabindranath Mitra, India's first Home Minister after independence. As a student he was one of the Indian Civil Service trainees to whom Woodroffe lectured on Indian Law at Oxford, after his retirement from India. His story about a visit to Woodroffe's house and a conversation he had with him was passed on to Pal by Hemendraprasad Ghose, at a meeting in the journalist's offices. Pal records that the former revolutionary Baren Ghose was also present and told Pal that he had heard the same story before from Rabindranath Mitra.[68]

On being invited into Woodroffe's drawing room, the student Rabindranath Mitra was astonished to see on the walls pictures and framed photographs of Hindu divinities and saints, including one of Sivacandra Vidyarnava with his wife. In another room of the house, he saw other pictures: of *tīrthas* ('holy places') and rishis living in caves. 'It was as if I were standing in some Indian temple or in any Indian *sādhak's* ashram', said Mitra. Joining hands and doing *praṇām*, Woodroffe said that it was through the grace of his guru that he had visited these places and seen these saints. 'Indeed I do not know,' Woodroffe said 'whether it was seeing those sights that has changed the course of my inner life since that time'.

Over tea in the drawing room Woodroffe spoke of 'his Gurudev Sivacandra' who was an enduring presence in his life. He told Mitra of many experiences of the guru's '*kṛpā*' (compassion) shown to him after his death, both in India and after his return to England. These were appearances to him in visions and dreams, bringing guidance and consolation. He said that on several occasions this happened to him in the High Court while he was trying difficult cases:

> One day I was listening to the arguments of a complicated legal case . . . I was noting down the important points and remarks . . . I was also looking at the faces of the witnesses and trying to guess their inner mind . . . whether they were speaking the truth or not. While looking at the witnesses from time to time, once suddenly my eyes fell on the wall opposite and there was a beautiful and pleasant sight waiting to feast my eyes on. I saw my gurudev sitting there and just as our eyes met he raised his hand and blessed me. Even in broad daylight at noon

> I saw this vision of my guru very clearly and I offered my obeisance to him in my mind. And he said: Kalyanam astu . . . And again another day I was sitting at home at night and writing the verdict of a difficult case. And suddenly I saw my gurudev standing in front of me clad in the tantric apparel with a trident in hand. Just as I rose from the seat to do the praṇām to him, touching his feet, he extended his hand and said: Kalyanam astu. And then that image multiplied into several such images and filled up the whole room with lots and lots of images of my gurudev, wherever I looked in the room. I was quite surprised and I felt the blessing of my gurudev on me and my eyes filled up with tears. When I wiped my eyes and looked again even then all the apparitions were present.[69]

A person like Sivacandra, Woodroffe is reported as saying, is impenetrable to ordinary people. His feelings and mental states (*bhāva*) cannot be comprehended. He is a great mystery.

Woodroffe's *sādhanā*

Plucking up courage, the student shyly asked the former judge how, with his different cultural background, he had managed to accept and adapt to a guru who was a Tantric. Woodroffe said that he had brought this difficulty to Sivacandra, who had replied that in the Hindu religion there were many paths (*paddhati*) and methods of practice (*prakriyā*). The guru would judge the correct initiation for his disciple, taking account of his mental tendencies (*mānsik prabaṇatā*), his character traits (*cāritrik lakṣana*), his skills (*dakṣatā*) and his suitability (*adhikāra*).[70] Consequently, said Sivacandra to Woodroffe: 'I have already decided . . . according to the indications given in the śāstras. *Vamācār* or *vīrācār* is not right for you and I know already that you are averse to such practices. I have decided to initiate you . . . through *divyācār* only.'[71]

Others did not get off so lightly. *Divyācār* – the 'divine practice', the highest of the three paths of *sādhanā* according to the Tantras – traditionally signified the practices of those who had gone beyond the stage of taboo-breaking *vāmācāra* rites by transcending social inhibitions as well as personal like and dislike. Sivacandra's use of the concept to enable Woodroffe to bypass *vāmācāra* sounds like an accommodation to his high-ranking disciple. Mr Bagchi, whose own guru was a disciple of Sivacandra, had to perform his *sādhanā* in the graveyard – which he intensely disliked – for a whole year until his guru allowed him to stop the visits, to the disciple's great relief.

The theme of personal disposition, suitability, or a person having *adhikāra* for certain practices and not for others, is prominent in the Avalon/Woodroffe writings. One of the reasons why Woodroffe praises Tantra is just such alleged insight into and tolerance of individual differences, of race and culture, temperament and capacity. It was also of course a useful way of dealing with the problem of the more controversial rituals.

How authentic is Rabindranath Mitra's picture of Woodroffe? His story is corroborated in one interesting detail: it is only in his section reporting Mitra's story that Pal uses the name of Jayakali Devi as the *bhairavī* who gave Woodroffe his second initiation. This was confirmed by the Ghose family who told me that she was also Atal Bihari's guru and they showed me two postcards he had received from her. I have not come across her name anywhere else and it looks as if Mitra may have learned it from Woodroffe himself. Secondly, although the passages about the suitability of disciples for different paths are a favourite theme of Woodroffe's *Shakti and Shākta*, the use of the term *divyācār* in the sense given here is not used anywhere in the Avalon/Woodroffe books, so Mitra would not have read about it there. As for Woodroffe remaining a disciple in later life: we have Pal's unquestionably accurate report of what happened when news of Woodroffe's death reached Sivacandra's disciples at Kumarkhali. A condolence meeting or *śoksabhā* was organized for him by the *Sarvamangalā Sabhā*, where a sacrifice (*āhuta*) was made and a song of tribute was specially composed and sung at the gathering. A photocopy of the sheet on which the song was printed and distributed is included in Pal's book.[72] Although Woodroffe's work in spreading knowledge of the Mother (*mātritattva*) is the theme of the tribute, Pal has also stated that Woodroffe sent money from England for the upkeep of the worship of the Mother at Sivacandra's ashram. That he had continued to be a major financial sponsor would seem to be a more immediate reason for the memorial meeting and the sacrifice. At the very least, it is much less likely to have taken place if Woodroffe had not maintained his relationship with Sivacandra's ashram during the fourteen years since his departure from India.

ALEXANDRA DAVID-NEEL

The final word on Woodroffe as a Tantric while he was still in India can be given to Alexandra David-Neel, the French explorer who visited the Woodroffes in 1912.[73] At that time she described Woodroffe as someone who was openly a Śākta and devotee of Kālī, and who practised rites to that goddess.[74] She mentions successive (*krama*) initiations called *abhiśekha*. She contrasts her own attitude, which she claims is that of the detached scholar, with Woodroffe's which was that of the '*dévot*'.[75] Many years after her visit she described an intimate domestic ritual where Woodroffe worshipped his wife as his *śakti*, tantric fashion, before they made love. She does not name the couple she is writing about – even though she says she is writing many years after their deaths – but it is obvious to whom she is referring in a book first published in 1951:

> If I dared to mention such a delicate subject, I would reveal that I have known a European, well educated and belonging to the highest society of his own country, who was a Śākta ... He took part in mystic cakras of an irreproachable purity. As for his wife, with whom he seemed very much in love, he looked on her as representing the goddess and before their intimate relations, he worshipped her as one worships the image of Śakti in the temples, presenting before her flowers, ritual lamps with many tiny flames and burning incense all the while chanting hymns in Sanskrit.[76]

She does not claim to have witnessed this scene, but only that it was told to her during confidences made in a spirit of innocence and religious reverence (*une gravitée toute réligieuse*). It made her wonder how such a prelude did not inhibit love-making, but the three children of the marriage proved that this was not so. 'Initiates', she continued, would understand, that the couple were not seeking true spiritual illumination through the rite, for properly speaking the tantric *maithuna* should not result in procreation.[77]

David-Neel may have added this aside because a little earlier she had just claimed that Woodroffe confessed to her that he saw tantric ritual as a sort of magic that would bring him material benefits. The French explorer had also made remarks about magic during her 1912–13 visit, expounding upon 'this unhappy mentality' in a letter where she wrote that 'there are English officials who secretly become disciples of Hindu sorcerers'.[78] Woodroffe, the 'devotee' (*dévot*) as she called him, had been captivated by Tantra *au dela des limites qu'on eut pu prévoir*, so presumably she included him in her comments about the disciples of sorcerers. As David-Neel's biographers remark, 'she was not given to praising her rivals'[79]: in fact she was usually disparaging about almost everyone. If Woodroffe's example had aroused some misgivings in her, she was soon to travel much further 'beyond the limits' herself, for she was to travel in Tibet as a Buddhist nun. David-Neel was a strange mixture of the 'superior' rationalist and the willing believer.[80] One wonders what other disciples of 'sorcerers' she had in mind – perhaps some of Woodroffe's European friends? Or was she implying that the fascination with Tantra was more widespread? If so, then our stereotypes of the typical servants of the British Raj are sometimes wide of the mark.

She has written: 'He took part in mystic cakras of an irreproachable purity.' Just what that meant is illustrated by the story of her own participation in a so-called *divya cakra*, presumably belonging to the *divyācāra* path in which Sivacandra initiated the Woodroffes. It was an entirely 'respectable' version of the *pañcatattva* rite.[81] She had been initiated by a guru – she does not say who this was – and invited to participate by a Western educated, middle class Indian couple. The atmosphere was opulent and refined. Each male participant brought along two *śaktis*: his *bhogya śakti* – partner of 'enjoyment' (the sexual partner) – had to be his lawful wife; she sat on his left. On his right sat his *pūjā śakti*, another woman who was to represent the Goddess. David-Neel attended in the latter capacity and was worshipped in an *ārati* ceremony with music and lights. She was presented with offerings which were definitely not meat, fish and wine, but a kind of sweet and what she thought was mildly fermented fruit juice, or perhaps rice–wine.[82] She was very curious to see what the fifth '*tattva*' would consist of. It consisted of the man wrapping himself fully clothed in his wife's capacious sari and the couple remaining immobile for a long time, rapt in meditation.[83]

She does not say if the Indian couple who took her to this *cakra* were the Ghoses, and we do not know who the guru was. But in any case, if John and Ellen Woodroffe did ever sit in tantric *cakras* with Mr and Mrs Ghose as they were rumoured to do, then it is highly likely that this was the kind of *cakra* it was. Sobhun Ghose passed on the family's image of Woodroffe: that he was *sattvic*. The highest of the three *guṇas*,[84] *sattva* is inevitably associated with *divyā bhāva* (the highest or most spiritual state of mind or feeling) and *divyācāra*. Sobhun translated it (wrongly but interestingly) as 'puritanical'. Woodroffe's writing on Tantra skirts around its sexuality, even to the extent of appearing naive. His inspiration appears genuinely to be predominantly mystical and metaphysical. Nevertheless we can assume tantric affirmation of sexuality was important to him. This is hinted at in his writings, sometimes concealed behind affirmation of the senses in general as opposed to the renouncer's rejection of them. Such an ethic could have been welcome to a British person of the early twentieth century – especially to a former pupil of Lord Petre who had witnessed his struggle against the world-denial and asceticism of the more stringent forms of nineteenth century Catholicism.

EPILOGUE

Each of Woodroffe's roles studied so far has contained a paradox – and this one is no exception. In his two most famous books *Shakti and Shākta* and *The Serpent Power*, he claimed that he was an 'outside' observer who was not an advocate of Tantra.[85] Not even in *Principles of Tantra*, his translation of Sivacandra's book, does he actually write of the book's author as a disciple might be expected to write of a guru; and in *Shakti and Shākta* he even hints at disagreement with him.[86]

We have seen how Woodroffe claimed that the abuse levelled at Tantra presented a challenge to him to investigate it 'impartially', and throughout his books there are appeals to tolerance and empathy as the ground for understanding the religion of 'another'. He is reported to have told his publisher in the 1920s that he was an impartial examiner not a practitioner of Tantra.[87] This of course could have been deliberate secrecy, but a statement in one of his last letters to Atal Bihari Ghose makes one pause for thought.

It was written in 1934, shortly before his death when he may have finally started to feel that his Indian life lay behind him. The letter concerned the Maharaja of Patiala, who had made a promise to purchase the copyright of the *Tantrik Texts* series. Maharaja Sir Bhupender Singh, the ruler of the largest Sikh kingdom in India, would seem to be an unlikely Tantric, but he appears to have had a tantric guru. He reneged on his commitment to give financial help, and discussing the reasons for the rebuff, Woodroffe first considered political difficulties to be the cause, but finally he wrote to Ghose:

> As regards P[atiala], the only rational explanation which presents itself to me is that his Guru has forbidden him to have any communication with me. You may ask why: and the answer would be that *I have not been initiated*.[88]

Even if we imagine that Woodroffe did not like to make his initiation public knowledge, it is strange he should deny it in a letter to Ghose of all people. A possible explanation is that Woodroffe meant that he had not accepted initiation from this particular guru, and this is how I take it. The evidence for Woodroffe having practised some form of tantric *sādhanā*, and therefore having accepted some form of initiation, is very strong, despite his disclaimers.

Besides prominent figures like Hemendraprasad Ghose and Rabindranath Mitra, we have seen that Pal includes testimony from several other people to Woodroffe's close connection with and deep feeling for Sivacandra, and the fact that he was widely believed to be a disciple. Woodroffe is portrayed as a practitioner of the Tantras in his obituaries in both *Baśumati* and *Bhārat Varṣa*, the former edited by Hemendraprasad Ghose and the latter by Jaladhar Sen, another prominent figure who, as we have seen, was present at Sivacandra's *śoksabhā*. The rumours of what went on at Konarak may have been wrong as regards *kuṇḍalinī yoga* but they are backed up by other stories of Woodroffe's involvement in forms of tantric practice. Alexandra David-Neel portrayed him as an initiated Śākta practising a form of tantric ritual, and she was a witness independent of both Sivacandra's circle and the art movement. Besides all this, there are stories of Woodroffe as a Tantric still current at the High Court of Calcutta even today. The evidence for his strong personal feeling for Sivacandra revealed in his grief at his death sounds authentic, and having such a strong bond it seems unlikely he would hold back from initiation. There are the photographs which Woodroffe permitted to be taken of himself in Indian dress at Konarak: a bold move for a British person in his position, and again, it seems unlikely he should go so far and yet hold back from initiation. Finally, there is the memorial tribute paid to him by Sivacandra's disciples at Kumarkhali in which (as we shall see below) they describe him as an advanced Tantric. They would not have done this only because he had authored some famous books: he also would have had to reflect his glory on to their guru because they believed him to be a disciple.

In the year following the letter just discussed – ie. some time in 1935, the last year of his life – Woodroffe was re-baptised into the Catholic Church. The reason, according to his son James, was some doubt as to whether his infant baptism was valid. This is puzzling. Woodroffe was first baptised as a Protestant, in an Anglican church in Calcutta, but one would have expected him to have been re-baptised when his parents converted to Catholicism and he was sent to a catholic school. In 1934, Ellen Woodroffe had been received into the Catholic Church.[89] According to James, this had nothing to do with his father's catholic background: on the contrary he thought it was the other way around, and that Ellen's conversion (which had come about through a woman friend), had influenced her husband. James thus saw his mother's influence on his father's religious life in both directions: towards Theosophy and Hinduism to begin with, and back again to Catholicism in the end. It does not necessarily follow, however, that the re-baptism implied a wholehearted rejection of Tantra. It is more likely that it was another example of Woodroffe's use of the notion of *adhikāra*: that he deemed the rites of the Catholic Church to be 'appropriate' for the European race which had evolved them. Later we shall see that Woodroffe continued faithfully (even if a little impatiently) to promote the publication of *Tantrik Texts* right until the end. Presumably he would not have done this if he was really beginning to experience serious 'repentance' for his tantric past, although a desire to honour commitments already entered into might have overruled such feelings, if he had them.

It may be the case however that the period of Woodroffe's most active and enthusiastic personal involvement in tantric *sādhanā* occurred rather earlier than the bulk of his writings and lectures on Tantra: during the period when he was also active in the art movement from around 1904–5 up until Sivacandra's death in 1914. Both his major books, *Shakti and Shākta* and *The Serpent Power*, were produced a few years after that event. By that time it is possible he was beginning to distance himself a little from his experience, perhaps through the very act of writing them. On the other hand, perhaps we may have to recognize that the split in his personality that we have already noted in previous chapters, operated in this sphere too.

Commenting on *The Serpent Power*, the tantric scholar M.P. Pandit described its author as 'truly an Indian soul in a European body'.[90] There seems to be little doubt that Woodroffe was granted by many in India the near-Indian religious identity he appears to have sought in at least part of his being. In their memorial tribute, the followers of Sivacandra praised him as an advanced Tantric. They addressed him: 'Oh calm, peaceful[91] Kaula Tantric Rishi' – high praise indeed. But there is even more: the heading of this tribute, photocopied in Pal's book, describes Woodroffe's death as *mahāprasthān*, the voluntary relinquishing of life of an advanced soul – the same term that Pal uses for Sivacandra's own death. Furthermore, although Pal himself refers to Woodroffe by the honorific *mahāday*, on the memorial leaflet he is called *mahātma*.[92] His obituary in *Bharat Varṣa* suggested he had been incarnated in the unfavourable environment of the West because of some sin in a past life, and that he had expiated this through his *sādhanā* in India.[93] The same idea is echoed in the preface to the Bengali edition of *Is India Civilized?* where Woodroffe was called a *śāpbhrasta mahāpuruṣa*, a great or highly advanced being who because of some small sin or ritual fault, has been reincarnated in an unfavourable condition: 'No other low caste person could be compared to him'.[94] Not only in Bengal but also in South India, Woodroffe acquired a near-brahmanical status. His obituary in *The Hindu* of Madras mentioned a legend that he took initiation in the *Gāyatrī* mantra, and that he wore the sacred thread beneath his judge's robes.[95]

If identity is connected to love, then it would seem that love of a tantric guru was a factor in bestowing upon Woodroffe his 'Indian soul'. It was however a divided soul. Woodroffe's chameleon-like quality, referred to in the last chapter, may have contributed to a split within him as he absorbed into his own identity the strongly conflicting influences to which he was exposed or to which he opened himself.

How far the 'Indian soul' that emerged in his writings reflected his close collaboration with Atal Bihari Ghose is an important theme of the second part of this book. As we shall see, for most people in his own lifetime, Indian or Western, the pseudonymous Arthur Avalon's status as a foreign orientalist was crucial to his authority and influence. But the situation would soon be the reverse. The hint of secret 'inside' knowledge, the suggestion that the author had received authentic initiations, greatly extended the influence of his books outside academic circles, not only in India but especially among subsequent generations in the West.[96] In Part Two we look at the Avalon/Woodroffe books and their interpretation of *tantraśāstra*. We begin with the study of Tantra in orientalism previous to Arthur Avalon and the prevailing attitudes which his books aimed to challenge.

Part Two

ARTHUR AVALON

The Creation of a Legendary Orientalist

Chapter Seven

THE STUDY OF TANTRA

A new orientalist appears on the scene

'Tantra'

This subject is discussed in greater depth in chapter 9. The term *tantra* 'means simply a system of ritual or essential instructions'[1] and strictly speaking refers to certain texts, related to or derived from another class of scriptures called *āgama*[2] – hence the name of the company which published Arthur Avalon's books, *Āgamānusandhana Samiti*, the Āgamas Research Society. It was said by a commentator in the fifteenth century: 'Śruti is twofold: Vaidik and Tāntrik', which shows how the Tantras were regarded as a separate kind of revelation (*śruti*) and a new source of authority from the Vedas.[3] Whereas the vedic tradition is synonymous with orthodoxy in Hinduism, the position of the Tantras and their followers has always been more ambiguous; the Tantras themselves however mostly claim to be in the vedic tradition.[4]

A typical Tantra, according to a traditional list, should contain seven subjects including cosmogony ('creation and dissolution of the world'), worship, meditation, *mantra*, and the *ṣaṭ-karma* or six magic acts.[5] The tantric literature is divided between original Tantras, which are usually anonymous and considered to be the Word of Śiva (or other deities), and digests and commentaries by named authors. The former possibly originated from around the eighth or ninth century, but the period when Tantrism flourished was from the eighth until around the fourteenth century; it is still practised today.[6]

Tantras prescribe individual practices (*sādhanā*) aimed at the goal of personal liberation (*mokṣa*) and/or the acquiring of magic power (*siddhi*). With the dual goal of knowledge as inner self-realization and as mastery over nature, Tantrics seek initiations (*dīkṣā*) from a Guru who imparts oral instruction and to whom the disciple submits. Tantric *sādhanā* has characteristic features by which it is usually defined.[7] Most important of these is the use of certain mental and physical objects which express or concretize, abstract principles and deities.[8] These are: *mantra* or *bīja* (sound-

'seeds') accompanied by *yantra* (geometric patterns representing *mantras* and divinities), *maṇḍala* (cosmos diagrams), *mudrā* (ritual gestures)[9] and figurative images (*pratimā*). Tantric divinities are those of the wider Hindu or Buddhist pantheon but conceived in many more forms and with a special iconography important for *dhyāna* – mental images constructed in meditation – which accompanies outer ritual worship (*pūjā*). Ideas of microcosm–macrocosm correspondence underlie Tantrism, where the bipolar, bisexual divinity (*Śiva–Śakti* in Śaiva and Śākta Tantra) resides in the human body, and is brought into conscious union through tantric or *kuṇḍalinī* yoga.[10] *Kuṇḍalinī* is a form of *śakti* – 'energy' or 'power' – the female, active, cosmogonic aspect of the divine polarity, which is conceived to permeate all things and is the most important concept of Tantra. In the theological context *śakti* means the activity of a deity in manifesting the cosmic cycles and dissolving them, or reabsorbing them into the Godhead.[11]

Eventually *śakti* became more significant than her consort – especially in the śākta literature that grew out of Śaiva Tantra – and the Goddess took central place, appearing in many forms and lesser emanations. Hence 'Tantra' in Hinduism became almost synonymous with Śāktism, although it originally had a wider reference, for there were tantric forms of Vaisnavism, Saivism, Buddhism and even Jainism.[12] Today, the term *tantra* (or 'Tantrism') is often used generically to cover the body of metaphysical, theological and cosmological ideas along with ritual and yogic practices, which are contained in, or derive from, the *āgamas* and Tantras but are also to be found in other texts which do not bear that label. This is the sense in which the term is used in this book.[13]

The prominence of the Goddess in itself appeared sinister enough, at least to English commentators on Hinduism and Buddhism who were mostly raised, unlike Woodroffe himself, in the protestant tradition where the 'maleness' of God is not compromised by the practice of devotion to the Mother of Jesus. To this was compounded Tantra's strong emphasis on ritual, with its images and mantras – seen as 'idols' and 'magic spells'. Moreover much of the imagery was associated with death and some rites (especially those of a more magical nature) took place in the cremation ground. This gave Tantra a particularly repugnant surface and was roundly dismissed as 'necromancy'. Last but not least, there was the sexuality of Tantra, derived at least in part from its concept of bisexual divinity. The notorious *pañcatattva* rite, or *cakra pūjā* (circle worship), was the main focus of notoriety in Woodroffe's time, in which male initiates worship female partners who represent *śakti*, through 'five substances' or 'five true things' (*tattvas*).[14] These are also known as the *pañca makāra*, or the five 'm's: wine (*madya*) meat (*māṁsa*), fish (*matsya*), grain (*mudrā*) and sexual intercourse (*maithuna*).[15] This deliberate ritual transgression was usually seen by orthodox Hindus and European observers as simply an excuse for licentiousness.[16]

The *pañcatattva* and the rites performed in the cremation ground remained secret, esoteric affairs, but the general features of tantric ritual and imagery gradually penetrated the Hindu mainstream and became allied to Vedanta philosophy. It was on this aspect of 'Tantra' that Avalon/ Woodroffe placed his emphasis. His approach was in striking contrast to that of nearly all previous European scholars who either ignored or vilified the Tantras.

I 'TANTRA' IN EUROPEAN ORIENTALISM

That the books of Arthur Avalon marked a turning-point was acknowledged by Ernest Payne, a missionary author who wrote *The Śāktas* in 1933, in a series on Hindu sects edited by J.N. Farquhar. He wrote of Woodroffe: 'The zeal of a convert often runs away with his judgement ... Students of Indian religion, however, owe him a great debt for having opened up this important and difficult field.' He noted a marked change of attitude 'almost entirely due to the publications of Arthur Avalon' reflected in recent writings on Tantra and Śāktism.[17]

Admitting that previous writers 'have been content to follow one another in expressions of disgust rather than embark on the difficult task of examining it,' Payne listed E.W. Hopkins,[18] William Ward ,[19] the Abbé Dubois ,[20] Horace Hayman Wilson, Monier Williams, A. Barth (see below) and William Crooke[21] Among this list, Ward was ridiculed by Arthur Avalon, and Dubois and Wilson strongly criticised in the same preface in which he attacked his contemporary L.D. Barnett (see above p. 1) [PT/1 pp. 1–6]. It was the orientalist use of language that Arthur Avalon confronted in this and his other books: language which he claimed was the result of a sense of racial superiority allied to ignorance and prejudice. Among writers on Buddhism he criticised L.A. Waddell, for phrases like 'silly mummery of unmeaning jargon and gibberish' [SS:68],[22] and he was fond of citing Brian Houghton Hodgson's similarly summary dismissal of buddhist Tantra as 'lust, mummery and black magic'.[23] The word 'mummery' seems to have been used to sum up succinctly for English-speaking commentators their perception of ritual as excessive or meaningless, and hence unworthy of hermeneutic effort.[24] Payne himself pointed to the frequent occurrence of words like 'bestiality', 'obscenity' and 'pious profligacy'.[25]

It was Tantric Buddhism (*vajrayāna*, or 'the Way of the Thunderbolt') which first made a strong impression on European minds. Peter Bishop in his history of European perceptions of Tibet, has described the reactions evoked among nineteenth century travellers when they encountered the *vajrayāna* with its frequently sexual or violent imagery. The ideal of the austere religion of Sakyamuni Buddha that was reflected in Sir Edwin

Arnold's *Light of Asia*, published towards the end of the nineteenth century, was contrasted with the 'degenerate' and 'superstitious' practices of *vajrayāna*. Buddhist Tantra became a target of abuse, and commentators wrote of 'the evil teaching of the Tantrik philosophy'. 'To those well-read travellers' comments Bishop 'it was simply inconceivable that such doctrines bore but the barest relation to the noble philosophy of self-denial that was believed to constitute original, pure Buddhism'.[26]

Intertwined with these adverse reactions, however, went also romantic idealizations: both originated in European perceptions of 'the other'. Bishop shows how Tibet became for the European imagination a sacred space on to which romantic and spiritual yearnings were projected. For this the landscape was crucial: a beautiful wilderness, vast, dangerous and hard to approach, helped to constellate the image.[27] Perhaps it is possible to view tantric Hinduism in Woodroffe's time as a similarly inaccessible country of the mind, sealed off from European penetration not by physical barriers but by the horrific exterior which its symbolism presented. Consequently Arthur Avalon's expedition into this 'forbidden' territory and his discovery of spiritual treasures within it earned him the accolades of 'pioneer' and 'explorer' by his contemporaries, both Indian and foreign (see next chapter).

If Arthur Avalon appeared to take on the mantle of the pioneer opening up a new field of knowledge then one of the original bearers of that image must surely have been Brian Houghton Hodgson. His lifelong labours brought to European scholarship the discovery of an entirely new literature – the Sanskrit *mahāyāna* buddhist texts of the *prajñāpāramitā* school as well as the Sanskrit and Tibetan scriptures of the *vajrayāna*. A British civil servant in Nepal, he pursued research into every aspect of his Himalayan environment, scientific, cultural and religious. Knowing neither Sanskrit nor Tibetan, he built up knowledge of the structure of the living Buddhism around him through oral inquiries. He attempted to map the literature and set about collecting texts from 1820 onwards. Eventually he donated literally hundreds of manuscripts to the libraries of Great Britain, India and France during the first half of the nineteenth century, which formed the basis for the study of Buddhism in European universities and in India for the second half.[28] He presented the fruits of his oral inquiries in papers to the Asiatic Society of Bengal in the 1820s and '30s, which included the first systematized description of the Tibetan pantheon of *dhyāni* Buddhas and Bodhisattvas.[29] Hodgson only gradually came to know of certain sections of the buddhist canonical texts called 'Tantra' or *upadeśa*: his verdict on them was that they were 'in general disgraced by obscenity and by all sorts of magic and demonology.'[30] But he added nevertheless that they were 'frequently redeemed by unusually explicit assertions of a supreme Godhead.' (This referred to the sixth *dhyāni* Buddha of the *vajrayāna* 'pantheon': *Vajrasattva*, who corresponds to the Mind governing the five who represent the senses.)

The first European academic to make use of Hodgson's material was the French orientalist Eugène Burnouf, who published his history of Indian Buddhism in 1844 through working on the many texts presented by Hodgson to the *Société Asiatique de Paris*. Hodgson is warmly acknowledged in the preface.[31] Burnouf devoted a chapter to tantric Buddhism in this book but saw little in it beyond tedious systems of magic for utilitarian ends, devoted to a cult of 'bizarre and terrible gods and goddesses'. 'These treatises' he wrote 'are merely sets of instructions for the guidance of devotees in the construction of circles and other magical figures (*maṇḍala*)'. He felt that in them Buddhism was reduced to human proportions and he was disappointed to see a facile cult aimed at temporal advantages displacing the cultivation of the virtues of a Buddha.[32] Derogatory phrases abound in his chapter: he described the Tantras as 'the books which seemed to me the product of ignorance and the grossest superstition'.[33] Noting that in many of the texts the name of Buddha was rarely mentioned whereas śaiva divinities were frequently named, he classified tantric Buddhism as a degenerate synthesis with Śaivism and Śāktism.[34]

During the same period as Hodgson collected his manuscripts, the legendary Hungarian traveller Csomo de Koros visited Tibet where he studied the language in the monasteries.[35] He too brought many texts to the Asiatic Society in Calcutta. Many of these Tibetan texts, it was realised, were translations of Sanskrit originals which Hodgson had acquired in Nepal. But whereas Hodgson had only found fragments of the literature, de Koros had discovered the whole canon.[36] De Koros published a dictionary and grammar of Tibetan in 1834; his summary of the Tibetan textual library – the *Kangyur* and *Tangyur* – appeared in *Asiatick Researches* in 1836. The *Kangyur* was the section containing the sacred scriptures; the *Tangyur* contained commentaries. De Koros listed nine divisions of texts in the former group, the seventh of them being called *gyut*, or *tantra* in Sanskrit. Unlike many later academic orientalists, but like Woodroffe himself, de Koros approached the texts with the help of the traditional interpreters, the Lamas whom he studied with. His language reveals a sympathetic attitude, which is not blocked by prejudices against the magical elements, which he merely notes objectively. He wrote of a 'mystical theology', and noticed that this class of text also included such subjects as astronomy, astrology, chronology and medicine. Several passages he considered expressed excellent ideas on the Supreme Being, and on diverse subjects such as the nature of the human body and soul. One text particularly appealed to him because it revealed its author's benevolence towards all living beings.[37] It was from de Koros' work on the *kālacakra tantra* that there penetrated into Europe the idea of the mythical land of Shambala, and its hidden wisdom which became the 'Shangri-La' of a popular book of the 1930s.[38]

The work of Hodgson, de Koros and Burnouf, then, formed the basis of the study of *māhayana* and *vajrayāna* Buddhism by later European orientalists. But the attitude towards the tantric strand, specially among English scholars, strongly contrasts with that of de Koros. Among writers on Hinduism, Horace Hayman Wilson in India and England, like Burnouf in France, was one of the great Sanskritists of the nineteenth century. Translator of the *viṣṇu purāṇa* and other texts, he occupied the first chair of Sanskrit at Oxford University from 1832. Before that he served for many years as a surgeon for the East India Company.[39] In the 1828 edition of *Asiatick Researches* Wilson published translations from the Sanskrit of three fragments of manuscripts from Hodgson's collection.[40] He characterised them as being of a 'popular not a scriptural' nature and as 'guides to the common and corrupt practice and belief'; they showed 'how far the Buddha creed has been modified by Tantrika admixture'.[41] The longest of the three fragments, called *ashtami vrata vidhāna*, consisted of instructions for a tantric ritual from which Wilson translated brief extracts. Writing in the early nineteenth century, Wilson was already well aware of distinctive features that were characteristic of the Tantras, whatever their doctrinal affiliation:

> The ceremonial of the Tantras is distinguished by the repetition of mystical syllables, the employment of Yantras, or diagrams, a superabundance of gesticulations, the adoration of the spiritual teacher or Guru and the fancied identification of the worshipper with the divinity worshipped.[42]

We can see that Wilson neither could nor wanted to penetrate the surface, but behind the dismissive language we can see that he already knows that '*mantra*, *yantra* and *mudrā*' are among characteristic features of what came to be known as 'Tantra'. He continued:

> In all of these, as well as in the order and nature of the presentations, the *Ashtami Vidhāna* is as applicable to Calcutta as to Kathmandu; the only difference being in the object or objects addressed.'

He dismisses this and other tantric texts as 'nonsensical extravagance' which one 'might be disposed to laugh at' if it were not for their interest for 'the study of human nature'.

The same edition of *Asiatick Researches* included the first part of Wilson's seminal essay on the religious sects of the Hindus.[43] Wilson characterised his account as 'necessarily superficial' being based on only a 'cursory inspection' of a few texts. These he augmented from oral sources.[44] In 1832 he presented the second part of his essay in the following edition of *Asiatick Researches*. This included a short section on 'the Śāktas', where he supports his account with short quotations in footnotes from the śākta Purāṇas and a few Tantras. The latter he has introduced as the collective term for the works containing 'the principal rites and formulae' for 'the worship of Śakti', having traced the history of the latter concept in the Vedas and

Purāṇas. The two-fold division of the Śāktas into a respectable branch and a so-called 'extremist' and unacceptable one seems to have originated with Wilson. He distinguished the *dakṣinācāris* or followers of the 'right hand path' from the *vāmācāris*, followers of the 'left hand'.[45] Under the former Wilson describes the public cult of the goddess, mainly in the forms of Durga and Kālī; while the latter term refers to those who adopt a ritual 'contrary to that which is usual, and to what indeed they dare publicly avow': namely the ritual known as the five *makāras*, or the *pañcatattva*.[46] Wilson described it through the medium of brief extracts from a selection of tantric texts. These were backed up by oral report ('a very general belief in their occurrence').[47] His account is purely descriptive: apart from expressions of disgust, it makes no attempt at commentary or interpretation. He believed, however, that the ritual was practised rarely. Far from using it for anti-Hindu propaganda, he sought to reduce the impact of *vāmacāra* by downplaying its importance:

> It is contrary, however, to all knowledge of the human character, to admit the possibility of these transactions in their fullest extent; and . . . there can be little doubt of its being practiced but seldom, and then in solitude and secrecy . . . it is usually nothing more than a convivial party, consisting of the members of a single family . . .[48]

A decade later his attitude seems to have hardened. Most of his phrases that Avalon selects for criticism were taken from two lectures Wilson delivered in Oxford in 1840.[49] In these he calls the texts themselves to bear witness against themselves. Having alluded to the quest for superhuman powers and control over spirits, he then mentions 'worse things' practised by 'the left hand Shakta sect':

> It is to this that the bloody sacrifices offered to Kālī must be imputed; and that all the barbarities and indecencies perpetrated at the Durga Puja . . . are to be ascribed. There are other atrocities which do not meet the public eye. It is not an unfounded accusation, not a controversial calumny. We have the books – *we can read the texts* . . . veiled necessarily in the obscurity of the original language, but *incontrovertible witnesses* to the veracity of the charge. Of course no respectable Hindu will admit that he is a Vāmācāri . . . although if the Tantras are to be believed many a man who calls himself a Śaiva . . . etc is secretly a Śākta and a brother of the left-hand fraternity.[50]

It is possible that this hardening of opinion might have had something to do with the fact that by the 1840s Wilson occupied the Boden chair of Sanskrit at Oxford, which had been set up with an expressly missionary purpose.[51] Nevertheless, here Wilson was touching upon more serious matters than simple magic, sexual or otherwise. In this passage he was bracketing together the secret 'left hand' *vāmācāra* practices, with the public animal sacrifices and sexual licence associated in some places with the public cult of Durga at that time – and 'the bloody sacrifices offered to Kālī', by which he undoubtedly meant the human sacrifices performed to that goddess which are prescribed in the *kālikā purāṇa*, and described in several eighteenth and nineteenth century reports.[52] Taken together with the secrecy of *vāmācāra*, this added up to a potent mixture of blood, lust and hypocrisy. It was the image of 'Tantra' and 'Śāktism', taken as a single phenomenon, which was to dominate European perception until the writings of Arthur Avalon marked a turning in the tide of opinion.

Wilson's successor in the Boden chair of Sanskrit was H.M. Monier Williams, who called the Tantras 'the bible of Śāktism', and defined the latter as 'the worship of force ... with a view to the acquisition of supernatural faculties...or to the destruction of enemies ...'[53]

> Unhappily a vast proportion of the inhabitants of India, especially in Bengal, are guided in their daily life and practices by Tantric teaching, and are in bondage to the doctrines inculcated in these writings ... Its demoralising effect ... cannot be doubted and indeed it can scarcely be doubted that Śāktism is Hinduism arrived at its worst and most corrupt stage of development.[54]

He equates this corruption with what he calls the *undue* adoration of the wives of Śiva and to the '*neglect*' of their male counterparts.[55] This author's division of the 'Śākta sect' into *dakṣina* and *vāma* branches is made to coincide with a greater or lesser emphasis on the feminine, thus enhancing the notion of *vāmacāra* practices as 'extreme Śāktism'. Like Wilson and Burnouf he perceived it almost entirely as a system of magic; he calls *mantra* 'a spell or charm' and dismisses other characteristic tantric concepts such as *bīja*, *nyāsa*, *yantra* similarly as magical terms. The philosophy of language (as a cosmogonic principle), which greatly attracted Woodroffe, is known to Monier Williams, but does not affect his perception of the associated practices as 'magic'. Nevertheless, he also conceded that the Tantras are 'theoretically very different' and not all were of the character he had described.[56]

The French scholar A. Barth, in his *Religions of India* (first published in French in 1881) described the philosophical notion of *śakti* sympathetically, but regarded the Tantras as literature detailing the 'sensual and obscene observances' which formed the 'other side' of śākta cults. For him 'a Çākta of the left hand is almost always a hypocrite and a superstitious debauchee', but he went on to note that 'among the authors of these contemptible catechetical books there was more than one who sincerely believed he was performing a work of sanctity'. Nevertheless 'No Hindu with any self-respect will confess that he has any connection with the Vāmācārins'.[57]

It is perhaps significant that Monier-Williams cited an Indian secondary source for his quotations from the Tantras: Gopāl Hari Deshmukh's *āgama prakāśa*. He quotes approvingly the strong condemnation of the magic practices of the 'Mantra Śāstrins' made by this 'enlightened Brahmana'.[58] Another example of such a European–Indian alliance against Tantrism is provided by the missionary writer Mrs Sinclair Stevenson and her Brahmin informants who shared her horror of *vāmacāra*.[59] Woodroffe, when he attacked Indian attitudes to Tantra, always had in mind the English-educated, whom he called the *mānasaputra* (mind-born sons) of the English [SS:71]. He was attacking the influence, not only of missionary education, but of Utilitarian and Rationalist thought:

> Theories stale in the West, but new in the East, were adopted by some with the same undiscriminating fervour as were the discarded fashions of English "art" and articles of commerce. Some there were who, judging all things by a narrow test of "utilitarian" principle, found every historic religion, whether of East or West, to be the outcome merely of the deceit of priests ... [and] ..."abomination worship". And of this in India, the Śākta and other cults were cited as the worst examples. [PT/1 p. 21]

This was an important insight into the root of attitudes stemming from Europe. Nevertheless, revulsion from the sexuality and magic of Tantra in themselves did not originate with Western education. Disgust and ridicule are well known in Sanskrit literature from the time when the *kaula* tantric sects flourished.[60] Moreover Tantrics when viewed as magicians evoke fear, and it was not only Western observers who associated some tantric rites with human sacrifice.[61] Where unconventional social behaviour was concerned, it is necessary to remember that Tantra was often *meant* to shock.[62]

Prominent Indian scholars writing in English tended to skirt around the subject of Tantra. Dinesh Chandra Sen, who wrote his history of Bengali literature in 1911, ascribed the śākta cult of female divinities to 'the primitive Asiatic races': ie the non-Aryan inhabitants of India, whose cult had gradually been absorbed into Saivism, where it was 'Sanskritized' and 'Aryanized' into a 'refined and spiritual faith'. Some forms of it (he probably meant the *pañcatattva*) were possibly imported from China.[63] The theory of the brahmanical synthesis as an 'Aryanizing' of 'lower' races in India that is put forward here is essentially a Hindu version of the orientalist 'myth' of the Aryan race, already mentioned.[64] The theory of the Chinese origin of the erotic rites was taken up by Woodroffe and Ghose.[65] D.C. Sen also ascribed the *pañcatattva* to a degenerate form of Buddhism, and this was how he explained the rite to the Marquis of Zetland.[66] This was not a new idea: *Prabodha Candrodaya*, a 10th century Sanskrit play, ridicules the sexual immorality of buddhist and jain monks and promotes devotion to Viṣṇu as its antidote.[67] The notion that Tantrism's sexuality had drained the Indian nation of its vitality, or that it was a kind of disease was shared by some Indians as well as Europeans.[68]

R.G. Bhandarkar whose influential *Vaisnavism, Saivism and the Minor Religious Systems* was published in 1913, did not either defend or condemn Tantrism. But his section on 'the Śāktas' was extremely slim, compared to the space devoted to other sects. It consisted of a discreet description of a sexual rite and its symbolism based on the erotic mysticism of the poem *saundaryalahari* ('Wave of Beauty') but he did not make any analysis or commentary.[69] Similarly discreet was Rajendralal Mitra, a prominent Indian historian and member of the Asiatic Society of Bengal. In his book about daily life in ancient India, he makes several references to the Tantras in the context of śaiva and śākta practices, and he clearly dislikes them. However, he concedes that the Tantras 'constitute the life and soul of the modern system of Hinduism', at least in Bengal.[70] Skirting euphemistically around the five *makāras* (he calls *maithuna* 'female society') he associates the Tantras with wine drinking pointing out that this is ordained in the daily prayers of a *kaula* Tantric, although not necessarily associated with drunkenness.[71] In his second volume he mentions human sacrifice, which Mitra believed (unlike many European idealizers) could be be discerned in the Vedas themselves. He also believed it to have been widespread in subsequent periods in India and even in recent times, and that is was associated with Durga and Kālī worship, and with *vāmācāra*.[72]

Indian scholars in English, then, seemed to share much of the foreign orientalist view of Tantra, but usually made less of it. They did not place emphasis on its exotic status. It was possible, also, to turn it around, and attach its opprobrium to the West. Rabindranath Tagore criticised European 'Śāktism' in the form of materialism and warfare ('the worship of force') in an article to which Woodroffe penned a reply in 1919.[73]

It would be superfluous to add further examples of the prevailing attitude to the Tantras prior to Arthur Avalon. He himself gives ample evidence for it throughout his writings. Among his contemporaries he quoted obscure writers like the missionary Harold Begbie [SS:74] and the privately circulated monograph by Edward Sellon (see below p. 180) as well as major scholars like Winternitz (see below p. 141) and L.D. Barnett. Edward Said's critique of orientalism is hardly more apt than when applied to attitudes to Tantra and Arthur Avalon would have agreed with him in this context. His condemnations attain a fine irony, as when commenting on Wilson's definition of a *bīja mantra*, he writes: 'We learn nothing from his definition "monosyllabic ejaculations of imagined mysterious import" beyond this – that he had nothing else to say.' [PT/1, p. 4]. His accusations raged against 'smart and cocksure judgments' [SS:174] covering up for racial prejudice and ignorance and lack of the quality he emphasized was the most important for studying the religion of another: empathy.

Apart from Csomo de Koros, few Western commentators before Arthur Avalon noticed anything 'mystical' in Tantra, except when this word itself was used derogatorily. An exception was Louis de la Vallée Poussin and even he used the prevailing language as well.[74] But he was commended by Arthur Avalon for making the observation that tantric concepts were of a 'metaphysical and subtle character'.[75] It was necessary to view rituals like the *maithuna* in their context, he claimed, otherwise one could be led to exaggerate their immorality. This was cited by Woodroffe when defending the *pañcatattva* [SS:619]. De La Vallée Poussin in 1896 published a short study of two buddhist *vajrayāna* texts, but took little further interest after that.[76]

To sum up: what European orientalists saw when they expressed revulsion against 'Tantra', which they also identified as 'extreme Śāktism,' were mainly three things: an intense ritualism which they perceived as magic mostly directed to worldly or utilitarian aims; that certain rituals promoted sexual licence and drunkenness; and that the worship of female divinities was associated with animal and even with human sacrifice. The combination of magic, lust and bloodthirstiness promoted a potent image. Ernest Payne, despite conceding many things to Arthur Avalon in his own book, still argued in his last chapter, entitled 'The Impermanence of Śāktism', that it was a degenerate form of religion which arose mainly in times of political and social instability. A believer in empire, Payne thought the stability provided by British rule would lead to the disappearance of Śāktism.[77]

Attitudes to History: the 'Aryans'

At the heart of romantic orientalism's view of India lay admiration for the Vedas and the philosophy of the *upaniṣads*, and also of the buddhist Pali canon. A divide was usually placed, however, between these earlier texts and what was seen as 'degenerate', popular religion. This was related to the perceived division between 'Aryan' and 'non-Aryan' elements in Indian religion and culture. A classical or 'high' tradition believed to derive from the Vedas and a 'golden age' of Indo-Aryan civilization was contrasted with cults of a subsequent period – roughly defined as 'medieval' – which were seen as 'popular or tribal, orgiastic and corrupt'.[78] Not all European orientalists idealized the Vedas or the Aryans (Wilson for example did not), but a powerful example of the duality in perception is given by L.D. Barnett, whom we have already encountered. Barnett opened his *Antiquities of India*, in which he made such strong condemnations of the Tantras, with a passage which epitomises orientalist idealization of ancient India.[79] He went on to present his own form of the standard picture of Aryan society with its three divisions:

> Its head was a foreign race of fairer skin and Indo-Germanic speech, warriors and priests proud and jealous of their blood and traditions; its feet was a mixed populace, of which the more civilized elements had learned something of the arts of peace from the Dravidians . . . while the lower strata were wallowing in savagery.[80]

Tantra in this view was a survival of, or a reversion to, that primitive savagery, and was associated with the original inhabitants of India prior to the Indo-Aryan invasions.

As has been pointed out by, among others, N.N. Bhattacharyya, ritualism and magic in the Vedas and the Tantras (although mostly independent of each other) in fact have many similarities.[81] But wherever the 'Aryan myth' held sway, they were perceived very differently.[82] Although Barnett acknowledged those vedic rituals which involved taking an intoxicating drink (*soma*), the sacrifice of animals, and the royal horse-sacrifice (where the chief queen had to mimic copulation with the dead horse), he could portray all these without undue expressions of horror. They did not interfere with his highly idealized vision of vedic society. While admitting a 'darker side' to vedic religion he asserted that: 'it was nevertheless in its official aspect a fairly bright and respectable system'.[83] Of the Tantras, however, whose rituals he does not describe at all, he writes, in the words quoted at the beginning of my Introduction to the effect that: 'Even the highly coloured Yogic imagination pales beside the doctrines of some of the innumerable sects which have pullulated on the fertile soil of India,' most infamous of which were the Tantras.[84] (Yoga was also regarded as 'non-Aryan' in origin, and hence could come in for criticism.) Whether idealizing the Aryans or not, most scholars, Indian and European, considered that the Tantras were symptomatic of the supposed degeneration of Hinduism.

Yet it is interesting to see how differently L.D. Barnett and D.C. Sen saw the 'great synthesis' between Aryan and non-Aryan which they both believed constituted the history of later Hinduism. Barnett saw this as a case of degeneration: the civilized 'Aryan' culture was infiltrated and swamped by 'non-Aryan' elements. For Sen it was the opposite: the 'primitive' cults were 'refined' (even if not completely) by being sanskritized and incorporated into the 'Aryan' mainstream.

While the vedic pantheon was predominantly male, Śāktism, the worship of female divinity, is associated with the numerous autochthonous local goddesses of India. In the 1920s with the discovery of the Indus Valley civilization, some links between India and the ancient Near East were established. Even before that, comparisons were made between India's Great Goddess traditions and those of the ancient civilizations of Greece and the Mediterranean.[85] For most nineteenth century Europeans the latter belonged to the 'paganism' that was supplanted by the higher religions of Judaism and Christianity with their monotheism and male divinity. Woodroffe however made creative use of such comparisons, as we shall see in the next chapter.

The tantric texts themselves claimed, for the most part, to derive from the Vedas, in order to enhance their authority. But in addition, the prevailing 'Aryan myth' meant that Indian followers of the Tantras would not like to be associated with a 'non-Aryan' religion. In frequent attempts to defend the three most controversial of the five elements of the *pañcatattva* rite – meat, wine and sex – Woodroffe and his collaborators pointed to precedents in the vedic rituals.[86] Although this may well have been unpalatable to some readers, it shows how the authority of the Vedas and the notion of the high civilization associated with them were strong enough to overcome questions of morality or immorality.

II THE WORKS OF ARTHUR AVALON

The majority of the Avalon/Woodroffe books were published rapidly during the last decade of Woodroffe's career in Calcutta, from 1913–23. 1913 alone saw the appearance of four publications: a translation of the *mahānirvāṇa tantra*; the anthology called *Hymns to the Goddess* produced in collaboration with Ellen Avalon; and the first two volumes of the series of editions called *Tantrik Texts*.

Arthur Avalon presented himself to the world as a European orientalist who unlike most of his colleagues had attempted to approach the Tantras with an open mind. He made the point that no other foreign scholar had at that time studied these scriptures in depth, whereas he had not only done this but his knowledge of them seemed prodigious. Yet no-one had heard of him when at the beginning of 1913 he published *The Tantra of the Great Liberation* [GLb], his translation of the *mahānirvāṇa tantra* [MNT]. This was a probably modern and very restrained anonymous original Tantra, but for that reason was extremely important in Bengal at the time, where it was popular with the English educated middle class (the *bhadralok* or 'gentle-folk') who were Arthur Avalon's first and most important readership. The translation was also welcomed by many European scholars, especially for its Introduction which outlined the conceptual framework of Tantra, and elucidated many technical terms. This introduction was not reprinted with the second edition of the translation: perhaps because sections of it were cannibalised in later works.[87] In 1952 Ganesh and Co. resurrected it and issued it as a separate book: *An Introduction to Tantra Śāstra* [ITS].

Tantrik Texts

The *mahānirvāṇa* remained the only complete original Tantra whose translation Arthur Avalon published. But he produced editions of several other Tantras and tantric digests in the mostly Sanskrit series called *Tantrik Texts*, of which he was the general editor. By 1922 eleven volumes of these had appeared, edited individually by eight named Indian scholars, most of whom were traditional pandits with titles to Sanskrit learning. The texts were accompanied by introductions, and sometimes by detailed summaries of their contents which provided an entry for readers without a proficient knowledge of Sanskrit. Nearly all of these were written under the name of the general editor, Arthur Avalon. Avalon's name was also given to two translations of short texts in the series: *karpūrādi-stotram* (a hymn to Kālī) and *kāma-kalā-vilāsa* (a short but very important text of fifty-five stanzas on the unfolding of the cosmos.) Out of eight later volumes published between 1926 and 1937, seven (representing five texts) were edited under Arthur Avalon's name alone. Finally, two volumes were brought out posthumously by collaborators – the last of them in 1940 – making twenty-one volumes in all. Two translations published by Avalon but not included in the *Tantrik Texts* series appeared in 1917: the mystical-erotic hymn to the Goddess 'Wave of Bliss' (*ānandalaharī*), traditionally ascribed to Śankarācārya, and 'Hymn to Śiva' (*mahimnastava*).[88]

Of the first two volumes of *Tantrik Texts* which came out in early 1913, volume 1 (*tantrābhidhāna*) was a reference book, a collection of seven dictionaries. Six of them gave access to the esoteric meaning of the letters of the Sanskrit alphabet – the *bījas* or monosyllabic components of tantric mantras – which were written in the texts in code to conceal them from the uninitiated. The seventh was a reference book for *mudrās*, the ritual hand gestures.[89] A revised edition of this first volume was published posthumously in 1937, edited by Pañcanan Bhattacharyya.

The second volume was *ṣaṭ-cakra-nirūpaṇa*, the text dealing with *kuṇḍalinī* yoga which was later translated in Avalon's *The Serpent Power* [SP]. It was part of a much larger work by the sixteenth century Bengali Brahmin Purnānanda [SP:xi–xii]. Several nineteenth century editions of *ṣaṭ-cakra* had been printed, some in 'cheap publications on yoga', with Bengali translations, indicating that the text was already popular.[90]

Volume 3 was *prapañcasāra tantra* [PST] first published in 1914, to which there was a revised edition in two volumes much later in 1935 and 1937 [TT/19 and 20]. *Prapañca* means the 'extended universe' – extended that is, from *bindu*, the dimensionless point (see below chapter 7); *sāra* means 'essence'.[91] The *prapañcasāra* is encyclopedic in character: it begins with the evolution of the cosmos by sound and speech through the concepts of *nāda*[92] and *bindu* and prescribes *mantras* and *dhyānas* for a large number of divinities. It, too, deals with the concept of *kuṇḍalinī* and the *cakras*. It describes cosmogony in terms of embryology through microcosm–macrocosm correspondences: the growth of the embryo in the womb recapitulates the evolution of the cosmos. This text was the only anonymous tantric digest, but being the oldest and most authoritative was attributed by traditional Indian authorities to Śankarācārya, though this was not accepted by Western orientalists.[93] It was the first of the series to be accompanied by a long introduction which took the form of a chapter-by-chapter summary in English. This for the second time after the *mahānirvāṇa* translation made the contents of a Tantra immediately accessible to an international readership.

The majority of the other editions in the series were also of Hindu śākta-tantric texts in Sanskrit belonging to the *kaula*[94] schools. Volume 5 was an important original tantra: *kulārṇava* ('The Ocean of Kula'), which, like *mahānirvāṇa*, was popular among Woodroffe's contemporaries in the Bengali professional class. Its date is uncertain but is estimated to be between 1000–1400 AD. The *kula* path (which is entered by initiation from a guru) is extolled above that of the 'Vedas', or the exoteric rites. The divinizing of the body through mantras, in the rite of *nyāsa* is prescribed in great detail, and the deities worshipped therewith. It gives instructions for the ritual *cakra* and the offering of the five *ma-kāras* or the *pañcatattva* by the *sādhakas* and their partners in the rite. This is accompanied by moral injunctions against lust and other vices, but a striking feature is a chapter on *ullāsa*, states of joy or ecstasy, which appears to prescribe a drunken orgy.[95] M.P. Pandit published his own translations of selected extracts of the *kulārṇava*, accompanied by the introduction to Avalon's edition. This book, published in 1973 by Ganesh & Co., was attributed jointly to M.P. Pandit and Woodroffe (see bibliography).

Tantrarāja tantra in two volumes was devoted to the *śrī vidyā* school of Kaulism and its worship focused on the *śrī yantra*, which is the great *maṇḍala* of the Goddess Tripurasundarī or Lalitā with her many subsidiary *śaktis* [TT/8 and 12]. This text was provided with a lengthy summary in English, later published separately by Ganesh & Co. under the name of Woodroffe in 1954. *Śāradātilaka*, also edited in two volumes with a summary in English [TT/16, 17], was a 'mantra digest' by Laksmanadeśika, a śaiva religious leader of the Kashmir school. Commonly ascribed to the eleventh century, it was best known for its fifteenth century commentary by Raghavabhatta. It is 'a liberal adaptation' of the *prapañcasāra*.[96] Its first chapter (on which Woodroffe drew heavily in his essays) describes cosmic evolution by speech in succinct stanzas.

Volume 7 of the series consisted of an edition and partial translation of a Tibetan text by Lama Kazi Dawasamdup: the *Demchog Tantra* in Tibetan.[97] The translated part consisted of a *dhyāna* (visualization) on the *maṇḍala* of *Demchog* or *mahāsukha* ('Highest Bliss'), who is the same as Vajradhāra the sixth and highest of the *dhyāni* buddhas, with his consort Vajra–yoginī or Vajra–varāhī.[98] Opening his Foreword to this volume Arthur Avalon stated that he intended to include in his series buddhist and jain tantras as well as vaisnavite, saivite and *śākta* texts, and translations from Tibetan and Chinese as well as Sanskrit. This was in order to point to the basic similarities of Tantra across different doctrinal affiliations.[99] But in the event the series was less ambitious.[100]

Some editions of Tantras had been published previously in either Bengali or *devanāgarī* script [TT/20:i], but Arthur Avalon's series rank among first attempts to collect and edit tantric manuscripts in a systematic way. Roughly concurrent with it was the *Kashmir Series of Texts and Studies* published from 1911 under the auspices of the maharaja of that state and edited by Kashmiri pandits, which aimed to publish all the major texts of Kashmir Saivism. These books, however, did not contain the sort of comprehensive summaries and commentaries in English that Avalon's work provided.[101] Moreover, Arthur Avalon's *Tantrik Texts* were the first to be brought to the serious attention of Western scholars, and this to a large extent was because their general editor was believed to be a European orientalist.

Tantratattva

1914 saw the publication of *Principles of Tantra* [PT] – Arthur Avalon's translation from the Bengali of Sivacandra Vidyarnava's *tantratattva*. The translation in two volumes was by Jñanendralal Majumdar [PT/1 p. 32] but Arthur Avalon wrote prefaces to both volumes and the introduction to the first one. In these as we have seen, he began his ideological defence of Tantra by addressing himself to its image in the works of previous European orientalists, and deplored their influence upon the Indian English educated public. He introduced the author, Sivacandra, as 'a well-known Tantric Pandit ... who, happily for our purposes, knows no English', whose 'modern orthodox views', were therefore, Avalon believed, independent of influence from Western education [PT/1 p. 31]. Arthur Avalon opened his defence of Tantra with a strong statement on its position within Hinduism: in the mainstream rather than on an esoteric fringe:

> Medieval "Hinduism" ... was, as its successor, modern Indian orthodoxy is, largely Tantrik. The Tantra was then, as it is now, the great Mantra and Sādhana Śāstra and the main, where not the sole, source of some of the most fundamental concepts still prevalent as regards worship, images, initiation, yoga, the supremacy of Guru, and so forth. This, however, does not mean that all the injunctions which are to be found in the Śāstra are of universal acceptance ... [PT/1 p. 1]

Both the author Sivacandra and the subject he was writing about were thus clearly labelled 'orthodox', while a sympathetic understanding of Tantra was declared to be essential for approaching Hinduism in general. This was a radical departure from previous orientalist perceptions of the position of Tantra.

Sivacandra's *tantratattva* had been published in Bengali twenty years previously, and as we have noted already was written to defend traditional Śākta Tantra against the modernizing sect, the Brāhmo Samāj, and other Indian opponents. Its style, as Avalon admitted, is often polemical [PT/1:13, 30–31], but the poetical and literary gifts of its author also come through strongly in the translation, which was an important and unique book for a Western readership.

One of the first European writers to make use of Avalon's material was Heinrich Zimmer. The German Sanskritist and writer on art and mythology described the impact the *Tantrik Texts* editions made on him when they first became generally available in European libraries around 1918. He acknowledged his debt to Arthur Avalon, whose example as a new kind of Indologist had inspired Zimmer to study Sanskrit.[102] *Principles of Tantra*, and several of the *Tantrik Texts* were substantially drawn on in Zimmer's first book, *Kunstform und Yoga im Indischen Kunstbild*[103] in which he formulated his theories of Hindu art and iconography. It contained the first European study of the *maṇḍala*, which soon took an important place in Jung's psychology, and Zimmer's book has subsequently been described as 'the work that introduced Tantric Studies to Jung and to much of educated Europe'.[104] The third chapter, on the linear sacred image (the *yantra* and *maṇḍala*), is based on Zimmer's reading of several of the *Tantrik Texts*. Its second chapter, on the figurative image, follows *Principles of Tantra* very closely, which led Zimmer to argue that form in Hindu art related to concepts beyond the visual sphere and should not be judged by Western aesthetic values. Although Sivacandra did not write about art theory as such, he wrote persuasively about the place of imagery, ritual and symbolism, and the use of the specific tantric ritual elements. Zimmer's book marked a new kind of understanding of Hindu religious philosophy and practice on the part of a European who had never been to India, and he owed this to Sivacandra and to Arthur Avalon.[105]

English Writings

Arthur Avalon's influence spread outside academic circles with the advent in 1918 of two books which were destined to have a long life. *Śhakti and Śhākta* [SS] was the first book to be published under the name of Sir John Woodroffe in its first edition in April 1918. It was compiled from talks and magazine articles, many of them addressed to followers of Swami Vivekananda [SS(1) p. i]. 'Tantra' is presented as *śaktivāda*, the doctrine of Śakti, a subtle monistic (*advaita*) philosophy allied to a psychologically profound ritual system with a spiritual or mystical goal, and supported by contemporary Western philosophical and scientific ideas. Replies to Western orientalist criticisms are prominent, but the preface to the second edition makes clear the readership at whom the book was primarily aimed: 'the English educated Indian . . . who has hitherto neglected his Scriptures' [SS (2):vii]. If this appeared arrogant from a foreigner to some of the Indian public, it was welcomed by most others at a period when, as we have seen, nationalist feeling and pride in Hindu identity were strong. *Shakti and Shākta* also had a wide appeal in the West, where it inspired an interest in

Tantra in several generations of readers, in both the academic and popular sphere. This was despite its style which in places is obscure and repetitive,[106] and – being written primarily for an Indian readership – it assumes much knowledge on the part of the foreign reader. But it is illumined in places by pieces of fine writing, and Woodroffe's attraction to metaphysics gave it an appeal to those drawn to Vedanta. His comparisons with fashionable occultist and contemporary scientific ideas helped to place 'Tantra' amidst the holistic world-view of the 'New Age' movement.

In September of 1918 *The Serpent Power* [SP] was published – the book above all others which introduced *kuṇḍalinī yoga* to the Western world.[107] The 'Serpent' of the title is of course *kuṇḍalinī*, the form of the all-pervading *śakti* or divine energy that lies dormant in the human body till awakened by yogic practice. The book contained the text and translation of *ṣaṭ-cakra-nirūpaṇa* ('Description of the Six Centres'). It deals with the 'anatomy' of the subtle body, with its 'centres' or 'circles' (*cakra*) of energy and the means of arousing the *kuṇḍalinī* power. The second and third editions (1922 and 1928) included some coloured prints illustrating the method of visualizing the *cakras*, but these were dropped from some of the subsequent editions. Like *The Great Liberation*, *The Serpent Power* has a long introductory section that is almost a book in its own right. It presents a view of anatomy which today we would regard as 'mystical' or magical because we view the body through the lens of Western biological science, where 'spiritual' and material aspects of mind and body are separate. It could be argued that *The Serpent Power* has itself almost become a tantric 'text' in its own right, and this too despite the fact that in many places it is very badly written. It has probably helped to standardize the number and positions of the *cakras* in modern works on yoga, for it was for long the major work on the subject in English. It has been quoted in nearly all subsequent secondary sources for decades, even by Indian yoga teachers and gurus themselves writing in English, who used it instead of going to the original texts.[108] Along with *Shakti and Shākta*, and *Hymns to the Goddess* it has been translated into other European languages.[109] The powerful symbol of *kuṇḍalinī* entered Western psychology when at some date C.G. Jung read *The Serpent Power.*[110] Jung assimilated it to his own system in a series of seminars in the 1930s.[111] Since then it has gained an ever wider currency and the 'awakening of *kuṇḍalinī*' is now used to explain many kinds of psychological and spiritual experiences.

The Serpent Power was attributed to Arthur Avalon. Three more books came out under the name of Sir John Woodroffe. *Garland of Letters* [GOL] appeared in 1922 during his last year in India; but its central core was a series of articles originally published in 1917–18 under the pseudonym and called *Studies in the Mantra Shāstra*. It is about the "science" of *mantra* especially in its cosmogonic aspect. The 'letters' of the title are the primordial phonemes or sound-seeds out of which the universe evolves, and their garland is the necklace of skulls that is such a prominent feature of the iconography of Kālī [GOL p. xiii–xiv]. This metaphysical transformation of her symbolism was what primarily interested Woodroffe. The first chapters outline vedic and tantric doctrines of *vāc* or Speech; for these Woodroffe acknowledged the help of his friend P.N. Mukhopadhyay [GOL p. xi], the philosophy professor who was later to become guru Swami Pratyagatmanand Saraswati. After Atal Behari Ghose, he was Woodroffe's second major collaborator.

Mukhopadhyay's collaboration was acknowledged in two other titles: *The World as Power* (1921–3) [WAP] and *Mahāmāya* (1929). The former was published as a series of essays on different aspects of what Woodroffe called 'Śākta Vedānta'. The 'Power' of the title is of course *śakti*, who manifests as the phenomenal world, and hence as Life, Mind, Matter, Causality and Consciousness. The sections devoted to each of these topics provide a glimpse of the philosophical questions that exercised intellectual Indians and Europeans in the light of scientific ideas at the beginning of the twentieth century in physics, chemistry, biology and psychology. Woodroffe's gift for metaphysical discourse comes into its own in this book. Space does not permit dealing fully with it but some topics are covered in chapters 14–16 of *Shakti and Shākta*, and discussed in chapter 10 below.

As we shall see in the next chapter, the Avalon/Woodroffe books made an immediate impact, and in a short time 'Tantra' was elevated from its status as a 'primitive', or 'degenerate' or 'extremist' cult, into a subtle philosophy that could stand alongside the foremost modern European thought. Besides Zimmer, Masson Oursel, the French philosopher of religion, and Julius Evola, the Italian esotericist, were both deeply influenced by Woodroffe. Drawn to 'eastern' spirituality in the 1920s, Evola discovered Tantrism through *Shakti and Shākta* and *The Serpent Power*, on which he drew extensively in his 'Man as Power' first published in Italian in 1925. We shall see in the next chapter that Masson Oursel was attracted to the 'immanentist' bias in the philsophy of *śakti*. Evola was attracted to the notions of 'will' and 'action' associated with the tantric path over the more passive and speculative path of Vedanta; and to Tantra's claim to provide practical means to spiritual experience.[112] All of these are prominent themes of Woodroffe.

Ernest Payne, who acknowledged how extensively Woodroffe had affected tantric studies, can himself be seen struggling between two opposing pictures of Śaktism in his own book. Basically he had inherited the older attitudes, but could no longer express them uncritically after the Avalon/Woodroffe books had become influential. He constantly engages with him, especially attacking his allegorising of and interiorizing of the more shocking images and rites.[113] In a passage on mantras, Payne cited J.N. Farquhar's contemptuous dismissal ('Many of them are mere nonsense syllables, sparks from the blazing furnace of aboriginal superstitions . . .') alongside Woodroffe's philosophical gloss: ('The whole idea of mantra in the Sākta system goes back to the conception of sound as an essential part of the Supreme . . .'). Payne himself turned to psychology, but his position remained closer to Farquhar's than to Woodroffe's.[114] He acknowledged, however, Arthur Avalon's influence on the German Sanskritist Helmuth von Glasenapp,[115] on Sten Konow,[116] and on Zimmer.

Mahatma Gandhi also read Woodroffe. When he caused consternation to his disciples and to the public by his experiments with what he called *brahmacārya* – which consisted of sleeping, chastely, alongside a young woman – Gandhi justified his practice by appealing to some Western writers, and then added:

> Even amongst us there is the Tantra school which has influenced Western savants like Justice Sir John Woodroffe. I read his books in Yeravda prison.'[117]

Despite the fact that there is nothing in Avalon/Woodroffe which could be taken to refer to Gandhi's practice, the fact that Woodroffe had made Tantra respectable is very obvious here. Another point of interest in Gandhi's statement is Woodroffe's status as a 'savant'. His association with great learning was a significant aspect of his image as Arthur Avalon, as we shall see in the next chapter where we continue to examine the impact of this new orientalist upon Indian and Western readers.

Chapter Eight

ARTHUR AVALON AMONG THE ORIENTALISTS

A public face and an open secret

After the translation of *mahānirvāṇa tantra* and the early editions of the *Tantrik Texts* were published, European orientalists readily accepted Arthur Avalon as a new member of their community. *The Tantra of the Great Liberation* made a strong impact. No previous translation of a Tantra had been published in Europe.[1] Extracts from numerous press reviews printed in the later books reveal the admiration evoked in India and abroad by the scholarship Arthur Avalon displayed, and his venture into an area of research previously almost untouched by Europeans.[2] Sylvain Lévy,[3] professor of Sanskrit at the Collège de France, commended Arthur Avalon for attempting to change the prevailing attitudes:

> Mr Avalon is, so far as I am aware, a new comer in Oriental studies, but he makes his entrance therein with 'eclat'. His book brilliantly inaugurates the study of the Tantras, the literature of which occupies a front rank in the religious life of Modern India . . . Nevertheless, the learned in Europe have hitherto put them aside, and have neither published any Tantrik text nor translation of them. Western opinion has crushed them all under the weight of a common ill-fame . . . Mr Avalon has therefore set himself to work for the rehabilitation of this calumniated literature, and announces for early publication a series of works on the Tantra and its texts. As a commencement, he has selected the Mahanirvana Tantra . . .[4]

But the text as translated by Avalon was not a typical Tantra in many respects. Today it is believed by most scholars to be a late eighteenth century or early nineteenth century work: a view that was also held by some of Woodroffe's contemporaries, although Arthur Avalon pronounced it to be genuinely ancient.[5] It was an important text at the time because it taught a 'reformed' or purified form of Tantra which appealed to members of the Brahmo Samaj and had been a favourite text of Ram Mohun Roy himself [GLb:vii]. The *mahānirvāṇa* tones down the two most objectionable aspects of Tantra from their point of view: the *pañcatattva* rite involving wine drinking and sex to which it gives an idealized interpretation [see Glb: 205]; and ritual worship to a variety of divinities ('polytheism'). After the opening chapter, which begins with the usual setting of a Tantra – that of Śiva and Parvatī discoursing on Mount Kailasa – the *mahānirvāṇa* presents a typically tantric form of ritual with *mantra* and *dhyāna* which is focused on the supreme Brahman. This is something unknown in any other Tantra.[6] The text's moral tone is strict, even "puritanical": it condemns drunkenness within and outside the ritual[7] and it prescribes substitutes for the five literal *tattvas* which it declares should not be used in the *kāli yuga*.[8] Entirely missing from the text translated by Arthur Avalon is a section on magic, especially the *ṣaṭ-karma*, or six magic acts, which were usually an essential ingredient of a Tantra.[9] Its special appeal for the *bhadralok* of nineteenth century Bengal among whom the Brahmo Samaj was influential, lay partly in the fact that they believed it placed Brahman knowledge above ritual. Avalon asserted that it was traditional while reforming only what he called 'abuses'.

Nevertheless the translation still needed to be read against a considerable background of technical knowledge, and Sylvain Lévy expressed his admiration at the new orientalist's textual competence and understanding, remarking:

> In his work he has not made even the least demand on European learning. He has, on the contrary, been able to dispense with it without prejudice to his research. On the other hand, he shows himself to be familiar with a considerable number of Tantrik works. He cites them with profusion in the original Sanskrit, and derives from them the explanation of technical terms of which the dictionaries do not give us the meaning.

He went on to state that it was the Introduction to the translation which was particularly valuable:

> His translation is preceded by an Introduction of 150 pages, which is the most solid and exact account that has as yet been written on the doctrines of the Tantras, their ontology, mystical phraseology, worship, yoga, and ethics. All items of information given in this exposition are supported by the authorities he cites . . .[10]

In fact both the footnotes to the translation and the Introduction were more than those words imply. What Arthur Avalon had produced amounted almost to a new commentary on the text, a modern commentary not aimed at the initiate in a secret cult nor the pandit steeped in Sanskrit learning, but at the modern general public. Two Sanskrit commentaries used in the translation were recognised as insufficient for the general reader. Therefore, Arthur Avalon declared:

> I have accordingly . . . written my own commentary, and added an Introduction, explaining certain matters and terms referred to or presupposed by the text which, as they require a somewhat more extended treatment, could not be conveniently dealt with in the footnotes. [GLb (1) p. xiv–xv]

Continuing in the same vein of modest understatement he described his Introduction not as an 'exhaustive treatment' but only as an 'extended note'. The enthusiasm and excitement Lévy expressed were not misplaced: nothing like this had been available hitherto in English or any other European language on a tantric scripture. For the foreign scholar and 'outsider' it was a door into a whole new world.

The contemporary missionary writer on Hinduism, J.N. Farquhar, had a very different attitude. He was not going to allow Arthur Avalon to change his own view of what he called the religion of 'the Left-hand Śāktas' which remained extremely negative.

> These books [the Tantras] are probably the worst that Hinduism has produced, for they consist in the main of grossly superstitious rites, charms and diagrams, and meaningless syllables said to be instinct with supernatural power, with here and there horrible filth.[11]

Nevertheless Farquhar – who wrote and edited historical studies of Hinduism which took a more sympathetic approach than was usual hitherto among missionaries – acknowledged that the *mahānirvāṇa* was an 'honourable exception' to this category. He welcomed Arthur Avalon's translation and introduction as a valuable contribution to knowledge. Farquhar lived for some time in Calcutta. Writing his review in 1915, he engaged in some speculation about the identity of the mysterious scholar and, unless he was "in the know", seems to have had an inspired guess:

> The translator, who writes under a *nom de plume*, is clearly a European disciple of some pundit belonging to the Left-hand Shaktas; and he shows great sympathy for the sect. He is always ready to defend any of its doctrines and practices, even the most shameful . . . On the other hand, his faithful discipleship has brought him a wonderful understanding of the teaching and cult of the sect . . . and his introduction and commentary (is) of great exegetical value.[12]

His reactions indicate a turning in the tide of attitudes towards Hinduism. In his case it was directly the result of accommodation to the new self-confidence and cultural self-assertion of Hindus which was associated with the early modern nationalist movement.[13]

Better placed than either Lévy or Farquhar to judge the value of Avalon's work was Otto Schrader, director of the Theosophical Society's library at Adyar, Madras, who reviewed the first Avalon publications at the end of 1913 for *The Theosophist*. As a scholar who was himself working on the vaiṣṇava Tantras with the help of an Indian pandit collaborator,[14] Otto Schrader was able to give a more expert opinion. Avalon's Introduction to his translation did not provide as much new information for him as it had done for Sylvain Lévy, but he still commended it as 'by far the most valuable part of the book', which 'must be welcome to both the general reader and the orientalist'. Although he pointed to 'a large number of small inaccuracies' in the translation, he praised its 'elegance' and 'the profound knowledge with which it is backed'.[15] Like Lévy and Farquhar, he was wholeheartedly enthusiastic about Arthur Avalon's work, which he looked upon as a 'scientific' venture.

> The Tantras have hitherto played in Indology the part of a jungle which everybody is anxious to avoid. It is therefore a matter of congratulation that at last somebody has made up his mind scientifically to explore the jungle ... That these books are likely to become a great boon, everybody will admit who knows to what an extent medieval and modern Hinduism are penetrated by Tantrism.[16]

In the same edition of *The Theosophist*, Schrader also reviewed *Hymns to the Goddess*, which he thought valuable for 'the science of religion', and the first two volumes of *Tantrik Texts*. He praised Arthur Avalon for seeking assistance from 'gurus and pandits'. The study of Tantra or any other Śāstra, he stated 'demands absolutely the help of the authorised custodians of its traditions'.[17]

In 1921 when eight volumes of the *Tantrik Texts* had been published, Woodroffe made a gift of the series to the newly formed *Association Francaise des Amis de l'Orient* in Paris. The French orientalist association was formed by Masson Oursel, Sylvain Lévy and others in 1921 at the time of Rabindranath Tagore's second visit to Europe where his astonishing reception bordered on worship and the atmosphere was one of powerful 'romantic orientalism'.[18] Acknowledging Woodroffe's gift in its bulletin the Association's first President, Masson-Oursel, declared that it was an astonishing event to see a whole class of literature being opened up by one single scholar:

> A chapter of Burnouf, some remarks of A Barth, various researches of Louis de la Vallee Poussin, constituted before 1913 all that was written on the Tantras, whose encyclopedic character, ritualistic nature and bizarre mysticism repelled the analysts. And then there appeared one after another the rudiments of a tantric library for which we thank the scholarship and courage of an Englishman concealed under the pseudonym of Arthur Avalon; texts, translations and historical studies in the form of prefaces ... a repertoire of tantric vocabulary.[19]

He congratulated Avalon on 'the work of a pioneer and explorer' which had dispelled a vast number of prejudices. The Tantras only appeared obscene, he wrote, when one did not understand their 'mystical grammar'. Masson-Oursel was a professor at the Collège de France, and one of the first phenomenologists of religion, pursuing a comparative approach.[20] In October of 1921 Woodroffe was invited to lecture in Paris at the end of his holiday in Europe. Sylvain Lévy was present and Masson-Oursel was in the chair and again praised 'Arthur Avalon' in extravagant terms: despite being a pseudonym, this name would attract *la gloire du savant*, he enthused. Avalon had taken a comparative approach and revealed the close connections between the Tantras and other modern religions. The tantric cult was not mere superstition, but a belief 'that Man can realize the divine in him and outside him.' Masson-Oursel knew who Arthur Avalon 'really' was of course, for all this was by way of introducing the speaker.[21] His fulsome praise was translated in *Shakti and Shākta*.[22] Masson Oursel's own writings continued to accord with Woodroffe's presentation of Tantra. His insights were cited approvingly in the third edition of *Shakti and Shākta*: that Tantra is 'a triumph of the conception of immanence' and Man's conquest of himself [SS:347]; that it teaches that the body is not an obstacle to Liberation, and that there is no opposition between Nature and Spirit [SS:478]. These, as we shall see, could be said to sum up Woodroffe's presentation of the significance of Tantrism.

Another eminent orientalist of the time – whom Tagore made a point of visiting on his European tour – was Maurice Winternitz in Czechoslovakia.[23] His *History of Sanskrit Literature* had been published in German from 1907. He reviewed *The Great Liberation* and other early works by Arthur Avalon at the beginning of 1916.[24] As part of his engagement with European orientalism, Woodroffe included a translation of Winternitz's review in the third edition of *Shakti and Shākta*, preceded by his own comments.[25] Like other orientalists Winternitz regarded 'the Tantras' as the sacred books of a single sect called 'the Śāktas', and he had a low opinion of them which was only slightly modified as a result of studying the translation of *mahānirvāṇa tantra*:

> If we have been accustomed, up till the present, to see nothing else in Śāktism ... than wild superstition, occult humbug, idiocy, empty magic and a cult with a most objectionable morality, and distorted by orgies – then a glimpse at the text made accessible to us by Avalon, teaches us that ... behind the nonsense there lies hidden after all much deep sense and that immorality is not the end and aim of the cult of the Mother.[26]

Winternitz appreciated many aspects, including the philosophical concept of *śakti* as 'Eternal Energy out of which everything has been created', and finding 'the highest expression for the divine principle in the conception

'Mother'.[27] In contrast to attitudes such as Payne's, he supported Avalon's protest against the idea that it was a 'debasement' (*eine Erniedrigung*) to conceive of the deity as feminine. He reluctantly conceded that *mokṣa* or Liberation was the soteriological goal of tantric practice, but still insisted on seeing magic as the 'chief aim, though not the final aim of Devi worship'. This for him clearly was the crux of the matter. Dealing with mantras, *bījas*, *yantras* and other features of tantric *sādhanā*, he saw these as nothing but magic. He translated *sādhaka* as 'magician' (*Zauberer*), one who used these means to 'force the Deity into his service'.[28] This led him to conclude by hoping that Europe and America would be spared the addition of the Śakti cult to its list of 'India-faddists' (*Indienschwärmern*), because he equated them with occultism and 'mystery-mongering' (*Geheimtuerei*). The place of the śākta texts, in other words, must stay firmly within the arena of the History of Religion, of academic study, not of personal belief or practice.[29]

Winternitz, then, was only partly won over by Arthur Avalon. It is interesting to note the style of Woodroffe's reply to this review. As we would expect, he criticised the choice of language, especially the use of derogatory words about 'magic' and 'magicians' [SS:115]. He criticised in a distinctly superior manner: 'The article does not show a complete comprehension of its subject-matter, nor was this to be expected.' Rather like a schoolteacher he awarded good marks for signs of a better understanding: 'Nevertheless, in reading this article one feels oneself in the presence of a learned mind which wills to be fair . . . Several appreciations are just . . .' Among those that were considered 'just' are precisely those points which Arthur Avalon himself always put forward: namely, that 'the Tantra Śāstras . . . are not merely some pathological excrescence on "Hinduism" . . . their metaphysics is that which is common to all other schools . . .' [SS:115–6].

Winternitz, whatever his difficulties with the Tantras, was at the time an eminent scholar of international standing. Granted that Woodroffe's comments were made in the third edition of *Shakti and Shākta* in 1927, when Arthur Avalon was established as an expert on Tantra, one can still pause to reflect on where this confidence in his own superior knowledge comes from.

The extracts I have given from Sylvain Lévy's and other reviews provides the answer: Arthur Avalon's textual knowledge was impressive. His position of authority was based on his superior knowledge of the tantric literature, which he was the first Westerner to study in any depth. As a Western scholar he pointed out further limitations in his colleagues – their failure in empathy:

> In giving an account of Indian beliefs and practices, we, who are foreigners, must place ourselves in the skin of the Hindu, and must look at their doctrine and ritual through their eyes and not our own.

> It is difficult I know for most to do this: but until they can, their work lacks real value . . . Many do not even make the attempt. They look at the matter from the point of view of their own creed, or, (what is much worse), racial prejudice may stand in the way of the admission of any excellence or superiority in a coloured people'.[30]

He has just claimed that empathy need not preclude objectivity:

> . . . though I have furnished argument in favour of this much-abused faith and practice, I am not here concerned to establish the truth and rightness of either. My attitude is an objective one. I have endeavoured to explain my subject as simply and lucidly as the recondite matters treated of allow, from an entirely detached and unprejudiced standpoint.[31]

Leaving aside here the problems around the question of 'objectivity' in religious studies, this statement sits uneasily with much of the material in the Avalon/Woodroffe books, which often have the character of apologetics in favour of a particular view of Tantra; and sometimes one can detect a conflict between the apologist and the 'scientific' or 'outside' observer Woodroffe claimed to be. But this is how Woodroffe presented himself and the pseudonymous Arthur Avalon: he was not an Indian but a foreigner, a Westerner; he was a sympathetic outsider, an observer, not a participating believer; he was an orientalist scholar with a prodigious knowledge of textual material; he criticised the attitudes of fellow-scholars from his position as one of their number. His attitude was impartial, whereas others were biassed by prejudice.

Understandably, it was the Indian reviewers who responded most warmly to his empathy with Hinduism. For many of them, Arthur Avalon's writing on Tantra was in striking and favourable contrast to that of other orientalist writers. Not only did he take a sympathetic attitude, but he appeared to understand from within. Pañchkori Bāndyopadhyay, whom we have already encountered among Sivacandra's circle[32] was a writer in Bengali on Tantra; he commented in the magazine *Sāhitya*:

> We could never have dreamt that it was possible for a modern Christian Englishman to so fully understand such matters as the mode of Tantrik Sadhana . . . (He) has certainly learnt a great deal of the inner and secret doctrine of the Tantra . . . We have never heard even from any Bengali Pundit such a clear exposition of Mantra Shakti as the author has given in his introduction to the Mahānirvāṇa Tantra.[33]

Translated extracts from this review article were included in *Shakti and Shākta* and in *Principles of Tantra*.[34] They show that Pañchkori Bāndyopādhyāy took for granted the close relationship between the *mahānirvāṇa tantra* and the Brahmo Samaj, and in so doing accepted the text as a modern authentic Tantra, suited to the modern age of English education when the influence of older Tantras had diminished:

> It seems to us that, considering the form into which, as a result of English education and culture, the mind of the Bengali has been shaped the Mahānirvāṇa is a proper Tantra for the time. Rājā Rām Mohun Roy endeavoured to encourage regard for the Mahānirvāṇa Tantra because he understood this. [SS:25]

The fact that Arthur Avalon was both a foreigner and a distinguished person socially, would help in its promulgation: '. . . a cultured, influential, rich Englishman like Arthur Avalon, honoured of the rulers, has translated and published (it) . . .' [SS:26. Bandopadhyay, too, knew his supposed identity.] Although a foreigner Avalon had not, like some other orientalists, projected his own interpretations upon his material but had been faithful to the vision of the insiders;

> Arthur Avalon has not spoken a single word to satisfy himself nor tried to explain things according to his own imagination. He has only given what are true inferences according to the principles of Śāstric reasoning. [SS:26]

He concluded: 'Will not the Bengali receive with welcome such a full offering made by a Bhakta from a foreign land?' [SS:26]. Thus he urges its acceptance as a *text*, brought about by the will of the World-Mother [SS:19], not as a contribution to the science of religion or to orientalist study.

A more critical reception was given to the translation in Calcutta's *Modern Review*, where a reviewer thought it superfluous for Bengali readers who had many cheaper translations in their own language. He thought Arthur Avalon was less critical than foreign scholars were expected to be and had not taken an historical approach. He also criticised *Hymns to the Goddess* for uncritically accepting Śankarāchārya as the author of several of the hymns.[35] An unnamed critic who had accused Avalon of misrepresenting the Vaiṣṇavas, was answered by Woodroffe in *Shakti and Shākta* [SS(2): ix–x].

On the whole the Indian reception to Arthur Avalon's books was even more enthusiastic than that of Western reviewers. We find that over and again reference is made to the sympathy and the understanding of Hinduism by Arthur Avalon, to his faithfulness in representing the Hindu tradition. Here was a foreigner who allowed himself to be a mirror and did not impose his own interpretations and judgments, whether hostile or romantic. One reviewer contrasted him with 'poor Max Muller who . . . was compelled to study in the Vedas . . . the religion of Paley and Addison.'[36] 'He has commenced his work with a Hindu's heart, with a Hindu's regard, and a Hindu's faith, and so his translation is what it ought

Plate 1 Sir John Woodroffe shortly after his retirement from India

Plate 2 The young Jack Woodroffe at Frensham Heights

Plate 3 Sir John Woodroffe in his garden at Oxford (between 1923 and 1930)

Plate 4 Ellen Elizabeth Woodroffe

Plate 5 Woodroffe wearing the *dhoti* at the Konarak Temple

Plate 6 Woodroffe, A.B. Ghose and H.P. Moeller at the Konarak Temple

Plate 7 The *Śri Yantra*

Plate 8 Atal Bihari Ghose

to be' wrote a reviewer in the Bengali journal *Hitāvadi.*[37] In fact, he sounded rather like an Indian pandit himself, remarked coincidentally both *The Nation* of New York and the *Bankipore Express.*[38] Other press extracts however showed that Indian reviewers just like those abroad whole-heartedly accepted Arthur Avalon as a foreign scholar, an orientalist, but one with an exceptional understanding of India; and as a scholar, his equally exceptional fund of knowledge is frequently the source of admiration [SS(3):iii–xxvii].

This continued to be the image of Woodroffe as Arthur Avalon among many people in India. A more recent writer on Tantra, M.P. Pandit, commenting on Woodroffe's statement about the need for a foreign scholar to 'place oneself in the skin of a Hindu', considered that Woodroffe himself had no need to do so:

> For the one thing that strikes a close reader of his exposition is that he is truly an Indian Soul in a European body ... The spirit of the original thought in Sanskrit drips through his transparent writing with a freshness that is invigorating.[39]

ALIAS MR JUSTICE WOODROFFE

In January of 1915, exactly two years after the publication of the first books of Arthur Avalon, Justice Woodroffe of the Calcutta High Court delivered a lecture at the Dalhousie Institute in the city. It was entitled 'Creation as Explained in the Tantra'.[40] The extremely eminent audience included not only Lord Carmichael the newly appointed Governor of Bengal, but even the Roman Catholic Archbishop of Calcutta, Cardinal Meulmann, who had been a personal friend of Woodroffe's father. Other prominent citizens who listened to him included the Chief Justice Sir Lawrence Jenkins and several other High Court judges; among eminent Indians present was Sir Gurudas Banerjea, barrister and politician, the leader of the 'Old' or 'moderate' wing of Congress. Among several ICS officials present was Nicholas Beatson Bell, later to be Governor of Assam. He had studied Sanskrit while he was an ICS probationer at Oxford around the same time that Woodroffe was there,[41] and that was perhaps why he was chosen to give a vote of thanks to the speaker. Perhaps some of the other people felt out of their depth, although, politely: 'His Excellency said that he was quite pleased to learn a great deal from what Mr Justice Woodroffe had said.' The account of the gathering given in the daily *Amrita Bāzār Patrika* continued with Beatson Bell saying he now recognised that he must change his opinion of Tantra:

> Sometimes he believed that Tantra was a sort of work that one did not like to read or place it on his table in case his wife or daughter

> happened to see it. Mr Justice Woodroffe however had entirely taken away that impression. They now came to know that it was of very great interest from the deepest philosophical point of view and he regretted very much that he had never read Tantra.[42]

So the same effect was being produced in Calcutta as on the European orientalists abroad – or at the very least it was considered necessary to pretend that it was – and many Indians declared themselves flattered. The *Amrita Bāzār Patrika* remarked: 'It is gratifying to note the high compliments thus paid to the Tantras ... by a European of the finest intellect.'[43]

You could not possibly have hoped to find a more "respectable" gathering than the one at the Dalhousie Institute on Monday afternoon of 18 January 1915, nor one more closely entwined with the British administration. Did it require courage to lecture before them on such a subject as Tantra? Perhaps: but it must be noted that Woodroffe presented himself before his audience as a scholar, not as a convert or initiate. He was firmly within the tradition of orientalism in India, like Sir William Jones before him. In his own time, his former colleague on the bench of the High Court, F.E. Pargiter, was a significant scholar of the Purāṇas.[44]

The substance of the lecture was extremely technical, explaining the difference between the *māyāvāda* metaphysics of Śankarācārya and the *ābhāsavāda* thought of the tantric schools.[45] It was full of Sanskrit terms with which some in the audience would be familiar but many would not. It represents the earliest of Woodroffe's lectures and articles on Tantra, and it marks his *début* as an authority on the subject in the public arena.[46] The fact that he gave such a lecture only two years after the publication of the first books of Arthur Avalon, tends to contradict the suggestion that is sometimes made that Woodroffe took a pseudonym to avoid scandal.[47] After that, he delivered the lectures on Tantra that were collected into *Shakti and Shākta* from the platforms of several literary and religious societies, while articles under the pseudonym were published in magazines.

And so Justice Woodroffe stood forward in person, clothing the pseudonymous Arthur Avalon with his judges' robes, donating to him his social prestige and winning for him popularity with a great number of Indian people. For Woodroffe was already well known in Calcutta as an Indophile, and a connoisseur and patron of Indian art. We have seen how the combination of foreign scholar plus profound textual knowledge gave Arthur Avalon his status and authority as an orientalist. When this was augmented by Woodroffe's public identity in Calcutta, one can begin to glimpse why the writer of an article in 1916 considered that this one man alone had been able to transform public attitudes towards Tantra. The article, in *Bhārat Varṣa,* was entitled 'A New Way of Learning Letters' and it consisted of a pictorial alphabet, each letter being illustrated with the photograph of some well-known figure of the Bengali literary world whose name began with it.[48] When it reached the long 'U' vowel there was no Bengali name to fit, so the writer decided on 'Woodroffe' in Bengali characters. The article ran:

> The Tantras are obscene, the Tantras are full of Indecency . . . the Tantras are loathsome . . . Such loud words of condemnation were wont to resound without pause in the mouths of the English-educated class . . . Having received an English initiation and education they were cutting with their own hand the branch on which they were seated. At that moment Arthur Avalon (people say he is Mr Justice Woodroffe) broke their false pride and revealed the greatness of the Tantra and the English educated Babus commenced to rub their eyes.[49]

The writer was being ironical. He remarked that this after all was nothing new: the English-educated in India were only too eager to follow after foreigners even in being nationalistic, as for example the followers of Mrs Besant in the Theosophical Society. The article however pays sincere tribute to Sir John Woodroffe's championship of Indian culture, which extended beyond his works on Tantra, and the writer finished by saying that everything he touched turned to gold.

THE LEGEND OF ARTHUR AVALON

There have always been two questions concerning Woodroffe's pseudonym: why did he take one at all, and why did he choose one so enigmatic and legendary? In view of Woodroffe's public lectures on Tantra, it is scarcely surprising that the supposed identity of Arthur Avalon seemed to become fairly well known even before the publication of *Shakti and Shākta* under his own name in 1918. In addition to the writer of the article in *Bharat Varṣa*, we have seen that Pañchkori Bandopadhyay wrote as if he knew Arthur Avalon, while J.N. Farquhar seems to have heard rumours. In February 1918, just before the appearance of *Shakti and Shākta*, Woodroffe's Theosophist friend in Madras, James Cousins, made an enigmatic reference in an article for Calcutta's *Modern Review* as if he believed no-one had yet penetrated the mystery. Acknowledging that Theosophists had previously been very suspicious of Tantra, Cousins wrote enthusiastically on the influence he believed Avalon's editions and translations would have in both 'East' and 'West'. Their success:

> . . . is all the time enhanced by the challenging phenomenon of a decried and abused Eastern scripture being championed with missionary ardour (albeit in the most judicial manner) by a writer

> whose name takes him outside India in race (though the suggestion of France in one magazine might be modified in front of Burne Jones' unfinished picture of *Arthur in Avalon*).[50]

Avalon was the Celtic island of the dead which was transformed in Tennyson's poem *The Passing of Arthur* into a place of healing to which, after his last battle, the fatally wounded King Arthur was taken on a ship by three mysterious women:

> . . . I am going a long way
> With these thou seest . . .
> To the island valley of Avilion;
> Where falls not hail, or rain, or any snow,
> Nor ever wind blows loudly; but it lies
> Deep-meadowed, happy, fair with orchard-lawns
> And bowery hollows crown'd with summer sea,
> Where I will heal me of my grievous wound.[51]

This poem was the subject of a famous painting by Burne-Jones: *Arthur's Sleep in Avalon* continues the story where the poem leaves off and shows King Arthur on the island, lying in an entranced sleep attended by maidens of typical pre-Raphaelite beauty. It was the artist's last painting and was unfinished at the time of his death in 1898.[52] James Cousins seems to be dropping a hint about the writer's nationality – British – and also perhaps hinting at Woodroffe's well-known interest in art. The words 'albeit in a most judicial manner' are another hint, this time at his profession.

So 'Arthur Avalon' was named after a painting. This is quite important to know, for here we have a writer on an Indian esoteric system taking a name imbued with western esotericism. The name at any rate seems to hint at initiations and the possession of occult secrets. The Arthurian legends are bound up with the story of the Holy Grail and its quest. This was a symbol of esoteric wisdom, especially to Theosophists who appropriated the legend. Anyone who named himself after King Arthur or the mystic isle of Avalon would be thought to be identifying himself with occultism, in Theosophists' eyes. James Cousins was not the only connection. As we have seen, Woodroffe's wife Ellen was a member of the Theosophical Society, though according to the membership lists in the International Headquarters in Madras, her husband did not join it himself.[53] As we have seen, both the Woodroffes were acquainted personally with Annie Besant.

Woodroffe in his writings certainly appears familiar with and sympathetic to modern occultism, and it is quite possible that he could at some stage have been personally involved in Theosophy or some other western occult society. But it is also just as easy to believe that he had not. The Theosophical Society was enjoying the peak of its influence in India during the first two decades of the century, when Annie Besant grew to prominence as a public figure. They called their system 'the higher Occultism', but associated 'Tantrikas' with 'sorcerers'.[54] Linking Tantra as he did to fashionable modern occultism could have been one more way of dispelling negative images. Apart from that, the Avalon/Woodroffe books are in fact almost entirely free from Theosophical or any other Western occultist terminology, and several pages of *The Serpent Power* are taken up with distinguishing Theosophist ideas about the nature of the subtle body and its *cakras* from the those of the Hindu texts [SP: 6–10] in a context where it is clear that Avalon regards the Hindu ideas as the correct ones. There is simply none of the syncretism or appropriation which might be expected from a Theosophical author. The contrast with Charles Leadbeater is especially striking.[55]

It looks as if the pseudonymous author was not therefore claiming to be a western occultist and that the name may have had no significance in itself. It was perhaps selected because Woodroffe was thinking of one of his favourite paintings. The name, however, helped to promote his own legend: that of the western adept who had gained arcane knowledge through initiation in a mysterious oriental cult. This is the image the name on the books tends to evoke in the minds of modern Europeans – an image, as it turns out, not so far from the truth. It is the fascinating image of the 'secret adept'[56] which his pseudonym enhances: an impression which can only be stronger today when 'Avalon' (Glastonbury) is associated with contemporary New Age occultism. But it seems that such associations were probably unintentional. To most of his Indian readers in his lifetime, 'Arthur Avalon' was just another European orientalist, but one with an exceptional understanding of and sympathy with India, and his identity was something of an open secret in Calcutta. I have already referred to the Bengali novelist Pavitra Gangopadhyay, who described meeting Sir John Woodroffe at a party in Calcutta, when he was astonished to see a British Sahib of the High Court wearing Indian dress:

> But the next moment I remembered that this was the lover of India, Sir John Woodroffe. For two generations his family had been living in India and drank Indian culture to their fill. He loved India and embraced the Indian way of life with respect . . . Woodroffe studied and explained in an incomparable way the most esoteric of Indian sādhanās, that of the Tantric path. Under the pseudonym of Arthur Avalon he wrote books on Tantra, but in those days there was no doubt in anyone's mind as to the true author of those books . . .[57]

The 'real' Arthur Avalon?

So if his identity was such an open secret, why did Woodroffe use a pseudonym? In fact, he gave the explanation just twice: in the prefaces to the first and second editions of *Shakti and Shākta*, where referring to his previous books, he declared that he had published them under the name of Arthur Avalon . . .

> to denote that they have been written with the direct cooperation of others and in particular with the assistance of one of my friends who will not permit me to mention his name. I do not desire sole credit for what is as much their work as mine.[58]

So the person who really wanted to keep his involvement secret was not Woodroffe but someone else. Nor did the pseudonym refer to a team of collaborators – the named editors of the individual volumes of *Tantrik Texts* for example. The passage clearly indicates one person.

We have seen that three books came out under the name of Sir John Woodroffe in their first editions: these were *Shakti and Shākta*, *Garland of Letters* and *World as Power*. Another other book (*Mahāmāyā*) came out in collaboration with P.N. Mukhopadhyay. None of these books was entirely to do with Sanskrit texts (except for certain sections of *Garland* to be discussed below). All the publications attributed to Arthur Avalon were, however, either translations, editions or commentaries. So it seems that Woodroffe was acknowledging that someone else did the work that involved Sanskrit, which represented the greatest part of it in terms of quantity at least, though later on it was the essays in English which made Tantra more widely popular. Nevertheless with time the sole credit Woodroffe wanted to renounce was eventually given to him, and this unknown and apparently very self-effacing friend has been forgotten.

One reason why this easily came about was because of a certain established relationship between European orientalists and their pandit collaborators, whereby the latter received very little recognition. An example of the prevailing attitude can be seen in a review by the Theosophist–orientalist, Johan Van Manen, on volume 7 of *Tantrik Texts*, Lama Kazi Dawasamdup's translation from Tibetan. While Arthur Avalon attracts warm praise, Van Manen scarcely acknowledges the Lama:

> We owe indeed a debt of gratitude to Arthur Avalon, whose enthusiasm for and insight into the Indian religious and philosophical mind have unearthed this particular gem for us . . . As far as this first Tibetan text is concerned . . . he has been . . . fortunate in having been able to secure a competent collaborator to undertake the philological portion of the work, the translating and editing labour.[59]

In such arrangements, the question of how much linguistic knowledge the European partner possessed seldom arose.[60]

Probably as strong a factor, though, was that once having made this acknowledgment of his anonymous friend in the preface to *Shakti and*

Shākta, Woodroffe never referred to him again and this remains the only place where he acknowledged that Arthur Avalon was anyone other than himself.[61] Thereafter he seemed all the more ready to subsume Arthur Avalon's identity under his own. In subsequent publications he listed books that had come out under his own name along with those under the pseudonym, describing them all neutrally as 'works which I have published',[62] while 'Arthur Avalon' was again used for *The Serpent Power* and for the later volumes of *Tantrik Texts*. In Paris in 1921, as we have seen, he openly identified himself with Arthur Avalon and his books.

Now in 1937 two volumes of *Tantrik Texts* were published posthumously. One was the second edition of the first volume of the series, the other a new work. The prefaces to both explained that Arthur Avalon had secured manuscripts for these volumes but had been heavily engaged in editing *śāradā tilaka* and *prapañcasāra tantra* before his death at the beginning of 1936 had left the rest of his work unfinished.[63] It is obvious that here the name Arthur Avalon referred to one person and that the pandit who wrote these prefaces did not consider that the person was Woodroffe, despite what was to me initially the mystifying reference to his death at the beginning of 1936. Just before his death in 1936, Woodroffe was suffering from Parkinsons's Disease in Monte Carlo.

There was one other person, however, who was very much still on the scene. His name did not appear on the covers of the books but did appear on a pamphlet put out by the *Āgamanusandhana Samiti* which published the *Tantrik Texts*. Arthur Avalon's name was given as the organizations's editor and its President was the Maharaja of Darbhanga, a well-known practising Tantric (see below, chapter 11). There were two joint secretaries, Sir John Woodroffe and someone who normally stayed very much in the background: Mr Atal Bihari Ghose.

The name of Atal Bihari Ghose was mentioned in a clause in Sir John Woodroffe's Will, where he referred to their long collaboration on a 'Shastric work'. An address of eighty years ago was printed in the membership lists of the Asiatic Society of Bengal and from there it was possible to trace his family to where they now live.[64] I was told by his granddaughter, Mrs Sumita Guha: "My grandfather wrote all the books except *Shakti and Shākta*." In chapter 11 I discuss to what degree I believe her claim was accurate. In the room which contained Atal Bihari Ghose's large library of books on Tantra and other philosophical and religious subjects there stood the trunk which contained his collection of tantric manuscripts. Among the letters found with the manuscripts were four addressed to Sir John Woodroffe from members of the public. Accompanying one of these was a note from Ghose to Woodroffe which seemed to indicate that as late as 1918 – the year in which both *Shakti and Shākta* and *The Serpent Power* were published – Woodroffe needed Ghose to translate for him even very simple Sanskrit quotations. It read:

> Dear Sir John, I return the letter with the Sanskrit parts (except for the quotation from the Upanishad) translated. I do not translate this as you can get it from Max Muller.[65]

On the accompanying letter, English translations were inserted above the correspondent's Sanskrit passages in the same handwriting as on Ghose's note. The quotations together with Ghose's translations of them were subsequently used in the second edition of *Shakti and Shākta*, with nothing to indicate of course that the author had been unable to read them without help. This indication as to how the pseudonymous Arthur Avalon's apparently very impressive knowledge of Sanskrit texts comes about, is pursued further in chapter 11 below.

The problem is not so much with the *Tantrik Texts* series. The early volumes of these mostly had named Indian editors anyway; and as we shall see in chapter 11 the correspondence confirmed that the later volumes were nearly all the work of Atal Bihari Ghose. A question still remains however over some of the English writings: over the various articles and lectures which became chapters in *Shakti and Shākta* and *Garland of Letters*, and the two long Introductions – to *The Serpent Power* and to the translation of the *mahānirvāṇa tantra*. One reason why many people have thought of Woodroffe as an orientalist scholar is surely that it is difficult to see how anyone could have written even parts of *Shakti and Shākta*, which was attributed directly to him, without a good knowledge of Sanskrit and this is even more true of *Garland of Letters* and the other books. *World as Power* – which was written with the acknowledged help of P.N. Mukhopadhyay – has notably less Sanskrit than the others.[66] Not only are many passages of these characterised by an immense, even superfluous fund of quotations, but in places it seems clear that the author thinks about the philosophical ideas he writes about through the medium of the Sanskrit technical terms. Moreover, if Woodroffe was as ignorant of the language as Ghose's note seems to suggest, it is difficult to see how he could have lectured in front of scholars like Sylvain Lévy and Masson Oursel without this becoming apparent – or was it the case, that attitudes such as those mentioned above, made the degree of Woodroffe's own knowledge, or lack of it, seem irrelevant? I think we shall have to conclude that it did.[67]

The mystery is pursued in chapter 11, where an analysis of the writings does suggest that Woodroffe drew very heavily indeed others, and especially on Ghose. The two men were fellow disciples of Sivacandra Vidyarnava. Publicly they merged their identities into 'Arthur Avalon', who wrote with the voices of both men and was a larger figure than either of them alone could have hoped to be. Atal Bihari Ghose's grandchildren actually said to me: 'No-one would have taken any notice of Mr Ghose of Calcutta.' Nor would Woodroffe have carried the authority of textual knowledge which Ghose could lend to the fictional orientalist.

As for the slight mystery over the date of Arthur Avalon's death – I discovered that all three of them did indeed die together, for Atal Bihari Ghose died just four days before his British friend. As the Bengali journal *Baśumati* put it: 'they have gone together to the lap of the Great Mother', and it expressed the hope that they would be born again 'in the same twin-form to spread knowledge of the principles of Śakti'.[68]

This concludes the section on Arthur Avalon's identity and significance. We have seen how the 'open secret' of Arthur Avalon worked in the public arena to raise the status of Tantra in Bengal, in other parts of India, and abroad. Far from being a pseudonym used to *conceal* Woodroffe's authorship, the name looks more like a 'legal fiction' that enabled him to claim authorship of books, or parts of books which were not entirely his own. In the last three chapters we turn to the content of the books published in the Avalon and Woodroffe names, beginning in the next chapter by outlining the area presented in them as *Tantraśāstra*, or *Śaktivāda*, the doctrine of Śakti.

Chapter Nine

ON TANTRA

Arthur Avalon and modern studies

The volume of study on Tantra (or 'Tantrism') is as prolific now as it was scant in the time when Woodroffe and Ghose wrote their books. This chapter is not a comprehensive survey of the field of modern tantric studies, for to do this would take us beyond the scope of a book about Woodroffe. Instead I have followed closely some scholars whose work I have found specially relevant. In particular, André Padoux's book on the doctrine of the Word revisits in greater detail the area which Avalon/ Woodroffe entered in his books, especially in *Garland of Letters*. His second chapter is also a useful survey of Tantrism.[1] Alexis Sanderson's articles on the history of the tantric cults and their literature throw much light on what were for Woodroffe and his collaborators the vexed questions of the relationship between Tantra and the Hindu mainstream, and the role of horrific symbolism and trangressive rituals. It also becomes possible to perceive the Avalon/Woodroffe writings themselves as an extension in the early twentieth century of the process of domestication which Sanderson defines.[2] For the theological and ritual world of Saivite Tantra – 'Kashmir Śaivism' – I have drawn mainly on the work of Debabrata Sen Sarma who is a disciple of the influential 'insider' Gopinath Kaviraj, and on Gavin Flood's study of body and cosmology. For *kuṇḍalinī* yoga, Eliade's *Yoga: Immortality and Freedom* is still a 'classic' and more recently the work of Liliane Silburn.[3]

'What are the Tantras and What is Their Significance?' The problems of defining 'Tantra'

Although they usually avoided using the word 'Tantra' for reasons discussed below, Woodroffe and Ghose nevertheless considered they were writing about a specific group of concepts, rites, symbols making up a definable whole, which was presented as the religion of the Śāktas, a sub-group within the wider religion they called 'Brahmanism'.[4] This chapter attempts to outline this area in the context of modern studies of Tantrism.

The problems of defining Tantrism were addressed by André Padoux in a 1981 review article, where he emphasized that 'the word "Tantrism" assuredly is a Western creation. India traditionally knows only texts called Tantras.'[5] The typical doctrinal and ritual features now known as Tantrism became so much a part of general Hinduism from around the seventh to eighth centuries onward, that it becomes difficult to delineate a substantive area called 'Tantra'. One of Avalon/Woodroffe's most persistent theses is just this: that it is not legitimate to separate 'Tantra' from general Hinduism, and Arthur Avalon too claimed that 'the adjective Tantric is largely a Western term.'[6]

Woodroffe and Ghose however were less intent on precise scholarly definition than on dismantling the image I have discussed in chapter 7: that of a distinct and degenerate sect or group of sects involved in obnoxious practices. Consequently their books generally attempted to remove what had become an offensive term – 'Tantra' – from the vocabulary of discourse and sought to redefine the area within wider frames of reference.

On the opening page of the first edition of *Shakti and Shākta* it is suggested that *Āgama* should be used as a generic term in place of *Tantra*, since the *āgamas* included the tantras:

> For what does Tantra mean? The word denotes injunction (Vidhi), regulation (Niyama), Śāstra generally or treatise ... We cannot speak of 'The Treatise' nor of 'The Tantra' any more than we can or do speak of the Purāṇa, the Samhitā. We can speak of 'the Tantras' as we do of 'the Purāṇas'. These Tantras are Śāstras of what is called the Āgama. [SS(1):1; DP:54–5][7]

By the same logic, however, *Āgama* would also be invalid. In fact Avalon/Woodroffe used many other terms as well: *Āgamaśāstra*, *Tantraśāstra*, the *Śākta Tantra*, merely avoiding the word 'Tantra' on its own. Even here, the writings give the appearance of inconsistency because 'Tantra' does occur in them. What seems to have happened is that Woodroffe and his collaborators used this term until around 1917 when they decided to reject it because of its negative associations in orientalist writings.[8] Arthur Avalon set out his reasons in two articles published in *Prabuddha Bhārata*, a journal of the Ramakrishna Mission and therefore aimed at readers influenced by the neo-Vedanta of Vivekananda. 'What are the Tantras?' was followed by 'The Significance of the Tantras' and they were amalgamated into a single chapter in *Shakti and Shākta* [SS(DP):54–69].

Avalon points to the practices of the *vāmācāris* (ie. the *pañcatattva* and other controversial rituals) as the crux of the matter, as he sees it:

> The secret Sādhanā of some of the latter ... has acquired such notoriety that to most the term "The Tantra" connotes this particular worship and its abuses and nothing else ... Now it is this Kaula

> doctrine and practice, limited probably, as being a secret doctrine, at all times to comparatively few, which has come to be known as "The Tantra". [SS(DP):61–2]

He has pointed out that such 'aberrations' were also to be found in the West and adds that, furthermore, they were not characteristic of all followers of 'the Āgamas':

> This is but one division of worshippers who again are but one section of the numerous followers of the Āgamas, Śaiva, Śākta and Vaiṣṇava. Though there are certain common features which may be called Tāntrik yet one cannot speak of "The Tantra" as though it were one entirely homogeneous doctrine and practice. Still less can we identify it with the particular practices and theories of one division of worshippers only. [SS(DP) 62]

The wording in the original article shows more clearly how he was struggling against the image of 'Tantra' as a single extremist sect of the Śāktas that indulged in disreputable practices:

> The *antinomian* Sādhana of the latter ... has acquired such notoriety that to most the term 'The Tantra' connotes this particular worship and its abuses and nothing else ... Now it is this *extremist* doctrine and practice ... which has come to be known as 'The Tantra'. Nothing is more incorrect. This '*left wing*' is but one division of the Shāktas ... Still less can we identify it with the particular practices and theories of one *sect* only.[9]

His insistence that not only Śāktas but also Vaiṣṇavas and Śaivas were followers of *Āgama* 'took the heat off' the former, so to speak. He added that the tantric texts were concerned with wider matters than simply ritual practice and included such things as science, medicine and law [SS(DP):62], a point developed elsewhere by pointing to a 'double framework' whereby tantric Hinduism mirrored vedic forms in every sphere [SS:147].

He returned to the issue of definition in the second of the two articles, repeating the assertions made in the preface to *Principles of Tantra*, that the negative image of Tantra was propagated by the language of Western orientalism:

> According to a common notion the word "Tantra" is (to use the language of a well-known work) "restricted to the necromantic books of the later Śivaic or Śakti mysticism" (Waddell's *Buddhism of Tibet*, p. 164). As charity covers many sins, so "mystic" and "mysticism" are words which cover much ignorance. "Necromancy" too looms unnecessarily large in the writers of this school. It is,

> however, the fact that Western authors generally so understand the term "Tantra" ... SS(DP):62.[10]

He went on to say that he was not concerned with the 'dangerous practices' of 'inferior persons' but with 'the practices which govern the life of the vast mass of the Indian people' and that these were to be found 'in the Tantras of the Āgamas of the different schools which I have mentioned' [SS:63]. As he put it later on: 'The Tantraśāstras or Āgama are not some pathological excrescence on "Hinduism" but simply one of its several presentations' [SS:115]. And: 'He who has not understood Tantra Śāstra has not understood what "Hinduism" is as it exists today' [SS:169]. As Eliade put it later on: Tantra had become a 'pan-Indian mode' for many centuries.[11] This was the result of the process described by Alexis Sanderson as 'exotericization', whereby elements of what originally belonged to taboo-breaking cults practised by renouncer-ascetics, were gradually absorbed by the Hindu mainstream. Thus the Hinduism of the ordinary householder had over centuries acquired more and more tantric features (see below).

Avalon nevertheless did believe in the specificity of the area he was writing about, and he defined it both ritually and doctrinally. In the first of the two articles in *Prabuddha Bhārata*, he listed features of what he called 'the Āgama'. His list is far from exhaustive and is very technical but he summarises it by stating: 'Where there is Mantra, Yantra, Nyāsa, Dīksā, Guru and the like, there is Tantra Śāstra', thus defining the phenomenon by its characteristic elements, as most scholars have done since [SS:61].[12] We have seen how H.H. Wilson had recognised some of these long before.[13] As long as some other term such as *Āgama* or *Tantraśāstra* was used, neither Woodroffe nor Ghose denied they were writing about a specific area of Hinduism that shared also with *vajrayāna* Buddhism certain distinctive features [TT/7 p. iii]. In one instance Woodroffe was forced to concede that the term 'the Tantra' was used in contemporary Bengal and that this may have 'misled' some Western writers [SS:460].

Padoux himself in his review article decides that there is indeed, as he puts it 'a Tantric specificity' which he defines not by a list of characteristic features but by particular doctrinal concepts and above all by certain values, attitudes and aims – a '*weltanschauung*'. First he quotes favourably a definition by Madeleine Biardeau who described Tantra as an attempt 'to place *kāma* – desire – in every sense of the term, in the service of deliverance ... not to sacrifice this world to deliverance, but to reintegrate it ... within the perspective of salvation.' Padoux then adds to this his own summary:

> Tantrism has recourse to a complex of ritualistic, psychic, and corporal practices that make use of elements of this world and of the

> body in particular, practices and notions that correspond to a certain conception not only of the godhead, conceived as polarised into masculine/feminine, but also of the universe and of man, both being immersed in that divine power. As a result, the quest for liberation is fundamentally nothing but a tapping, a using, or even a manipulating of that power. Tantrism, thus, closely associates a doctrine, an aim, a 'weltanschauung' and certain practices which are grounded in that doctrine . . .[14]

Tantra as Woodroffe encountered it was of course the product of a development through time, in which the meaning of the word itself had changed, but he would not have disagreed significantly with Padoux's *weltanschauung*.

ŚAKTI: THE GODDESS

The 'power' of which Padoux writes is of course *śakti*, the most quintessential concept of Tantra, which led to the increasing significance of female divinity. An extensive pantheon of goddesses are regarded as expressions, emanations in hierarchical order, of the one Śakti, usually conceived as the consort of Śiva, but with strikingly independent power. The typical tantric images of the Goddess show Her seated or standing upon one or more corpses, which are those of Śiva and sometimes other male divinities. Historically this can be seen as a statement of the triumph of the Goddess in her cult over the male divinity she has supplanted.[15] Metaphysically it is interpreted as a symbol of the active power of divinity represented by Śakti being upheld by the transcendent Śiva who is so passive with regard to this world that He appears corpse-like. Viewed either way the Goddess has gained in significance over her consort as far as this world is concerned. Woodroffe presented his readers with a metaphysical interpretation of an image which in varying forms can nowadays be seen everywhere in Bengal, especially at the time of the Kālī *pūjā* festival. Kālī stands astride an inert Śiva; she holds in her hands an axe and a severed head; she has a long, lolling red tongue; she wears a belt of human hands and a necklace of severed heads.[16] Woodroffe wrote:

> The scene is laid in the cremation ground (Śmaśāna), amidst white sun-dried bones and fragments of flesh . . . Here the 'heroic' (Vira) worshipper performs at dead of night his awe-inspiring rituals. Kālī is set in such a scene, for She is that aspect of the great Power which withdraws all things into herself at, and by, the dissolution of the universe. He alone worships without fear who has abandoned all worldly desires, and seeks union with Her as the One Blissful and

> Perfect Experience. On the burning ground all worldly desires are burnt away ... She stands upon the white corpse-like body of Śiva. He is white, because he is the illuminating transcendental aspect of consciousness. He is inert, because he is the changeless aspect of the Supreme and She, the apparently changing aspect of the same ... [SS:517–8]

Ernest Payne in his book on the Śāktas referred to in chapter 7, quoted this passage in order to illustrate Woodroffe's naivety. Believing its transparency so obvious as to need little comment he dismissed it by saying: 'All this means little more than that it is now felt necessary to have some ideal explanation of the more repulsive features in the description of the Goddess.'[17] To this Woodroffe replied that he had not invented this explanation but was only repeating what was presented in the texts themselves.[18] The cremation ground – *śmaśāna* – is indeed the great sacred space of Tantra, the conceptual as also often the actual place of transformation for the *sādhaka*, whether seeking liberation or supernormal powers. The imagery of death and eroticism, together with its metaphysical interpretation both belonged to the phenomenon that Woodroffe knew as 'Tantra'.[19]

Mastering the Excluded

The iconography was the outcome of the historical process analysed by Sanderson. The symbolism of the severed heads and the cremation ground relate to the origins of Tantrism in the ancient saivite cults of the *kāpālikas* ('skull-bearers') and other sects of ascetics. They sought supernormal power through rites performed to Śiva in the fear inspiring form of *Bhairava*, who was associated with death, pollution and sexuality: that is, with all that was kept ritually at bay by the purity rules and caste restrictions of the orthodox Brahmanical system. The Feminine was also located in this realm of the excluded, and hence was associated with its power.[20]

While tantric elements have gradually permeated the Hindu mainstream, Sanderson shows how Tantra itself was from the beginning an esoteric affair, initially restricted to the domain of renouncer-ascetics. From whatever sect they emerged – Saivite, Vaisnavite or Buddhist – the tantrics held the same relation to the orthodox practice: they transgressed boundaries and infringed the rules whether ritual or ethical. Thus the *kāpālikas* made offerings to the deities of 'impure' substances such as blood, meat and alcohol, and engaged in caste-free sexual intercourse in rituals which took place in the cremation ground – the most inauspicious and polluted of all places.[21] However, two processes were at work: on the one hand a movement towards further esotericism, on the other a reverse process of domestication or what Sanderson calls 'exotericisation' whereby the esoteric sects were reincorporated into the orthodox mainstream, but with their rituals 'purified'. The effect of this was that gradually what was considered orthodox in Hinduism acquired more and more tantric features, the same deities being worshippedy and retaining much of their iconography, but being conceived in milder forms and without the transgressive practices.[22] Thus *Śaiva Siddhānta*, the basic saivite mainstream in south India, though socially conforming and caste-observing, has as its texts the twenty-eight *Śaiva Āgamas* – originally anti-vedic – which were among the earliest of the scriptures first classed as 'tantric'. Here Śiva is worshipped as *Sadāśiva*, whose iconography preserves the symbolism of the cremation ground but the image of the deity 'lacks the aura of terrifying and ecstatic power' which belongs to his manifestation as Bhairava ('the Fearsome')'.[23] Bhairava too, however, became domesticated, in the cult of *Svacchanda Bhairava* which represented the orthodox saivite mainstream in Kashmir at the time of Abhinavagupta and his disciples. Here scented water was offered to the divinity instead of wine.[24]

It can be seen then how there was scope for confusion as to what was or was not regarded as genuinely 'tantric', especially as the more esoteric sects used the exoteric public cult as a lower or outer level from which one could enter their secret initiations.[25] This situation is reflected in the famous maxim quoted by Woodroffe: 'At heart a Śākta, outwardly a Śaiva, in gatherings a Vaiṣṇava, in thus many a guise the Kaulas wander on earth' [SS:160–1].[26] It is the situation reflected in the seven *ācāras* (grades of ritual practice) listed in the *kulārṇava tantra*, which place the Kaulas (see below) at the top of the esoteric hierarchy, with *vedācāra* at the bottom [SS:152–3 and 243];[27] and the threefold division of worshippers into *paśu* (animal or unspiritual),[28] *vīra* (heroic) and *divya* (divine) [SS:163]. The first grade is the ordinary worshipper in the public cult, who is bound by convention, the second the practitioner of the esoteric rituals, the third has transcended the need of either.

Sanderson proceeds to show how within the saivite tradition the feminine – the Goddess and her retinue of subsidiary female divinities – became related to increasing degrees of esotericism. Sects continually bifurcated, with more esoteric variations of a cult arising from within it. The many lists and groupings of Tantras which occur in this literature, of the kind reproduced uncritically by Avalon/Woodroffe [eg.SS:149–52] are thus to be seen as maps which place the text in which they occur at the summit of the esoteric hierarchy. As we ascend through these levels, Sanderson explains, 'we find that the feminine rises stage by stage from subordination to complete autonomy.'[29] The Goddess ceases to be a consort and acquires supremacy in her own right.

The basic structure of a tantric cult comprised: the deity (usually a form of Śiva or *Bhairava*), seated alone or embracing his consort, surrounded by circles of lesser divinities who are considered to be emanations of one or both of the central couple. These *āvaraṇa devatās* – 'covering divinities' – are assigned places in the deity's *maṇḍala* ('enthroning diagram') within which he/she is worshipped and which represents the cosmos. For purposes of ritual, it can be inscribed on the ground, or on metal, stone or wood.[30] Conceptually, it is a cremation ground, which is regarded as a *pītha* ('seat') of the divinity's power.

Sanderson shows how in some of the sects this system was feminized by stages.[31] First, the attendant divinities became female spirits called *yoginīs*; then the 'union' (*yāmala*) of the central divine couple was emphasised; finally this couple was replaced by one or more goddesses either reigning alone or with subordinate male consorts: here we are in the cults of the triple goddess (*Trika*) and the various cults of Kālī.[32] In her supreme form as *kālasaṁkarṣinī*, the Destroyer of Time, this goddess's iconography presents us with one of the prototypical images of a tantric deity, images which also permeate *vajrayāna* Buddhism:

> Conventionally beautiful but holding such Kāpālika emblems as the skull-staff (*khaṭvānga*) and the severed head (*muṇḍa*), wearing a tiger skin dripping with blood, trampling the body of Kāla (Time) beneath her feet, she holds a trance-possessed Bhairava in a two-armed embrace in the centre of a vast, many-circuited *maṇḍala* of goddesses enclosed by cordons of male servant-guards and an outer ring of cremation grounds. In the elaborate form of worship both the goddesses and the guards embrace consorts.[33]

In still more esoteric forms she is not beautiful but 'a hideous emaciated destroyer'. The shift towards the feminine and the more terrific corresponded with an increasing emphasis on non-dualism in philosophy: the deity representing the non-dual Absolute appearing inimical at first to the ego-consciousness.[34] In the southern tantric sect called *śrī vidyā* however, the 'Triple Goddess' *Tripurasundarī* kept some of her gruesome accoutrements but acquired others that were not so – like her flowery arrows to inspire passion – and became beautiful, erotic and benevolent.

There are other explanations of the violence and eroticism of tantric imagery, Buddhist or Hindu. The deities could be seen as representing the violence of human passions harnessed and transcended in the quest for *mokṣa* or Liberation. Among the methods (*upāya*) of transformation of consciousness described by Abhinavagupta, one involved the upsurge of sudden violent emotions such as anger, fear, desire etc.[35] The tantric divinities also often have a history as local or tribal deities incorporated into the Buddhist and Brahmanical pantheons.[36]

The feminine was consistently associated with what was considered more esoteric, more transgressive, and more fearsome. Although Sanderson does not state it this way, the implication is that because the cults of the male forms of the deity tended to become domesticated first, the female forms were left to represent what was wild, uncivilized, and excluded. It also underlines how despite the feminine imagery, the tantric cults were predominantly male-oriented and that part of their esoteric secret was to do with the mastery of the feminine, of sexuality, pollution and death, which were all linked together and located in the realm of the excluded.

The Kula Path

It was the *kaula* movement, by which the śākta sects too were domesticated and refined, which was to give to Tantra its quintessential aspect of 'spiritual' sexuality. The word comes from *kula* which means primarily 'family'[37] and refers to the eight families of the *yoginīs*, who originally formed the retinue of Śiva as *Bhairava*. The Kaulas transformed and internalized the mainly magical sexual rites of the earlier sects into a system of erotic mysticism where orgasm itself was seen as a vehicle of illumination or spiritual experience.[38] Thus they exemplified the *weltanschauung* described by Padoux as definitive. In accordance with microcosm–macrocosm correspondence, sexual union was seen as a recapitulation on the individual level of the cosmic union (*maithuna*) of Śiva and Śakti.[39]

The Kaulas aestheticised the ritual, although the true place of performance remained conceptually the pollution-carrying environment of the cemetery or cremation ground and it still contained the basic *kāpālika* offerings of alcohol, meat and sex. Two ritual systems are prescribed in the twenty-ninth chapter of Abhinavagupta's *tantrāloka*, of which one involved sexual practice and one did not – called the *kula prakriyā* and the *tantra prakriyā* respectively. In the *tantra prakriya* an elaborate ritual is prescribed with the typical tantric elements, aimed at purifying and divinizing the body, mind and senses and ending with external worship in which meat and alcohol were offerings. (The purpose was to show that the adept had transcended distinctions of 'pure' and 'impure'.) To this in the *kula prakriya* was added ritual sexual intercourse with a consecrated partner – the *dūtī*, *yoginī* or *śakti*.[40] The *kula* path however had a tendency to transcend and minimalise ritual, concentrating on spontaneity, possession (*āveśa*) and intuition as immediate means of experiencing the ultimate unity of Consciousness, which was the aim of the practice.[41] In the course of time the basic three offerings were expanded to include five elements: the well-known *pañcatattva*[42] which were the cause of much of the notoriety of Tantra in Woodroffe's time.

The male adept's sexual partner in the ritual represented or was considered to be possessed by, the spirit *yoginīs* who were part of a tantric deity's *maṇḍala*. These consecrated women were considered the male adepts' spiritual superiors and the vehicle of transmitting the tradition (*āmnāya*), and initiation was passed to an adept through the partner of his guru. The most important qualification for a *yoginī* or *śakti* was that she should be initiated – whether the wife of the adept or not – but in the 'respectable' form of Tantra which was acceptable among Woodroffe's middle class acquaintance she was the practitioner's wife. Woodroffe, however, was aware of another tradition: that the *śakti* should be *parakiyā* – 'the wife of another' [SS:610]. In this latter case, the distinction is maintained between the ordinary household life with the *dharmapatnī*, the wife married by orthodox rites, and the partner in the ritual who belongs to the esoteric domain.

The most famous Kaula was the great Kashmiri philosopher Abhinavagupta (fl.975–1025 CE). By his time secret societies practising the cult were widespread among the social élite and the court in Kashmir, for the sect already had a wider social base than the circles of ascetics and appealed to ordinary householders.[43]

'KASHMIR ŚAIVISM'

Abhinavagupta's synthesis and exegesis of various schools of śaiva and śākta thought and practice formed the basis of a metaphysical Idealist Tantrism that spread outside Kashmir to other parts of India, especially South India and Bengal.[44] He and his disciples produced commentaries upon the older texts, the anonymous Āgamas and Tantras, in the light of the saivite non-dual (*advaita*) philosophical schools known as *spanda* ('vibration')[45] and *pratyabhijñā* (recognition),[46] in which cosmological speculations were intricately connected with certain yogic practices and tantric rituals. This was 'Kashmir' or 'northern Śaivism' although the later texts placed more emphasis upon Śakti.

Woodroffe was one of the first European writers to become captivated by Kashmir Śaivism which Gavin Flood has described as 'stupendously vast and intricately precise, and also a teaching of salvation . . . a cosmological soteriology'.[47] Here notions about sexuality are interwoven into a wider complex of cosmological ideas which can be viewed from a number of different perspectives according to which factor is given prominence, but most important among them all is *mantra*. The Goddess is hypostasized Speech, and the cosmos an emanation through sound and language. Light and its reflection form another complex of symbols. Śiva is radiance (*prakāśa*) and Śakti His reflection (*vimarśa*) – paired concepts which also convey the sense of Consciousness and what it reflects *upon*: Śakti becomes the cosmos, making the manifest world a reflection of the deity and at the same time the product of his thought.[48]

Śaktivāda – 'The Doctrine of Śakti'

At the heart of this doctrine is the divine bipolarity (or *advāya*, 'two-in-one'), Śiva–Śakti. It was set against the *advaita* or non-dualist doctrine of Śankarācārya, in which the sole ontological reality and transcendence of the

Ultimate Principle (Brahman) is not compromised by his having anything to do with either creating or manifesting a cosmos. This 'work', according to Śankara's teaching, is not really an act at all, for the existence of the manifest world is the result of illusion, or primal ignorance (*avidya*). The cause of this illusion is *māyā*, which has an undefined ontological status ('of the nature of neither IS nor IS NOT'). Neither is *māyā* conscious, or personified: 'it' does not partake of the *sat-cit-ānanda* that is Brahman. Śakti however, in the Tantras, while pervading and becoming the manifest cosmos also shares in the ontological status and pure consciousness of Śiva. 'She' is *cit* or *caitanya*, 'essentially Divine and Spiritual'.[49]

Saivite non-dualism thus differed fundamentally from Śankara's *advaita vedānta*. In place of the inactive Brahman, was placed Śiva as Supreme Lord and Free Agent (*svatantra kartā*), who through His Absolute Freedom (*svātantryā*) causes himself to appear as the universe. Śakti is identified with His five powers or aspects: consciousness (*cit*) and bliss (*ānanda*) are also attributes of Brahman, but Śiva in the Āgamas and Tantras has three more: will (*icchā*), knowledge (*jñāna*) and action (*kriyā*). The first two of the five were identified with His supreme state 'before' the manifestation of a cosmos; the last three, through which 'creation' or manifestation occurs, were associated with Śakti. Will, Knowledge and Action are Her three forms [SS:361] – the famous triple Goddess with whom many other triads in mind or cosmos were homologised.[50]

Tattva

Śiva is the divine Subject, the supreme 'I' (*ahaṁta*) from which all human sense of identity (*ahaṁkāra*) emanates,[51] and Śakti is his self-reflection or self-awareness (*vimarśa*). The cosmos is the object of Śiva's knowledge (which is also self-knowledge), in increasing degrees of separateness from Himself in each successive stage of its evolution or unfolding. These stages are the cosmic planes called *tattva*. This word, which literally means 'that-ness', when used in cosmology denotes a reality, a fundamental phase of manifestation, a 'real state'.[52] (This is different from its meaning as one of the five 'substances' in the *pañcatattva* rite.) They are also present within the individual where they are states of consciousness and parts of the body and mind. This is because of the belief in the fundamental unity of all phenomena. The evolution of the cosmos is thus both an outer and an inner event, or both a material and a mental or psychical one.[53] The Tantras took over the ancient *Sāṁkhya* system of cosmic genesis, which had a system of twenty-four *tattvas*, or evolutionary stages, in an essentially atheistic cosmology.[54] To this the śaiva and śākta Tantras grafted on twelve more representing the absolute Śiva-Consciousness gradually evolving or transforming itself into the dualistic perception of an outer cosmos. These thirty-six *tattvas* form an ascending and descending series of planes leading from 'earth' or the material world perceived by outward-directed sense perception, through the subtle origins of these perceptions in consciousness to the ultimate source of the manifest cosmos in the 'pure', ie. non-dual consciousness of Śiva or the Godhead. The higher or purer *tattvas* are inhabited by different 'supernatural' beings who exist in the state of consciousness to which the *tattva* or level corresponds, thus creating the cosmic planes or *lokas*. The yoga practitioner's ascent through them is an inner return journey towards Śiva-Consciousness.[55]

Ābhāsa

Kashmir Saivism retains a non-dual metaphysics while leaving room for a more personal divinity. Śiva is closer to a deity in the theistic sense than Brahman: He projects the universe as an act of His divine Will, although it is also a reflection of Himself. The universe is not a creation out of nothing, but an emanation, a projection out of its latent state within the Śiva Consciousness. As Padoux describes it, the cosmos

> . . . is emitted as a throbbing, radiating light as a shining forth or a luminous projection, which is then reflected on ever lower levels, where gradually losing its initial power and radiance, it will gradually reveal all the cosmic levels down to the lowest one. But while in the course of the process the manifestation condenses . . . progressively losing its initial freedom and light, it does not . . . cease to share in the effulgence, the consciousness and life of the primary principle . . . The light is just obscured, never does it cease to be present, for otherwise the world would be inert (*jada*).

This is the doctrine of *ābhāsa* which means 'shining forth'.[56] The word in Śankara's metaphysics implied an illusory reflection, but here it is used to express the universe as a theophany.[57]

It was these metaphysical aspects of Tantrism, rather than the erotic rites, which Arthur Avalon emphasised. Woodroffe's first public lecture on 'Creation'[58] dealt with this saivite and śākta doctrine of cosmic emanation, which made use of *śakti* as a principle uniting the Absolute with the material world. He presented what he called *śaktivāda* as a reconciling third position transcending the opposition between the uncompromising monism of Śankarācārya, and the dualism of the *sāṁkhya* philosophy which had placed 'spirit' (*puruṣa*) and 'world' (*prakṛti*) in separate categories.[59] The theme was one of great importance to him and he devoted many pages of his books and lectures to it.[60]

Here Woodroffe had discovered what has been called the 'Realist Idealism' of Kashmir Saivism which countered the kind of doctrine associated with Śankarācārya that held the phenomenal world to be illusion. It allowed for the reality of the senses since the world derives reality from Śiva whose experience it is, 'and Śiva's experience is not unreal' [SS:362].[61] In the contemporary context, *śaktivāda* – as opposed to Śankara's doctrine which Woodroffe called *māyāvāda* – could withstand criticisms aimed by Westerners at the latter's 'illusionism'. Because the doctrine of Śakti was not world-denying or ascetic, it could not be accused of being 'weakening', for it had 'a strengthening pragmatic value' [SS:364]. Vivekananda had called for such virtues in his own modernised interpretation of *advaita vedānta*, although he made less use of *śakti*. There was another advantage: the concept of *śakti* could be presented as a kind of principle of Consciousness or Life-force pervading matter, expressed in Sanskrit terminology by saying that matter is not *jada* – not inert (see above). Therefore the doctrine could be presented in terms of contemporary Western philosophies of science which attempted to unite the categories of matter and spirit (see below pp. 194–202ff). As Woodroffe summed it up: 'The Natural and the Spiritual are one' [SS:408]. To him, this is what 'the doctrine of Śakti' primarily meant.

'THE GARLAND OF LETTERS': THE COSMOS AS MANTRA

We have seen that Ernest Payne could not take seriously the assertion that the gruesome iconography of Kālī could be symbolic of abstract principles. The passage he quoted from Woodroffe was from a short essay entitled 'The Necklace of Kālī' which was included in *Garland of Letters* as well as *Shakti and Shākta*. Here the Goddess's necklace of skulls – an essential aspect of her iconography – is transformed into the *varṇas* or *bījas*, the 'letters' or cosmogonic syllables of the Sanskrit 'alphabet'. *Garland of Letters* opens in its first chapters with the doctrine of the Word or *vāc* in the Vedas and Tantras, leading to an explanation of *bīja* (a 'sound-seed') as what Woodroffe calls 'natural name' – or rather 'approximate natural name', the nearest that the human ear can perceive to the divine creative 'Word' (*śabda*) which gives rise to the cosmos [GOL:70ff]. The *bījas* are 'seed-syllables' formed from the letters or phonemes of the Sanskrit 'alphabet' – the *varṇa* or *akṣara* (a word which means 'indestructible' and conveys the sense of the eternal nature of sound). Combined with the nasal *anusvāra* they are recited as monosyllabic mantras. The entire alphabet being recited in this way mentally 'unwinds' the cosmos into manifestation, and if recited in reverse 'rewinds' it again into dissolution in Śiva-Consciousness which is its source. This is because the *bījas* are identical with the *tattvas*, and hence the elements of mind, body and cosmos.[62] Combinations of them also make the characteristic mantra-form of the tantric deities.[63]

Chapters 10–21 of *Garland of Letters* represent the *Studies in the Mantra Shāstra*, which describe this mantra cosmogony, found mainly in the śākta texts which emerged out of Kashmir Saivism. Here we meet with the world of *śrī vidyā*, a sect of Kaulas whose worship is focused upon the beneficent and beautiful[64] triple Goddess Tripurasundari (also called Lalitā). The name *śrī vidyā* refers to this Goddess' sixteen-syllable mantra (a *vidyā* is a special kind of mantra) which is also expressed in geometric form in her *maṇḍala* called the *śrī yantra*, or the *śrī cakra*, thus uniting form and space with sound.[65] It has now become a very familiar image in the West.[66] This rich geometric symbol is loaded with referents on many inter-related levels.

Consciousness, sound, light and erotic symbolism are intricately combined in this complex imagery. At the heart of the *śrī yantra*, lies the inverted triangle called *kāma-kalā* which represents śakti in her three forms. The letters or *varṇas* in three groups reside along its sides, expressing the fact that this triangle is the 'root of all mantras' [GOL:184]. The word *kāma* – 'desire', which Avalon translates, not incorrectly, as 'will' – is not intended to lose its erotic connotation. *Kalā* means both 'part' and 'manifestation'. The Goddess is the supreme *kalā*, the manifestation of the unseen Śiva, and as the cosmos emanates she diffuses herself as sixteen lesser *kalās* who are her aspects and subordinate divinities residing in her *maṇḍala*.[67] Within the *kāma-kalā* triangle is the dot – *bindu*– from which the cosmos emanates. *Bindu* has many referents. It is born from the sexual union (*maithuna*) of the god and goddess within the inverted triangle, where the *bindu* is a drop of the semen of Śiva, the triangle the womb of the Goddess. But *bindu* is also the condensation of Śiva-consciousness as the geometric point which is about to expand into the world of multiplicity during cosmic emanation (or 'creation') [GOL:130]. As a point, *bindu* is also the *anusvāra*, the nasalization-mark of the single-syllable *bīja* mantras. It emerges out of its own resonance which is called *nāda*.[68] *Nāda* is identical with the vibration (*spanda*) with which the cosmos both begins and ends. It is everlasting and imperceptible sound, called *anāhata* ('unstruck'), but which is heard by yogis in trance. It is approached through the resonance which follows upon the pronunciation of a *bīja* mantra, or of the *praṇava* (the sacred syllable '*Oṃ*').[69] For in yoga, which reverses the process of creation or emanation, the sound of the mantra is gradually reabsorbed into the initial energy of vibration, which in turn is absorbed back into the silence of supreme consciousness.[70] The three points of the *kāma-kalā* triangle thus represent *bindu* and *bīja*, the sound and the mantra, with *nāda* the resonance between them.[71] *Nāda* also represents the 'union and mutual relation' of Śiva and Śakti (that is, their 'sexual' relation).[72]

Sound, in this synaesthetic world of Tantra, is also light and consciousness. *Bindu* is also a drop of light[73] which is reflected in ever widening circles as the central triangle unfolds into the *śrī yantra*, the *maṇḍala* of the Goddess Tripurasundari, which is the body of the cosmos. The whole universe is contained in potential within the *kāma-kalā*, expressed by the letters in three groups, along with other essential trinities around the triangle's sides.[74] Just as the *bindu* expands into the triangle (the 'one' has become 'three'), so the triangle transforms itself into the *maṇḍala* (the 'three' have become many). The *śrī yantra* is like a great source of light and sound which is radiated outwards in echoes and circling reflections.[75]

It is composed of forty-one triangles arranged in four concentric circles around the central one. (see Plate 7) These are surrounded in turn by two circles of eight and sixteen lotus petals. Beyond these are three circles of plain lines and the whole is enclosed in a yellow square with four entrances representing the four directions: this is the earth-plane, or the fully manifest cosmos. The total makes nine circuits, which have a central axis of nine triangles, four with the apex pointing upwards and five pointing downwards. These make up the nine enclosures (*āvaraṇas*) of the Goddess.[76] They represent the *lokas*, worlds or cosmic planes inhabited by the *kalās* who are lesser śaktis making up the retinue of the Goddess in her *maṇḍala*, and are present in their mantras which are inscribed within it. They are related to groups of the thirty-six *tattvas* or planes of the cosmic evolution, which in turn are correlated to four stages of speech: from the transcendent or ineffable, through two levels of subtle or mental speech to audible language.[77] The *sādhaka* worships each circuit in turn, moving from the outer limits inward to the central point, the *bindu*.[78]

The unity of the world in Consciousness, its source and end, is the dominant theme of *Garland of Letters* as of all the Avalon/Woodroffe books. The author's interest is not only metaphysical but also experiential, as frequent references to sādhana imply. To 'realise' a mantra is to pierce to the subtle 'Light' form of the Divinity whose Sound-form it is. The aim, as of all tantric practice, is to pass from the 'gross' (material, here audible) world to the subtle (unheard) forms of speech or thought behind it, and thence to the Supreme Speech or Creative Thought (*Śabda Brahman*) whose 'meaning' is the whole cosmos.[79]

TANTRIC YOGA AND KUṆḌALINĪ: THE 'SERPENT POWER'

In Tantra there is an intricate connection between cosmology and yoga because the human mind and body is experienced as a reflection of the cosmos. The body is itself a *maṇḍala*.[80] The triangles on the central axis of the *śrī yantra* are correlated to the spinal chord with its six *cakras* or 'centres', while the *kāmakalā* is situated in the seventh *cakra* at the crown of the head, which is thus the centre of the cosmic *maṇḍala*. *Kuṇḍalinī* yoga is understood as a recapitulation within the individual *sādhaka* of the evolution and dissolution of the cosmos, but especially the latter. Hence it is also called *lāya*, or 'dissolution', *yoga*.

'The Worlds are dissolved (Laya) from time to time for all beings. The perfected Yogi dissolves the Universe for all time for himself. Yoga is thus Laya.' [SP.48] It is a return to the source, from human to divine

Consciousness, by an ascent through the cosmic levels or *tattva*. These are present in the body in the six *cakras* – 'circles', 'centres', 'regions'[SP:114]; or 'wheels'.[81] In *ṣaṭ-cakra-nirūpaṇa* they are also known as *padma* – 'lotus' – and are conceived as flowers with *bīja* mantras on their petals.[82] The *cakras* and the *nāḍīs* ('currents' or 'channels') which branch out from them are 'subtle organs' of a system of yogic anatomy, imperceptible to ordinary senses, but 'real' to yoga experience. The 'mystical physiology' of which they are a part concerns the divinization or cosmicization of the body.[83] As Flood points out, the concept of the evolution of the *tattvas* implies that the cosmos itself is perceived as a kind of collective body, or a hierarchical series of such bodies; in Kashmir Śaivism these are all reflections in greater or lesser degree of Śiva – or rather 'grosser' or more 'subtle' condensations of the Consciousness of Śiva. These collective bodies are also the worlds or cosmic planes (*loka*), to which the *cakras* of the body correspond. Consciousness being seen as primary, the body itself is an expression and product of Consciousness, not the other way around as is the predominant conception in contemporary Western culture.[84]

The six *cakras* are named, and are visualized within a narrow channel called *suṣumṇā* rising within the spinal cord. The system described in *ṣaṭ-cakra-nirūpaṇa* and *The Serpent Power*, placed them at levels corresponding to the following: the base of the spine (*mūlādhāra*), just above the penis (*svādhiṣṭhāna*),[85] the navel (*maṇipūra*), the heart (*anāhata*), the throat (*viśuddha*) and between the eyebrows (*ājñā*) [SP:141]. The body besides being a *maṇḍala* is also a great mantra, and is produced by mantras [SP:166]. The phonemes or *bījas* are visualized on the petals or spokes of the 'lotuses', thus the *cakras* 'spell out' the body, mind and senses as a manifestation of Śakti, just as the cosmos is. They give rise to, first – in the *ājñā cakra* – the three levels of the mind.[86] The mind and the highest centre come first in the order of creation as the life force, *śakti* descends from above. In dissolution or *lāya* they are the last to disappear. Then, in the other bodily *cakras*, come the five faculties of sense perception with their sense-organs (the *indriyas*), and the five subtle elements which are their fields of operation (the *tanmātras*: sound, touch, form-and-colour, taste, smell)[87] and the five 'gross', ie material, elements (the *bhūtas*) which correspond to the latter: ether, air, fire, water and earth.[88] Only with these last, with the 'gross' elements or *bhūtas* does the system concern itself with the material world. All the others relate to the subtle or mental layers behind or beyond it and form the 'subtle body'. As Arthur Avalon points out, the order of 'creation' or evolution (*śrsti*) is from subtle to gross, from the imperceptible to the perceptible; consciousness appears first, then matter. *Kundalinī* yoga, which is a process of involution, reverses this order: the gross is dissolved into the subtle (or mental) and that into the still more subtle [SP:82]. Various parts of the body, and aspects of the mind and the cosmos – a multitude of referents, physical, mental and spiritual are loaded into this system by being localized in the cakras.[89] As well as unifying various different symbolic schemes, this is a way of placing the whole phenomenal world within the body.

Most important of all, the *cakras* are seats of the conscious energy called *kuṇḍalinī*, who is the form of Śakti who dwells in the individual mind and body. She is 'the coiled one' (*kuṇḍala*) [SP:1–2].[90] The concept is descended from the ancient Vedic idea of the cosmic serpent encircling the universe, guardian of treasures of immortality. *Kuṇḍalinī* is a reservoir of immense power. Unawakened, her 'poison' is what binds man in *saṁsāra*; awakened by yoga, she unwinds herself and her 'poison' becomes nectar, the source of liberating knowledge, power and conquest over death.[91] She is fire ,[92] sexuality [SP:224],[93] supreme Consciousness [SP:245–6] but, above all, Speech and Breath. Her body is composed of letters – the *bījas* and mantras [SP:165–6, 226];[94] and she is *prāṇa*, the breath of life, in its five-fold division [SP:73–4, 77].

In normal, outwardly directed waking consciousness, *kuṇḍalinī* is 'asleep'; she resides unawakened in the lowest of the *cakras*, the *mūlādhāra*. Her sleep is the 'bondage of the ignorant' [SP:245]. She lies at the base of the spine, coiled around the entrance to the central yogic channel, the *suṣumnā* – the centremost of the three principal *nāḍīs* of the yogic anatomy which rise within the spinal cord, which is also Mount Meru, the axis of the world.[95] On either side of *suṣumnā* lie two other *nāḍīs* (called *iḍā* and *pingalā*) which are the channels of the in-breath and out-breath [SP:110–1]. *Kuṇḍalinī* is awakened by a combination of mental and physical practices: primarily by yogic breathing or *prāṇāyāma* combined with certain postures, and by mantras combined with visualization.[96] By these means the vital breath, *prāṇa*, which is identical with *kuṇḍalinī*, ceases its in-flow and out-flow, which sustains normal consciousness, and is forced into the central channel – *suṣumnā* – where it is drawn upwards and gradually pierces (*bheda*) through the six *cakras* in the spinal chord [SP:228–9].[97] At the summit of *suṣumnā* – at the crown of the head, which means also at the summit of the world-axis – is the seventh and highest *cakra*, which is not of the body: *sahasrāra*, the lotus of a thousand petals [SP:143–4].[98] This is the abode of Śiva; it is the goal of *kuṇḍalinī's* ascent through the body, and the place of Śiva's love-union (*maithuna*) with Śakti. This is also a kind of inner sexual union for the yogi [SP:238–40]. Here one has entered the higher *tattvas*, the planes of divine, pure (*śuddha*) or non-dualist Consciousness both beyond and prior to the cosmos. Since *Kuṇḍalinī's* ascent is an unwinding or reversing of the process of cosmic evolution, her descent again is its re-creation. For the yogi the whole process is a kind of death and rebirth [SP:241].

As she ascends *kuṇḍalinī* 'pierces' each of the six *cakras* on her way, activating and then dissolving them into herself [SP:237–8]. At each she awakens certain supernormal powers (*siddhi*) and various kinds of bliss [SP:293]. Her arrival at *sahasrāra* can bring *mokṣa* or Liberation from the phenomenal world for the practitioner. But this is only one goal of the practice, and perhaps not the main one. Another kind of Liberation, implying agelessness and power to die at will, is achieved by those who can keep *kuṇḍalinī* at the supreme *cakra* permanently while still living. This is one meaning of the frequent claim that tantric practice brings both *yoga* – in the sense of renunciation and self-control – and *bhoga* – enjoyment or success in this life as well as beyond it. This Avalon recognises as an important part of the goal for most practitioners, for he considers that if Liberation alone is sought, other and simpler forms of yoga are resorted to [SP:288, 293–5].

Avalon himself interprets the claims about *yoga* and *bhoga* being reconciled in terms of general values of world-affirmation, and the non-separation of the categories of 'spirit' and 'matter' – one of Woodroffe's favourite themes [SP:290–3]. This sidesteps the issue of acquiring powers, or *siddhi*. It is clear that the author of *The Serpent Power* has an ambivalent relationship to the subject matter. Although he stresses the 'spiritual' aim of *kuṇḍalinī* yoga, as opposed to acquiring occult powers or the practice of sexual magic,[99] he does not always sound convinced. Asserting the 'scientific' purpose of his work he insists this is value free – he is not advocating the practice of *kuṇḍalinī yoga* [SP:22]. Elsewhere he states that he has not practised it himself [SS:679]. It seems that over time Woodroffe's doubts grew stronger. By 1927 in a foreword to another writer's book, he wrote: 'What may be its value is . . . a matter upon which I am not so sure as I once was'. While other forms of yoga were 'of certain worth' to him, he confessed that the value of *kuṇḍalinī yoga* from what he called the spiritual aspect, 'is not now so clear to me'.[100] Furthermore he felt that in *The Serpent Power* he had undervalued some adverse criticism of this form of yoga. This may refer to remarks by 'a Brahmo author' which appeared in the introductory chapter in the first edition, but in later editions were transferred to chapter 7, where they have more weight. Despite answering the critic, Arthur Avalon clearly agrees with some points he makes about concentration on the lower centres which are associated with sexuality and the passions [SP:283–7].

The system of six bodily cakras (*ṣaṭ-cakra)* plus the seventh at the crown of the head was the one which had become standard when the *ṣaṭ-cakra-nirūpaṇa* was written, but it was not the only one. There were others with more or fewer centres; the earlier texts seem to mention four. Being based on visualization, the number 'varies according to need', although most texts are agreed on the main centres in the navel, heart, throat and head.[101] The system and locations given in *The Serpent Power* seem to have arisen in the western kaula tradition of the worship of *kubjikā* ('the crooked one', an early name for *kuṇḍalinī*), but later became pan-Hindu.[102]

Correlations between the yogic system and Western physiology of the sympathetic nervous system were the subject of speculation among

Woodroffe's contemporaries. The *cakras* were identified with the various nerve plexuses and the *sahasrāra* with the upper cerebellum, the *ājñā* with the pineal gland and so forth, and the *nāḍīs* (currents or channels of energy) became 'yogic' nerves or arteries [SP:103–15, 147–58]. The chapter on the 'Centres or Lotuses' in *The Serpent Power* opens with such an attempt at correlation. Several books on the brain by Western scientists are cited, but the main inspiration for this section was a recently published essay by Brajendranath Seal: *Positive Sciences of the Ancient Hindus*.[103] Seal commented on an article that had appeared in the previous century in *Calcutta Review* entitled 'The Physical Errors of Hinduism' which ridiculed the notion of the *cakras*, among many other things.[104] Though derogatory, it inadvertently revealed just how much anatomical knowledge there possibly was in the Tantras – a fact pointed out by Seal, who averred that the Tantras had discovered that consciousness resides in the cerebro-spinal system and the brain.[105]

Passages in Avalon's chapter appear to move indiscriminately between the Western scientific and yogic terminologies suggesting that he accepted the identification between them. However, he eventually expresses caution, emphasising the point that the *cakras* are to be located in the 'subtle' and not the 'gross', ie. material body [SP:158–61]. He writes: 'to connect or correlate and to identify are different things'; and himself defines the *cakras* as 'extremely subtle vital centres . . . ', the 'subtle forms of that which exists in gross form in the physical body . . .' which 'vitalize and control the gross bodily tracts . . . in these respective regions' [SP:161]. By making the *cakras* invisible to 'gross' (sensual) perception, he nevertheless is able to allow them the ontological status which later Western writers denied them.[106] For Eliade they were 'images expressing transmundane experiences',[107] but for Arthur Avalon they were more actual than that. He recognizes that certain aspects are possibly symbolic and guards against too much literalism: '. . . one must be constantly on guard against falling into a possible trap – namely taking the prescribed methods of realization for actualities in the common sense of that term. The former are conventional, the latter are real' [SP:92]. He thus accepts certain features as symbolic – for example, the numbers of petals to each lotus, and the letters on them – but accepts that the *cakras* themselves are in the category of actualities. 'There are . . . certain facts of objective and universal reality. Thus, for example, there are certain centres (Cakra) in the spinal column' [SP:95].

It was natural that the incursion of Western science into contemporary consciousness should lead Indian thinkers to attempt to unite the yogic with the scientific anatomy. Avalon's placing of the *cakras* and *nāḍīs* of the *kuṇḍalinī* system in the realm of the 'subtle' as centres of consciousness, was a form of compromise, moving away from too literal identifications which could leave the Hindu system vulnerable. But recognition that the latter system was symbolic and related to visualizations in *sādhanā*[108] need not obscure the fact that for its practitioners it was also objective. Inaccurate in terms of modern scientific facts,[109] the yogic anatomy was considered 'scientific' in its day and was used in medicine. The divinized body which was the goal of *sādhanā* was still the living physical body which the practitioner possessed, which thus united him to every level of the cosmos. The very physical methods used to arouse *kuṇḍalinī* – the postures, the notions of forcing or 'churning' the *prāṇa*[110] – shows that what was at issue was a quasi-physical force, which was nevertheless also identical with imperceptible and non-material power.

All the thirty-six *tattvas* or stages of the cosmic evolution, together with all that they contain or represent, along with the stages of speech, and many other aspects of the divine and human realms are thus symbolically distributed among the six *cakras* in the human body plus the seventh at the crown of the head. Outwardly, they are present in the nine circuits of the *śrī yantra*. Tantra has the appearance of a many-pointed search for origins, a constantly repeated attempt to discover the most subtle point of emergence of the perceptible from the imperceptible. The growth of the embryo in the womb from the implantation of the male seed,[111] the growth of individual consciousness out of the universal divine Consciousness, the growth of spoken language out of the unheard (*anāhata* – 'unstruck') Word, and the evolution of the universe out of the divine creative idea (*sṛṣṭi kalpana*, GOL:197) – all are homologised in a highly complex interweaving system. English words like 'evolved' and 'growth' need to be qualified, however, because here 'evolution' represents a fall, a separation from Wholeness [GOL:150; SS:31] while involution or dissolution means the return to the divine Source: a return which, when permanent, becomes Liberation. The loading of many referents into the symbolic systems of the *śrī yantra* and of the *cakras* in the human body has a special role in the quest for the non-dual Absolute; it is one way in which the multiplicity of the world-experience can be compacted and dissolved into unity. In the 'gnostic' philosophy of Tantra as well as of other branches of Hinduism, the simple and homogeneous source is always 'higher' than its complex and evolved manifestation.

This chapter has considered 'Tantra' or the Doctrine of Śakti as it is presented in the work of Avalon/Woodroffe as a whole. The next chapter examines particular apologetic themes that Woodroffe drew out of his material and it focuses upon *Shakti and Shākta*. This book never appeared under the pseudonym, and much of it was made up from lectures which Woodroffe delivered in person. We can therefore more easily distinguish in it when he was speaking in his own voice. In the final chapter, we will look for Atal Bihari Ghose's voice.

Chapter Ten

'ŚAKTIVĀDA'

Soul and body united

Woodroffe was President for a time of Calcutta's Vivekananda Society,[1] and between 1917–18 he delivered lectures to them which formed the core of his first edition of *Shakti and Shākta*. Four magazine articles accompanied them, one of which reproduced a lecture he had given to another organization in Calcutta.[2] The second and third editions of the book included several more lectures Woodroffe delivered, both in India and Europe. The present chapter concentrates on themes from all of these lectures.

SOME POINTS OF DEBATE

As we have seen, Woodroffe presented the Śākta Tantra as a form of philosophical non-dualism (*advaita*) that could be interpreted in a positive sense that did not treat the world as illusion. This was in accord with Swami Vivekananda's 'Practical Vedanta',[3] although the Swami did not examine the metaphysical implications as closely as Woodroffe did. Like other neo-vedantists, Woodroffe believed that experience of the essential unity of Consciousness represented the one truth underlying all religions (the 'perennial philosophy'). He presents the path of the Tantras as one means towards this 'spiritual realization', or knowledge (*jñāna*).

Vivekananda had roundly condemned what he called 'vāmāchār' in his lecture at the Star Theatre in Calcutta on his return in triumph from his first visit to the West, as well as on other occasions.[4] The challenge which Avalon/Woodroffe faced was to reconcile tantric ritual and symbolism with the legacy of nineteenth century Hinduism which was influenced by sexual puritanism and by the protestant-rationalist rejection of 'idolatry'. The emphasis of neo-Hinduism is on 'spiritual experience',[5] and this is where he placed his own emphasis. But Avalon/Woodroffe's 'neo-tantrism' unites a high valuation of transcendent experience with affirmation of 'this world', of sense experience and of matter seen as permeated by *śakti*.

Doctrine or Practice?

Through the philosophy of *advaita vedānta* Avalon/Woodroffe positioned Tantra in the mainstream of Hindu life and thought. In a lecture in his series delivered to the Vivekananda Society ['Tantra Śāstra and Veda' SS:70–115], Woodroffe claimed that he had 'never properly understood the Vedānta' until he had studied the Tantras and their ritual [SS:80]. The purpose of the ritual was 'to gain realization' which he called *aparokṣa jñāna* (knowledge of the unseen). In another, shorter, address to the society [SS:457–62] he said that Sādhana brought 'knowledge to gain liberation', and distinguished this from intellectual or book knowledge: it was 'actual immediate experience' (*sāksātkāra*) [SS:458]. He called it 'spiritual experience' which one could only acquire by 'adopting some definite means' [SS:461–2].

This spiritual experience was 'Brahman-knowledge' – the truth, by actual experience, of the great upanishadic sayings: 'Thou art That', 'I am Brahman' [SS:81]. Thus the Śākta Tantra was 'the Sādhana Śāstra of Advaitavāda' [SS:80]. This was its true aim, not the acquiring of occult powers (*siddhi*) which could be an obstacle [SS:79–80]. Thus the tantric goal was the same as that of general neo-Hinduism, with the emphasis on spiritual experience rather than on *mokṣa*, Liberation, as such.[6]

Woodroffe frequently repeated the formula: 'Tantraśāstra is a Sādhana Śāstra', and moreover 'the chief Sādhana Śāstra for the orthodox Hindu' [SS:80], the vedic rites having mostly passed away [SS:458]. The term *sādhanā* covers yoga, meditation and ritual, and its aim is transformation of the practitioner. Woodroffe quoted his friend P.N. Mukhopādhyāy, who proclaimed that Tantra offered a practical system that 'not merely *argues* but *experiments*' [SS:66, 461]. He also cited 'a Tibetan Buddhist' (in fact Dawasamdup) who claimed that the Tantras were regarded more as scientific discovery than as revelation [SS:460–1]. He liked to reiterate that the test of truth is experiential:

> The authority of a Śāstra is determined by the question whether siddhi is gained through its provisions or not ... The test is that of Ayurveda. A medicine is a true one if it cures. *The Indian test for everything is actual experience.* It is from Samādhi that the ultimate proof of Advaitavāda is sought. [SS:142. Emphasis in original]

Avalon/Woodroffe makes this point so frequently and emphatically that it may have influenced later scholars to restrict definitions of Tantra to its ritual or *sādhanā* and to deny the significance of distinct doctrines. Agehananda Bharati defined Tantra as 'psycho-experimental speculation' and denied that there was any tantric philosophy 'apart from Hindu or Buddhist philosophy, or to be more specific, from Vedāntic or Māhāyāna Buddhism'.[7] While it may be true in general that 'what defines Tantra is practice (*sādhanā*) rather than thought',[8] as Padoux has pointed out 'there is no religious or 'magic' practice that does not reflect an ideology.[9] Without the specific doctrinal emphasis that underlies them, there would be no point in the distinctive elements of tantric *sādhanā*.

It is easy to quote statements from the unsystematic Avalon/Woodroffe works out of context. That the Tantras presented no significant departure in doctrine but merely an innovative form of *sādhanā*, is an apologetic point, aimed at establishing their orthodoxy before an audience and a readership that would have been inclined to be suspicious of Tantra. Woodroffe devoted many pages of his lectures to the Vivekananda Society to the doctrinal conformity of Tantra with the rest of Hinduism, by which he meant primarily that it was non-dualist but also that it shared many other essential beliefs [SS:89–92]. But even in the lecture on 'Tantra Śāstra and Veda' there are suggestions of doctrines that he found specifically in the Tantras: the 'subtle philosophy' that a friend had written about, which was an exception to his statement that nothing entirely new was to be found in the Tantras [SS:81]; the 'philosophical and religious aspect' which he found personally important [SS:79]; the 'essential concepts' which Louis de la Vallée Poussin was praised for finding to be 'of a metaphysical and subtle character' [SS:77]; and his own discovery that: 'the Tantras contained a remarkable philosophic presentment of religious teaching, profoundly applied in a ritual of psychological worth' [ibid].

In the second edition of *Shakti and Shākta*, Woodroffe quoted a letter he had received from Sivacandra Vidyarnava just before the guru's death. Philosophy (*darśana*) declared Sivacandra, was an integral aspect of the Tantra Śāstra, but 'it is scattered through the Tantrik treatises and is dealt with, as occasion arises, in connection with Śādhana and Siddhi'. Woodroffe reveals here that he had suggested to Sivacandra that he should write a third volume of his book *Tantratattva*, concentrating on these doctrines, but the guru died before this project could begin. The quote from Sivacandra's letter continues:

> Could ... such parts be collected and arranged, according to the principles of the subject-matter, they would form a vast system of philosophy wonderful, divine, lasting, true, and carrying conviction to men. As a Philosophy it is at the head of all others.' [SS:16]

Woodroffe agrees with him: 'I think that those with knowledge and understanding ... will allow that it contains a profoundly conceived doctrine, wonderfully worked out in practice' [SS:17]. It seems he would have agreed with Padoux's point about ritual and doctrine being closely intertwined.

Tantra and Veda

Even so, Woodroffe devoted a large part of the lecture on 'Tantra Śāstra and Veda', to assuring his listeners and readers that doctrinally the Tantras were in accord with 'Veda'. He cited numerous references from the Tantras to show that these texts claimed to be based on 'Veda' [SS:85–7], and that they regarded themselves as the expression of vedic truth that was suitable for the *kāli yuga* [SS:90].

While appearing to relate to history, the question of whether the Tantras stood in the tradition of the Vedas really concerned questions of authority, authenticity, and morality. Through the process of 'exotericization' described in the last chapter, deities and scriptures which were once classed as 'tantric' became '*vaidik*', in the sense that their followers conformed to *varṇāśrama dharma* and avoided practices considered impure or immoral. Just as the terms 'Tantra' and 'tantric' are rather ambiguous in scope, so 'Veda' and 'vedic' do not necessarily refer strictly to the contents of texts. For Woodroffe's listeners and readers in India, the word *vaidik* was synonymous with orthodoxy in doctrine and practice and social respectability. To insist that the Tantras were opposed to the Vedas was to declare them heterodox. A letter from a reader which will be discussed in the next chapter, shows how one member of the public protested over an implication that the twenty-eight major *Śaiva Āgamas* were non-vedic.

Woodroffe brings out in his lecture that by 'Vedic' was meant first and foremost conformity with *advaita vedānta*, with upanishadic monism. (See SS:85–8 in which he declares (p. 87) 'Advaitavedānta is the whole day and life of the Śākta Sādhaka.') He interprets 'Veda' in the abstract sense of knowledge or 'ultimately Spiritual Experience' [SS:81]. Conformity with *advaita vedānta* seems in itself to provide reassurance to his readers that tantric practice is not immoral, as when he defends the *pañcatattva* by declaring that it is a practical application of *advaitavāda* [SS:99–100].

Another line of 'defence' against the 'charges' [SS:99] of heterodoxy or immorality (the two being equated) was to draw parallels between tantric rituals and vedic ones, pointing out that animal sacrifice, consumption of alcohol, and even *maithuna* can be found in the Vedas and Brahmanas. [See Brajalal Mukherji's appendix SS:103ff].

Questions over the actual historical origins of the Tantra Śāstra and of Śāktism are brushed aside in this lecture [SS:70]. Woodroffe himself seems personally to have accepted the theory favoured by most western orientalists that these were 'non-Aryan'; but he was perhaps aware that this would not be welcome to some of his Indian readers or teachers, especially to tantric 'insiders'. We shall see below how he tackled this issue, in another lecture belonging to the same period.

Tantra and Śāktism

When Avalon did use the word 'Tantra' in his writings he usually qualified it by writing of 'the Śākta Tantra'. We have seen that he did this, not in order to associate the two terms but rather the reverse. We have seen in chapter 7 how for most orientalists the identification of Tantra with 'extreme Śāktism' tended to increase the notoriety of both. The issue of whether Tantrism and Śāktism are always to be identified with each other is a complex one,[10] and Avalon/Woodroffe was not really concerned with it. His aim was to distance what he called *śaktivāda* or the Religion of the Śāktas, from the notoriety implied by the word 'Tantra', while still defending the distinct ritual and doctrinal elements which are commonly associated with the Tantras. After Avalon scholars were more inclined to distinguish Tantrism from Śāktism in the sense of worship of the Goddess *per se.*[11]

The most famous example of a śākta devotee is of course Ramakrishna, the saintly *bhakta* of Kālī. Kālī is very much a tantric divinity, being the most important of the ferocious forms of the Goddess. Her gruesome iconography did not prevent her from being also perceived as a benevolent mother and saviouress. Ramakrishna is often classed as a tantric as well as a śākta saint because of his devotion to Kālī and because he practised tantric *sādhanā* for a time with a female guru, his *bhairavī.* There is a suggestion, however, that this tantric experiment proved distasteful to the young Ramakrishna leading to his strong condemnation of Tantra later on.[12] Ramakrishna declared that his exploration of Tantra was motivated by the same quest which led him into exploring other forms of '*sādhanā*' including versions of Christian and Islamic devotion. His purpose was to prove the equal validity of all paths to the goal of *samādhi.* This is more of a neo-vedāntic attitude than a traditional śākta or tantric one.

Another famous example of a śākta saint, whose memory was very much alive at Woodroffe's time, is the eighteenth century poet Rāmprasād Sen. Although he too placed devotion above ritual as the highest means to approach the deity, he is usually classed as a Tantric.[13] For an example of someone who was both a śākta devotee and also very definitely a tantric ritualist, we can turn to Sivacandra Vidyarnava himself. Sivacandra displays in his *Tantratattva* all the characteristics of a fervent *bhakta* saint in the mould of Ramakrishna, and this is also how he is portrayed in his biography by Pal. But Sivacandra was also very particular as to the importance of ritual and he was known for his performance of elaborate tantric *pūjās*. He also practised *sādhanā* in the cremation grounds.

THE RELIGION OF THE ŚĀKTAS

As for Woodroffe himself, he was strongly attracted by the idea of the feminine aspect of God, and we have seen that this may have been what first aroused his interest in Tantra. He talked specifically about Śāktism to the Howrah Literary Association in 1917 in a lecture which subsequently gave its name to his book ['*Shakti and Shākta*' SS:136–88]: '. . . a beautiful and tender concept of the Śāktas is the *Motherhood of God*' he says [SS:170] and he shows how the Goddess's fearsome and benevolent aspects can be integrated:

> The Divine Mother first appears in and as Her worshipper's earthly mother, then as his wife; thirdly as Kālikā, She reveals Herself in old age, disease and death . . . Lastly She takes to herself the dead body in the fierce tongues of flame which light the funeral pyre. [SS:171]

According to the Ghose family, Woodroffe displayed a deep personal devotion to The Mother: they said he would not even wear sandals which had writing on them, because that required treading upon letters, Her symbols. However, such emotions do not come over in his writings where his interest seems purely intellectual and philosophical. Socially he considered that worship of the feminine aspect of divinity could promote progressive attitudes to women:

> A high worship therefore which can be offered to the Mother today consists in getting rid of abuses which have neither the authority of ancient Śāstra, nor of modern social science and to honour, cherish, educate and advance women (Śakti) [SS:172]'

Striyo devās striyaḥ prāṇaḥ' he quoted – the same quotation as in his strongly worded speech to the Mahākālī Pathśāla.[14] Yet here he proceeds in the following pages to declaim against associating Śāktism with what he calls 'sociology which is concerned with gross matter'; and he eventually manoeuvres himself into making a sweeping statement that: 'The doctrine of Śakti has no more to do with "Feminism" than it has to do with "old age pensions" or any other sociological movement of the day' [SS:174]. The reason however is that he has been stung by criticism from a reviewer – an 'American Orientalist critic' who had called tantric philosophy 'religious feminism run mad' [SS:173].[15] Reaction to his critic has pushed him into an extreme position that he may not have wanted to stand by.

In this lecture the passage about 'Feminism' is followed by a succinct summary of five 'characteristic features' of the religion of the Śāktas:

> The characteristic features of Śākta-dharma are thus its Monism; its concept of the Motherhood of God; its unsectarian spirit and provisions for Śūdras and women, to the latter of whom it renders high honour, recognising that they may be even Gurus; and lastly its Sādhana skilfully designed to realise its teachings. [SS:174]

Although here Woodroffe carefully avoids the word 'Tantra', the Sādhana of which he writes is of course tantric *sādhanā*, presented as the spiritual practice of a doctrine called '*Śākta dharma*.' His fourth point ('provisions for Śudras and women') is the closest Woodroffe comes to claiming social egalitarianism as a virtue of tantric tradition. Woodroffe's preceptor

Sivacandra was a Brahmin, and Woodroffe seems to have little contact with, and no preception of, low-caste people. So although elsewhere he praised Tantra for providing rites 'even for the lowest castes' [SS:172; PT/1 p. 77–8] he did not place emphasis on this or draw social implications from it. His third point, what he saw as Tantra's unsectarian spirit is something which certainly was important to him personally. Woodroffe comes over as someone who placed a high value on tolerance in religious matters (perhaps a reaction to his father's ardent Catholicism, or his own inheritance from Lord Petre?) However, he possibly idealised śākta Tantrism in this respect. We sometimes see him toning down instances of intolerance among his collaborators, and he almost apologises for the strong tone of parts of Sivacandra's work.[16]

It is the first and last features of his list to which he gives most attention: the Śākta Tantra's conformity with *advaita* philosophy and the psychological value of its *sādhanā* as a means to achieving the unitary experience which is the proof of that doctrine. If this appeared to eliminate differences between Tantra and other forms of Hinduism, this was a matter of emphasis.

Origins: Woodroffe's historical hypothesis

In this same lecture Woodroffe attempted to deal with the question of the historical origin of Śāktism despite Arthur Avalon's avowed contempt for orientalist preoccupation with such matters – something which might have reflected the feelings of Atal Bihari Ghose.[17] He states:

> For when we throw our minds back upon the history of this worship we see stretching away into the remote and fading past the figure of the Mighty Mother of Nature, most ancient among the ancients; the Ādyā Śakti, the Dusk Divinity, many breasted, crowned with towers whose veil is never lifted, Isis . . . Kālī, Hathor . . . [SS:137].[18]

In what was perhaps a tactful manner, Woodroffe has emphasised the attraction and romance for him of the ancient lineage and universality of the Goddess. Later in the lecture he argues for the 'non-Aryan' or pre-vedic origin not only of Śāktism but for much of Tantra also.

As he often did, he used material from a book he had been reading: this time by an obscure writer called Edward Sellon who had drawn comparisons between various Hindu sects and the mystery cults of European antiquity.[19] Sellon's interest as well as his language was typically 'orientalist' (in Said's sense): his book places the śākta cults, as it were, in a museum alongside the works of European classical and other ancient art he often refers to. For Woodroffe by contrast it is the parallels with antiquity which serve to add lustre to the modern living cult, and he appears impressed and proud of the ancient roots of Śakti-worship in the passage just quoted.

Woodroffe presents his historical thesis in a careful way, aware no doubt that to argue that the tantric tradition had a separate origin from the vedic was not merely a question of history, but affected the authenticity of the texts. However, the idea he wanted to counteract was that the Tantras were of recent origin. As was so often the case, the *pañcatattva* was the focus of the problem. Woodroffe suggests:

> Perhaps the *Pañcatattva* Ritual followed by some of the adherents of the Tantras is one of the main causes which have operated in some quarters against acceptance of the authority of these Scriptures and as such responsible for the notion that the worship is modern. [SS:139]

This is the crux of the matter, as far as 'insiders' were concerned, for here 'modern' equals not only 'unauthoritative' but also 'degraded'. It is in this context that Woodroffe draws parallels between tantric rituals and practices to be found in the Vedas themselves:

> If the subject be studied it will, I think, be found that ... those worshippers who practise these rites are (except possibly as to Maithuna) the continuators of very ancient practices which had their counterparts in the earlier Vaidikācāra. [ibid]

The qualifying phrase in brackets was not present in the first edition. But it seems that before long Woodroffe and Ghose had discovered another way around the problem of *maithuna* – the suggestion that it might be 'foreign' and imported from China or Tibet [SS:140], a theory discussed in three chapters including one entitled 'Cinācāra' which were added in the second edition of *Shakti and Shakta* [DP chapters 8,9,11].

Woodroffe next goes on to discuss questions of age and authenticity. While the western orientalist and 'outsider' might approach – or claim to approach – questions of date and authorship from a purely factual historical point of view, Woodroffe recognised that this was not what concerned 'insiders'. What he does is to attempt a reconciliation between the historian and the believer: first he distinguishes between the date of a written manuscript and the age of the tradition which informs it [SS:140] then he argues against a too literal interpretation of authorship [SS:141]. Finally he reiterates his point that the proof of authenticity is experiential and practical: 'The authority of a Śāstra is determined by the question whether *Siddhi* is gained through its provisions or not' [SS:141–2]. Given this, and a 'spiritual' and non-literal definition of inspiration, Woodroffe suggests that the authority of a scripture does not need to be affected by historical questions about its date. 'This is the way in which the question of age and authority is looked at on Indian principles,' he concludes [SS:142]. In fact it is not traditional. Woodroffe here is devising an imaginative method of dealing with the question of scriptural authority in the light of orientalist uses of history.

At SS:145–8 Woodroffe develops a theory of the historical origins of Tantra, but the argument is a curious one. He cites an obscure reference to show that followers of the class of tantric texts called *yāmala* claimed that their tradition actually *preceded* the Vedas: each of the four Vedas being said to have developed out of one of the four *yāmalas* [SS:148][20]; and he proceeds to take this literally. He has just drawn attention to what he calls a 'double framework' in the body of Hinduism whereby the tantric tradition mirrors the vedic one in every sphere: in scriptures, rituals, initiations and mantras, even in medicine and law there were tantric equivalents to vedic forms [SS:147]. From these two points he draws out his hypothesis that Tantra was in fact a separate religion, distinct from the vedic one, and possibly older as well:

> . . . it indicates that there were originally two sources of religion one of which (possibly in some respects the older) incorporated parts of, and in time largely superseded the other. And this is what the "Tāntriks" impliedly allege in their views as to the relation of the four Vedas and Āgamas [SS:148]

He goes on to present the theory of the non-vedic or non-aryan origin of Tantra and the subsequent synthesis that took place, in which it was mostly the vedic rituals which were superseded. He concludes by suggesting that in the history of Tantra . . .

> the beliefs and practices *of the Soil* have been upheld until today against the incoming cults of those "Āryas" who followed the Vaidik rites and who in their turn influenced the various religious communities without the Vaidik fold [SS:149. Emphasis added]

So the theory of the non-aryan origin of much of present-day Hinduism[21] and the eclipse of the vedic religion through the influence of non-vedic cults has been placed before the 'insiders' in a tactful way, carefully pinning his theory onto a tantric textual source. He comes to a completely different conclusion to his theory, however, from those European orientalists who used such ideas to portray later Hinduism as degenerate. For significantly, here the great 'Aryas' are dethroned and the phrase 'of the soil' suggests, at least, the possibility of valuing the primitive, something which became more fashionable later on, especially with historians of a Marxist slant.[22]

That Woodroffe was here putting forward his own opinion and not that of any of his collaborators, is suggested by the tentative tone which creeps into his writing: 'These are speculations to which I do not definitely commit myself' [SS:148]. The theory, or hypothesis, contradicts the assertion that Tantra follows in the tradition of Veda which is put forward in most other portions of the Avalon/Woodroffe writings. For example, the new first chapter in the second and subsequent editions of *Shakti and Shākta* placed the 'religion of the Śāktas' within what is called 'Bhārata

Dharma' which alongside Buddhism and Jainism is an 'Aryan religion (Ārya Dharma)' [SS:1,9]. This as we have seen was also the position in *Is India Civilized?*.

ON RITUAL

Defending the 'Indefensible': the *Pañcatattva*

When Woodroffe declared that its *sādhanā* was the most valuable aspect of Tantra, he did not claim to refer to the *pañcatattva*; he meant all other aspects of tantric practice – *dhyāna*, *mantra*, ritual worship with images and *yantras*, yoga. While privately he seems to have accepted the sexual ritual, at least within marriage, publicly his attitude was a mixture of denial and defensiveness. He considered that it was the *pañcatattva* which deprived 'Tantraśāstra' of authenticity in the opinion of the public, and he returns to the theme repeatedly as if it was a nuisance to him that would not go away:

> The notoriety of the Śākta Pañcatattva ritual with wine and women has thrown into the shade ... every other [topic] including the valuable philosophical presentment of Vedānta contained in the *Śākta Tantra* ... It is necessary ... to at least touch on the matter because as against everything one says about the Tantra, there is raised the express or implied query "That may be all very well. But what about the infamous Pañcamakāra"? Anything said in favour of the Śāstra is thus discounted in advance. [SS:590]

These words occur at the beginning of a chapter devoted to the rite in *Shakti and Shākta* [SS:590–648]. Originally this was part of the previous chapter on 'Śākta Sādhana' [SS:523–89] and was one of the series of lectures of 1917–18 to the Vivekananda Society. Therefore, like the two magazine articles discussed in the last chapter, that dealt with the negative images evoked by the word 'Tantra', it would have been aimed at an audience composed mostly of middle class English educated followers of the Swami. It is obvious that Woodroffe found difficulty in defending the tantric ritual that appeared to give religious sanction to intemperance and sexual immorality. His arguments can seem spurious, even sometimes ludicrous,[23] and his attempts to justify self-contradictory. Hence he can write in one and the same chapter: 'It is Śiva in the form of the universe who enjoys, and the manifested bliss is a limited form of that Supreme Bliss' [SS:626] and in another place of eradicating 'poison': 'Poison is the antidote to poison. This is the right treatment for those who long for drink or lust after women' [SS:632]. (It must be admitted however that both these strands of argument are to be found in the texts themselves.) On the one hand he defends the *pañcatattva* by declaring its purpose to be a cure for lust: an attempt to control what he calls the 'physical appetites' not by 'a forced abstention but a regulated use' [SS:626]. On the other hand, he reassures us that the rite is disappearing and is of historical interest only, 'with other ritual customs of a past age' [SS:647].

The point, when he eventually comes to it, is that the *pañcatattva* or *pañca makāra* far from being marginal was, according to the texts, essential for worship of Śakti [SS:603]. Even the "respectable" *mahānirvāṇa tantra* says:

> O Ādya! the five essential Elements in the worship of Śakti have been prescribed to be Wine, Meat, Fish, parched Grain, and the Union of man with woman.
>
> The worship of Śakti without these five elements is but the practice of evil magic. That Siddhi which is the object of Sādhana is never attained thereby . . . [MNT:V:22–3, translated GLb p. 86]

This text deals with the five elements of the ritual by analogy to the five elements of nature, thus making them symbols for the offering of the universe to the Goddess in a rather beautiful passage paraphrased by Woodroffe [SS:603]. Continuing to follow the text he points out that the five were not always offered literally. Only the *vīra*, the 'hero', the second grade of initiate was considered fit for them. He lists some of the substitutes that can be offered by the *paśu*, the initiate in the lowest grade who is not considered spiritually strong enough for the literal *tattvas* [SS:608]. On the other hand for the *divya*, the highest grade, they were understood symbolically, as inner yogic operations or as kinds of spiritual knowledge [SS:606–7].

The quotations from *mahānirvāṇa tantra* were added in the second edition of *Shakti and Shākta*, in which there were many interpolations. The original lecture as printed in the first edition was more straightforward [SS(1):143–68]. The section concerning the *pañcatattva* began by distinguishing between what Woodroffe calls 'general principles' and their 'particular application' [SS(1):158, DP:590–1]. The principle he explains as regulation of the 'physical appetites of man' by the tantric method which was anti-ascetic: by transforming the feelings and attitudes (*bhāva*) of the *paśu* (the ordinary person) into those of the *vīra* (the 'hero'). The latter experiences all his actions as those of Śiva because he has transcended, or is schooling himself to transcend duality; he knows 'that it is the One Śiva who appears in the form of the multitude of men and who acts, suffers and enjoys through them' and Śiva is 'Bliss itself'. Thus 'It is a fact that right sexual union may, if associated with meditation and ritual, be the means towards attainment of liberation' [SS (1):160; DP:628].[24] In the same way the *vīra* takes wine knowing that he is one with it: 'I myself offer . . . to myself' [ibid]. This is what Woodroffe had previously called 'a practical application of *advaita*' [DP:99–100]. (The other three elements of the rite, not presenting the same degree of difficulty, are mentioned only briefly.)

The 'notions of the Paśu' are described as the reverse of those of the *vīra*; they are dualistic and so the *paśu* makes a distinction between 'God' and 'His handiwork' [SS(1):160; DP:629]. Hence he has feelings of shame and considers that his 'natural functions' of eating, drinking and sex must be kept apart from his religious observance. Not so the *vīra* or true Tantric.

Woodroffe considers the practice (the 'application') of less interest and importance than the principle [SS (1):161, DP:629]. No doubt the principle alone provided fewer problems. Once again, he appeals to the Vedas, pointing out that meat and alcohol once had a place in vedic rituals but were subsequently excluded under Buddhist influence and that Tantrics were therefore simply following an earlier tradition [SS (1):161; DP:630]. He then claimed that the ritual was being domesticated in modern times. He hints: 'It is capable of application according to the modern spirit without recourse to Chakras and their ritual details in the ordinary daily life of the householder within the bounds of his Dharmashāstra' [ibid].

However, Woodroffe could not altogether deny what he called the 'antinomian' aspects of tantric practice: that the partner in the sexual ritual was often not the practitioner's wife but 'the wife of another' (*parakiya*) and that the highest grade of Kaula was one who was free to act according to his own will (*svecchācāri*) – ie. that he was said to be above good and evil and social conventions [SS (1):161, DP:619, 624]. Here Woodroffe does not attempt to justify but resorts to comparative material to draw parallels with 'antinomian' sects in the history of European religion [SS (1):164–6; DP:633–42]. He admits that in India, as well as Europe, such doctrines sometimes led to 'abuses', but quickly balances this concession by condemning the evils of contemporary western society, and claiming that the 'abuses' by Tantrics had in any case been exaggerated in order to make them a weapon with which to attack Indian religion [SS(1):165–6; DP:644–5]. He concluded his lecture however by cautiously distancing himself from the *pañcatattva*:

> All this again is not to say that I counsel the acceptance of any such extreme theories or practice ... It is necessary for me to so guard myself because those who cannot judge with detachment are prone to think that others who deal fairly and dispassionately with any doctrine or practice are necessarily its adherents and the counsellors of it to others. [SS(1):166–7; DP:646]

Finally he re-asserted that the true principle of Tantra is self-control, and that the true *vīra* is one 'who has controlled his passions ... has sacrificed lust and all other passions' [SS(1):167; DP:648].

In the second edition many interpolations and re-arrangements of the material served to highlight the inconsistencies. While adding considerably to the comparative material from European antinominianism Woodroffe also tried to distance Indian Tantra from such movements and to declare that it was anti-libertarian. Thus the rather puritanical tone of most of the chapter was enhanced. What could be called the homeopathic theory of the *pañcatattva* – alluded to above – is given more emphasis: the idea that 'Poison is the antidote to poison'. This passage is part of a quotation from Pandit Jaganmohan Tarkālankāra's notes to the *mahānirvāṇa tantra*, and thus were a nineteenth century interpretation of a modern text [DP:631–2]. Although such arguments were also traditional and are to be found in the much older *kulārṇava tantra* which Woodroffe also quotes in this context, in the latter text there are other passages (alluded to at SS:616) which carry a very different flavour. His treatment of these will be discussed in the next chapter in the context of Woodroffe's relationship to the texts.

If Woodroffe's arguments sometimes appear spurious, they are no more or less so than arguments put forward in the texts themselves to justify a ritual which was already old when many of them were written. Woodroffe's most perceptive comment is that: 'The true Sādhaka does not perform the ritual for the purpose of drinking wine . . . but drinks wine in order that he may perform the ritual' [DP:613]. The same would be taken to apply to sexual intercourse. The very fact that substitutes for the literal five *tattvas* were sometimes prescribed reveals the intrinsic importance of the rite itself.

In other places in his writings, Woodroffe shows that whatever ambiguous feelings he may have had about the practice of the *pañcatattva*, he appreciated the anti-ascetic, incarnational ethic he could draw from it. He presented affirmation of the reality of the world and of the senses as one of the great advantages of *śaktivāda*. By implication this includes affirmation of sexuality, as opposed to the position of the celibate 'renouncer'. Both Vivekananda and his master Ramakrishna had placed a higher value on celibacy than on the life of the married householder.[25]

The *vīra* or true Tantric is not afraid of the senses or of matter, or of this world. To contemporary western society this is not a particularly significant achievement, since the opposite pole – Renunciation – has been removed from the scales. In the context of a society which placed a high value on asceticism and distrusted the senses because they were regarded as illusory, and the source of spiritually dangerous desires, the *vīra's* 'heroism' becomes more apparent as a genuine union of opposites. In a short chapter called 'Matter and Consciousness' Woodroffe writes of the *vīra* in idealized terms with overtones of western occultism:

> The Vīra or heroic Sādhaka does not shun the world from fear of it. But he holds it in his grasp and wrests from it its secret. Realizing it at length as Consciousness the world of matter ceases to be an object of desire. Escaping from the unconscious drifting of humanity which has not yet realized itself, He is the illumined master of himself, whether developing all his powers, or seeking liberation at his will. [SS:347]

Despite the apparently 'puritanical' tone of most of this chapter. Woodroffe's work contained sufficiently differing messages for later commentators to choose what to take from it. It is interesting to see how Heinrich Zimmer uses passages quoted from Woodroffe in his own account of Tantrism. Zimmer focuses on the tension between 'renunciation' and 'enjoyment' and places 'Tantra' (which he identifies with 'nirvana') in a position transcending these opposites. But Zimmer's transcendence actually amounts to the abolition of the polar tension. The tantric goal, he writes, is to 'experience ... the essential non-existence of the antagonistic polarity – its vanishing away, its nirvana'. Release from the 'world illusion' comes from its 'full enjoyment' and the *vīra* overcomes the passions by 'embracing them'.[26]

It is not really any transcendence of upanishadic asceticism which lies behind this interpretation, but the post-Freudian dialectic of inhibition – liberation, whose atmosphere permeates Zimmer's paper. Woodroffe had heard of the psychology of the unconscious [see eg. WAP p. 104–5], but no more than that: it had not influenced him. Read against a post-Freudian discourse, quotations from Woodroffe could be taken to give subtle permission for an abandonment of inhibition which he himself would not have recognised. It was not far from here to Bhagavan Rajneesh.[27]

Tantra and Roman Catholicism

In the chapter on the *pañcatattva* a specific comparison is made between the wine and *mudrā* (grain) of the *pañcatattva* with the bread and wine of the Christian Eucharist [DP:613]. In the first edition the word 'sacrament' is actually used [SS(1):163]. Elsewhere Avalon had written: 'Tantrik Hinduism is in its more common aspect, essentially of a sacramental and ritualistic character' [PT/1:20]. This added to its difficulties in the eyes of those influenced by Protestantism, which was true of most of those who had introduced English education to India [ibid].

There can be little doubt that his Roman Catholic education prepared Woodroffe to envision Tantra as a mystical religion conveyed through ritual and imagery, and that this placed him at a distance from writers who were influenced by protestant and/or rationalist prejudices against 'idolatry'. He pointed out that the catholic tradition of devotion to Mary the Mother of God caused Vivekananda to recognize Italian Catholics as Śāktas [SS:176].[28] Despite her often gruesome imagery the tantric Goddess can be seen as a tender Mother, while Our Lady in Catholicism, though not strictly divine, often appears to be treated as such in practice. To Protestants on the other hand, this too would be dismissed as polytheism or paganism.

Woodroffe expressly compares the outer forms of tantric practice to the catholic ritual which he calls *sādhanā*: 'Thus amongst Christians, the Catholic Church, like Hinduism, has a full and potent Sādhana in its sacraments . . .' There follows here a long and interesting list of external ritual similarities [SS:175–6], which he concludes by drawing a specific parallel between the Christian sacrament and the wine of the tantric rite:

> In the Eucharist the bread and wine are the body and blood of Christ appearing under the form or "accidents" of those material substances; so also Tārā is Dravamayī, that is, the "Saviour in liquid form". [SS:176]

The point he claims to make here is simply that eating and drinking during ritual are not inconsistent with the 'dignity' of worship, 'since Christ instituted his sacrament at a meal'. Woodroffe holds back from identifying the two: 'Whilst however the outward forms in this case are similar, the inner meaning is different'. With regard to Our Lady, he makes a slightly odd use of Hindu terminology to express the differences between Śāktism and Catholicism: 'Whilst, however, the Blessed Virgin evokes devotion as warm as that which is here paid to Devi, she is not Devi for she is not God but a creature selected as the vehicle of His incarnation (Avatāra)' [SS:176].[29]

We can see that Woodroffe does not allow himself to be carried away by comparisons at a superficial level. Yet clearly for him Catholicism and Hinduism stand together on one side of a religious divide, while Protestantism is placed on the other – and he affirms the former strongly:

> It is because of its powerful sacraments and disciplines that in the West the Catholic Church has survived to this day, holding firm upon its "Rock" amid the dissolving sects, born of what is called the "Reform" . . . All things survive by virtue of the truth in them. The particular truth to which I here refer is that a faith cannot be maintained by mere hymn-singing and pious addresses. For this reason too Hinduism has survived. [SS:177]

Ritual in Tantra however occupies a very different place from the one it occupies in the Catholic Church, which sees its sacraments as universal and absolute. In another chapter Woodroffe describes the 'Brahmanic' position as mid-way between the catholic and the protestant, able to acknowledge the value of both: that is, recognizing both the need for ritual and the necessity for its transcendence at higher levels of spiritual discipline.

> Its [Brahmanism's] view is that all men need Ritual, but in varying degree and various kinds, until they are Siddha, that is, until they have achieved the end which Ritual is designed to secure. [SS:436]

Ritual is an *art* [SS:435, 464], and a psychological tool which is described in a quasi-scientific way which is closer to western Occultism than to Christianity. The Mind is treated as a quasi-physical force which can be shaped by, and can exert power through, concentration on prescribed images (*dhyāna*). Most important of all, rituals and the images associated with them are *not* universal: choice can be made between them, according to the spiritual capacity of the practitioner, as to their usefulness as different methods of achieving the goal of spiritual knowledge. This is not in accord with the Catholic Church's claims for its sacraments. Nor is Avalon's assertion that each race must evolve the ritual forms suitable to it – which is an interpretation drawn out of the ancient brahmanical idea of a person having *adhikāra* for some rituals and not others.[30] It was mainly this notion of *adhikāra* that Woodroffe had in mind when he praised the tolerance of Hinduism, and especially of the Śākta Tantra, for making allowances for individual psychological and racial differences. 'One goal may be reached by many paths. What is the path in any particular case depends on considerations of personal capacity and temperament, race and faith.' [SS:66] The idea of certain people having *adhikāra* for certain rituals also played a useful role in defending the *pañcatattva*, as it could be argued that the rite is only enjoined on those to whom it is psychologically and spiritually suited. In chapter 6 we were shown Woodroffe making use of this idea to justify his own non-participation in *vāmācāra*.

Woodroffe stated that 'Christianity is dualism' [GOL p. 5] in a passage where he pointed to the similarities and differences between Christian and Hindu-tantric doctrines of the Word. Unlike some neo-Vedantists he never obliterated differences in an attempt to produce a syncretistic system. Nevertheless like Vivekananda's neo-Vedanta, Avalon's 'neo-Tantra' is hegemonic. Christianity, being 'dualism', is subsumed within it as a valid but by implication lower religious stage leading towards the same goal as Hinduism – that of 'non-duality'. All rituals are relativised as they are subordinated to this end, which is defined as a state of mind or being, in non-dual terms as recognizing one's identity with Divinity, or transcendent Being [SS:467–8].

Tantra as Magic and Occultism

When Woodroffe described Tantra Śāstra as 'the Sādhana Śāstra of Advaitavāda' he declared its goal to be 'spiritual experience', Brahman-knowledge or *mokṣa*. He distinguished this from the acquisition of 'Powers' [SS:79] while admitting that tantric ritual magic, along with *vāmācāra* was one of the chief reasons for its unpopularity [SS:92]. There are similarities between Woodroffe's way of handling the magic of Tantra and his treatment of its sexuality. He universalises it [SS:95 'Magic is common to all early religions']; and points to its existence in the history of the West [ibid: the witchcraft trials of medieval Europe], and in the Vedas [SS:94 the *athārvaveda*]; he emphasises the good intentions of the texts which condemned magic for harmful ends [SS:92]. Last but not least there was the 'recrudescence today' in the West of renewed interest in magic in the more fashionable and scientifically respectable forms of modern Occultism and of interest in the paranormal [SS:95–7].

Woodroffe called Tantra 'the storehouse of Indian Occultism' [SS:79; SP:3]; and the traditional European Occultist and the Hindu Tantric do seem to have lived in similar worlds.[31] The two terms, 'Occultism' and 'Esotericism' are said to have been first used, in their modern sense, by the French 'Occultist' or magician Eliphas Levi (1810–1875); while 'Occultism' was first employed in English in 1881 by Alfred Sinnett, Madame Blavatsky's English disciple, who denoted by it the philosophy he claimed was taught to him by Theosophy's Masters.[32] Theosophy was the most influential of the nineteenth century esoteric organisations which claimed to have inherited an older tradition that included Gnosticism, Alchemy, and Jewish and Christian Cabala. 'Eastern' traditions of Hinduism and Buddhism were absorbed into the synthesis by Madame Blavatsky and Colonel Olcott, who founded the Theosophical Society in America in 1875 and first visited India in 1893. During the first decade of the twentieth century the Society grew into a strong international organisation and as we have seen, under Blavatsky's successor Annie Besant it played an influential role in Indian nationalism.[33] Other esoteric movements of the time were the Order of the Golden Dawn, to which Yeats belonged; and the Order of Oriental Templars (OTO) headed by the "infamous" Alisteir Crowley who borrowed from Tantra in his own systems of erotic magic.[34]

Woodroffe liked to quote from the *viśvasāra tantra*: 'What is here is elsewhere: what is not here is nowhere'.[35] He compared it with the Hermetic maxim: 'as above so below'. The famous saying from the Hermetic corpus refers to the occultist's world of analogical correspondences between the divine and human levels, uniting human beings, divinities and nature in a hierarchical order.[36] Woodroffe wrote:

> All occultism whether of East or West posits the principle that there is nothing in any one state or plane which is not in some other way, actual or potential, in another state or plane. [SS:276–7]

This applies to the doctrine of the *tattvas*, for these cosmic levels exist both without and within the individual, and each of the 'higher' *tattvas* contains within itself those 'lower' levels which succeed it.[37]

The quotation from *viśvasāra tantra* is also cited in *The Serpent Power*, in the chapter on 'Embodied Consciousness' dealing with the physiology of the *kuṇḍalinī* system. Here Avalon summarises the principles and purpose of tantric yoga: to raise and utilise in the practitioner divine powers that already reside within him:

> Man is a microcosm (Ksudra-Brāhmānda). The world is the macrocosm (Brāhmānda). There are numberless worlds, each of which is governed by its own Lords . . . In everything there is all that

> is in anything else. There is thus nothing in the universe which is not in the human body. . . . In fact, the body is a vast magazine of Power (Śakti) . . . The object of the Tāntrik rituals is to raise these various forms of power to their full expression. [SP:49–50]

This is consistent with the 'magical universe' of western Occultism, where:

> The universe is regarded as a human organism on a colossal scale and man as a copy of it in miniature. Man is also a miniature replica of God and so, by a process of mystically expanding himself, a man can become the sum total of all things, and the wielder of supreme power.[38]

This applies to Hindu Tantra as much as to western 'magic'. Seen from this point of view the Tantrics' *siddhis* or supernormal powers are seen not merely as a by-product of spiritual development but as its very essence, because they are a sign of the unveiling of the divine omnipotence which is inherent in the soul but obscured by ignorance [see SS:465]. Western Esotericism, Occultism or magic, like Hindu Tantra, represented the continuation of ancient, pre-secular ways of thought which some considered more holistic than modern consciousness.[39]

In the Avalon/Woodroffe books Occultism is presented 'scientifically' as the attempt to affect matter through thought. An essay on *mantra* which found its way in slightly differing form into *Shakti and Shākta*, *The Serpent Power* and *Garland of Letters* puts forward 'the power of Thought' as an explanation of the supernormal powers sought by Tantrics, as well as various paranormal phenomena which were currently arousing interest in the West:

> Thought-reading, thought-transference, hypnotic suggestion, magical projections . . . are becoming known and practised in the West . . . The occultist . . . will understand the Indian doctrine which regards thought like mind . . . as a Power or Śakti; something therefore, very real and creative by which man can accomplish things for himself and others. [SS:495]

In the same passage 'the Orientalist and Missionary' are depicted as people who misrepresent Indian teaching because they 'know nothing of Occultism.'[40]

Shakti and Shākta contains several references to an offshoot of American Christian Science called 'New Thought' which was first expounded by Dr Heber Newton in a series of articles in the New York journal *Mind*, and aroused interest among followers of neo-Vedanta.[41] Woodroffe may have known the works of the pseudonymous Yogi Ramacharaka who wrote on Hindu Yoga but seems to have been a western practitioner of New Thought.[42] Woodroffe stated: '"New Thought" as it is called and kindred movements are a form of Mantravidyā' [SS:79].[43] Directed mainly towards healing, the New Thought taught that Universal Mind is immanent in everything in varying degrees and that the universe is its expression – an idea which echoed śākta doctrine as Woodroffe presented it 'scientifically' (see below). This Mind-power was present in Man, who by the exercise of his 'will and imaging faculties' could transform not only his character but his environment and physical health.[44] The New Thought, however, did not have a supernatural dimension, and though Woodroffe seems to bracket it with Western occultism [SS:79] this was probably not strictly accurate.

Three chapters of *Shakti and Shākta* are devoted specifically to ritual other than the *pañcatattva* [DP chapters 21, 23, 26] and a fourth to the philosophy of *mantra* [chapter 24], indicating the importance of the subject to Woodroffe. The chapter on 'The Psychology of Hindu Religious Ritual' [SS:463–82] originated in a lecture delivered in England in 1925. The 'psychology' is occultism, set in a framework of Śiva-Śakti metaphysics, while ritual is an art: 'the Art both of Religion and Magic' [SS:464].

The primacy of consciousness and the power of thought to affect matter are the underlying theme of the lecture. Thought itself is a force (*cit-śakti*) which can be shaped and directed by concentration on certain objects – outer and inward images (*yantra* and *dhyāna*) and *mantras* – with which the practitioner identifies himself [SS:471–2].[45] In this view, magic – defined as the development of super*normal* rather than super*natural* power [SS:469] – is inherently possible [SS:470: 'Mind-Rays, the Hindus would say . . . are more powerful than X-Rays']; but belongs to the dualistic world which is to be transcended [SS:468]. Those forms of Sādhana defined as specifically 'religious', however, go beyond this: there the aim is to be 'raised from Limited to Perfect experience', and this includes a moral dimension. Such Sādhana Woodroffe defines as 'a spiritual effort to achieve a moral and spiritual aim, though it may also seek material blessings from the Divinity worshipped' [SS:469]. Thus while praising Occultism, Woodroffe also declared it should be transcended.

The word 'Psychology' in the title attempts to present the subject in a scientific light. Of tantric ritual Arthur Avalon had written:

> The Tantra further claims not only to be practical . . . but also to be fundamentally rational . . . The virtue of its general method . . . is inherent in the mental states induced by dhyāna and other physical and mental processes . . . chiefly explained by the fact that as at base all existence is of the nature of mind, the transformation of mind is the transformation of existence itself. [PT/1:80]

By presenting tantric *sādhanā* as a system founded on psychological principles (albeit of an occult psychology) it could be described as 'rational'

– a means by which Theosophists also justified their beliefs and practices in contrast to the reliance on faith of conventional Christianity.

Woodroffe and Sivacandra on the Psychology of Imagery

Woodroffe's ideas about ritual reflect the teaching of Sivacandra Vidyarnava in his *Tantratattva*, in which he defended Tantra against modernizing critics of traditional Hinduism, among whom it was seen as 'idolatrous' because of its emphasis on ritual [PT/1:13, 17]. Arthur Avalon supported Sivachandra's vigorous attack on liberal protestant and rationalist attitudes which led to a rejection of the outward forms of religion [PT/1:24]. Sivacandra criticised religious outlooks which rejected the senses and insisted that it is not possible to worship a deity that has no form or attributes [PT/1:222]. He devotes much of his book to explaining the function of *mantra, dhyāna* and other ritual elements in tantric practice. He does so from a psychological stance in that his reference-point is the working of the human mind, according to Hindu theories. Although this enabled tantric ritual to be portrayed as rational, the term 'psychological' should not be taken to imply that Sivachandra taught that the forms of tantric deities had no existence outside human consciousness. On the contrary, he devoted a large part of his discussion to counteracting just this idea among Brahmos and other modernizers.[46] The argument turned on the interpretation of a verse from the *kulārṇava tantra*: a verse which was taken by his opponents to mean that 'forms have been imagined by Sādhakas in relation to Brahman', but which Sivachandra insisted meant the exact opposite: ie. that Brahman Himself builds forms (of Himself) for the benefit of Sādhakas.[47] In other words, the imagery through which deities are contemplated is not arbitrary or subjective, but given by the Deity Himself, or Herself.[48] As Sivachandra puts it: 'Bhagavān Himself takes his own portraits in His own camera' [PT/1:225]. This leads to two consequences which are not 'rational' in the sense in which European Rationalists would use the word. For it means that the images of deities are *more* not less real than the images perceived by the senses of objects in the 'real' world – and moreover, more 'real' even than the individual soul (the *jīva*) himself in his separate identity, for the latter belongs to the world of duality, which is ignorance (*avidyā*). The form of a deity, on the other hand, whether male or female (*Īśvara* or *Īśvarī*) belongs to an intermediary realm of 'true forms' created by *māyā*. This, in Tantra unlike in Śamkara's school, is not regarded as illusion, but belongs to the intermediate *tattvas* between non-dual and dualistic perception [PT/1: 246–7, 276–7, 281]. Thus the images of the divinities which are the objects of ritual worship as well as their *dhyānas*, the subjects of mental concentration, have not been produced by individual human minds: they are what in Jungian terms would be called 'archetypal images'. In Sivacandra's terms, they are supramental forms created by the essentially unknowable and unthinkable supreme Divinity. We have seen that these ideas influenced Heinrich Zimmer's theories of Indian art. Something similar also seems to have emerged in Havell's art theories as we saw in chapter 4.

Emphasizing ritual as *sādhanā* for attaining transcendent states of mind or powers, acted as a defence against accusations of 'idolatry'. At the same time it relativised all religious rituals by subordinating them to the goal of *samādhi*. Because deities – although closer to reality than ordinary persons or objects – still do not belong to the highest state of knowledge, it follows that: '. . . for him who realises that all things are Brahman, there is neither yoga nor puja' [PT/1:81]. But this applies emphatically only to those who have reached the goal: 'ordinary' people cannot transcend either rituals or the deities worshipped through them.

Such a degree of transcendence was not, however, Sivacandra's goal who, like Ramakrishna, wanted to preserve the condition of duality in relation to the Goddess in order to remain Her son [PT/1:361, 462]. For both these *bhakta* saints immersion in the supreme but impersonal Brahman was not regarded as the highest state. Woodroffe himself however seems to retain non-duality as an ultimate goal – though we do not know whether that more impersonal aim represented his own position or was an apologetic stance to win over followers of Vivekananda and other western educated Hindus.

MĀYĀ-ŚAKTI: TANTRA AND WESTERN SCIENCE

By presenting *śaktivāda* as a form of *advaita* philosophy that did not deny the reality of the phenomenal world and of matter, Woodroffe and his friend P.N. Mukhopadhyay attempted to situate it among contemporary philosophies of science. This is one of the themes discussed in *The World as Power* which Woodroffe published (with acknowledged help from Mukhopadhyay) a few years after *Shakti and Shākta*. But it is touched upon in the latter book, particularly in two chapters headed 'Cit-Śakti' [SS:256–90] and 'Māyā-Śakti' [SS:290–337], and the short talk 'Matter and Consciousness' [SS:337–47]. The first two were originally subtitled 'The Spirit aspect' and 'The Matter aspect' of the universe respectively:[49] titles that reflected current scientific-philosophical preoccupations with the relationship between these two categories. The three chapters all originated in lectures by Woodroffe: the first two were among those delivered to the Vivekananda Society in 1917–18, while 'Matter and Consciousness' was originally an address to the Dacca Literary Society in 1916, reprinted in *The Theosophist* in 1918 [SS:337]. Two of Mukhopadhyay's books are referred to: *Patent Wonder* and *Approaches to Truth* [SS:263, 291]. A review of the latter book said that its author attempted to synthesize the principles of the radical empiricists with Vedanta.[50] This is also what Woodroffe attempts in these chapters; but it was a form of *vedānta* that held the dual principle of Śiva–Śakti in the place of the neutral Brahman as the Absolute. This 'śākta monism' in a modernised world-affirming garb was shown to be corroborated by the 'scientific monism' of the West which was fashionable at the time.

Western monism was placed opposite the 'dualism' of Christianity and other theistic systems: the aim was initially to subordinate 'God' or 'spirit' to 'matter'.[51] Hindu 'monism' on the other hand seeks to subordinate all phenomena including 'matter' to Brahman. But the materialistic bias of mid-nineteenth century Western science was counterbalanced, especially towards the century's end, by thinkers who posited 'an inner life force manifest in man and also in physical nature'. Such 'pan-psychism' was part of the quest for 'a new spirituality which must be authorised by science and yet contain a religious value'.[52] Woodroffe presented a pan-psychism with Śakti as the underlying essence of everything; but he also hinted at a more theistic or devotional direction too, with an 'immanentist' bias: a seeing of 'the Mother' or 'God' in all things [SS:334–6].

It has been suggested that the second half of the nineteenth century was the last period when a layman could sufficiently comprehend current ideas in all the sciences to form a coherent world view from them.[53] The picture of the unity of existence through the sciences of physics, chemistry and biology which Woodroffe presents was derived from the books by scientists which he had been reading, especially the physicist-philosophers Gustave Le Bon and L. Houllevigue, who wrote at the beginning of the twentieth century, and Ernst Haeckel, the most influential philosopher of science of the nineteenth.[54]

Three Sanskrit terms could be used to correspond to Western notions of 'matter'. *Śakti* represented the concept of energy, which increasingly was coming to be seen as more fundamental than matter itself [SS:306]; *māyā* was suggested by the insubstantiality of matter as revealed by new discoveries about the atom [SS:303], while *prakṛti*, like *śakti*, corresponded to philosophic concepts about a fundamental Substance which underlay spirit and matter [SS:304]. *Śakti* in addition, as *prāṇa* or 'Life', was correlated with ideas about the 'life' of Matter, which were current among Western philosophers of science, who were opposed to notions of a separate 'spiritual' source of life, or Soul [SS:313ff]. *Śakti* being presented by Woodroffe as the fundamental essence of everything within and beyond the phenomenal world, was an extremely fluid concept which could be used in any number of ways.

Cit corresponded to 'Spirit' but was called 'Consciousness' in later editions. It is the *sat-cit-ānanda* that is Brahman of the Upaniṣads [SS:259]. As supreme unitary consciousness it is identified in śākta theology with Śiva–Śakti in union. Rejecting Western theories that declared there could be no such thing as a consciousness without content, Woodroffe and Mukhopadhyay described *cit* as Pure Consciousness, beyond the mind, absolutely quiescent and all-pervading, like the scientific 'Ether' (see below) [SS:268, 274]

Spirit, Matter, Energy

During the first two decades of the twentieth century the mechanistic Newtonian science of the eighteenth and nineteenth centuries was being undermined by discoveries which led up to the splitting of the atom and the formulation of the theories of Quantum Mechanics in the 1920s.[55] New mysterious non-material forces had become known: electricity had been discovered in the mid-nineteenth century by Faraday; Clerk Maxwell formed his theories about electromagnetic fields in 1873 ,[56] but X Rays and radioactivity, as new kinds of forces different from electricity, were only beginning to be discovered at the very end of the nineteenth century. The discovery of radioactivity opened the door into the new world of the atom and showed that the most fundamental constituent of matter was not after all so fundamental or so solid as was thought before.[57]

The revolutionary new ideas were becoming generally known a few years before Woodroffe delivered his lectures in 1916–18. *The Theosophist* regularly commented on the new discoveries. In April 1913 its editorial noted that newspaper headlines were full of 'The Birth of the Atom' and commented:

> Modern chemistry doubts whether there is any such thing as matter; it analyses the atom and finds it to be a transient manifestation of energy, which has a birth, a "life", and a death, but a death which leaves no corpse to bury, for the energy that was the atom is restored to the general energy of the universe.[58]

Such ideas carried exciting implications to those seeking a monistic philosophy that united 'matter' and 'spirit', from whichever side of the divide they placed their emphasis. Woodroffe asks: 'Where does it [matter] go according to śākta doctrine, but to that Mother-Power from whose womb it came, who exists as all forms ... '[SS:305]. Energy – non-material, invisible and slowly being revealed as more powerful and all-pervading than had been dreamt of before[59] – could be assigned to the mysterious realm of 'spirit'. So could the related quasi-material concept of the Ether.

The 'Luminiferous Ether'

Despite having heard of the theory of Relativity and perceiving its possibilities,[60] Woodroffe and Mukhopādhyāy still did not themselves yet live in a universe of 'empty' Space–Time. The Ether theory held sway in this period and was only beginning to be discarded by some scientists.[61] The Ether was conceived of as a special kind of very attenuated 'matter' which filled Space forming a continuum in which light waves and other forms of electromagnetic radiation were propagated, as well as accounting for action-at-a-distance (gravity). It was only gradually that the concept of the Ether was replaced by that of outer space as a vacuum, in which electromagnetic fields could travel without any intervening medium.[62]

All theories concerning electromagnetism were therefore at first closely bound up with the notion of the Ether. Material qualities such as inertia, density, elasticity were attributed to it, and even measured by some scientists. This was encouraged by the calculation of a definite uniform speed of light. As Oliver Lodge wrote: 'the possession of these properties makes the Ether very real'.[63]

Yet at the same time it was an ancient concept that retained its philosophical and spiritual qualities. It formed the key element in Oliver Lodge's own religious beliefs. A prominent psychical researcher as well as a physicist, he speculated that after the death of the physical body, a body composed of ether could still be a vehicle for the personality.[64] 'Ethereal' bodies and 'ethereal' vibrations were part of the stock-in-trade of Theosophy's terminology, as well as of Spiritualism – both of them late nineteenth century movements. Ether, according to Oliver Lodge again '. . . is the primary instrument of mind, the vehicle of the soul, habitation of the Spirit. Truly it may be called the living garment of God'.[65]

If for Lodge the Ether could be the 'garment of God', for contemporary Hindus it was the *cidākāśa* or the 'Ether of Consciousness'. The parallel between the scientific Ether and the Indian *ākāśa* seemed obvious, for *ākāśa* was the first of the five elements (*mahābhūta*), which contained and transcended the other four [SS:274].[66] The mysterious nature of the scientific Ether, which 'differs profoundly' from ordinary matter 'in the physical sense, which alone is known by our senses' [SS:302], no doubt contributed to its mystical significance. P.N. Mukhopadhyay seems to have developed an elaborate theory of consciousness in terms of the 'Ether' and the 'Stress' (current terms of electromagnetism), and the notion of Ether as a continuum [SS:268, 274, 293]. Woodroffe, as with the subtle body notions (above p. 000) sometimes accepts this identification and sometimes emphasises that it is analogy:

> I do not say that scientific "ether" is Ākāśa, which is a concept belonging to a different train of thought . . . But it is important to note the agreement in this, that both in East and West, the various forms of gross matter derive from some single substance which is not "matter". Matter is *dematerialized* . . . [SS:339–40 emphasis in the original].[67]

The prevailing theme of tantric cosmogony, the emergence of the 'gross' from the 'subtle', was echoed in the scientific view of matter 'condensing' out of the Ether and mysteriously fading back into it through radioactivity.

Monism: the Search for Unity

Woodroffe opened his lecture entitled 'Māyā-Śakti' by declaring confidently: 'Spirit and Matter are ultimately one, being the twin aspects of the Fundamental Substance or Brahman.' [SS (1):77][68]

Here he has borrowed a term – 'Fundamental Substance' – from Ernst Haeckel's 'scientific monism'. Haeckel (1834–1919), the German naturalist and philosopher of science, wrote mostly before the new discoveries about radioactivity. His 'Substance' was an attempt to reconcile the older scientific theories about the duality of 'matter' and 'energy' as the two fundamental unchanging principles of nature.[69] By equating 'energy' with 'spirit' he was able to place the categories of 'God' and 'spirit' within not beyond 'nature':

> Monism . . . recognizes one sole substance in the universe, which is at once 'God and Nature'; body and spirit (or matter and energy) it holds inseparable'.[70]

His 'Substance' sounded 'spiritual' enough, however, being infinite, eternal (with 'neither genesis nor annihilation') and the source of all the changing phenomena of nature.[71] This was reminiscent of the notion of *prakṛti* in classical *sāṁkhya*, while the notion of two opposite aspects of one fundamental unity whose forms appeared and disappeared also suggested the *śiva–śakti* polarity. Woodroffe in this chapter soon replaced 'Substance' as the fundamental reality of *his* version of monism with 'Consciousness', 'Life', and of course with *Śakti* itself, or Herself.[72]

Haeckel's monism was part of the 'Religion of Science' which swept Europe during the second half of the nineteenth century. Sometimes called 'scientific naturalism' it has been defined as 'an implicit faith that by the methods of physical science . . . alone could be solved all the problems arising out of the relation of man to man and man towards the universe'.[73] An earlier figure associated with it was Herbert Spencer (1820–1903), whom Woodroffe also brings into his chapter, calling him 'the Philosopher of Modern Science'. He identified Spencer's concept of 'Primal Energy' with *ādya śakti*, and both with Haeckel's 'Spirit-Matter Substance' [SS:304].

With the discovery of radioactivity the 'Religion of Science' began to seem obsolete by the beginning of the twentieth century, when it seemed to be proved as a matter of empirical fact that matter was merely an aspect of energy.[74] Woodroffe paid little attention to the differences between the various Western scientific thinkers he cited, and the new theories fitted his own preferred world view even better:

'Matter' (in the scientific sense) *disappears*, and we and all that surround us are physically, according to these views, mere disturbed regions of the ether determined by moving electric charges – a logical if impressive conclusion, because it is by increasing their knowledge of 'matter' that physicists have been led to doubt its reality. [SS:303][75]

The living and the non-living: *śakti as prāṇa*

Another passage from Haeckel was also quoted by Woodroffe at the beginning of 'Māyā-Śakti':

> . . . in this universe immaterial Spirit is just as unthinkable as spiritless matter. The two are inseparately combined in every atom which, itself and its forces, possess the elements of vitality, growth and intelligence in all their developments. [SS:291][76]

As well as uniting 'matter' and 'energy', a further duality which Haeckel's monism sought to transcend was that between 'life' and 'matter'. He held that the most subtle qualities of organic life were present in some form in inorganic matter itself, and added a third term to his fundamental 'Substance': that of 'sensation'.[77] Haeckel even believed that the attraction and repulsion of molecules in chemical reactions were an illustration of sensation at the inorganic level and amounted to a rudimentary form of 'will'.[78] His idea grew mainly out of studies of the cell as the simple foundation for more complex life.[79] For Haeckel this elementary form of sensation did not amount to consciousness, which was something that evolved out of sensation: what the concept did in his system was to enable him to discount the idea of 'soul' and 'body' as separate entities.[80]

Other scientific thinkers also sought to probe the boundaries of the living and the non-living at this time, especially the Indian physicist Jagdish Chandra Bose (1858–1937), whose experiments Woodroffe mentions in this chapter [SS:320]. Bose was his contemporary in Calcutta, and a friend of Nivedita and of the Tagores. So it is quite likely that Woodroffe would have known him personally, but by 1918 Bose's experiments would have been widely known anyway, and had begun to find acceptance. In that year he retired from his post as Professor of Physics at Calcutta's Presidency College and devoted his time to his research institute in the city. His first book: *Response in the Living and Non-Living* had been published in 1902.

Bose worked on electro-magnetism and designed some early forms of radar equipment and radio receivers. He was among the first to discover the phenomenon of metal fatigue – something which appeared to show a similarity in metals to the response to stimuli of living tissue. He then extended his experiments to plants, devising complex equipment which could detect tiny electrical responses in plants that were similar to those of animal tissue in reaction to external stimulations such as shock. He believed he had shown that: 'Life's response is carried unbroken in the same form from metals to plants and then to animals.' Although his experiments aroused some amusement and scepticism at first both in the press and in some scientific circles, they were treated with respect by others, and by 1919 he was received in Europe with acclaim.[81] When he lectured at the India Office in London summaries of his lectures were cabled to Europe and America. Neither did the implications for monistic philosophy go unheeded. The *Times* reacted with a piece of 'romantic orientalism':

> While we in Europe were still steeped in the rude empiricism of barbaric life, the subtle Eastern had swept the whole universe into a synthesis and had seen the *One* in all its changing manifestations.[82]

But such views were not confined to 'the East'. They were part of the quest for scientific 'monism' and considered 'modern', if controversial. Woodroffe cites the physicists Ernst Mach [SS:321] and Gustave Le Bon, and quotes the latter:

> This sensibility of matter, so contrary to what popular observation seems to indicate, is becoming more and more familiar to physicists. That is why such an expression as the 'life of matter', utterly meaningless twenty-five years ago has come into common use. [SS, p. 316][83]

Having shown how *śakti* transcends the duality spirit/matter, Woodroffe turns to that of living/inert, or organic/inorganic at SS:313. Again, *śakti* is an underlying absolute or essence: this time it is 'Life ... beyond form ... for in a sense it is Eternal Life whence all life in form proceeds' [SS:313–4]. The significance is in the philosophical implication for the unity of being:

> There are no absolute partitions or gulfs. All is continuous, even if we cannot at present establish in each case the connection. That there should be such gulfs is unthinkable to any one who has even in small degree grasped the notion of the unity of things. [SS:315]

The notion of Life as an Absolute derives from *prāṇa* the 'vital breath' [SS:317]. Since this is only present in living bodies it contradicts the ideas just expressed about there being no boundaries between living and non-living. But *prāṇa* is also identified with consciousness. It was something of a leap in logic to use the appearance of sensibility in matter to argue for the presence of consciousness in it. Woodroffe gets around this by also identifying *prāṇa* with the *organization* of matter, an idea borrowed from his friend Pandit J.C. Chatterji [SS:317, 319]. Houllevigue had pointed out the 'extraordinary power of organization' which resides in matter.[84]

Here the concept of the three *guṇas* of *prakṛti* was given 'scientific' corroboration. *Śakti* as Consciousness is revealed most clearly by *sattva*, the first and 'highest' of the *guṇas* and is veiled by matter which is *tamas*, the 'lowest' of the three [SS:321]. This doctrine was considered to be proved by the experiments of Bose, whose responses in metal and plant tissue suggested the presence of *śakti* veiled by *tamas* inherent throughout matter, which is thus not *jada* ('inert', see above p. 165). It was seen as equivalent to Haeckel's 'Sensation' in inorganic and organic matter.

'Reality'

Woodroffe sets his chapter in the context of the ideas of his friend P.N. Mukhopādhyāy who elaborated on the world-affirming monism of the Śākta Tantra, as against the *vedānta* of Śankarācārya. Mukhopadhyay was a follower of William James[85] who is frequently referred to in *World as Power.* James, one of the first psychologists of religion who placed his emphasis upon experience and intuition, has been described as the first 'democrat of metaphysics'. An opponent of the European Idealists he affirmed 'the democratic consubstantiality of every entity and experience with every other'.[86]

Mukhopādhyāy set up a polarity between what he called 'the viewpoint of Siddhi' (here meaning Gnosis or transcendental experience) and that of 'Sādhana', the view of those who are still on the path towards the final goal (ie 'practical' as opposed to 'transcendental' experience). He placed the Śākta Tantra in the higher position, reconciling this opposition, accepting as real the twin poles of transcendent and empirical experience – 'the whole of experience without any reservation whatever – the whole concrete Fact of Being and Becoming' [SS:291].

It was a matter of definition. William James attacked in the European Idealist philosophers such as Bradley the dismissal of time and change as mere 'appearances';[87] Woodroffe and Mukhopadhyay reject the same in Śankarācārya. For Śankara, the Real is the state of *sāmādhi*, which is unmoving, and contrasted with the illusory universe which comes and goes – namely the three states of ordinary consciousness: waking, dreaming and dreamless sleep [SS:292–3]. Here Woodroffe specifically rejects 'changelessness' as alone categorizing ultimate Reality [SS:293–4] opening the way to more dynamic concepts which include the universe as constant flux – ideas to which he returns in his concluding chapter of *Shakti and Shākta* in the third edition [SS:708–17].[88]

Having thus established that the Śākta Tantra affirms the reality of the world and is 'scientific', Woodroffe asserts its value for modern times. The *māyāvāda* of Śankarāchārya which denies the world, he claimed, can have a deleterious effect on those who do not have sufficient strength for world-renunciation. 'They become intellectual and moral derelicts who . . . have neither the strength to follow worldly life, nor to truly abandon it.' In the Śākta Tantra, by contrast it is not necessary to renounce because 'all is seen to be Her' [SS:334]. He sums up its value at the end of his chapter:

> The Śākta doctrine is thus one which has not only grandeur but is greatly pragmatic and of excelling worth. ... Like all practical doctrines, it is also intensely positive. There are none of those negations which weaken and which annoy those who, as the vital Western mind does, feel themselves to be strong and living in an atmosphere of might and power. For Power is a glorious thing. What is wanted is only the sense that all Power is of God and is God ... [SS:335].

He concludes by calling this 'the pearl which those who have churned the ocean of Tantra discover' [SS:336].

So like Vivekananda's neo-Vedanta, this new Tantrism was called 'practical'. I discussed in chapter 5 the resonances which words like 'pragmatic', 'positive', 'vital' and 'power' carried in the contemporary scene. Lectures such as this one would have contributed to Woodroffe's appeal for his western educated science-loving admirers like Nolini Mohun Chatterji. The 'pearl' he presented to them was a world-affirming 'religion of Power', which could be defended rationally and in 'scientific' terms. Like Vivekananda's Practical Vedanta it presented a monist philosophy pointing to the experience of ultimate unity transcending worldy experience, but without denying the validity of the latter. Unlike Vivekananda's religion, this one did not place a value on celibacy but affirmed sexuality (though not sexual licence). The concept of *śakti* was used to reconcile expressly or by implication a whole range of opposites: spirit/matter, religion/science, superconscious experience/ordinary experience, renunciation/sexuality, timelessness/change.

The Avalon/Woodroffe books attempted to integrate Śākta Tantra within modern Hinduism, by drawing out of it immanentist and 'scientific' doctrines that were currently fashionable in India and in the West. Behind their appeal lay Arthur Avalon's impressive textual knowledge, without which his modern reinterpretation would not have carried so much authority. We shall see in the final chapter how both the hermeneutics and the textual scholarship reflected Woodroffe's use of and interaction with the knowledge of many Indian people, both middle class *bhadralok* and more traditional pandits. It examines Woodroffe's relation to his closest friend and teacher Atal Bihari Ghose and attempts to reconstruct his relationship with the Sanskrit language and with the texts.

Chapter Eleven

COLLABORATORS, SANSKRIT AND THE SCHOLARSHIP OF ARTHUR AVALON

I WOODROFFE'S COLLABORATORS

Atal Bihari Ghose [plate 8]

Atal Bihari Ghose is the unseen presence behind Arthur Avalon. He was just one year older than his British friend and died on 12 January 1936, just four days before him. His short obituary followed the longer one of Woodroffe in *Baśumati*, the journal edited by Hemendraprasad Ghose, Vasanta Kumar Pal's informant who knew both men (see above p. 105). It said the two friends came to know each other through the practice of their legal professions and 'took initiation together from the same guru'. But *Baśumati* described Ghose (not Woodroffe) as 'the famous founder of the Āgamānusandhana Samiti' and several volumes of the *Tantrik Texts* were stated to be his work.[1] The longer obituary of Woodroffe did not mention either the *Tantrik Texts* or the Samiti, though it praised *The Serpent Power* and *Shakti and Shākta*, and especially *Is India Civilized?* It said that Woodroffe and Ghose delved into the Tantras together and described them as guiding lights for India.[2] *Bhārat Varṣa* (whose editor was also at Sivacandra's memorial meeting)[3] gave Woodroffe credit for a revival of Tantra which made it attractive to modern educated people, both in India and abroad, and said that Woodroffe and Ghose formed the Samiti together and were jointly responsible for publications resurrecting the Tantras from oblivion.[4] This was also how the relationship was described in other obituaries and notices in India.[5]

Woodroffe's friend and chief collaborator was born in 1864 and lived in Calcutta. His family were traditionally Śākta, though not Tantrics, and his grandchildren were not sure what had led Atal Bihari to seek initiation. He received the typical English education of the Bengali middle class. He was a classmate of Narendranath Datta, the future Swami Vivekananda, at the Metropolitan Institute founded by Vidyasagar, and afterwards graduated at Ripon College in Philosophy and English. He then studied Law and practised as a *vakil* at the Alipore district court and at the Court of Small Causes in Calcutta.

His family did not believe he had introduced Woodroffe to Tantra, but rather that it was Tantra that had brought them together. They confirmed that Ghose was also a disciple of Sivacandra Vidyarnava, but said that he was closer to Jayakali Devi, the *Bhairavī* we have mentioned several times who performed the *siñcan* ceremony for Woodroffe.[6] Two postcards from her were found among the papers in the house, thanking him for gifts of money and inviting him to stay at her ashram in Benares. Ghose is also thought to have practised tantric *sādhanā* in the crematoria of Birbhum and Bankura with Mrtyunjaya Vidyalankara, a pandit from the Sanskrit college who eventually left his post to become a *sannyāsi*. Another of his mentors in later years was Pandit Pañcānan Bhattacharya editor of two volumes of *Tantrik Texts* published after the death of Arthur Avalon, who was a famous expert on Tantra and author of many books in Bengali.

Ghose married twice: Mr Sobhun Ghose and Mrs Sumita Guha, whom I met, were the children of his son by his second wife, Gauramma, and they were both born long after their grandparents had died. Gauramma came from a South Indian family who had lived a long time in England, and so the language of the home was English. She was a disciple of Vivekananda and a close friend of Josephine Macleod, whose photograph was in the house.

A fund-raising pamphlet issued by the Samiti under the name of its President the Maharaja of Darbhanga significantly plays down Ghose's role. It declares the society was formed 'to take over and continue the work begun by Sir John Woodroffe to collect, preserve and publish and also correctly to interpret the Philosophy of the Agamik Scriptures'. The pamphlet states that: 'Sir John Woodroffe has practically single-handed laboured at this task for several years, and has published and translated some original texts.' As he approached his retirement 'he made over the work to this Samiti'. Atal Bihari Ghose is described as 'one of his collaborators ... who is associated with him in this work from its very inception'. He was designated joint secretary of the Samiti, with Woodroffe. 'Arthur Avalon' is named as General Editor, but otherwise is not mentioned.[7]

It is significant that this pamphlet was published after Woodroffe's departure from India, for it looks as if the pseudonym was something insisted on by Woodroffe himself. Ghose on the other hand seems to have wanted his collaborator to claim direct responsibility for all the 'Arthur Avalon' works while he himself chose to stay in the shadows. In one of two short articles which Ghose wrote for an American occultist magazine in 1930 he states:

> Sir John Woodroffe in his book "*Serpent Power*" published under the assumed name of Arthur Avalon, has shown ... in VV–44–49 of the scriptures translated therein ...[8]

– thus implying (if not exactly stating) that Woodroffe even translated the textual part of that book himself, something which I believe was not possible. An American contact on the magazine, who sent Ghose copies of the published articles,[9] apologised that they had appeared under his name with a brief biographical introduction – it seems Ghose had wanted to write anonymously. In one of his letters to Ghose, Woodroffe insists that the new Sanskrit edition of *mahānirvāṇa tantra* to be published as volume 13 of the *Tantrik Texts* should be ascribed to 'Arthur Avalon' [see Letter 6]. It is not clear what Ghose had proposed to him but as we shall see, there is evidence that Ghose had at first wanted *The Great Liberation*, the translation of *mahānirvāṇa*, to go by Woodroffe's name.

It is not clear how Ghose himself acquired the Sanskrit knowledge which made 'Arthur Avalon' a famous orientalist, since he had the normal English education of the Bengali middle class. But that he did acquire it appears beyond doubt, even if we allow for his having himself received the help of pandits from the Sanskrit College, as his granddaughter acknowledged. That Ghose translated several of the texts published or planned in the name of Arthur Avalon is proved by the fact that copies were found in his house and they were in his handwriting. These were drafts and final copies of the published translation of *kāma-kalā-vilāsa* [TT/10] and fourteen chapters of an unpublished translation of *kulārṇava tantra*. There were also handwritten draft translations and notes on other texts which he was working on when he died. Ghose published under his own name in Bengali, including a study of the Tantric poet-saint Kamalakānta.

Correspondence of Woodroffe and Ghose

The collection of letters in the Ghose family house consisted of twenty-one from Woodroffe to Atal Bihari Ghose, one from Ghose to Woodroffe (mentioned above in chapter 8), seven to Woodroffe from other people and ten to Ghose from other people.[10] Of those in the first section, only four were written before Woodroffe's retirement from India in 1922. After that date it seems that the two collaborators kept in regular contact, for in a letter written as late as 1933 Woodroffe explains why he has not written for several weeks. Only a small fraction of the correspondence therefore has been recovered: apparently a random selection. Letters were found haphazardly in drawers and in the pages of books, and among the manuscripts which Ghose had collected before his death.

As we saw in chapter 6, some referred to Ghose as a guru (above p. 95). But these letters show nothing of a guru–disciple relationship between the two men. On the contrary Woodroffe is in the dominant role, reflecting his more powerful position in the colonial society, although the two men and their families are also clearly friends. Despite the fact that it is Ghose who has the knowledge on which Woodroffe needs to draw, Woodroffe is in authority and issues instructions. Their roles are therefore more like 'orientalist' and 'collaborator' than disciple and guru. In Calcutta we see Woodroffe politely summon Ghose to work with him during a spare couple of hours (letter 1). In letter 2, which was discussed in chapter 6,[11] he gives instructions about the printing of *ṣaṭ-cakra-nirūpaṇa* ('shatcakra'). He asks Ghose to correct a proof for him (letter 3); while letter 4, probably written from England while Woodroffe was on vacation in 1920, shows him passing on a book and manuscript sent by a correspondent, and asking Ghose to look through it.

After his departure from India in 1922, Woodroffe continued to issue instructions by letter to Ghose who had by now been left in sole charge of the *Tantrik Texts*. That he was alone is shown by a letter of 11 February 1931 which mentions possibly appointing some pandits to help him.[12] Some did help, especially Pañcānan Bhattacharya, but of eight volumes of the series published between 1926 and 1936 seven were edited by 'Arthur Avalon' himself. These included editions of *mahānirvāṇa tantra*, *śāradā tilaka* and *prapañcasāra tantra*, all of which are discussed in the correspondence. There was a lull in publications between the date of Woodroffe's retirement in 1922 – by which time eleven volumes had already been produced – and the second part of *tantrarāja tantra* (edited by Sadasiva Misra) which appeared in 1926. This may suggest that it was Woodroffe's initiative and probably also his money which had collected the team of Indian pandits who edited the earlier volumes. That the series lost momentum for a while after his departure is shown in an undated letter that must have been written between 1923 and 1925[13] where Woodroffe writes:

> I was surprised to read in your letter that you have *nothing to do* except Mahanirvana. What has become of *2nd vol of Tantraraja*? I have several times asked about this. When shall I see the Introduction? I sent it to you last summer and you were to add to it & to return it for me to revise. How does this stand? We must show M of D [the Maharaja of Darbhanga] something *done*. So far as I know nothing has appeared since I left. [letter 5, emphasis in the original]

'Arthur Avalon' was not directly responsible for *tantraraja tantra* but its lengthy introduction (which included a summary of the text) went by the name of the general editor in its first edition, and by Woodroffe later on.[14] The letter shows that the two collaborators worked on it jointly. If the correspondence with Dawasamdup is anything to go by (see below), Woodroffe's initial contribution would have emerged from written questions put to its pandit editors. Apart from Introductions, before 1922 'Arthur Avalon' had only directly contributed two translations to the series: *kārpūrādistotram* and *kāma-kalā-vilāsa* [TT/9 and 10].

This same letter reveals several sides of the Ghose–Woodroffe relationship: it begins with Woodroffe looking to Ghose for clarification over some details of Śiva–Śakti symbolism about which a friend had queries,[15] and continues with Woodroffe giving his collaborator instructions over the practical aspects of publication, even to the use of paper. Ghose seems to have got into difficulties over money and sponsors and Woodroffe tells him how to handle the situation, clearly still feeling himself in charge. Finally the letter turns to the only personal subject mentioned in this correspondence: the health of both the families, especially the Woodroffes. Their younger daughter, Barbara, was suffering from anorexia, from which she died in 1925.[16] Her father calls her illness neurasthenia and poignantly describes trying to stir her 'will'. A short note written the year after her death was almost illegible: it was to be a few more years yet before his Parkinson's Disease made Woodroffe's handwriting deteriorate so badly.[17] Eventually he had to dictate his correspondence. Other letters mention frequent illnesses in the family, including that of his other daughter Nancy, and the illness or death of their mutual friends: the Blounts, the Moellers, and Havell. In one letter he sadly comments that he seemed to be surrounded by sickness and death on all sides [letter 6].

The letters however predominantly concern the *Tantrik Texts*, with Woodroffe continuing to issue instructions on matters of publication and finances up until the end. He gives advice to Ghose over his relations with their sponsor the Maharaja of Darbhanga, and potential sponsor the Maharaja of Patiala. We can see that Woodroffe considered he had the right to vet the final version of whatever was signed by the joint pseudonym even as late as 1935. This is evident from the only example in these letters of a disagreement between the two men, which occurred in the last letter in the collection dated March 1935, nine months before their deaths. Here we see that Ghose's draft Introduction to the revised second edition of *prapañcasāra tantra*[18] has prompted a letter in which Woodroffe sounds unusually irritated. Objecting to what he considers the polemical tone of Ghose's draft, he comes close to claiming ownership of the identity of Arthur Avalon:

> I have cut out in blue pencil the bulk of the proposed introduction as unsuitable and irrelevant ... I am not concerned with orthodox polemics. These constant jibes at the modern Hindu become tiresome to the public. Moreover a polemic is more fittingly conducted in an article signed by the person who carries on such polemics. [letter 11]

Woodroffe refused to countenance a compromise suggestion by Ghose that the introduction should go out under the initials A.S.[19] and insisted on his right to approve the final product. (The initials probably stand for Atalānananda Saraswati, the name which appears on the Sanskrit – but not the English – title page.)

The disagreement was over the authorship of the text. Ghose vehemently supported the traditional ascription to Śankaracharya, but

Western orientalists did not accept this. Woodroffe's instinct was to treat controversial questions with great care, and as far as possible to be 'balanced'. In the end the original introduction to the earlier edition was preserved while the new introduction was transformed into a Postscript to it. If we compare the two we see the difference clearly: the earlier introduction attempts to leave the question open; the later postscript decides firmly in Śankara's favour, even if less polemically than might have been the case without Woodroffe's intervention [TT/18:1–4 and 67–73].

Against this background, we can see a glimpse of how Woodroffe had reacted to pressure from his collaborator when he wrote the original introduction. There, after presenting arguments for both sides of the dispute, 'Arthur Avalon' had left the matter like this:

> I leave however others, who may think that the contents of the work itself notwithstanding its authoritative tone and general style tell against the tradition as to its authorship, the development of their thesis. [ibid, p. 2]

This confusing sentence, which attempts to be "balanced" yet leaves us wondering just what is his own position, probably results from Woodroffe attempting to satisfy all sides. Chapter 10 has already shown how he dealt carefully with other matters he knew would be controversial. At the end of his life, it seems Woodroffe was reacting against a strain of intolerance that was present in both Ghose and Sivacandra. The 'polemics' and 'jibes against the modern Hindu' which Woodroffe complains of in this late letter are prominent in many passages of the Avalon/Woodroffe writings.

The letters during his last two years of life show Woodroffe beginning to tire of the *Tantrik Texts*. In a letter dated February 1934 he had said he wanted the Samiti to be wound up after the edition of *prapañcasāra tantra* was completed. This might have been because of his Parkinson's Disease, whose distressing symptoms were increasing;[20] or it might have had something to do with his return to the Catholic Church discussed in chapter 6. As it turned out, he continued to be involved and to worry over the *Tantrik Texts* almost till the end of his life. Ghose however was the one who worked hard on them, through several bouts of illness, till the very end.

Woodroffe usually addressed his correspondent 'My dear Ghose', occasionally 'My dear Atal' but only once by the more familiar 'Dear Atal'. Though their style is courteous and usually gentle, Woodroffe's reserve and dominance is very apparent in these letters. There are signs of genuine affection for his friend displayed by his anxious concern over a break in the regular correspondence due to Ghose's severe illness in 1929 [letter 9], and another break in 1933 (when Woodroffe, unusually, signed himself 'yours affectionately'). Nevertheless there is a strong contrast between the Woodroffe correspondence and two letters in the collection which were written to Ghose from amidst a small circle of American friends in the 1930s. These letters express a flood of personal feelings and reflections, as well as showing how they looked up to Ghose as a teacher. Woodroffe on the other hand, although he constantly drew on Ghose's fund of scholarship, does not acknowledge it and passes it on as his own (albeit with Ghose's connivance). Perhaps it was because the later friends were American, or because they were younger, or because the date was into the third decade of the century, but the pattern of relationship between Ghose and these other Westerners seeking oriental knowledge was quite different. The 'orientalist-and-collaborator' pattern with its overtones of colonial hegemony was replaced by one closer to that of guru and disciple, or at least of teacher and pupil.[21] By this time Ghose's contacts with Westerners had widened to include not only the United States, but also Germany. A telegram of sympathy on Ghose's death was sent to his son by a bookseller in that country who paid a moving tribute to his father's scholarship:

> We have learned of the death of the scholar Babu Atal Bihari Ghose through the German Consul General. It is my duty to convey to you the sympathy of German scholars for his death, as I know from my many contacts with them, how respected Mr Ghose was in Germany.[22]

Considering that Woodroffe and Ghose were dedicated to a common goal and had worked together for several decades, the lack of intimacy in these letters of Woodroffe's is very striking. Only one letter refers to general topics – the financial crisis of the 1930s – and speculates on the 'new world' they both might not (and did not) live to see [letter 8]. Although we have very little from the period when they met constantly in Calcutta, even in the four notes from that period, the tone is distant, even peremptory. Woodroffe's open display of grief at the death of his guru shows that he could have strong feelings for other men (although even this does not come through in his writings when Sivacandra is mentioned). Whatever was the nature of the bond between Woodroffe and Ghose it is so far hidden from us. Their very long collaboration, the evidence for Ghose's influence upon Woodroffe, the photographs taken at Konarak, the reports that they were frequently together, suggest a far stronger bond than is revealed in this correspondence.

The Lama Kazi Dawasamdup

Woodroffe informs his readers that he first met the Lama Dawasamdup when the latter was translator to the Tibetan Plenipotentiary for the Government of India. Besides other posts as an official translator he was a headmaster at Gangtok, Sikkim [TT/7 p. vii]. He is best known for his collaboration with W.Y. Evans-Wentz on a translation of the *Tibetan Book of the Dead* which went thereafter by Evans-Wentz's name, and to which Woodroffe wrote a Foreword.[23] Another book published by Evans Wentz – *Tibet's Great Yogi Milarepa* – was also based on a translation by Dawasamdup. The correspondence reveals that Dawasamdup had been trying to get his Western contacts to take an interest in *Milarepa* for some time, and he tried unsuccessfully to persuade Woodroffe to publish it.

The collection of letters was thirty-two, written between 1916 and 1918, and concerned Woodroffe's commissioning the Lama to edit and translate one out of a collection of eight manuscripts of the *Demchog Tantra*,[24] which Woodroffe had acquired in Nepal. In the event he only translated part of one, a *sādhanā* based on the *maṇḍala* of Demchog [TT/7]. Although more of this correspondence has survived and the letters are also much longer than those to Ghose, they reveal even less relationship between the two men. Dawasamdup was not a collaborator of the kind that Ghose was; Woodroffe simply employed him to work on the manuscripts he had acquired. There is an arrogant, sometimes bullying tone in Woodroffe's letters, which overall leaves an unpleasant impression. He often demands rather than requests information from Dawasamdup, whom he rather arrogantly upbraids in one letter for not being sufficiently knowledgeable in his own tradition, while another suggests he had made his collaborator feel inadequate over continuing his task.[25] He was impatient to have the volume finished, for he said he wanted to complete the publication of the *Tantrik Texts* before leaving India, which he intended to do as soon as the European war would be over.

But this correspondence also reveals how Woodroffe exerted himself to understand the text for which he was working, despite his lack of linguistic skill or previous knowledge. It shows him grappling with the Tibetan *vajrayāna* and *mahāyāna* concepts and attempting to relate them to what he knew of Indian Śākta Tantra. He could only approach the subject through comparison with what he already knew and so he tended to interpret the buddhist concepts in the light of Vedanta.[26] He asked for Sanskrit equivalents to the Tibetan terms, and in one instance asked Dawasamdup to write the former in *devanāgarī* (though there is a question as to whether Woodroffe could read this script, see below.) He plied his collaborator with questions in meticulous detail – for example, about the five *dhyāni* buddhas and their corresponding 'wisdoms' or qualities of Enlightenment – and most of the information he gleaned from the correspondence went into his Foreword to the volume and into footnotes to the translation. They thus give an interesting glimpse of Woodroffe at work with one of his collaborators and the thoroughness with which he attempted to grasp the subject through question-and-answer. His lack of Tibetan did not prevent him from taking an active role in directing Dawasamdup's translation, and he made efforts to understand precisely the concepts expressed by Tibetan terms. Here he acknowledged the assistance of the Indian Principal of the Calcutta Sanskrit College, who was also a Tibetan scholar.[27] He also made use of the work of Masson Oursel and La Vallée Poussin, and has consulted other Lamas, besides Dawasamdup.[28] Woodroffe ordered Dawasamdup not to resort to the works of orientalist scholars but to seek out senior Lamas to get the traditional interpretation of the text.

Dawasamdup was a traditional scholar whose role as a channel for knowledge about the Tibetan language and religion was significant, though he was never in any sense a guru. Besides Woodroffe and Evans Wentz, Alexandra David-Neel and two British Residents in Sikkim (Charles Bell and David Macdonald) studied and corresponded with him. Charles Bell who wrote books on Tibetan language and religion called him 'that tower of learning' and expressed his debt to the Lama.[29]

Ghose was also involved with the work on Tibetan texts and corresponded with Evans-Wentz who acknowledged his help and Woodroffe's in the preface to *Tibetan Book of the Dead*.[30] A letter from Evans-Wentz to Ghose in 1927 acknowledged help for *Milarepa* too, and mentioned his forthcoming book on Tibetan Yoga in which Ghose was taking a keen interest.[31]

Ghose and Dawasamdup belong to a class of people who have perhaps not been much noticed by historians: learned local scholars who played an important though often humble role in bridge building for Westerners interested in Hinduism and Buddhism, from the late eighteenth century through till recent times. Dawasamdup was closer to the older model of the pandit-collaborator or 'informant' working for an orientalist. Woodroffe's relationship with Ghose was different. Ghose was not a traditional pandit, he was a member of the English educated middle class. He had excellent English and could easily have translated on his own without Woodroffe's help, and was also skilled at presenting his knowledge to Westerners. The basis of their collaboration was closer to equality: their common purpose to further the world-view in which they both shared. Although Woodroffe was still in the dominant role socially, in other ways his work marks the beginning of a new relationship between Western enquirer and Indian knowledge, in which the foreigner takes a less powerful position. Woodroffe placed himself (even if not always humbly) at the feet of Indian teachers and accepted their hermeneutics. This did not only include pandits but also contemporary Bengali middle-class adherents, represented by Ghose, Mukhopadhay and others among his collaborators.

The Samities, the Maharajas and Money

The *Āgamānusandhana Samiti* was a publishing company set up specially for the *Tantrik Texts*, though it may have owned the copyright of some of the other books as well.[32] Its publicity leaflet, mentioned above, reveals it to have had a distinctly propaganda purpose, specifically aimed at the English educated Indian public. Its President, the Maharaja of Darbhanga, seems to have been the main financial sponsor after Woodroffe's departure, and was succeeded on his death in 1931, by his son who took over as President [TT/20 p. ii]. Other sponsors may have commissioned particular volumes.[33] According to his correspondence with Dawasamdup, Woodroffe had already put a lot of his own money into the *Tantrik Texts*: he paid Dawasamdup and therefore presumably paid the other Indian editors of the earlier volumes. The money was not recovered through sales, which seem to have remained poor.[34]

The Maharaja of Darbhanga, Rameshwar Singh, was a fellow disciple of Sivacandra and a renowned tantric practitioner. He was described by the Marquis of Zetland as a 'notorious' Śākta, patron of the temple to the Goddess at Kāmākhya where the 'erotic ritual' was performed.[35] Vasanta Kumar Pal refers to him several times: as sponsor of a spectacular tantric *pūjā* performed by his guru; as someone who practised *sādhanā* in the crematoria of Bihar and Bengal along with Sivacandra; and as sponsor of many of the saint's publications.[36] He was a founder and General President of the *Śrī Bhārat Dharma Mahāmaṇḍal*, a neo-conservative Hindu organisation which nevertheless had a universalist attitude and sought to make the scriptures available to all castes and to women.[37] His sponsorship of the *Tantrik Texts* probably reflected this aim. Rameshwar Singh was a colourful character who had a reputation among his subjects as a *siddha* Tantric: he was credited with having changed the course of a river through performing *sādhanā* thus diverting a flood. He was called a *rājaṛṣi*, a King-rishi.[38] He was relatively unusual in being a member of the princely class who was also a Brahmin, and took a leading role in the movement to prevent inter-caste marriage, and in the defence of brahmanical interests generally. His 'kingdom' was really no more than a particularly large estate, but he was extremely wealthy.[39]

One other prince supported the Samiti – the Maharaja of Cossim Bazaar, Mahindra Chandra Nandy, who was named vice-President on its pamphlet. The Maharaja of Patiala, who reneged on his offer to contribute funds (above p. 112) although a Sikh, sponsored Hindu projects including Benares Hindu University.[40] He was perhaps approached for sponsorship after Woodroffe was told of his meeting in London with Ellen Woodroffe's sister-in-law, the American sculptress Malvina Hoffman, an encounter which she described in her travel book. Finding the maharaja proud and cold at first she related how the atmosphere changed dramatically as soon as she mentioned the name of her brother-in-law. He immediately relaxed and warmth came into his voice: there were only two or three men left in the world, the maharaja told her 'who have such authentic knowledge of our people and our religion'.[41]

The Varendra Research Society

We have seen that Pal, who thought Woodroffe was introduced to tantric scholars through the Agamas Research Society, may have confused it with the *Varendrānusandhana Samiti* or Varendra Research Society (above p. 101). The latter was founded in 1910 to promote study of Bengali history, especially of the local Rajshahi area – the medieval kingdom of Varendra which was rich in tantric lore. Its Director A.K. Maitra, a lawyer by profession, was a swadeshi historian writing in English and Bengali but mainly in the latter. His aim was to reconstruct Bengali history and counter the influence of orientalist historians. He denied the existence of the 'black hole of Calcutta', and attempted to rehabilitate Siraj-ud-daula and other late Moghul rulers usually vilified by British historians. He also turned his attention to pre-Moghul Bengal with its buddhist and hindu tantric legacy. He was a dynamic personality, very well-known in his time, and was close to Rabindranath Tagore.[42] Maitra believed, like Arthur Avalon, in restoring the image of Tantra as a 'mystic faith'. Maitra explained that the purpose of his society was to educate the opinions of scholars:

> But it is chiefly as a centre of Tantrika activity that Varendra deserves to be specially explored, to discover the images and manuscripts which alone are capable of explaining the various stages in the development of that mystic faith, which are now only dimly seen, or more frequently, vaguely imagined, to suit the theories which the students of Indian history are so eager to advance'.[43]

The Avalon/Woodroffe works are in this same spirit of re-evaluation of Tantra while emphasising its mystical element. Maitra wrote the introduction to volume 4 of the *Tantrik Texts* and introduced its editor to Woodroffe.[44] He is mentioned several time as a source of information, [GOL:105; SP:xi] and the Varendra Research Society as a source of manuscripts. The society had a museum and engaged in its own manuscript search. Its contacts among local people and 'traditional' scholars included descendants of Pūrṇānanda, the sixteenth century author of *ṣaṭ-cakra-nirūpaṇa* [SP:xi]. Atal Bihari Ghose was a member and wrote for the society's Bulletin (see below).

II 'ARTHUR AVALON'S' SCHOLARSHIP

While it is easy to appreciate that Woodroffe published the *Tantrik Texts* with the help of Ghose and other collaborators, what is not so easy to imagine is how he managed to produce even the English writings which are attributed to him without a knowledge of Sanskrit. Some parts of these are so technical and display so much apparent erudition with a wide range of quotations from and references to texts that it is almost impossible to believe at first sight that they were not the work of a Sanskrit scholar. They comprise: *Shakti and Shākta*, *Garland of Letters* and *World as Power*; and the long introductions to translations – *An Introduction to Tantra Śāstra* and the seven introductory chapters of *The Serpent Power*.

Along with *Principles of Tantra* they have been published by Ganesh and Co. in Madras since the early 1920s. This was a family company founded by a Madras coffee merchant to whom Woodroffe was introduced by his Theosophist friend James Cousins. Mr Ranganadhan, the younger brother of the founder, was still faithfully turning out reprints of the books when I visited him in 1991. The work was seen by both brothers as an act of religious devotion, which never made a profit except from *Shakti and Shākta* and *The Serpent Power*, for which Dover Press acquired the American rights in the 1970s. Mr Ranganadhan had no doubt that Sir John Woodroffe wrote all the books of 'Arthur Avalon' and that he was an orientalist scholar. It was interesting to find that his publisher did not see Woodroffe as specifically a scholar of the Tantras, but as an exponent of Hindu religion and culture in general. He did not believe that Woodroffe had been a Tantric, for he told me that he had emphasised to his brother the impartiality of his position: 'I do not propose, I do not oppose, I merely expose', he was quoted as saying. Ganesh and Co. also published his nationalist writings discussed in chapter 5.

It is necessary at this point briefly to review the English publications on Tantra again, taking note of the dates when they were produced.

Shakti and Shākta (SS)

We have seen that the first edition contained Woodroffe's lectures delivered in 1917–18, plus four magazine articles which had appeared during the same period.[45] The book was revised and expanded in the second edition which appeared between 1918 and 1920, published by Ganesh and Co.[46] An introductory first chapter entitled 'Bhārata Dharma' was added plus three short chapters on the connection between Chinese and Indian Tantra (DP edition: chs 8,9 & 11). For two of these the source was a book by a Jesuit missionary in China [SS:207, 227], while the one on *cīnācāra* [SS:192–204] is drawn from Sanskrit texts. An earlier article entitled 'The Origin of the Vajrayāna Devatās' was also included: this was first published in *Modern Review* in June 1916 under the name of Arthur Avalon. ['Matam Rutra', DP ch.28]. Here the pseudonym has been used to cover the help of Dawasamdup, for the chapter is a summary of a translation by him [SS:650] which is referred to in their correspondence. A third edition in Woodroffe's lifetime appeared in 1927 and this represented its last revision. It introduces both earlier and later material: three lectures delivered before or at the beginning of 1917 (DP chs 16, 19 & 22); two delivered in 1925 and 1926 in London (chs 20 & 23); plus two articles in Indian magazines published in 1919 and 1920 (chs 12 & 13), and two articles of unknown date (chs 18 & 21). A fourth edition produced by Ganesh in 1951 was based on the third edition and remained largely unchanged in the many subsequent editions and reprintings. Although a few typographical errors have crept in, the only deliberate changes Ganesh have made are to omit the lectures which Woodroffe delivered in French and to update his transliteration system.[47] Careless editing in the second and third editions has made some of the chapters confusing, where long interpolations have been placed in the text without sensitivity to context, and the first edition generally reads more clearly.

Garland of Letters ('Garland' or GOL)

The preface states that most of this book was also composed of lectures and articles, except for the first nine chapters on the philosophy of the Word, for which the collaboration of P.N.Mukhopādhyāy is acknowledged [GOL p. xi]. These were presumably written close to 1922 when the book was published and he was also collaborating with Mukhopadhyay on *World as Power.* The central section of *Garland* – chapters 10–21 plus chapter 24 – were first published in *Vedānta Keśari*, one of the journals of the Rāmakrishna Mission [GOL:xii]. Chapter 24 (*Varṇamālā*) is a general essay on Mantra, parts of which also occur in *Shakti and Shākta* and *The Serpent Power.* Chapters 10–21 we know appeared under the title *Studies in the Mantra Śāstra* (hereafter *Studies*) by Arthur Avalon in 1917–18, because most of the series were published as offprints in pamphlet form in those two years.[48] Many of these *Studies* focus on passages from texts.

The first part of *Garland* is on the whole much better written than the *Studies* section, which contain passages which are almost incomprehensible, being smothered by Sanskrit terminology and strained English. The book thus highlights two aspects of the Avalon/Woodroffe style which will be discussed later in this chapter.

The Serpent Power ('Serpent' or SP)

In the first edition of *Shakti and Shākta* and in *Studies, The Serpent Power* is referred to as a 'forthcoming publication', and it is closely linked thematically to these earlier books. Although the translations of the two Sanskrit texts with their detailed footnotes are unlikely to have been the work of Woodroffe, the seven introductory chapters most probably are. Ghose almost certainly helped him, but one reason for detecting Woodroffe rather than Ghose as the chief author of these chapters is that they rely even more heavily than any other of the Avalon/Woodroffe books on secondary sources in English (see below). The ascription to Arthur Avalon would have covered their collaboration, but mainly the fact that the Sanskrit text was translated by Ghose.

The World as Power (WAP)

This book originated as a series of long pamphlets or short books published between 1921–3. Mukhopadhyay's help is acknowledged throughout, but he only wrote one section himself, the last one, which was not included until the second edition in 1929 [WAP: 3,8,297]. This book, like all the Avalon/Woodroffe works contains a large range of references, but here they are all to books in English or occasionally other European languages, and there is noticeably less Sanskrit (although Sanskrit terms are still often used in parenthesis). Woodroffe's erudition here reflects that of the English educated Bengali intellectuals of the time. Nirad Chaudhury's autobiography – which covers the entire period of Woodroffe's life in Calcutta – reveals how very extensive and eclectic their reading could be.[49] P.N. Mukhopadhyay does not appear to have assisted Woodroffe with Sanskrit texts, and the pseudonym 'Arthur Avalon' never refers to his help which is always acknowledged under his own name.

Use of the pseudonym

The pseudonym was used for *Serpent*, for *Studies* and for some of the original articles that made up *Shakti and Shākta*. As we have seen, all of the last book and most of *Garland* consist of articles and lectures. In every case where a provenance is available for a particular chapter the pattern is the same: where it was first published as an article it was ascribed to Arthur Avalon; where it originated in a public lecture it was ascribed to Sir John Woodroffe. So it seems that at first Woodroffe used his own name only when he could not avoid it: he did not ascribe his public lectures to Arthur Avalon. *Shakti and Shākta* went out under his own name probably because it contained his lectures. By 1922, when he collaborated with Mukhopadhyay on *The World as Power* and there was no need for the assistance of a Sanskrit scholar, he felt able to use it again. *Garland* as a whole went by the name of Woodroffe, but the *Studies* were first published under the name of Arthur Avalon. It seems the pseudonym mainly covers collaboration over texts but not necessarily only the help of Ghose. We have seen it apply to Dawasamdup (above p. 214), and in *Studies* it may include the Kashmiri pandits who helped Woodroffe (see below).

Order of writing

Arthur Avalon's first English writings were *Introduction to Tantra Śāstra* and the preface and introduction to the first volume of *Principles of Tantra*. Apart from these, nearly all the remaining English writings on Tantra were published, firstly between 1915–19, and then between 1921–3 when Woodroffe's sections of *World as Power* were first published, as well as (probably) the first nine chapters of *Garland*. Looking in more detail, we can see that the *Studies* section of *Garland*, along with most of *Shakti and Shākta*, and the first edition of *Serpent* were completed in a very short time – in 1917 and 1918. They are closely linked, with some passages being repeated in them. Altogether the first publication of about thirty-four of the chapters of these three books can be firmly dated to the two years 1917 and 1918, with a little over half that number (about nineteen) probably falling outside them.

The interval between 1919 and 1921 corresponds with a period of furlough in England in late 1919–20, where Woodroffe would not have had the assistance of his collaborators. Very few English writings were initiated after 1923 following Woodroffe's retirement from India, although there were revisions for the third editions of *Shakti and Shākta* and *Serpent* in 1927 and 1928 respectively. We have seen that the *Tantrik Texts* also diminished in momentum for a while after 1922, suggesting that it was the relationship between Woodroffe and his collaborators, especially the two chief ones Ghose and Mukhopādhyāy, which was inspirational for both English and Sanskrit publications.

What about the period before 1915? We are told that *Serpent* (1918) was five years in preparation, which takes us back to 1913, the year that marks the beginning of all the publications.[50] For stylistic and other reasons to be discussed later, we can probably assign *An Introduction to Tantra Śāstra* first published in that year, to Atal Bihari Ghose rather than to Woodroffe. Although we cannot be certain whether it was Woodroffe or Ghose who wrote the introduction and preface to *Principles of Tantra* part 1 (1914), it is possible that, like the introductions in the *Tantrik Texts* series, they worked on it jointly. Certainly, attacks on missionary and orientalist writers and their influence over the Western educated public which is the main theme of this book, was also a major preoccupation of Ghose.[51]

Sanskrit

We can now turn to the puzzling question of Woodroffe's relationship with Sanskrit. We know for certain that he tried to learn it: the Foreword to the third edition of *Bhārata Shakti* records a conversation with 'a distinguished European Sanskritist' who asked Woodroffe if he had learned the language. 'My reply', reported Woodroffe 'was that I had not learned Sanskrit, but that I had been and was still learning Sanskrit in this country.' To which the European scholar is quoted as replying: 'What a pity! They cannot teach Sanskrit in this country, they have no system.'[52] Woodroffe reported this conversation in 1921 but did not say when it took place. It suggests that his studies continued for some time and that he was taught in the traditional manner of the pandits (which he is here defending). What is significant is that he was careful to claim not that he *had* learned Sanskrit, but only that he *was* learning it.

Let us now take a closer look at Ghose's note to Woodroffe referred to at the end of chapter 8, and the letter it accompanied [letters: 12 & 13]. 13 is a photocopy of part of a letter addressed to Woodroffe from a correspondent in South India, Mr Sentinath Iyer, who seems to have been a follower of the southern saivite sect of *Śaiva Siddhānta.* He made markings of his own on the pages, but the writing of Atal Bihari Ghose can be seen clearly above the passages in *devanāgarī* script and alongside in the margins. It is the same handwriting as on his own note, letter 12. I will return to the substance of these quotations later, but for the present we need only to note, first that the Sanskrit is very simple, and secondly that one of the passages consists almost solely of a list of sects:

> Kapāla, Lakula, Vāmā, Bhairava, Purvam, Paksitam Pancharatra, Pashupata and others of thousands.

This seems to suggest that Woodroffe needed help even with the *devanāgarī* script. Although *kāpāla* and *lākula* might have been unfamiliar names to him, *vāma, bhairava* and *pāñcharātra* he should have recognised because he used the words frequently in his writings.

Strange as this may seem, it is borne out by remarks made by someone who claimed to have taught Woodroffe Sanskrit. In chapter 6 we saw that according to Pal his teacher was Pandit Haridev Sastri, the High Court interpreter. But I was able to obtain a tape of an interview that took place in the 1960s on West Bengal Radio with professor Suniti Kumar Chatterji, by then a leading expert on Bengali linguistics, who claimed that when still a student he was recruited by Atal Bihari Ghose to teach Sanskrit to Woodroffe and his wife Ellen. S.K. Chatterji was quite scathing and said emphatically: 'Woodroffe did not know Sanskrit'; and then he told an anecdote about how he had been asked the meaning of a word which did not exist because Woodroffe could not even read the script properly. So it would seem that Ghose really did feel it necessary to transcribe the list of sects – although his note was written *seven years* later than the time Chatterji was talking about (see below). It is possible that Woodroffe had been accustomed to read Sanskrit in Bengali characters, as some Tantras had been published in that script, including *mahānirvāṇa*, *kulārṇava* and *śāradā tilaka.*[53] But if so it would seem a comparatively easy matter to learn *devanāgarī* too, especially as that was the script in which the *Tantrik Texts* editions were published.

S.K. Chatterji laughed at Woodroffe's ignorance, and implied that Ghose did so too. He recounts how Ghose had told him that Mrs Woodroffe was particularly interested in reading texts of Śankarācārya, whereupon Chatterji had protested that he was merely a student who had just completed his BA, and this did not qualify him to teach Sanskrit philosophical texts. According to him, Ghose simply laughed and said: 'That doesn't matter, it will be quite enough for them!'[54]

The date of Chatterji's BA was 1911.[55] If his story is quite true it certainly follows that Woodroffe did not translate the *mahānirvāṇa tantra* and publish it two years later in 1913. Neither did he and his wife translate the collection of *Hymns to the Goddess* which came out in the same year. The *Hymns* was an anthology drawn from a range of texts. What Chatterji says of Ellen Woodroffe agrees with what is written in the preface to the first edition: that she collaborated with the translations from texts ascribed to Śankarācārya, while Arthur Avalon alone was responsible for the rest;[56] and the fact that one of the first 'Avalon' publications came out jointly with his wife agrees with Chatterji's picture of the couple studying together at the beginning. Chatterji also states in this interview that Atal Bihari Ghose initially wanted the translation of *mahānirvāṇa tantra* to be published under Woodroffe's name but that it was Woodroffe who refused and chose the name Arthur Avalon to indicate their collaboration.

That Suniti Kumar Chatterji was Woodroffe's first teacher does not mean that he had no others as well; therefore his story does not necessarily contradict what Pal writes. What is problematical is that Pal states that Woodroffe met his Guru Sivacandra through Haridev Śāstri, 'his Sanskrit teacher', and that Woodroffe then introduced Havell to Sivacandra. If both statements are right then Woodroffe would have had to meet his Guru before 1906 when Havell left India. If he was already studying Sanskrit by then, it seems strange that he was still so ignorant in 1911. In either case, whether Woodroffe began his Sanskrit studies in 1906 or in 1911, Ghose's letter was written much later. It is dated 12 June 1918 when Arthur Avalon's books had been before the public for nearly six years. In fact it was written in the middle of what turns out to be Woodroffe's most productive period (see above). The first edition of *Shakti and Shākta* had already been published and the first edition of *Serpent* was about to come out in September of that year. The *Studies* had already been serialised in a journal; and eight volumes of *Tantrik Texts* had been published.

'Creation in the Tantra'

If Woodroffe began studying Sanskrit with Chatterji in or around 1911, he was four years into his studies when he gave his first public lecture on 'Creation in the Tantra' at the Dalhousie Institute in Calcutta – the gathering which was described in chapter 8.[57] The lecture was first published as a pamphlet by the Samiti in 1915, the year it was given, and there is little change from the text in that pamphlet and the chapter as it now stands in *Shakti and Shākta* [SS:379–408].[58] It is full of Sanskrit philosophical terms which Woodroffe appears to use very fluently. A degree of familiarity with philosophical vocabulary however does not imply the ability to read an unseen passage of text. But the second part of the lecture is based on the first chapter of *śāradā tilaka* with the commentary of Rāghava Bhatta, which was to be edited later by Ghose as *Tantrik Texts* 16 and 17. The chapter follows the text and commentary very closely: in fact passages of it are simply quotes in translation [SS:396ff]. It looks as if Woodroffe had studied the first chapter of the *śāradā tilaka* with the help of Ghose and perhaps a roman transcription of the text, or a Bengali edition.

A comparison between the pamphlet and the more polished version of the lecture in later editions of *Shakti and Shākta* shows that a few changes were made but the alterations are fairly minor.[59] It is characteristic of one of the Avalon/Woodroffe styles: rather convoluted, technical and "heavy", and surely confusing to those in his audience without a knowledge of the subject. Woodroffe has another, far easier style and this occurs when there is less use of Sanskrit quotations and when he is not closely following texts. A comparison of the 'Creation' lecture, with two lectures delivered later in London illustrates the difference. Although the London lectures might have demanded concentration from his audience, they are not so confusing to read. There are fewer textual references and the few Sanskrit terms used are explained in parenthesis [SS:409–34 and 463–81].

Woodroffe could quote Sanskrit *ślokas* when he gave a public lecture.[60] That he would have learned to do this if taught Sanskrit in the traditional manner is very likely, but that, too, does not imply an ability to read unseen texts. Taken together with his constant use of Sanskrit terminology, however, it would have helped to create the impression of Sanskrit erudition to the general public, and this was an important aspect of the image of Arthur Avalon as an English orientalist. If Woodroffe really was as ignorant of Sanskrit as appears from Ghose's letter and Suniti Kumar Chatterji's story, one wonders how he would have managed to keep up such a performance in a public lecture. If anyone had stood up and quoted a *śloka* which he did not understand he would have been exposed. More significantly, it appears as if the author of *Shakti and Shākta*, *Garland* and *Serpent* <u>thinks</u> about philosophical concepts through the medium of Sanskrit terminology.[61] Although even this can be achieved without needing to be proficient in grammar and translation, the mystery remains.

'Studies in the Mantra Shāstra'

The letter marked 3 in the appendix deepens it. This was a scribbled pencil note on High Court paper and though it is undated we can surmise it was written in 1917 or 1918:

> Dear Mr Ghose, Please run through this proof and make what corrections are necessary specially noting the Sanskrit quotations marked in red pencil.
>
> I shall be glad to have it back soon as it is the next article to appear in the Vedanta Kesari.

The articles in *Vedānta Keśari* as we have seen were the *Studies in the Mantra Śhāstra* which later became chapters 10–21 of *Garland*. Now, while the 'Creation' lecture could possibly have been written by someone without a reading knowledge of Sanskrit, it is harder to believe this of *Studies.* They have the appearance of extremely scholarly productions, with short quotations from texts which are commented on in detail, many references to other texts, and an even greater profusion of Sanskrit terminology. The brief note reveals that Ghose assisted Woodroffe with the Sanskrit quotations; but it was Woodroffe who was responsible for the article, since the proofs were sent to him, not Ghose. Moreover, if Ghose had written the article himself, or even produced it jointly with his friend, he presumably would not have needed to be told that it was for *Vedānta Keśari*.

Moreover the author of the *Studies* informs us that they resulted from his visit to Kashmir which he had undertaken in order to investigate what he called 'the northern Śaiva school' (ie 'Kashmir Śaivism'). He wanted to understand the relationship between the śaivite doctrine of the thirty-six *tattvas*, and the parallel śākta cosmogonic system concerning *mantras* and the *śaktis* associated with them, which as we have seen is the theme of *Garland* [GOL:185]. Although this does not rule out the possibility that Ghose contributed to the *Studies*, Woodroffe did visit Kashmir himself at this time. Some of his letters to Dawasamdup mention a journey to Kashmir and Ladakh where he visited the famous Hemis monastery, in the summer of 1916. This was just before the first of the *Studies* was published: from a reference in the second article in the series, the first one seems to have appeared in the December 1916 issue of *Vedānta Keśari*.[62]

The chapters as they stand in *Garland* reproduce the offprints from the magazine as published in 1917 and 1918: there are only a few very minor differences between the pamphlet versions and the book. It is very difficult to believe that Woodroffe could have written any of them in the year before he needed Ghose to translate Sentinath Iyer's quotations for him in June 1918.

In the *Studies* Arthur Avalon added significant Kashmir Śaivite texts to his repertoire of quotations and references. He mentions the Kashmiri pandit Harabhatta Sastri who provided him with a summary of the śaivite doctrine of cosmic evolution extracted from two texts: the *netra tantra* and the *tantrāloka*, but Avalon does not note that this latter text is by the great Abhinavagupta. Several quotations from the pandits's summary are printed, accompanied by English translations.[63]

In the other articles, Avalon pursues his study through quotations of verses from *tattva saṁdoha* by Kṣemarāja (again he does not note that this was Abhinavagupta's disciple) and *Īśvara-pratyabhijñā*, one of the core texts of Kashmir Śaivism, though again, he does not inform us of this fact. Indeed Avalon appears so unfamiliar with these texts that when citing the *tantrasāra* – another of Abhinavagupta's famous works – he has to distinguish it from the seventeenth century Bengali treatise of the same name [GOL 160–1]. Scholarship in English on Kashmir Śaivism was of course very much in its infancy at that time. (But see below on J.C. Chattopadhyay.)

The text which is quoted far more often than any other is, once again, the first chapter of *śāradā tilaka* with Rāghava Bhatta's commentary, the text which featured prominently in Woodroffe's 'Creation' lecture of 1915, before his Kashmir visit. Woodroffe, it seems, was trying to penetrate more deeply the world of ideas which this text had introduced to him. The doctrine of cosmic evolution through the thirty-six *tattvas* and the cosmogonic role of *śakti* became one of his major themes. It appears in the chapter entitled 'Cit Śakti' in *Shakti and Shākta* [SS:256–89] where the diagram at SS:285 illustrates the scheme, and this chapter and *Studies* were written around the same time. Woodroffe returned to the theme again in 1926 in his London lecture on the worship of the Goddess, in which he describes the *śrī yantra* [SS:409–34].

Apart from the texts named above, most of the other references in *Studies* are very brief but what they lack in length they make up in quantity. The impression these *Studies* give is of very extensive textual knowledge indeed. The extremely technical style, with Sanskrit terms and phrases constantly being used, sometimes in parenthesis and sometimes not, at times suggests that passages are translated directly from some Sanskrit commentary. As examples I will quote from just two passages: (The transliteration has been modernised in the 9th edition.)

> . . . it is said that ether is hollow or pitted (*Suśiracinam*), air is moving (*Calanaparah*), fire is digesting (*Paripākavān*), water is tasteful (*Rasavat*) and earth is solid (*Ghana*). All the universe is composed of the four Bhūtas entering into one another (*Parasparānupraviṣṭaih mahābhūtaiś caturvidhaih*) pervaded by ether (*Vyāptākāśaih*). [GOL:189][64]

And an example of his mingling of Sanskrit terminology in English sentences:

> Above Bindu, the Śaktis . . . become more and more subtle until Niṣkala Unmanī is reached which, as the Yoginīhṛdaya says, is uncreate motionless speech (*Anutpannaniṣpandāvāk*), the twin aspects of which are Samvit or the Void (Śūnya-Samvit) and Samvit as tendency to manifestation in a subtle state (*Utpatsuh samvid utpattyavasthā sūkṣmā*). Unmanī is beyond Kāraṇarūpā-Śakti; where there is no experience (Bhānam) or Kāla or Kalā nor of Devatā or Tattva, in the sense of category, as that which distinguishes one thing from another. It is Svanirvāṇam param padam, the Nirvikalpa-nirañjana-śiva śakti which is Guruvaktra. [GOL:120–1]

If Woodroffe wrote this, then even allowing for Ghose's revision of his Sanskrit quotations it seems superficially impressive. It is hard for the reader to follow, however, and one wonders in passages such as this last one whether the author himself altogether understood it, and the translation is somewhat garbled.[65] Nevertheless the author is attempting to understand the philosophy through the medium of the language. Reading such passages is like reading a text alongside a literal translation, and this may be a clue to what has happened. It looks as if Woodroffe is passing on the substance of his lessons, reproducing passages he has read with Ghose or other teachers, with the explanations he has been given by them; and sometimes he is confused.

If reading some of these chapters is like reading passages of text with the help of a teacher, it looks as if this is just what Woodroffe did with the 'traditional' scholars he met in Kashmir, especially Pandit Harabhatta Sastri whom he named. The pandit was a member of the team working for the *Kashmir Series of Texts and Studies* which had just started to be published from Srinagar. Its first volume appeared in 1911 edited by Jagdish Chandra Chattopadhyay, who was editor-in-chief of the whole series; he too acknowledges considerable help from Harabhatta Sastri.[66] Woodroffe called J.C. Chattopadhyay 'my friend' in 1917.[67] His *Kashmir Śaivism*, which was an introduction to the Kashmir series, had been published in 1914. It presents a detailed and rationalized account of the evolution of the *tattvas* and also contains in its first section an outline of the textual sources. Woodroffe does not appear to have read it when he produced his *Studies*. He does draw on it slightly later in the chapter on 'Embodied Consciousness' in *Serpent* [SP:58ff].

That Woodroffe had little Sanskrit is something alleged by Agehananda Bharati – formerly Leopold Fischer – who took *saññyās* and wrote an autobiography entitled *The Ochre Robe*. He studied at Benares in the 1950s and would have met people still living there at the time who had known Woodroffe. Bharati stated that Woodroffe knew very little Sanskrit himself but relied closely on pandits and others who did.[68] Read in the light of this statement, the *Studies in the Mantra Shāstra* suggest that the author did indeed rely totally on others' translation and interpretation. Although he makes references to many texts, he seems only to have actually studied short portions of a very few selected ones. It is interesting to see that some of the ideas he focuses on seem to be connected to ritual or *sādhanā* and inner experience. He also seems sometimes to be out of his depth. The *Studies in the Mantra Śhāstra*, although Ghose may have contributed to parts of them, do not need to have been written by an expert in Sanskrit, despite the very impressive knowledge their author appears to display.

If we concede this, then we must assume that others provided Woodroffe with most of his copious textual references which are such a feature of parts of his work. Some of them seem to be taken from the

Sanskrit commentators he has mentioned.[69] Others could have been supplied by his pandit teachers, and of course by Ghose himself. But a further look at Sentinath Iyer's letter also suggests another source and shows us the process in operation.

Sentinath Iyer's Letter

Returning now to letter 13 in the appendix, if we take note of all the *ślokas* which Ghose translated for Woodroffe, we can see that these have been incorporated into *Shakti and Shākta*, in the chapter entitled 'The Tantras and Their Significance' [DP ch.3].

The passages of interest begin at the top of SS(DP):56, where after the untranslated Sanskrit quotation from the *śrīmad bhāgavata*, the first edition had originally continued:

> According to a quotation which has been given me from the Vayu Samhitā the latter speaks of a twofold Shaivagama namely one which is based on Shruti and another independent of it. [SS(1):2]

This was followed by the transliterated Sanskrit text from *vāyu saṁhitā* of which this sentence was a paraphrase.[70] Now the Sanskrit word for the 'independent' branch of *śāivāgama* in the quotation was *svatantra*. This led Sentinath Iyer to complain that this term referred to some of the texts of *Śaiva Siddhānta*, and therefore the *śloka* appeared to state that these scriptures were not based on *śruti* – ie. that they were non-vedic or heterodox. He suggested that Woodroffe replace the quotation from *vāyu saṁhitā* with one from *sanatkumāra saṁhitā*, which he wrote out in *devanāgarī*. In the second and subsequent editions Woodroffe not only substituted a translation of this latter *śloka*, but he also inserted before it a paragraph incorporating Iyer's other quotations – from the *kurma purāṇa* – on the southern śaivite sects. He followed Ghose's translations of them fairly closely, though not exactly [SS(DP):56–7]. It is interesting to see from the letter that Ghose translated even the *śloka* from the *vāyu saṁhitā* which Woodroffe had already used in his first edition. Woodroffe also took from another part of Iyer's letter a quotation from the *kāmika āgama* on the definition of Tantra, which appears on the previous page [SS(DP):55, top].

These lengthy interpolations in the second edition have greatly expanded what began as a short article,[71] but they have also disturbed the flow of the original. The passage on the śaivite sects reads as if Woodroffe has inserted it without much understanding. After it, he writes: 'Into this mass of sects I do not attempt here to enter, except in a general way.' [SS(DP):57, top] It seems that he found all this confusing, and he inserts his summary of Iyer's quotations without much relevance to context. It is not really so important at this point to know the status of these different sects, some of them very ancient and obscure, such as the *lākula paśupatas*.[72] The sentence: 'It is Śuddhādvaita because in it there is no Viśeṣana' [SS(DP):56, bottom] comes from another of Iyer's letters. There is no obvious need for it, apart from keeping Iyer happy.

The significance of this, is that it shows us how Woodroffe took care to satisfy his correspondent's objections and to get the matter exactly right in the eyes of his Indian readership. He did not exclude anything Iyer gave him, whether relevant or not. Many other interpolations in this and other chapters of the expanded second and third editions of *Shakti and Shākta* may have originated in similar correspondence with readers, or from conversations with friends and contacts. Passages like this one give an impression of great meticulousness at the cost of clarity, but it begins to look as if this was done not so much out of pedantry – as might at first appear – as out of a desire to satisfy as many people as possible.

Woodroffe does not acknowledge Iyer as the source for these references, but he has told us that the original quotation from the *vāyu saṁhitā* in the first edition, which prompted Iyer's letter, was given to him by someone else. In SS:509, he mentions a passage in the *Ṛg Veda* similar to the biblical story of the Tower of Babel and says a friend has told him of it but has forgotten to send the reference. (The story is repeated in another chapter, still mentioning the friend and still without the reference: p. 521]). We can assume that besides Ghose himself, there were many such friends and correspondents like Iyer who provided references. On the whole Woodroffe was scrupulous about acknowledging his sources, other than Ghose, where he has drawn extensively from them, but to have done so for the great number of short quotes and references to texts which fill his work would obviously have been impracticable.

Most of the numerous Sanskrit references in the books are very brief and many are repeated in several different places. It might seem obvious that referring to a text, even providing a short quotation, does not imply having direct access to it oneself, but the large number of such references in his writings contributes to the impression of great Sanskrit learning which belongs to Woodroffe's image as Arthur Avalon.

Woodroffe's relationship to the texts

There are some texts, however, like *śāradā tilaka* – referred to above – which Woodroffe mentions especially frequently, portions of which he seems to have studied in the original. In most cases he probably did so with Ghose, though sometimes with others, as we have seen. Most important among them are the two Tantras which were specially popular with the Bengali *bhadralok*: the *mahānirvāṇa*, and the *kulārṇava* which was edited as TT/5.[73] We have seen that the former was considered a very restrained Tantra as far as "immoral" practices were concerned.[74] Despite describing the *pañcatattva* and other sexual rituals in detail *kulārṇava* too could be presented as having a high moral, even "puritanical" tone if quoted selectively and some passages were used to this effect by Woodroffe.[75] But it also contains passages which might have shocked, and this could perhaps be the reason why the promised translation, that Ghose was working on, was never published. The Foreword to the Sanskrit edition of the text stated that a translation on the same lines as that of *mahānirvāṇa* would be published shortly and therefore no detailed summary of the contents was provided. As already stated, the incomplete translation was found in Ghose's house. Some of Woodroffe's references to *kulārṇava* in *Shakti and Shākta* are more detailed than his usual quotations. A long quote from its 'grand opening chapter' on the frailty of Man, in a lecture of January 1917, is a fairly close paraphrase of Ghose's translation [SS:457].

The eighth chapter of *kulārṇava* describes seven *ullāsas* – states of ecstasy approaching a condition where all constraints are dissolved and 'the command (of Shiva) is that which is willed (by the Sādhaka)'.[76] These passages appear to describe a drunken orgy. They certainly suggest a cult of ecstasy. Ghose in his notes interprets the *ullāsas* as symbolic of states of mystical union.[77] Woodroffe makes a brief reference to this passage in his chapter on the *pañcatattva*, where he provides several explanations from which his readers may take their pick: that *ullāsas* are stages of initiation; that a pandit has told him the passage is not authentic; that it is not meant to be taken seriously [SS:616–7].[78] Other passages in *kulārṇava tantra* make fairly clear that sexual intercourse takes place within the ritual. Woodroffe is aware of this but allows it no more than a passing reference, which is immediately followed by citations of the text's moral injunctions [SS:593]. In presenting the *kulārṇava tantra* as a text preaching restraint of the senses, Woodroffe has told only half the truth.

The Ocean of Kula (*kulārṇava*) was advertised on early lists of forthcoming publications, along with *The Six Centres and the Serpent Fire* before the latter finally took shape as *The Serpent Power* about five years after the first publications appeared. By this time all mention of *The Ocean of Kula* had disappeared. Even so, the three texts, *mahānirvāṇa*, *kulārṇava*, and *ṣaṭ-cakra* seem to have been selected for translation very early on and to have formed the basis for Woodroffe's own study of Tantra. He also studied the first chapter of *śāradā tilaka* with the interpretations of its commentator Rāghava Bhatta in very great detail, but he does not to refer to any other chapter of that text. Although all of the texts in the *Tantrik Texts* series are referred to occasionally in Avalon/Woodroffe's English writings, the most frequently cited are these four: *mahānirvāṇa*, *kulārṇava*, *ṣaṭ-cakra* and *śāradā*. Of these, we have seen that *mahānirvana* and *sāradā* were edited by Ghose himself, and of the other two, he translated *ṣaṭ-cakra* for *The Serpent Power*, and *kulārṇava* he translated but never published. So this is strong evidence that Ghose was Woodroffe's most important – though not sole – source of textual knowledge. We have seen that Woodroffe was very far from being completely dependent on him, for he also sought out other scholars and pandits in many places.

Two other texts referred to several times in *Shakti and Shākta*, though far less frequently, are the unpublished *sammohana tantra*, of which there was only one manuscript [SS:348], and the tantric anthology called *sarvollāsa*, whose author Sarvanandanatha was the subject of an article by Woodroffe in 1920 in which he states that he came across the manuscript 'three years ago' [SS:251–5]. There are three other references to *sarvollāsa*, all occurring in passages dating from 1917 [SS:146, 172, 349].[79] In this connection, Woodroffe acknowledges Dineśa Candra Bhattāchāryya [SS:251], who had provided him with his unpublished article on Sarvanandanātha, because he wanted the latter's place 'in the history of the so-called "Tantricism" of Bengal duly recognized [SS:251]. So here we have another instance of someone inviting Woodroffe to use the fruits of his own research because of his high public profile. Like Sentinath Iyer's letter, it suggests the way in which Woodroffe in the role of Arthur Avalon was used by the Indian public to reflect back to them (with added prestige) their own knowledge.

For the *śrī vidyā* school, Woodroffe drew on two texts substantially quoted in *Serpent*: *ānandalaharī* (Wave of Bliss) with Laksmidhara's commentary, and Bhāskararāya's eighteenth century Sanskrit commentary on *Śrī Lalitā Sahasranāma* (the 'Thousand Names' of the Goddess), which is also quoted in *Garland*. These texts describe the worship of Tripurasundarī in her *maṇḍala*, the *śrī yantra*. But although a translation of the former text was published by Arthur Avalon,[80] Woodroffe's English writings know both of them only through the English translations of R. Anantakrishna Sastri, a pandit who worked for the Theosophical Society at Adyar.[81] Another text of one branch of this school was the *tantrarāja tantra* [TT/8 and 12]. Its detailed introduction signed Arthur Avalon provided material for Woodroffe's London lecture of 1926 on the 'Magna Mater' [SS:409–34]. *Kāma-kalā-vilāsa*, another very important text on the *śrī yantra*, translated by 'Arthur Avalon' as *Tantrik Texts* vol.10, Woodroffe refers to only very rarely.

Secondary sources

Thus we can see a third important element in Woodroffe's knowledge, besides the texts he read with Ghose and others and his wide contacts and correspondence – namely his very wide reading in secondary literature. His works are as full of English references as Sanskrit ones and occasionally French, German or Italian authors are also mentioned. Where other European orientalists are referred to, it is usually in order to refute them, though scientific or philosophical writers are used to endorse śākta-tantric ideas or to provide comparative material. Among the few exceptions in the former category was Otto Schrader, librarian at the Theosophical Society[82] whose introduction to his edition of *ahirbudhnya saṁhitā* (a Vaiṣṇava

Pāñcarātra text) Woodroffe cites [SS:59]. He has also benefitted from Louis de la Vallée Poussin who gets several favourable references – especially in regard to Buddhism – as does his French contact Masson Oursel.[83]

Secondary literature on Tantra and related subjects by contemporary Indian writers, on the other hand, whether in English or Bengali, is often drawn on and deferred to. As already mentioned, Pandit Anantakrishna Sastri,[84] J.C. Chattopadhyay (above p. 223) and Brajendranath Seal (above p. 172) are all extensively quoted in *Serpent.* Besides his *Kashmir Śaivism*, Chattopadhyay's *Hindu Realism* ,[85] is a prominent source in *World as Power.* A notice in *Modern Review* describes both Seal and Chattopadhyay as leading modern reinterpreters of Indian philosophy. They both belonged to the *bhadralok*; the latter combined the status of traditional 'pandit' with that of modern Western trained scholar.[86] Brajendranath Seal was Professor of Philosophy at the Calcutta University, and a member of the *Sādhāran Brahmo Samaj*, who later became a secular humanist.[87]

Apart from these major sources long extracts covering several pages are lifted directly from other Indian writers – for example, Saccidānanda Swāmi, whose 'modern' account of the grades of Kaula practice are paraphrased over several pages [SS:155–60]; and Jādaveśvara Tarkaratna's 'orthodox' views – from his article on the history and antiquity of Tantra – are quoted at length in the introduction to *Principles of Tantra*, and his textual references are used and acknowledged in *Shakti and Shākta* [PT/1:48–66; SS:145]. An article on the origins of Tantra by an anonymous Indian writer in the journal *Prabuddha Bhārata*, and Panchkori Bāndyopādhyay's lengthy review of Avalon's *mahānirvāṇa* translation were both reproduced in the introduction to the second volume of *Principles of Tantra* [PT/2:11–16, and 16–22]. Finally, there are whole sections or chapters which are direct contributions from Indian scholars – for example the long introductory chapter to *Principles of Tantra* volume 2 was written by Barada Kanta Majumdar, and a Note to a chapter in *Shakti and Shākta* on precedents for tantric practices to be found in vedic rituals, was contributed by Braja Lal Mukherji [PT/2:25–153; SS:103–114].

Then there was of course Woodroffe's friend and second major collaborator, P.N. Mukhopadhyay, later to become an influential guru in Calcutta. Apart from *Garland* and *World as Power* to which he made major contributions, his pseudo-scientific theories about *kuṇḍalinī* were worked out in correspondence with Woodroffe. This was summarized in the short chapter on *kuṇḍalinī* in *Shakti and Shākta* and at greater length in *Serpent* [SS:695–700; SP:297–313]; and his explanation of Pure Awareness found a place in the chapter on Consciousness in the former book [SS:267–8]. P.N. Mukhopadhyay was, as one reviewer put it, 'unnecessarily technical' and his books could 'scare away not only lay readers but also many philosophic students'.[88] But Woodroffe made a serious attempt to unpack his ideas and present them in accessible form.

Briefer references are made to many other Indian writers, for example: Nallaswami Pillai, author of a book on *Śaiva Siddhānta* and its Introduction by V.V. Ramana Śāstrin [SS:59, PT/1 pp. 42–3, 45]; J.N. Mazumdar's paper to the Indian Research Society [SS:375]; Pandit Jayacandra Siddhāntabhūṣana, who wrote an essay explaining the *pañcatattva* [SS:605]; Professor S.N. Dasgupta (soon to publish his standard history of Indian philosophy in 1920) [SS:54, 323]; and Pandit Candrakānta Tarkālankāra's Bengali lectures on Hindu philosophy [SS:308, 324].

Apart from long passages quoted from Anantakrishna Śāstri and Brajendranath Seal, the whole of *Serpent* draws heavily on secondary sources. A section on *rāja yoga* seems closely based on a pamphlet by Dayananda Saraswati published by the *Ārya Samaj*. This makes for some confusion as the writer of the pamphlet considered *rāja yoga* superior to *kuṇḍalinī yoga*, but Woodroffe placed it as the culmination of his chapter on 'Practice'.[89] This might have reflected his later misgivings about *kuṇḍalinī yoga*, referred to above in chapter 10.

In *Serpent*, as in *Shakti and Shākta* and *Garland*, some paragraphs are quotes from translated Sanskrit texts or their commentaries, along with the references cited by the commentator. For example, a sentence beginning 'The Ācārya . . .' in a chapter of *Serpent* is confusing, until one perceives that one is actually reading the translation of a Sanskrit commentary by Bhāskararāya.[90] This book quotes so frequently that it sometimes becomes difficult to establish where one cited author or text ends and another begins. Yet it is the very abundance of references to texts and to other sources that makes it encyclopedic in scope, if also confusing in places.

The first chapter of the first edition of *Serpent* included two long quotations exemplifying 'modern criticism' of *kuṇḍalinī yoga* which were then answered by Woodroffe, or possibly by Ghose. The first was a letter from the disciple of 'an English educated Guru' – giving rise to an acerbic footnote to the effect that it was always necessary to note such a fact [SP:273, ftnt.2]. Perhaps this indicates the influence of Ghose. The second extract was taken from a book by an unnamed 'Brahmo author'. These two sections have been displaced in the later editions from the introductory chapter, where they were much better suited, to chapter 8 [SP:273–87]. Thus the first edition of *Serpent* began with an introduction along the lines of that to *Principles of Tantra*, addressing the already existing images of its subject matter in the minds of the English educated public. Displacing them to a later chapter might have been intended to give the critics' opinions more weight – especially to the second, the 'Brahmo author' some of whose ideas appeal to Woodroffe [SP:286]. Some of the other long quotations in Woodroffe's books are also there for discursive reasons – to present one side of an argument which is then discussed or criticised, as happens for example following Jādaveśvara Tarkaratna's contribution [PT/1:66–7].

This list could be longer but these examples have been given to show how Woodroffe's books could be seen in the light of a compendium of contemporary Indian scholarship and hermeneutics in the field of Tantra. Indian writers, except when they are considered to be influenced by Western orientalist prejudices, are usually treated with respect, and even when criticised are never condemned in the tones directed at foreigners. Thus Pandit Anantakrishna Shastri's negative attitude to the *kaula* sects is gently and respectfully disputed [SP 250–1, footnotes].[91] If some Indian writers have ideas that seem extravagant or unconvincing, Woodroffe adds his own balanced commentary afterwards. Sometimes he uses their contributions as points for discussion; sometimes he answers their criticisms; but whenever he can, he accommodates their views. Above all, they were a major source of his own knowledge.

It becomes clear then how Woodroffe made very extensive use of secondary sources, whether these were literature, personal contacts, or correspondence. He usually gives his references, and although we cannot be sure that he always does so, this provides understanding of how his books were built up. Writing in the tradition of the nineteenth century 'gentleman scholar' and amateur – which was of course much more acceptable in his day than in our own – he evidently read as much as his Sanskrit knowledge permitted him in the original texts, though presumably always with the help of written or oral translations. Even allowing for Atal Bihari Ghose's close assistance, it is still a very impressive performance. It shows us how far a skilful and dedicated use of 'informants' and secondary sources could take a scholar who had no direct access to Sanskrit at this period, when Indian scholarship in English was abundant. It took Woodroffe further into the realm of the 'insider' than those among his European contemporaries who could rely on their own linguistic skills. It was a paradox: Arthur Avalon was meant to be a western scholar, but what he presented to his Indian readers was their own interpretation of their own religious culture, to which he acted as a mirror and mediator.

III STYLES – GHOSE OR WOODROFFE?

One solution to the problem of Woodroffe's apparent Sanskrit expertise might be available if there were an obvious difference between an 'Arthur Avalon' style and a Woodroffe one. Then one could attribute the former to Atal Bihari Ghose, as might seem to be implied by Woodroffe's disclaimer in his preface to *Shakti and Shākta*. A thorough stylistic comparison of the different portions of the Avalon/Woodroffe works would probably not be of great interest, especially as we can assume that the two collaborators often worked closely together. The following are put forward merely as suggestions that might indicate how the two contributions could be distinguished.

Some examples of Ghose's writing in English under his own name are available and do bear resemblances in style and content to passages of *Shakti and Shākta* and *Serpent*. The two short articles from the American *Occult Digest* already mentioned,[92] summarised Śākta Tantra as an integral part of what Ghose called 'Brahmanism' or *Brahmanya Dharma* – which we have seen is one of Woodroffe's themes. They do so with a simplicity and economy unusual in the Avalon/Woodroffe books and with a minimum of Sanskrit terminology. The contents of one of these articles is close to a chapter in *Shakti and Shākta* entitled 'Alleged Conflict of Śāstras' [SS:235–50] which describes the doctrines of *adhikāra* and *bhumika*: 'competency' and 'grades' of spiritual knowledge. It says that differing philosophical views (*darśanas*) should not be treated as conflicting versions of 'truth', but as varying levels of understanding according to the 'competence' (*adhikāra*) of the individual. This is the basis of Hinduism's 'tolerance' that we have seen deeply appealed to Woodroffe.

Other examples of Ghose's writing are: an article entitled *Śiva and Śakti* published in the Varendra Research Society bulletin;[93] and 'The Spirit and Culture of the Tantras' in a collection entitled *Studies on the Tantras* published by the Ramakrishna Mission.[94] These contain more Sanskrit than the two short articles for the American periodical, but not to the extent that it overloads the English text. Both their style and content would be familiar to anyone who has read *Shakti and Shākta*, except that Ghose, even more than Avalon/Woodroffe, stresses the symbolic over the literal aspects of sexuality in Tantra. These articles are written in a simple style and do not tax the reader with complicated terminology. Yet Ghose keeps close to his Sanskrit texts: he cites them frequently, but in context. He does not refer to any secondary source in English, but on the contrary seems completely at home in the Sanskrit literature. Nor does he occupy himself with much metaphysical discussion of the different forms of *advaita*, of the *tattvas* and other matters, which so fascinated Woodroffe.

Ghose's style is similar to that of the *Shakti and Shākta* chapter on '*cīnācāra*' [SS:192–204], which we can almost certainly ascribe to him, since it summarises texts. 'Alleged Conflict of Śāstras' [SS:235–50], which has just been mentioned, was an article for *Indian Philosophical Review* signed with the pseudonym. It contains much Sanskrit terminology, but considering its readership, that is not inappropriate. The writer cites many texts whose contents he expounds in a clear and fairly simple style. The theme – that 'Brahmanical' schools of thought form a coherent whole which caters for all grades of spiritual development – is pursued without digressions into metaphysical discussion. This chapter of *Shakti and Shākta* too may be by Ghose. So might some of the later chapters of *Garland*, which originated in articles other than those of the *Studies* series, and while containing frequent references to texts, are in a simpler style.[95] Woodroffe himself could write reasonably clearly, but this was usually when he was *not* referring closely to texts. These however are conjectures. Since Woodroffe studied from Ghose, it is likely that he frequently wrote up in his own style material with which his collaborator had provided him. For example we have seen how 'someone' (and it may well have been Ghose) gave Woodroffe a 'note' about the *Gāyatri mantra* which he then used as the basis for a lecture (above p. 84).

There are some instances, however, when I believe it is both possible and significant to separate them. Ghose's chapter in *Studies on the Tantras* covers its subject matter in short paragraphs under subsidiary headings. This is not at all like Woodroffe's writing which tends to be more discursive and rambling. It is however similar to the earliest of the Avalon publications, the Introduction to the translation of *mahānirvāṇa tantra*, later published separately as *An Introduction to Tantra Śāstra*. The writer of this book seems to experience less difficulty in explaining tantric concepts with comparative economy than Woodroffe appears to have had later on, and passages from it have been reproduced in *Shakti and Shākta* and *Serpent*, suggesting that Woodroffe could not find a better way of explaining some points. This *Introduction* has the familiar Avalon/Woodroffe style of using a lot of Sanskrit terminology, sometimes in parenthesis, sometimes in the text and without always translating it – but, again, not to the extent that occurs in the *Studies in the Mantra Shāstra*. *An Introduction to Tantra Śāstra* is written in a clearer style than many passages in the later books. It is simple and factual, confining itself to imparting information and not embarking on philosophical discourses. Nor does it rely at all on secondary sources, but on the other hand quotes frequently from the relevant texts. It lives up, in fact, to its name, for it is a compact introduction to the whole field of Tantra. Its author obviously has very wide knowledge and never gives the impression of being confused by his subject matter. For these reasons, and also because it was the earliest publication we can probably consider Ghose to be at least the leading collaborator if not the sole author of this Introduction. That would make the whole *mahānirvāṇa* translation with its introduction in its first edition, in effect the work of Ghose rather than Woodroffe, and it is significant to recall that it was this publication which first established the reputation of the pseudonymous Arthur Avalon among the Indian public and foreign orientalists, as we saw in chapter 8.

The 'heavy' style, the confusing proliferation of quotes and references, and overloading with Sanskrit that occurs in some parts of the other books look like the direct result of Woodroffe's collaboration with others. One gets the impression that he was sometimes confused by Ghose or his other informants, who had supplied him with more information and references than he could assimilate. The result in *Studies* and in Woodroffe's use of Sentinath Iyer's letter, are examples of what could happen.

On the other hand, Woodroffe has a talent for writing about metaphysical subjects, in which he has more interest than Ghose has.

When he has distanced himself from the texts – and perhaps from his collaborators too – Woodroffe's writing can also be distinguished for being far more romantic, and more philosophical in the popular sense, than that of Ghose. Woodroffe's romanticism is revealed most clearly in passages of writing which are not about Tantra: in his description of the landscape by the sea near Konarak [GOL:xiii]; in his writings on art appreciation – for example a short article in the Madras magazine *Sha'ama* describing his impressions of Japanese temples[96] – and Ganguly remarked that Woodroffe's early reviews of Indian art exhibitions 'created mild sensations'.[97] This romanticism also penetrates the tantric writings in many places and adds touches of beauty or spirituality. An example can be given from the lecture on the 'the Indian Magna Mater' which Woodroffe delivered in London, long after his researches were complete. This lecture is a summary of what he had learned in India; its third and last section is specially fine. It concludes:

> The Śākta unites himself with this joyous and liberating Mother, saying *Sā'ham* – "She I am". As he realizes this he is the fearless Hero or *Vīra* . . . and fearlessness is also the mark of the Illuminate Knower . . . Such an one is not troubled for himself by the thought of Death . . . An imperishable instinct tells him that if he, like the leaves, is about to fall he is also the tree on which they will come out again, as also the Earth in which both grow, and yet again . . . the Essence which as the Mother-Power sustains them all . . . Either man's consciousness expands into that Lordliness which sees all as Itself, or he and all lower beings are withdrawn into the Womb of Power in which they are conserved to reappear in that *Sphurana* or Blossoming which is the Springtide of some new World. [SS:433–4]

This is not at all like Ghose's style, which is much more pedestrian, though it has the virtues of clarity and simplicity.

Several articles which did not find their way into the books were published in *Vedānta Keśari* in 1922 and 1924. The shortest, entitled 'The Wise Childhood', was signed 'Sir John Woodroffe'. Four others are on tantric ritual and are signed Arthur Avalon.[98] Themes familiar from *Shakti and Shakta* are present in them, especially in one on 'Pūjā' which recalls parts of Woodroffe's lecture on 'The Psychology of Hindu Religious Ritual' [SS:463–81] which was delivered in London shortly afterwards, in 1925. (Perhaps this article was a source of 'raw material' for that lecture). They are mostly factual, and closely related to texts. There is much use of Sanskrit terminology, not all of it translated; there are no references to secondary sources. The articles are straightforward and economical, apart from the occasional jibe at foreign orientalists or 'modern' Hindus. They could very well be the work of Ghose. 'The Wise Childhood' is a striking contrast. It is Woodroffe at his simplest. It seems to have been inspired by

'Alleged Conflict of Śāstras' and refers to the main text around which that chapter was built [see SS:236]. It discusses the meaning of a short sanskrit phrase, where Woodroffe's gramatical argument has presumably followed that of Ghose; but he then departs from the text into meditation in a philsophic and romantic vein, connecting the simplicity of childhood with the 'Beautiful ... vision of the sage-child in which naturalness is suffused and enriched by knowledge.'[99]

These are only hints, but perhaps they help us distinguish the two personalities whose distinctive gifts merged to create the figure of 'Arthur Avalon'.

CONCLUSION

In the last edition of *Is India Civilized?* Woodroffe prophesied that the philosophical concepts of India would be appropriated by the West and added to its cultural wealth.[1] He probably could not have imagined the extent to which he would be proved correct, nor have known the part he himself was playing in the beginnings of this process. From being seen as a primitive system of magic, the image of Tantra was transformed rapidly into that of a subtle philosophy that appealed to sophisticated minds in the West, thus greatly enhancing the prestige of Hindu thought.

It was not only as a writer on Tantra that Arthur Avalon was influential, but also as an interpreter of Hinduism. M.P. Pandit's remarks, quoted in chapter 8, about the transparency of Avalon's writing to the 'original thought in Sanskrit' point to an important though paradoxical ingredient of this. For those prepared to persevere with them, the books provided an education in Hindu thought that was unique for a long time, despite their many obscurities and confusing passages. I have attempted to show how this came about despite Woodroffe's own comparative ignorance of Sanskrit, but with the help of Ghose's knowledge of it. Indeed, the very limitations to Woodroffe's knowledge increased that of 'Arthur Avalon', by making Woodroffe more dependent than academic Sanskritists of the time on sources among modern 'insiders' to the tantric tradition. Paradoxically, too, Woodroffe's very inability to translate philosophical vocabulary into English for himself made him rely on the Sanskrit terms and phrases which occur so frequently in his work, and he passes this familiarity on to his readers.

In India, the books represented a re-interpretation of the tantric tradition, which could now take its place as an accepted aspect of modern Hinduism. This re-evaluation was presented under the name of a foreign orientalist. The prestige of European scholarship was less than it had been a generation earlier, before the revival of confidence in Hindu identity at the beginning of the twentieth century. Orientalists who condemned Hinduism no longer carried the weight that they had done once; but when they approved and eulogised, their prestige was still alive and was welcome because it could be appropriated. This is illustrated by the response to the 'Arthur Avalon' legend in India. But in contrast to orientalists such as Max Muller of a previous generation, Avalon's hermeneutic method was wide open to interpretations that originated in India itself. However much European idealization and projection upon an essentialised 'spiritual India' contributed to the attraction of the books in the West, my contention is that the story that unfolds in this book is mainly one of Indian agency. The prestigious image of European orientalism was harnessed to a modern Indian agenda: the propagation of an updated and 'purified' Hindu Tantrism, and a reversal of Western valuations of it.

This brings us to Atal Behari Ghose, who has not had as prominent a place in this book as he could have had, and who could be the subject of another study himself. 'Arthur Avalon' appropriated much of his life's work. When Woodroffe called the *Tantrik Texts* 'his' publications, he was right insofar as his own money and organizing drive lay behind them, but without the textual scholarship of Atal Behari Ghose in the background they could not have existed. Furthermore the translation and introduction to *mahānirvāṇa tantra* which launched Arthur Avalon's reputation with such *éclat*, as we saw at the beginning of chapter 8, must have owed very much more to Ghose than to Woodroffe. Even the influence of *Shakti and Shākta* was greatly enhanced by the belief that it was written by the same person who possessed the textual knowledge of the translator of *mahānirvāṇa* and the editor of *Tantrik Texts*.

Ghose was a gifted teacher and a channel of knowledge to other Westerners besides Woodroffe. He could present ideas in a more easily accessible form than Woodroffe could, though without the latter's romanticism. However much or well he wrote however, he could never at that time have carried the weight that 'Arthur Avalon' could carry without Woodroffe's mediation. The desire to propagate his own religious beliefs and to raise their status in modern opinion, was his motive for actively promoting the deception that Woodroffe was the real Arthur Avalon. It would not be true to say, however, that the latter was 'really' Ghose either: he was a symbiosis of the two. Woodroffe's contribution was more than merely social prestige. He had an unerring instinct for public relations. He was a skilful apologist. Whenever he felt himself sufficiently master of his material, he could write in a style that was inspiring and won over the public through the width of his tolerance and his capacity to interpret Tantra in popular modern ways. This is as important a feature of the books as their textual knowledge.

The 'Arthur Avalon' symbiosis meant a certain loss of identity to both partners. On the one hand it can be looked upon as an instance of a British person, with greater power and social status in the colonial society, appropriating the knowledge of an Indian scholar. Although Ghose actively promoted this, Woodroffe's dominating tone in his correspondence reveals that he did not consciously acknowledge the extent of his reliance on his collaborator's expertise, while the fame and status of the pseudonymous Arthur Avalon was entirely reflected onto him. Yet not only was Ghose's textual knowledge essential for Woodroffe to play the orientalist's role on the public stage, but his skill in teaching has obviously benefitted Woodroffe himself, as well as those parts of the books which directly emanated from his collaborator.

There was also a subtle current that ran in the opposite direction. There are suggestions in his books that Woodroffe, too, felt that he lost out to 'Arthur Avalon'. We find him struggling not to have opinions expressed through 'his' name that he does not want to claim. His repeated insistence that he was an outside observer not a participator in Tantra could reflect an internal conflict. While it had the effect of consolidating the image of Arthur Avalon as the orientalist scholar studying the subject impartially, it most probably reflected his own ambivalence about the collaboration. 'Arthur Avalon' was a kind of 'legal fiction' that resulted in books (or parts of books) being attributed to Woodroffe that were not entirely his. But the pseudonym may also have served as a protective barrier that Woodroffe attempted to place between himself and Ghose, who seems to have wanted to make even greater use of his British friend's social identity. Ghose, it seems, would have preferred all the books to go by Woodroffe's own name: it was Woodroffe who invented the pseudonym and insisted on it.

Whatever the intricacies of this subtle story, and whatever the degree, or lack of it, of conscious deception, 'Arthur Avalon' was a project that worked extremely well – drawing prestige to Tantra from the status of the British partner in the symbiosis, and from the history of European orientalism. Arthur Avalon was a greater figure than either Woodroffe or Ghose alone could hope to be. In his own early foreword to the *prapañcasāra tantra*, Woodroffe had written:

> It is common knowledge that in the history of all religions, works are attributed to great names to gain for them an authority which their real author could not perhaps have achieved. [TT/18:2.]

One wonders if he ever perceived the connection with his own contribution to the modern tantric 'texts' he was helping to create.

This book has also been a study of a British supporter of Indian nationalism, of the same time and milieu as Annie Besant, Nivedita, and C.F. Andrews. Here, instead of the orientalist projection on to, and distancing from, the 'other', we have instances of identification with that 'other'. Woodroffe seemed ambivalent about his British identity, and escaped from it on occasions into a private Indian one; the former was 'official', the latter was personal; the former was public, the latter half-secret. His concern to defend the Indian 'Self' from the inroads of westernization may have reflected his need to protect an aesthetic, spiritual identity of his own, perhaps identified as 'feminine' within the colonial context of rugged stereotypes of 'super-masculinity'.[2] It certainly reflected a felt need to defend the quality of 'soul' or 'spirit' in an atmosphere of increasing secularism spread by Western influence.

Finally there is the attitude to sexuality implied but not explicitly stated throughout the Avalon/Woodroffe work. The 'sexual revolution' in Western society was still to come when Woodroffe was writing, and there is nothing in his work, ostensibly, that even points towards it. Nevertheless 'Tantra' in modern popular consciousness is about the 'spiritualization' of sex, and Arthur Avalon is generally believed to be an early exponent of it. What is actually present in his work is something more subtle: an 'incarnational' theology linked to affirmation of the life of the senses, of 'this world', of matter, in opposition to the values of the renouncer and ascetic. It also appropriated current scientific ideas, which attempted to unite the spiritual and 'magical' world-view of occultism with the terminology of contemporary science – a project that was then, as it is now, a fashionable one. It reflected a need for a more holistic interpretation of reality than that felt to proceed from modern scientific consciousness. In this Woodroffe as Arthur Avalon was an early herald of the 'New Age'.

Last but not least there is the story of a remarkable collaboration that crossed the colonial divide and to which both partners remained faithful for several decades, until death, by taking the two friends at the same time, seemed to seal the hidden bond that forged Arthur Avalon.

Appendix 1

LETTERS

N.B. Woodroffe's handwriting is difficult. Illegible words or phrases are indicated by dots.

LETTER 1: NOTE FROM WOODROFFE TO GHOSE (handwritten)

(no address)

Sunday (no date)

Dear Mr Ghose –

As my wife is in town & cannot return before 11.30 or 12 and I have nothing to do between 10 or when I finish my bath & 12 I want you to come to me if you will. If you will come now the driver will bring you to the Sanitarium[1] Park Street near Morello's & then we will go together to Mr Hirsh's house 5 Mission Row[2] where we can do some work until my wife is ready when we can all return to Barrackpore.[3] If you will be with me at Park Street about 10 o'clock I will wait for you there. Don't forget to bring all the papers.

Yours
John G Woodroffe

LETTER 2: WOODROFFE TO GHOSE (handwritten)

13(?15) Alexandra Court,
3 Middleton Row

Dear Mr Ghose

I enclose a/c made up by Mr Moller & which I have been through showing our respective indebtedness to him on a/c of our trip to Konarak last Easter and the two railway tickets he took for you & Mrs Ghose. You owe him 96/2 of the 60/- I gave you. If as you said there is anything over (?) this should be divided in three parts you keeping one third & returning 2/3 for Mr Mueller & self.

Now if I remember rightly you paid for Mr Wurthle's carts which came (?) I suppose out of the 45/- we have credited you – In that case please let me know what was paid for the carts for we are entitled (?) to get this back from Hoffmann's & when so obtained (?) it should be divided in three amongst us – When I hear what the amount (?) is I will write to Mr Hoffmann. Mr Wurthle only returned the day before yesterday.

As regards the printing of the Shatchakra you had better send a few lines to Bannerjee (?) to be printed to see the effect. If the margin is too small then we must increase the size of the page. Please do this at once as we cannot continue(?commence?) until the size of page for the ... (?lines? ?text?) is determined on.

Yours sincerely (?)
John G. Woodroffe

LETTER 3: PHOTOCOPY OF LETTER

(see above p. 220)

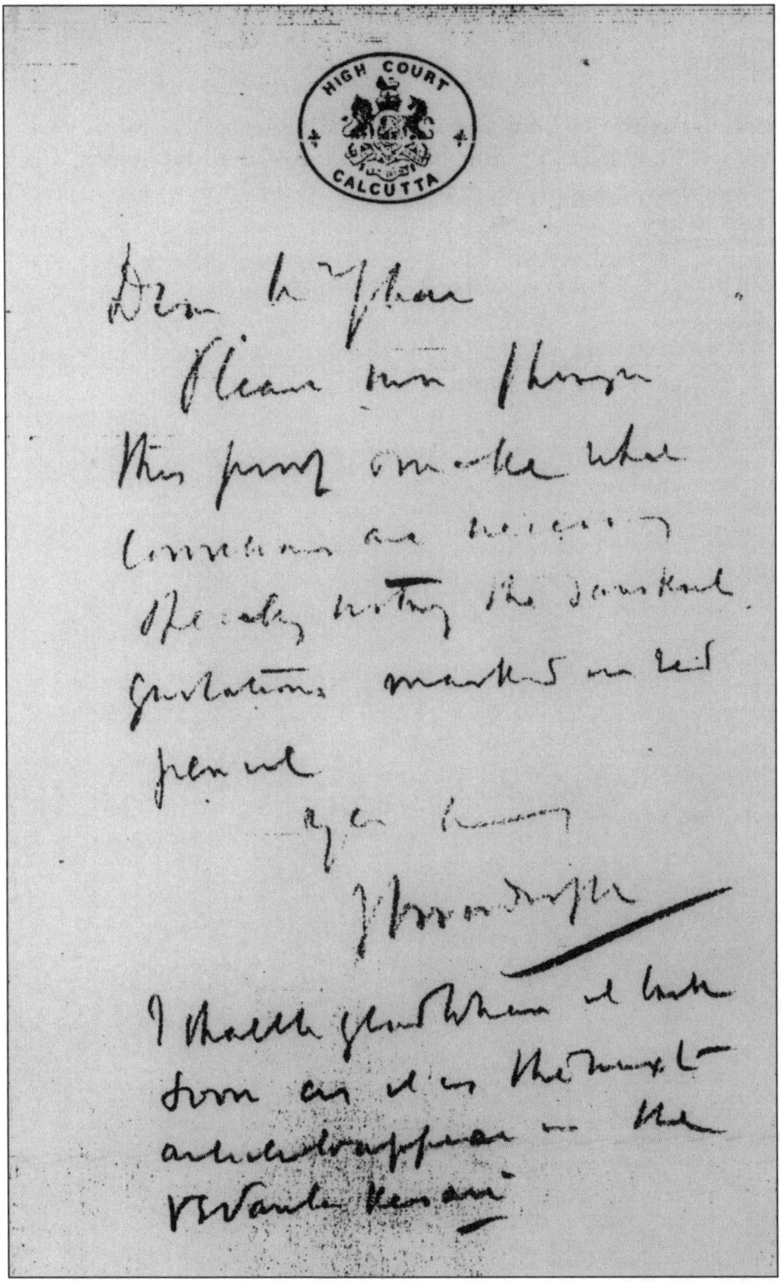
HIGH COURT
CALCUTTA

Dear Mr Ghose
Please run through
this proof & make what
corrections are necessary
specially noting the Sanskrit
quotations marked in red
pencil
yours sincerely
J Woodroffe

I shall be glad when it [illegible]
soon as it is [illegible]
article to appear in the
Vedanta Kesari

LETTER 4: NOTE FROM WOODROFFE TO GHOSE (handwritten, no address)

15 Jan 1920[4]

Dear Atal

I send herewith two copies of the . . . (illegible) sent to me as a useful work on Shastra. Look through it and keep it until my return. I have sent you this week a Mss from the Shangkarācharya in (?) Trivi(?)krama[5] & two letters.

Yours sincerely
John G Woodroffe

LETTER 5: WOODROFFE TO GHOSE (handwritten (c.1924–5)[6]

17 Bradmore Road,
Oxford

My dear Ghose

Thanks for your note about the 3 bindus. I know that Setu(?) Bindu = Shiva(?). What struck me as odd is that Shiva is Fire (Agni) and Shakti Moon. One would have thought it was the other way about because moon is white and fire is a reddish colour.

My Italian friend also wants a difficulty solved. He finds that on Hangsah[7] it is stated sometimes that Hang = Shiva and Sa = Shakti and sometimes the reverse.

I have always understood and said that Hang, that is breath out, is Shiva and Sah, inspiration, is Shakti. Hang must be expiring and Sah inspiring for we breath out in saying Ha and indraw in saying Sa. But the question is whether Ha is Shiva or not.

As Prasara is "going forth" it might be that Ha = Shakti. The active going forth is hers but it is His will which sends her forth. You mentioned this point or rather I did before but I do not think you gave any explanation beyond saying that there are statements both ways.

The commentary to Ānanda Lahari says Ha = Shiva (verse 1). In v.3 of Kāmakalāvilāsa,Ha = Vimarsha.

This account is all confused to me at present and the only explanation I think of is that the Hindu is not exact in our sense . . . primarily(?) according to circumstances. However let me know so that I can satisfy (?) P. . .[8]

I regret to find that in an article he(?) cites "Pandit" Chakrabarti of the Tantrik Order of America[9] I warned him not to do so and I have since written him that he will only dishonour himself and myself(?) by introducing(?) these men.

The Italian magazine "Netra" has now asked me for an article which I will send them on Sādhanā.

I was surprised to read in your letter that you have *nothing to do*[10] except Mahānirvāna. What has become of *2nd vol of Tantrarāja*? I have several times asked about this. When shall I see the Introduction? I sent it to you last summer and you were to add to it & to return it for me to revise. How does this stand? We must show M of D something *done*. So far as I know nothing has appeared since I left. Do let me know when I may see the Introduction and what is the state of this book.

I am sorry about BC but as I told you and I hope it will never happen again, do *not* incur any expense before you receive the cash. If you do not care to say so yourself put the responsibility on me and say that I as your co-secretary insist on cash as matter of business.

You must also avail yourself of the opportunities you have of seeing M of D. He is a busy man. I do not see that any good will come of making it a State Department so long as he finances the series. But we on our hand must show something for the work done. If you can get him to take over(?) the paper then use it for some other book[11] after first telling BC and finally(?)asking for payment(?). Say point blank that you cannot yourself find the money to finance Sharada and if he wants it done let him put *down* the whole cost in cash. Why should you worry yourself because of his failure? You have got the paper. You can't use it for Sharada Tilaka until *paid for the paper & for the printing*. If he does not produce the money then ask M of D whether he will take(?) over(?) the paper for some other book. Anyhow do not let yourself in again and never work except for cash ... yourself now on Tantrarāja & Mahānirvāna and let M of D see some completed work.

My wife is getting better but is not yet fit again and has one or two slight relapses which shows she is still sensitive.

Doctors say that Barbara's illness is neurasthenia one of the symptoms of which is self-starving. They have . . . diet (. . . for her & she is manfully doing her best to take it. I have stirred her *will* & told her to keep the body as her servant but the difficulty in such cases is that the disease affects the mind. However she is doing her best at present and we are pleased at it. She is also being massaged(?) . . . flesh. I think she has let herself down with too much work & too little food. Keep this private except for your wife. Nancy is at home and this has done her good as she is now sleeping which she has not been doing well lately.

Best Xmas greetings again to you both.

Yours sincerely
J G Woodroffe

LETTER 6: FROM WOODROFFE TO GHOSE (handwritten)

29 Nov (no year)
17 Bradmore Road, Oxford

My dear Atal

Do *not* as you propose have Mahanirvana text[12] . . . (illegible) name of any Editor. Put down (?) as Editor *Arthur Avalon*.

I was glad(?) to get(?) your photo. You look well though a bit(?) off colour(?) ... I would(?) not(?) have thought(?) that you had been through a severe illness. I am glad thus to have it & . . . proof of your state.

I am keeping well having gone to Boars Hill 500 ft up near Oxford a very healthy place. I can walk miles here(?) but live(?) in Oxford which is a relaxing pleasure. Moreover I have a peaceful time here.

My wife writes that she is not at all well and the Doctor there says she is very much run down. She has a bad cough and has been Xrayed & we await the doctor's report.

My daughter Nancy is better but far from well as she should be. The doctor says defective glandular action is interfering with her whole system. – Anyhow it's my sister in law Amy (?) who had what . . . was a cancer is making apparently a wonderful recovery. The tumour in the face . . . discharging into the mouth – a horrid business but apparently a liberating (?) one. As . . . to be surrounded by sickness and death on all sides.

I feel personally better than I have been either in India or leaving it. I left your country just in time as far as health is concerned. I wish you as many years as you want & remain with all good wishes

Yours ever
John Woodroffe

LETTER 7: FROM WOODROFFE TO GHOSE (typed)

11th February 1931
Villa Paulette
Boulevard D'Italie
Monte Carlo

My dear Ghose,

There have been a number of things which prevented my writing to you during the last two or three weeks. I am glad to see from the letter of yours which arrived today that you are well enough to write your own letters. From the last two or three which I had had [sic] I see that they were written for you. You say that you feel rather shaky in the morning. What is this? Your writing seems good. I have done nothing since I wrote as regards either of the Maharajas. I had thought of writing to D.[13] but deferred doing so as I thought it better to write to P. and D. at the same time. But the M. of P. has been down with influenza. I expect by the end of this month or the beginning of next, he will be thinking of returning to India. I leave here in May as we have settled not to spend the summer here. I may go for another cure at the waters where I was before. After that things are unsettled.

Yesterday Mrs Blount received a telegram from Moller to say that his wife had died the day before. The poor woman must have had a terrible time with her successive operations, anxiety for her children and for her husband down with consumption. However she is released from her troubles, but I doubt much whether Moller will recover from this new blow. Everything has been shattered around him, but perhaps it may operate in another way, and steel him against all disasters.

I asked Mrs Blount about the book on Appollonius of Tyana. She says that practically all his books are with his things in Calcutta. She says that you can see them there, but you will require a permit from Mrs Blount which I will ask her to send you when next I see her.

I note that you have done a third of the Sharada, as regards which you have sent some moneys to the printer. I want you now to settle up the printer's bill up to date. I wish this matter to be settled, for at the age at which you and I are anything might happen at any time, and if it was my duty to deal with the matter I should be unable to do so for I have had nothing to do with the matter financially.

I hope you will go very slowly yourself with the work until some other pundits are appointed to help you. And stick to one work at a time. What is the name of the printers who are doing the book? If you will do as I want and get a receipt from the printer, keep the receipt with you and pay all charges by cheque so that there may be a record of it.

You are worrying too much about P.[14] This is a mistake, as also the suggestion as regards his resigning the Presidency.[15] For my part I would let things go on as they [are] without intervention, and in the belief that what is right and suitable will be done. There may be something in what you say as regards his entourage including his guru, but I am inclined to think that the cause is as I have stated, – namely a rash promise made without reference to his being able to afford it. His finances appear to be in a bad way, as shown by the guru's communication to you, and the appointment of an Englishman as Minister of Finance. Izzat prevents him from saying so. Either then his funds will not allow his doing anything, or as much as he promised, or he will do what he can. I expect to see the solution of this matter in March or April, if not earlier.

Ever yours and with all good wishes
John Woodroffe

LETTER 8: FROM WOODROFFE TO GHOSE (typed)

16th December 1931
Villa Aureglia
Beausoleil
France

My dear Ghose,

Your letter has arrived very a propos, for it reached my hands the evening of the day of my birthday. Many thanks to you for all your good wishes. You say nothing about current affairs but I suppose you read the papers which will tell you something of what is going on. Judging from the Statesman which I see in weekly form they do not give you much news. We are witnessing the birth of a new world and the final disappearance of the one which you and I have known. One of the most sacred things for the English is sterling, but now England has gone off the gold standard and is followed by many other countries. One hears of debts and deficits everywhere. Every pound which I draw from England for my expenses here is shorn of six shillings and more, – a loss of about thirty per cent. And that may not be the worst, for the exchange may go to one half or even more. Everywhere one hears of failures, non-payment of dividends and so on. A propos of this, how did Thacker Spink & Co come to grief? I read today that great hoards of gold are now being sent from India to Europe. We have lived to see a very eventful time, and I hope that we may live to see at least the beginnings of the new world that follows ours. Both my wife and I desire to be remembered to you both. This letter will arrive round and about Christmas and we both send you good wishes for that season as also for the coming year.

Yours affectionately,
John Woodroffe[16]

LETTER 9: NOTE FROM WOODROFFE TO MRS GHOSE (handwritten)

15 July 1929
Bygdin, Norway

Dear Mrs Ghose,

This is the third letter which I have written (?) to you about Atal. As I have heard nothing I am very anxious about him. Please send me news if only a word and give him our sympathy & good wishes for his safe recovery. I have not written to him directly for according to what you write he is not fit to receive letters.

I hope to . . . hear from you. . .

I am yours truly
John Woodroffe

PS Please reply to *Oxford* as usual. I have mail forwarded.

LETTER 10: WOODROFFE TO GHOSE (handwritten by someone else).

16th February 1934
Villa Aureglia,
Beausoleil

My dear Ghose,

I think I have had now all the letters which you have sent to the bank. Every week I look forward to getting an announcement that the Prapanchasara is finished. I was glad to hear of your interview with D. I have written to him myself – thanking him for his interest, & regretting the loss which he has sustained in the great earthquake which you have had.

I should have preferred that the Samiti was wound up, on completion of the Prapanchasara and gloss. As regards P. the only rational explanation which presents itself to me is that his Guru has forbidden him to have any communication with me. You may ask why: and the answer would be that I have not been initiated. Otherwise his conduct is wholly inexplicable.

With many affectionate greetings
I remain

Yours ever
J Woodroffe

P.S. I shall be glad to have some chavyapracha, if it will travel. And if you can prepay the duty as otherwise it will be difficult for me to do so here. I must know what are the exact ingredients in any case.

LETTER 11: WOODROFFE TO GHOSE (handwritten by someone else)

March 9th 1935
Beausoleil

My dear Ghose

Yours of the 6th February to hand. I have now read and return your proposal for introduction to Prapanchasara . . . note that the manuscript sent to me is incomplete. I have cut out in blue pencil the bulk of the proposed introduction as unsuitable and irrelevant. We are not concerned with the Ain Soph, the parentage of Jesus, the marriage of the Queen of Spain and so forth. I am not concerned with Orthodox polemics. These constant jibes at the modern Hindu become tiresome to the public. Moreover a polemic is more fittingly conducted in an article signed by the person who carries on such polemics. You suggest that if I do not approve the introduction might appear under the initials A.S. but to this I cannot consent. I only consent to the insertion of such matter as I have not blue pencilled. I also should like to see the remaining portion of the introduction not now sent to me.

I do not wish to sell the copyright of Isha Up to Mazumdar. If he tells me what he wishes to do in particular, how many copies he wishes to print, I may be able to license him to do so. I will write to Luzac to send him his account since the last settlement.

The proceeds of the last settlement were sent to you and were, I think, received by you. This is not an unfitting time for a further account, if I am correct as to the date on which the last settlement was made. As to Thacker Spink's account you might write or . . . them and get their account sent on to me.

Yours ever with all good wishes,
John Woodroffe (not signed)

P.S. I have not yet heard from Ganesh to whom I have written a number of times. I asked you, in one of my last letters to find out from him why I got no reply. Have you been able to do so?

LETTER 12: PHOTOCOPY OF LETTER FROM GHOSE TO WOODROFFE

(see above p. 152)

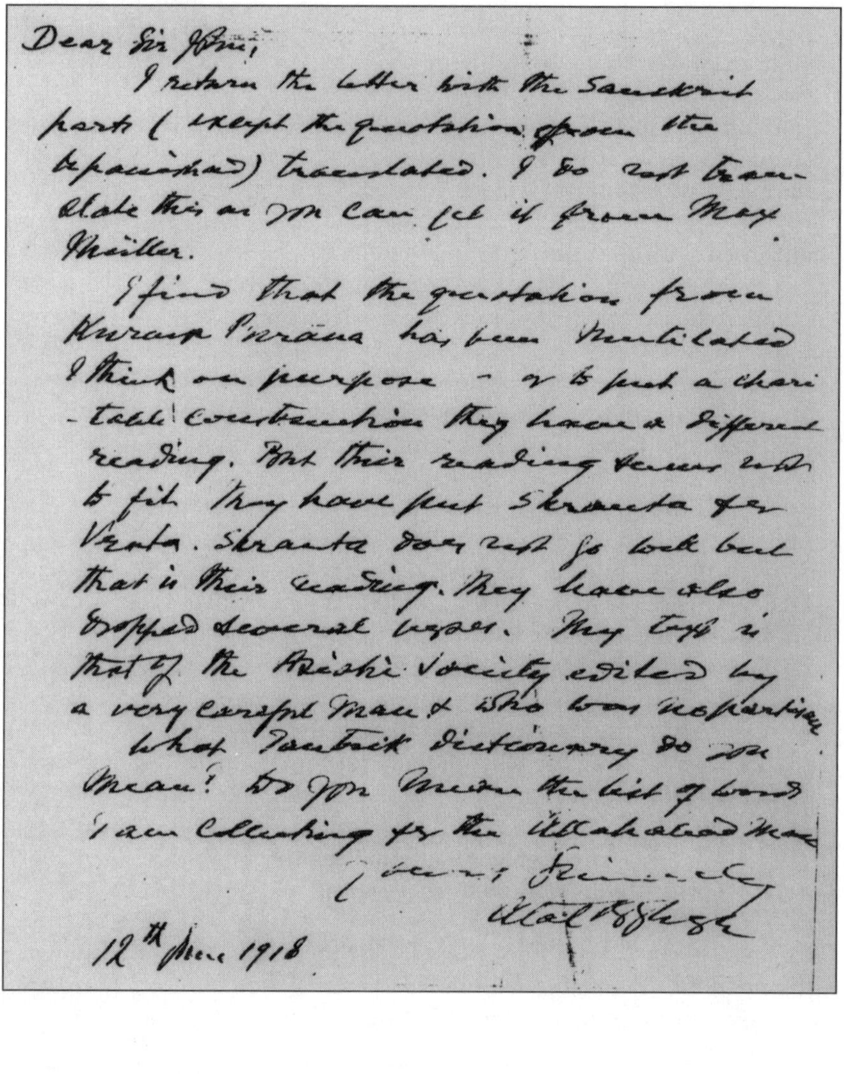

Dear Sir John,

I return the letter with the Sanskrit parts (except the quotation from the Upanishad) translated. I do not translate this as you can get it from Max Müller.

I find that the quotation from Kurma Purana has been mutilated I think on purpose – or to put a charitable construction they have a different reading. But their reading seems not to fit. They have put Shrauta for Vrata. Shrauta does not go well but that is their reading. They have also dropped several verses. My text is that of the Asiatic Society edited by a very careful man & who was no partisan.

What Tantrik dictionary do you mean? Do you mean the list of words I am collecting for the illustrated man[illegible]

Yours sincerely

Atal B Ghose

12th June 1918

LETTER 13: PHOTOCOPY OF EXTRACTS FROM SENTINATH IYER'S LETTER TO WOODROFFE

(see above p. 224).

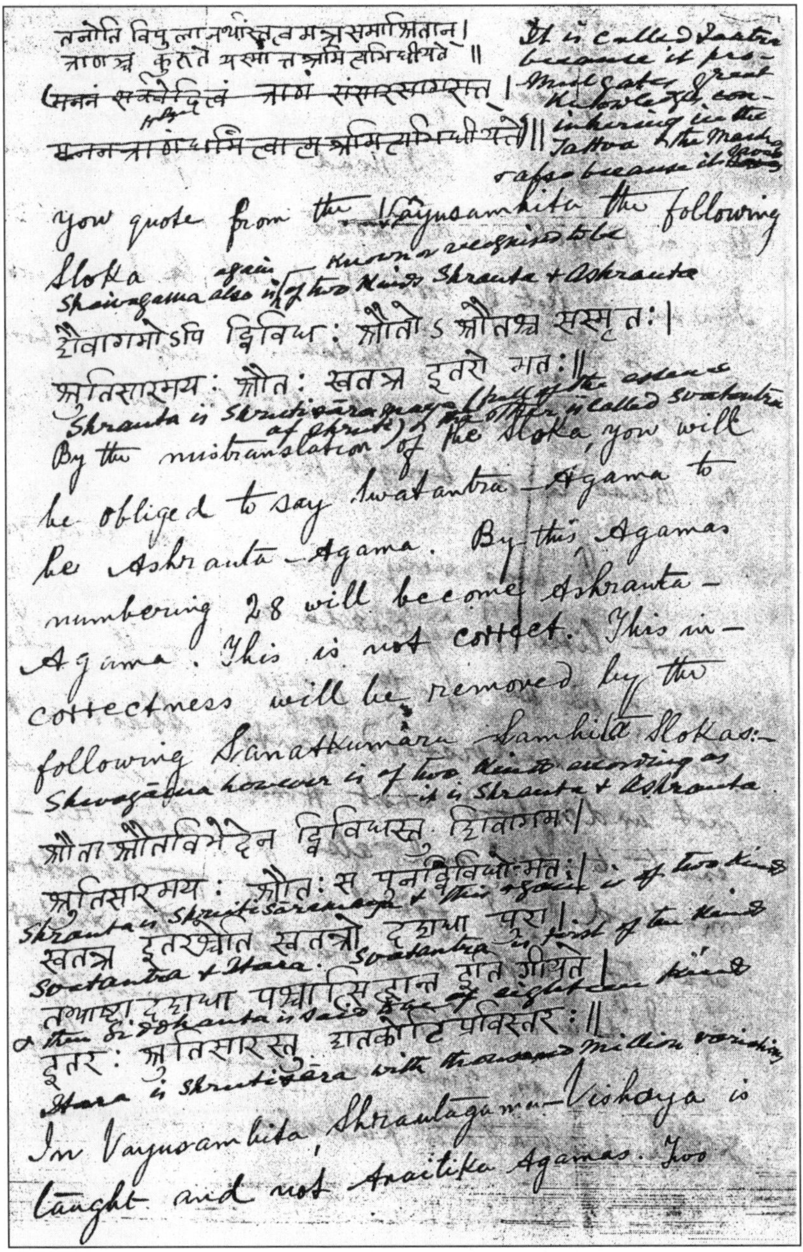
तनोति विपुलानर्थान् तत्त्वमन्त्रसमाश्रितान् ।
त्राणञ्च कुरुते यस्मात् शास्त्रमित्यभिधीयते ॥
~~मननं सर्ववेदित्वं त्राणं संसारसागरात् ।~~
~~मननत्राणधर्मित्वात् मन्त्र इत्यभिधीयते ॥~~
It is called Sastra because it promulgates great knowledge concerning the Tattva & the Mantras & also because it saves

You quote from the Vayusamhita the following Sloka
Shaivagama also is of two kinds Shrauta & Ashrauta again known or recognised to be
शैवागमोऽपि द्विविधः श्रौतोऽश्रौतश्च संस्मृतः ।
श्रुतिसारमयः श्रौतः स्वतन्त्र इतरो मतः ॥
Shrauta is Shrutisaramaya (full of the essence of Shruti) & the other is called Swatantra
By the mistranslation of the Sloka, you will be obliged to say Swatantra-Agama to be Ashrauta-Agama. By this Agamas numbering 28 will become Ashrauta-Agama. This is not correct. This incorrectness will be removed by the following Sanatkumara Samhita Slokas:-
Shaivagama however is of two kinds according as it is Shrauta & Ashrauta.
श्रौताश्रौतविभेदेन द्विविधस्तु शिवागमः ।
श्रुतिसारमयः श्रौतः स पुनर्द्विविधो मतः ।
Shrauta is Shrutisaramaya & this again is of two kinds
स्वतन्त्र इतरश्चेति स्वतन्त्रो दशधा पुरा ।
Swatantra & Itara. Swatantra is first of ten kinds
तथाष्टादशधा पश्चात् सिद्धान्त इति गीयते ।
& then Siddhanta is said to be of eighteen kinds
इतरः श्रुतिसारस्तु शतकोटिप्रविस्तरः ॥
Itara is Shrutisara with thousand million varieties
In Vayusamhita, Shrautagama-Vishaya is taught and not Avaitika Agamas. Too

LETTER 13: CONTINUED

3

Kinds of Agamas, Shrauta and Ashrauta, are found in the 38th Chapter of Kurma-purana Uttara-Bhaga. They are these:

By me was composed first Pashupata which is Shrauta which is most sacred & subtle and is Vedasara — for attainment of liberation

निर्मितं हि मया पूर्वं श्रौतं पाशुपतं शुभम्।
गुह्याद् गुह्यतमं सूक्ष्मं वेदसारं विमुक्तये॥

वेदाभ्यासरतो विद्वान् ध्यायेत् पशुपतिं शिवम्।
एष पाशुपतो योगः सेवनीयो मुमुक्षुभिः॥

The learned man devoted to the Veda should meditate on Shiva Pashupati. This is Pashupata yoga to be practised by the seekers of liberation

वेदवादविरुद्धानि मयैव कथितानि तु।
वामं पाशुपतं सोमं लाकुलं चैव भैरवम्॥
असेव्यमेतत् कथितं वेदबाह्यं तथेतरम्।

By me have been spoken Vāma, Pashupata, Sōma, Lākula & Bhairava which are opposed to the Vedas. These should not be practised; they are outside the Vedas.

The names of Avaitikagamas are found in the 16th Chapter 1st Pt. Kurmapurana as Kāpāla &c.

Kāpāla, Lākula, Vāma, Bhairava, Purva, Pashchima
कापालं लाकुलं वामं भैरवं पूर्वपश्चिमम्।
Pāncharatra, Pashupata & others of thousands
पाञ्चरात्रं पाशुपतं तथान्यानि सहस्रशः॥

There are two kinds of Pasupadas. One is Vaidika and other is Avaidika. The Pashupada, which we know and teach, is Vaidikapashupada.

LETTER 14: TELEGRAM TO ATAL BIHARI GHOSE'S SON

(see above p. 209).

FROM: Deutsch-Ausländischer Buchtausch, Berlin
TO: Herrn Babu Ajay K Ghose

DATE: 16.6.1936

Sehr geehrter Herr Ghose!

Von dem Tode des hervorragenden Gelehrten, Herrn Babu Atal Behari Ghose haben wir durch das Deutsche Generalkonsulat erfahren.

Es ist mir ein Bedürfnis, Ihnen das Beileid der deutschen Wissenschaft zu seinem Tode zum Ausdruck zu bringen, weiss ich doch aus meinen vielfältigen Beziehungen zu allen Gelehrten, wie angesehen Herr Ghose in Deutschland war.

In grösster Hochachtung!

i.A.
Dr. Jürgens

Appendix 2

'THE WISE CHILDHOOD'

By Sir John Woodroffe

Reprinted from *Vedānta Keśarī* (Madras) vol.9 no.4 (August 1922)

The Brihadāranyaka Upanishad (3–5–1) contains a beautiful saying which has been mistranslated and misunderstood. *Tasmād Brāhmanah pāndityam nirvidya bālyena tishthāset.* "Therefore let the Brahman-knower who is satiated with knowledge of the Self remain like a child," that is, simple, free from all conceit, and guileless. The saying has been said (Farquahar, Crown of Hinduism 260: citing Deussen 58) to mean that the Brāhmana should reject learning and be a child. This learning which is to be "rejected" has been supposed to be that contained in the Brāhmanical literature for which the followers of the "Ātman Philosophy" are supposed to have felt contempt. This is wrong. Why should a Brāhmana who "rejects" the literature then remain like a child, a foolish one in any event if that literature has worth, and if it has none why should the Brāhmana be a child? What connection is there between such rejection and childhood? The Sanskrit word *Nirvidya* does not mean to reject or to abandon. It comes from the root *vid*, to know. The word *Nih* or *Nir* signifies intensity, fullness and the like. *Nirvidya* therefore means having fully and detachedly known and thus attained the state of *Nirveda* or satiety of knowledge. This Nirveda is detachment from the world due to full knowledge. It has thus two meanings, namely, full mastery of the subject, and the indifference to further enquiry and argument, which is the result of such full knowledge. Then who is the subject of the verb *Nirvidya*? Sangkara says that it is a Brāhmana by which is meant a man entirely devoted to Brahman-Knowledge (Brahma-nishtha purusha). Lastly the object of Pānditya (Bhāskararāya reads Pānditỵan), which does not mean any learning but knowledge of the Self (Ātmatattva). The meaning of the saying will be understood by reference to the commentary where it is cited.

Bhāskararāya cites the text in his Commentary on the Nityashoda-shikārnava Tantra when discussing the stages or Bhūmikā of knowledge. He says that a man advances from one stage of secular knowledge to another and higher stage until he reaches the highest. He finds that even this is inadequate for the understanding of the ultimate Reality (paratattva). He therefore pursues the path of Devotion (Bhakti mārga). In this there are seven stages (Bhūmikā). When he has got beyond all these, there is nothing for him to learn or do; but he should live as a simple and guileless child in constant communion with the Divine Mother.

There is a very fine thought expressed in this saying. There are two kinds of children, the natural child before the acquisition of available knowledge, and after such acquisition the man-child. There are two kinds of ignorance – the ignorance of the child which as such may be removed. The ignorance which attaches to man however learned is irremovable so long as he remains man. There are two states of knowledge – the state of the child who does not know because he does not know, and the state of the wise who does not know because he knows. He knows how little he knows and that some matters are wholly beyond his ken. He knows that he does not know. The child is ignorant but is not aware to what extent. The beautiful simplicity and guilelessness of childhood is due to its innocence. The child-man regains this state after knowledge of evil. Both simplicities are beautiful; – the spring-like beauty of the natural child so unconsciously close to nature, and the autumnal richness of the mind which has known and understood all, has achieved freedom from all conventional and partial judgments and which battling through all confusions has won to simplicity. To continue childlike is to continue young, the natural child's youth being the youth of years, and the childhood of age being the youth which is the reward of the wise. The outlook of the child is natural and therefore beautiful. Beautiful also is the vision of the sage-child in which naturalness is transfused and enriched by knowledge. All that is ugly and weak, false and absurd lie between these two limits, the sphere of sophisticated men, of unripe or spoiled intelligence.

NOTES

INTRODUCTION

1 Avalon quotes Barnet's *Antiquities of India* London 1913.
2 Said E: *Orientalism* London 1995 (first published 1978).
3 For a survey of Western attitudes to Tantra see D. Kopf 'Sexual Ambivalence in Western Scholarship on Hindu India', *Comparative Civilizations Review* vol.13 (1986) pp. 143–57. To bring the picture right up to date see H.B. Urban 'The Cult of Ecstacy: Tantrism, the New Age and the Spiritual Logic of Late Capitalism' in *History of Religions* 39/3 pp. 268–304.
4 K. Taylor: 'Arthur Avalon, the Creation of a Legendary Orientalist', in J. Leslie (ed.) *Myths and Mythmaking* London 1996 pp. 144–63.
5 The pseudonym refers to Ghose above all, but occasionally to others who provided Woodroffe with textual knowledge. (See below chapter 11).
6 P. Marshall & G. Williams (eds) *The British Discovery of Hinduism in the Eighteenth Century* London 1970; E. Stokes *The English Utilitarians and India* Oxford 1959. For a summary of the problems around the nature of knowledge and European perceptions of India, see R. Inden 'Orientalist Constructions of India' in *Modern Asian Studies* 20/3 (1986) pp. 401–46, and the same author's *Imagining India* Oxford 1990.
7 Inden 'Orientalist Constructions . . . .' p. 430 writes of 'romantic, spiritualistic or idealistic' orientalism which was opposed to utilitarianism while both shared the same image of an essentialized 'East'.
8 See Raychaudhury T: *Europe Reconsidered: perceptions of the West in nineteenth century Bengal* Oxford 1988 pp. 176–82 on Bankim Chandra's criticism and parody of European orientalists.
9 The complete collection is at OIOC Mss Eur F285/4 & 5. (The system of numbering individual letters there is different from mine.).
10 OIOC Mss Eur F285/1,2,3 and 6.
11 O.C. Gangopadhyay *Bhārater Śilpa O Āmār Kathā* Calcutta 1969.
12 V.K. Pal *Tantrāchārya Sivacandra* Cooch Behar 1972 (1379 BE).
13 S. Sarkar *The Swadeshi Movement in Bengal* New Delhi 1973.
14 P. Mitter *Much Maligned Monsters: a history of European Reactions to Indian Art* Oxford 1977; *Art and Nationalism in Colonial India 1850–1922: occidental orientations* Cambridge U.P. 1994; T. Guha-Thakurta *The Making of a New 'Indian' Art: artists, aesthetics and nationalism in Bengal c.1850–1920* Cambridge U.P. 1992.
15 A. Padoux *Vāc: The Concept of the Word in Selected Hindu Tantras* New York 1990.

16 A. Sanderson 'Purity and Power Among the Brahmins of Kashmir' in Carrithers et. al. (ed.) *The Category of the Person: Anthropological and Philosophical Perspectives* Cambridge 1985; 'Śaivism and the Tantric Traditions' in S. Sutherland (ed.) *The World's Religions* London 1988 pp. 660–704.
17 D. Sen Sarma *The Philosophy of Sādhana with special reference to the Trika Philosophy of Kashmir* New York 1990.
18 *Body and Cosmology in Kashmir Saivism* San Francisco 1993.

CHAPTER 1

1 IOLR Baptism Records, Bengal: N/1/Vol 115/31.
2 *Curzon Papers* OIOC Mss Eur F111/202, Jan-June 1900, no.88.
3 He controversially defended O'Hara, an Irish soldier accused of murdering an Indian, when it was a matter of surprise that a penniless soldier should be defended by 'such a gigantic figure'. (The case caused a furore, being seen as a race issue; but probably was more to do with solidarity to a fellow Catholic). See K. Leslie, *The Red Judge and other anecdotes*, Rangoon, 1934, pp. 29–31. Other sources refer to his prominence at the Bar, his success, his powerful personality or his 'prodigious wealth'. See his retirement tribute: *Calcutta Weekly Notes* vol.xii p. 164–5.
4 It also made those who were very successful at the Bar reluctant to accept promotion to the Bench. The comparative values of the estates of the two Woodroffes, father and son, on their deaths look like confirmation of this fact. James Tisdall Woodroffe left a total estate of 140 thousand pounds in 1908 whereas his son left 6000 in 1936 [Public Record Office, St Katharine's House, London. Probate register].
5 His father was John Woodroffe, Rector of Glenmire in County Cork [*Who was Who*, 1908]. Other family members were also clergymen.
6 Wedderburn *A Life of Alan Octavian Hume* London 1916.
7 C. Ray *Calcutta a Hundred Years Ago – Excerpts from The Statesman Calcutta* 1987.
8 After being first drawn to Madame Blavatsky and Theosophy, Hume later became a disciple of a Hindu guru [Marion Meade *Madame Blavatsky: the woman behind the Myth* New York 1980].
9 *The Letters and Diaries of John Henry Newman* (ed. C.S. Dessain & T. Gornall) vol.xxvi, Oxford, Clarendon Press, 1974, p. 351.
10 Provence Belge de la Compagnie de Jesus: *La Mission du Bengale Occidental du Archidiocès de Calcutta* Bruges 1921 vol.1, p. 442 mentions his donation to the building of a church in 1877 and says he was converted two years previously.
11 See obituary in *The Catholic Herald* (Calcutta), 10 June 1908. He was made a Knight of St Gregory in recognition of his generosity to catholic causes (which included being one of the founding donors for the building of Westminster Cathedral in London).
12 *Historical Register of the University of Oxford to 1900*, Oxford Clarendon Press. See *Oxford Magazine* vol.3 (1885) pp. 24, 38, 41 for articles defending the recent changes to allow for an Honours degree in Law.
13 G.A. Beck *The English Catholics 1850–1950* London 1950, pp. 299, 305.
14 Nirad Chaudhury *Scholar Extraordinary* London 1974.
15 *Oxford Magazine* 27 June 1889, p. 2.
16 V.H.H. Green *Religion at Oxford and Cambridge* London 1964, p. 315.
17 See also SS:27–53 his chapter on 'Śakti: The World as Power', especially p. 41–2.
18 See especially WAP:9–50, his pamphlet on 'Power as Reality'.

19 W. Halbfass *India and* Europe, New York, Suny Press, 1988. See Sitanath Tattvabhusan *Autobiography*, Calcutta, Brahmo Mission Press (no date). A Brahmo, he recounts his enthusiasm for the Idealists, first Berkeley, then especially T.H. Green. His chapter on 'Study of philosophy, Eastern and Western pp. 57–103 (his longest) shows the reading of a philosophically inclined intellectual Bengali of the time.
20 *The Law Relating to Injunctions in British India* 1900 and *The Law Relating to Receivers in British India* 1903.
21 Woodroffe and Ameer Ali: *The Law of Evidence Applicable to British India* 1898, was a commentary on the Indian Evidence Act of 1872. Its 14th revised edition was published in 1979–81. Woodroffe's *The Code of Civil Procedure* was published in 1908.
22 See *Thackers Indian Directory 1887–1961.*
23 O.C. Gangopadhyay *Bhārater Śilpa O Amār Kathā* Calcutta 1969, p. 87–8.
24 SS:466. He refers to him as 'the "mad" wine-drinking Sadhu Bhāma'.
25 He was Reader in Indian Law but did not hold the All Souls Readership as stated in *Who's Who* as this was for English Law. *Historical Register: Supplement 1901–1931.*
26 IOLR Marriage Records Bengal: N/1/301/232.
27 Annie Grimsom was a pianist who performed at the proms in 1899 and composed a symphony at the age of 17. Jessie Grimson was a violinist, and Amy Grimson won a scholarship to the Royal College of Music at the age of only 14. All were trained by their father. [J. Warriner (ed.) *National Portrait Gallery of British Musicians* London, Sampson Low & Co., 1896].
28 K.K. Aziz *Ameer Ali, his life and work* Karachi 1968.
29 'Echoes of British India' chapter 2 p. 1, draft in *Ameer Ali papers* OIOC Mss Eur C336/3.
30 *Denison Ross Papers* SOAS PPMS 8 file 11 vol.4: letter dated 12 April 1904.
31 ibid: letter of 6 April 1904. 'I have been nearly three years in India and this is the first mixed party at which I have been present.' In his autobiography he confessed he could not imagine having an intimate friendship with an Indian. [E. Denison Ross *Both Ends of the Candle* London 1943, p. 147.].
32 The Woodroffes had many addresses in Calcutta. According to Thackers Directory they lived at 4 Camac Street from 1916 until Woodroffe's furlough in England in 1919. Before that they lived round the corner in Alexandra Row. Denison Ross wrote to his fiancée that 'to have a house of one's own is more than half the battle in Calcutta' and European residents moved frequently. (*Denison Ross papers* file 13 vol.6: letter dated 1 July 1904).
33 'Echoes of British India' p. 2.
34 ibid p. 3. He does not say which modern Indian language Woodroffe was attempting, though it was not Bengali.
35 ibid p. 1.
36 Louisa M Finn c.1980 *Was the Scholarly Advocate a Secret Adept?* I am grateful to Dr Finn for generously giving me her unpublished article and allowing me to make use of it.
37 See previous note.
38 *The Times*, London, January 18 1936 p. 14(e).
39 P. French *Younghusband, The Last Great Imperial Adventurer* London 1994.
40 *The Englishman* 17 December 1918 p. 10 notes the start of a new series of symphony concerts at the Calcutta School of Music, with Lady Woodroffe performing as solo pianist.
41 Denison Ross *Both Ends. . . .*
42 *Denison Ross Papers* file 10 vol.3: letters dated 13–27 February 1904. On the 13th

he wrote: 'I am flattered at being asked to sing at the Woodroffe's home for it is tantamount to be considered the best singer in Calcutta'. He adds however that 'the competition is not great'. He had been asked to sing at several other parties and was anxious because he was unwell. He said he cared 'much more how I feel on the 26th and 27th. On the former date I am to sing at the Woodroffe's evening party and on the 27th at the Town Hall.

43 ibid: letter dated 18 March 1904.

44 He retired three years before the usual age of sixty. This is discussed in chapter 3.

45 SS:vii. (Preface to the third edition).

CHAPTER 2

1 Letter of John Woodroffe dated Eastbourne 18 June 1872, given to me by James Woodroffe.

2 C.R. Chichester *Schools* London 1882.

3 The Hon. & Rev. W.J. Petre *The Position and Prospects of Catholic Liberal Education* London 1878 p. 14.

4 V.A. McClelland 'The Liberal Training of England's Catholic Youth: William Joseph Petre (1847–93) and Educational Reform', *Victorian Studies* March 1972 pp. 257–77.

5 W. & R. Elwes *Gervase Elwes: the story of his life* London 1935.

6 S. Foster 'The Thirteenth Lord Petre', *Essex Journal* Winter 1984, pp. 69–71; 'A Pillar of Downside: Lord Petre' in *The English Benedictine Historical Symposium* pp. 24–33.

7 Petre '. . . *Catholic Liberation Education*' p. 14.

8 Chichester *Schools* pp. 58ff.

9 ibid p. 65–6.

10 ibid p. 67–8.

11 ibid p. 70. It is not clear whether this was expulsion from the school, or only from the parliament.

12 ibid p. 60. P.J. Rich *Chains of Empire* London 1991.

13 McClelland 'The Liberal Training of England's Catholic Youth . . .' p. 266, 268–9.

14 ibid pp. 269–71. Science had just been introduced at Eton at the end of the 1870s when Curzon was there. [See Ronaldshay: *A Life of Lord Curzon* London 1972 chapter 2.].

15 *The Amoeba* no.4, Nov. 1881, p. 9.

16 ibid no.1, March 1881, p. 4.

17 ibid no.9, Nov. 1883, p. 13. The story of the sudden closure of Woburn is told by Foster and McClelland. The school had a hundred pupils on its register when it closed, which McClelland points out indicates it was still successful; but it seems it was proving too much of a drain on Petre's family fortunes. By a strange twist of fate, his father died, bringing Lord Petre into his inheritance only three weeks after he was persuaded to sell the site of Woburn to the Josephite Fathers. They founded St George's school Weybridge, which still occupies the house and grounds today. Petre made an attempt to revive his school the following year on the Isle of Wight, with just forty of his former pupils, but his own ill-health together with an epidemic of influenza combined to bring this experiment, too, to a close after just one year. After that, sadly, Lord Petre's own health and spirits declined rapidly and he died when he was still only in his mid-forties.

18 For example, rules regulating duties on the cricket field, and use of the library. But, as we see below, there were deeper issues to do with real power struggles beneath the surface.

19 *Gervase Elwes* p. 32.

20 *Schools* p. 65.
21 *The Amoeba* no.4, Nov 1881, p. 11.
22 ibid no.2, May 1881, p. 1. This was probably written by Petre himself.
23 ibid no.9, Nov. 1883, p. 2–3.
24 *Gervase Elwes* p. 31–2.
25 McClelland 'The Liberal Training' pp. 257 & 267.
26 *The Amoeba* no.5, April 1882, p. 13.
27 ibid no.4, Nov. 1881, p. 3.
28 ibid no.3, June 1881, pp. 2, 20.
29 ibid no.6, July 1882, p. 9.
30 Petre ... *Catholic Liberal Education* p. 5.
31 *The Amoeba* no.6, July 1882, p. 12.
32 ibid no.7, Dec. 1882, p. 18.
33 ibid no.9, Nov. 1883, p. 18.
34 ibid pp. 12–14.
35 *Gervase Elwes* p. 54.
36 McClelland 'The Liberal Training' p. 265.
37 Petre '... *Catholic Liberal Education*' p. 5. He is referring to the *Index Expurgatrius*, of books banned to Catholics by their church.
38 *Chains of Empire* p. 95.
39 It hangs today in St George's School, Weybridge, which stands on the site of Woburn.
40 Foster 'A Pillar of Downside' p. 27–8.
41 *Gervase Elwes* p. 34.
42 *Schools* p. 64–5.
43 *The Amoeba* no.1, March 1881, p. 5.
44 McClelland 'The Liberal Training' p. 276.
45 *Schools* p. 64–5.
46 McClelland 'The Liberal Training' p. 267.
47 *Gervase Elwes* p. 33.
48 Foster 'A Pillar of Downside' p. 27–8.
49 No.4, Nov. 1881, p. 2. Also cited by McClelland 'The Liberal Training' p. 272.
50 *Chains of Empire*. See especially preface p. 13.
51 *The Amoeba* no.2, May 1881, p. 10.
52 *Chains of Empire* p. 97.
53 Petre ... *Catholic Liberal Education* p. 35.
54 ibid p. 4.
55 ibid pp. 36–9.
56 Indira Chowdhury-Sengupta *Reconstructing Spiritual Heroism* in Leslie (ed.) London 1996, pp. 124–42.
57 Every issue of the magazine was headed by a quotation from a contemporary book containing this description of the amoeba.
58 Letter to P.N. Mukhopadhyay, quoted in Woodroffe's *Bhārata Shakti*. See chapter 5 below.
59 *The Times* London, 18 January p. 14(e).

CHAPTER 3

1 Personal communication by Mr Somarendranath Bagchi, retired judge.
2 See below.
3 *The Statesman* Calcutta 1 Sept. 1922, 'Occasional Notes'. Also in *Calcutta Weekly*

Notes (henceforth CWN) xxvi pp. 162–4 (Notes section).

4 London 1917. Both books are discussed in chapter 5.

5 *National Archives of India* Nehru Memorial Museum and Library, New Delhi: Home Dept. Public File No. 1022.

6 N.C. Sengupta *Yuga Parikrama* Calcutta 1961, p. 136–7.

7 N.C. Chaudhuri *Hinduism* London 1979, p. 251.

8 S.B. Bhattacharje *Encyclopedia of Indian Events and Dates* [henceforth EIED], New Delhi 1995, Section A p. 147.

9 G. Ashe *Gandhi* London 1968, p. 184–5. The Rowlatt Acts were the cause of the demonstration which triggered Dyer's action.

10 For a selection of press comments see under 'Press Reviews' in GOL (1) pp. v–xi.

11 The relevant files both of the Government of India Home Dept in New Delhi and of the India Office in London, are listed as destroyed.

12 *Calcutta Review* 3rd series vol.5 (Oct. 1922) pp. 111–16, p. 112.

13 IOR L/R/5/42 p. 971 Indian Newspaper Reports Bengal, *Hitāvadi* on 25 June 1915.

14 *Chelmsford Papers* OIOC Mss Eur E264/42, letter dated 8 July 1919. In Home Dept Judicial Proceeding No.390, Aug. 1919, Sanderson says that if Woodroffe did come back in 1920 'it will not be for long, probably about a year.' [NAI, New Delhi].

15 *Havell Papers* OIOC Mss Eur D736 folio 2, letter dated 3 September 1919.

16 *High Court at Calcutta: 125th Anniversary Souvenir*, published by the High Court, Calcutta 1987.

17 Anniversary souvenir p. 59.

18 CWN viii p. 149 (Notes): 'The selection of Mr Woodroffe is very welcome as a recognition of local talent. It is certainly a pity that vacancies on the Bench are not more largely filled from the local Bar'.

19 Anniversary souvenir pp. 66, 70.

20 CWN ix p. 17 (Notes). There were still many European barristers, of course, but the majority of the members of the Bar were Bengali.

21 CWN xii p. 233 (Notes).

22 Sumit Sarkar *The Swadeshi Movement in Bengal 1903–8*, New Delhi, 1973.

23 ibid pp. 74, 313.

24 P. Heehs *The Bomb in Bengal: the Rise of Revolutionary Terrorism in India 1900–1910* Delhi 1993.

25 *Autobiography of an Unknown Indian* New Delhi 1976, p. 247.

26 Heehs *The Bomb* ... pp. 109–16; 143–9.

27 EIED Section A p. 140.

28 Heehs *The Bomb* ... pp. 167–9.

29 ibid pp. 204, 227, 189.

30 ibid pp. 208–9, 215–16.

31 ibid p. 226.

32 CWN xiii p. 44 (Notes).

33 A quote from the *Graphic* of December 1908, a British paper, in CWN xiii p. 69 (Notes: 18 June 1909). *Asian Quarterly Review* vol.1/1 (April 1913) had an article on the High Court of Calcutta entitled 'The Ulcer of Empire'.

34 One reason why the partition of Bengal was viewed with alarm in these pages was that it was feared the administration would have more control over the proposed new court at Dacca than it could exercise over the Calcutta High Court. See eg. vol.x p. 10.

35 *Papers of Sir Asutosh Mukherji* National Library Calcutta, letter from C.J. Stevenson-Moore, 21 Sept. 1911. N.K. Sinha *Asutosh Mookerjee: A biographical study*, Calcutta 1966 p. 143. A comment from Justice Harrington that he (Harrington) had 'only had one threat', on the back of a pamphlet sent by post, suggests other High Court

judges were threatened too [*Erle Richards Collection* OIOC Mss Eur F122/7, letter dated 29 March 1910].
36 Heehs *The bomb* ... pp. 241–50.
37 Lord Hardinge of Penshurst *My Indian Years* London 1948, pp. 14, 80–1.
38 W.A.J. Archbold in N.H.E. Carmichael *Lord Carmichael of Skirling: A Memoir by His Wife* London 1929, p. 193.
39 *Autobiography* ... p. 309.
40 EIED Section A p. 145; Heehs *The Bomb* ... pp. 248–50.
41 R. Kumar *Annie Besant's Rise to Power in Indian Politics* New Delhi 1981; A. Taylor *Annie Besant: a biography* Oxford 1992.
42 Quoted by Kumar *Annie Besant's Rise* ... p. 111.
43 Personal communication.
44 J.H. & M. Cousins *We Two Together* Madras 1950, pp. 315–6.
45 Actually, Cousins was an Irish nationalist, while Woodroffe, Besant and Nivedita all had Irish Protestant ancestry.
46 Hugh Tinker: *The Ordeal of Love: C.F. Andrews and India*, Delhi, New York, OUP, 1979.
47 The reforms inaugurated the system of 'dyarchy' where Indian elected assemblies took over certain areas of government but central power remained in the hands of the British [Kumar *Annie Besant's Rise* p. 125–6].
48 EIED Section A p. 146.
49 J. Brown *Gandhi's Rise to Power: Indian Politics 1915–1922* London 1972.
50 Sarkar *Swadeshi Movement* pp. 79, 371.
51 *śakti* especially means the cosmogonic energy of the Goddess, the 'power of creation' which in Tantra is feminine. See below pp. 118ff.
52 V. Chirol *Indian Unrest* London 1910, p. 10.
53 ibid p. 30.
54 Sarkar *Swadeshi Movement* pp. 313, 495. But Sarkar points out that this use of religion was 'not traditional'.
55 ibid p. 485, 495.
56 ibid pp. 52–7.
57 *Autobiography* ... p. 240.
58 Quoted in K. Singh *Prophet of Indian Nationalism: a study of the political thought of Sri Aurobindo 1893–1910* London 1963, p. 70–1. Bhawani Mahisha Mardini is the goddess Durga of the *Devī Māhātmya* at war with the demons. She takes form out of the lesser *śaktis* who are the feminine aspects of the male members of the Hindu pantheon. [T.B. Coburn *Devī-Māhātmya: the crystallisation of the Goddess Tradition* Delhi 1984.].
59 Quoted by Chirol *Indian Unrest* p. 94.
60 'The world was a manifestation of Divine Power (Śakti) and each man was himself ... a fragment (*aṁśa*) of that great Power'. Address to the Friends' Union Club. See below chapter 5.
61 *Bhārata Shakti* (3rd ed.) p. viii.
62 See Heehs *The Bomb* ... p. 73 especially the first of the three points of Aurobindo's 'religious nationalism': the idea of India as a living goddess.
63 In 1912 a newspaper report noted that 'swadeshi' was no longer an objectionable term to government. [IOR L/R/5/39 Reports on Indian Newspapers, Bengal, No.31/92, *Hindi Bangavāsi* 29 July 1912].
64 IOR L/R/5/41 Reports on English Newspapers in Indian Ownership No.10/14, *Amrita Bāzār Patrika* 26 February 1914.
65 Sir E. Montagu *An Indian Diary* London 1930, p. 81–2.
66 Sinha *Asutosh Mukherji* ... p. 107.

67 Zetland (Marquis of) *Essayez* London 1956, pp. 124–6. See next chapter.
68 See GOL(1) p. x–xi (press notices on *Bhārata Shakti*).
69 Reviewer in the *Madras Mail*, cited at GOL(1) p. viii.
70 Sarkar *Swadeshi Movement* p. 33–4 distinguishes four trends within the swadeshi movement, one was 'moderate, and three were called 'extremist'.
71 See Wedderburn, *A Life* ...
72 Sarkar *Swadeshi Movement* p. 36.
73 S. Sarkar: 'The Kalki-Avatar of Bikrampur: A Village Scandal in Early 20th Century Bengal' in R. Guha (ed.) *Subaltern Studies: writings on South Asian history and society* VI, Delhi, OUP, 1989, pp. 1–53.
74 ibid p. 30.
75 ibid p. 31–2.
76 IOR L/5/42 Indian Newspaper Reports, Bengal, No.24/20–1: *Dainik Chandrikā* 2 June and *Bangabāsi* 5 June.
77 Clerk of the court.
78 Translation by Satyakam Sengupta. The story with the extract of the poem was published in Mr Bagchi's biography of Woodroffe serialised in the magazine *Bhāvmukhe*. (See below chapter 6).
79 The references are so frequent that it is superfluous to cite examples, but see the Notes section, CWN ix (1905–6), the year of partition; vol.x p. 61 (no vested rights of the judiciary are safe from the encroachments of the civil service) and p. 69 (complaints that magistrates placed themselves above the law).
80 CWN xiii p. 205–6 (Notes, June 14 1909; comment on the Nattore Mail Robbery Case) 'The methods of the police ... seem to bear a marked family likeness ...'.
81 Heehs *The Bomb* ... p. 122.
82 *Judicial and Public Department Annual Files* 1909, IOLR L/J&P/6/951 (henceforth *Annual Files*: subsequent references come from the 1909 volume. All related papers were filed under the year in which the issue originated.).
83 CWN xviii p. 198.
84 CWN xiii pp. 861–95 *Santosh Das ... versus King–Emperor*, p. 894, and p. 880: The Chief Justice commented: 'It is difficult to avoid the conclusion that the arrest [of Peary Mohan Dass] was a move towards getting from Santosh the statement he had hitherto withheld'.
85 *Annual Files*: notes and telegrams from June 1909; CWN xiii p. 229–30 (Notes).
86 *Annual Files* 12 June 1909, 1 March 1910.
87 Harding *My Indian Years* p. 15.
88 'Clarke's case': CWN xii p. 973 (Reports).
89 CWN xiii p. 458 (Reports) *L.O. Clarke versus Brajendra Kishore Roy Chowdhuri*.
90 CWN xvi pp. 865–74 Report of Privy Council decision.
91 CWN xiii p. 895 (Reports) *Lāla Lājpat Rāi versus the Emperor*; ibid p. 237–8 (Notes), CWN praises Fletcher's judgement.
92 CWN xiv pp. 201–3 (Notes, 6 June 1910). Here, as later, Woodroffe upholds the 'official line' (more than did his fellow judge on the bench). 'He [Woodroffe] was satisfied that the Government would not have taken this exceptional action against the Plaintiff [ie his deportation] unless, after the most careful consideration, his conduct appeared to justify it.' CWN commented that 'this begs the question' and was irrelevant to Fletcher's original decision. There is a distinct similarity with the Midnapore case. For trial report see ibid pp. 713–41 (11 March 1910).
93 CWN xvi pp. 145–216 (Reports): *Peary Mohan Das versus D. Weston and others*; *Annual Files*: notes and telegrams from Aug 1911.
94 CWN xvi p. 41 (Notes, 8 Jan 1912); *Annual Files*: 26 July 1910.
95 *Annual Files*: Oct. 1911.

96 According to CWN, this was because he had 'not been swayed by executive influence' in coming to his decision [CWN xvi p. 205 (Notes, 1 July 1912)]. 'Clarke's case' is also discussed in ibid pp. 197, 221–2.

97 CWN xviii pp. 185–245 (Reports) *D. Weston and others versus Peary Mohun Das*: 'Where an officer causes the arrest of a person under the authority of law and in the bonafide belief in his right to do so, the fact that he might also be shown to have been actuated by other motives, for example to induce his son to make a confession, would not make such act actionable.' (p. 185).

98 ibid p. 231.

99 *Annual Files*: 7 Feb 1913.

100 *The Englishman* August 19 1912 p. 2 col 4 (also cites *The Pioneer* and *The Statesman*). See also *The Statesman* (overseas weekly) August 29 1912 p. 4 col.1–3a.

101 IOR L/R/5/39 Indian Newspaper Reports Bengal for 1912.

102 CWN xvi p. 261 (Notes).

103 IOR L/R/5/39 Indian Newspaper Reports Bengal, p. 518: *Amrita Bāzār Patrika* 21 Aug 1912.

104 CWN xviii p. 191 (Reports).

105 ibid p. 217.

106 Sarkar *Swadeshi Movement*, p. 372–3. The Raja of Narajole, who featured prominently in the case, supported the revolutionaries with funds.

107 Heehs *The Bomb* . . . p. 124–5.

108 Woodroffe several times makes the observation – but only in passing – that it would have been open to the magistrate to have granted bail to the elderly Peary Mohan Das instead of keeping him in prison.

109 CWN xviii p. 218.

110 ibid p. 224.

111 CWN xiii p. 894 (Reports). See Binoy Jiban Ghosh *Murder of British Magistrates* Calcutta 1962. A nephew of one of those put on trial writing long after the events, claims that bombs had been manufactured in Midnapore but not by those put on trial. He claimed police had planted evidence after failing to find the bombs made by Hem Chandra Das and Satyendranath Bose. Heehs *The Bomb* . . . p. 162 says the police failed to search Hem Chandra's house in time.

112 CWN xviii pp. 245ff (Reports).

113 An attempt was later made on the life of his informer, Abdur Rahman [Heehs *The Bomb* . . . p. 245].

114 Home Dept (Judicial Branch) Proceeding No.226 dated 26 Sept. 1912. [NAI, New Delhi].

115 CWN xvi p. 261 (Notes).

116 *Hardinge papers* vol.50, f.63, letter dated 13 June 1911, Cambridge University Library.

117 *Morley Collection* OIOC Mss Eur D573/46: letter dated 18 July 1909.

118 *Nāyak* 22 August 1912 scornfully states that Woodroffe was 'preparing a table of contents for the *mahānirvāṇa tantra*' and that in his judgement 'the Tantra was made manifest' (ie as rubbish). [IOR L/R/5/39 Indian Newspaper Reports, Bengal No.35/71].

119 See below pp. 94–5ff.

120 See above endnote 92.

121 CWN xi p. 181 (Notes, May 29 1907).

122 CWN xiii p. 229–30 (Notes).

123 In July 1919 we see him rejecting an appeal by the English Language *Amrita Bāzār Patrika* against forfeiture of funds on account of two articles which Woodroffe found 'were indeed likely to stir up feelings of hatred and contempt towards Government . . .'. He had just exercised his own freedom of speech to produce *Is*

India Civilized?. No doubt he felt the cases were different. [CWN xxiii p. 1057; in this case Fletcher was on the bench too and agreed with Woodroffe's decision].

124 CWN xix p. 150 (Notes, 31 May 1915); *Jyoti* on 3 June 1915, *Charu Mihir* on 8 June, and *Dainik Chandikā* on 20 June support Woodroffe, as does *Hitāvadi* on 25 June (which however saw his appointment as opening the way for Sir Asutosh Mukherji to succeed him). [IOR L/R/5/42 Indian Newspaper Reports Bengal, nos 905, 946, 971].

125 CWN xix p. 153 (Notes, 7 June 1915).

126 CWN xxvi p. 162. (Notes).

127 CWN xix p. 217ff (Notes, 30 August 1915).

128 *Hardinge papers*, Telegram No.97. Dated Aug 18th 1912.

CHAPTER 4

1 J.H. Cousins *The Renaissance in India* Madras 1918; Sarkar *The Swadeshi Movement in Bengal* New Delhi 1973 p. 497.

2 *Art and Nationalism: occidental orientations* Cambridge 1994.

3 *The Making of a New 'Indian' Art: artists, aesthetics and nationalism in Bengal c.1850–1920* Cambridge U.P. 1992. The new orientalists and nationalists 'veered closely together' (p. 8, p. 163).

4 *Rūpam* No.12 (Oct. 1922) p. 144 describes him as 'the Founder and soul' of ISOA.

5 O.C. Gangopādhyay *Bhārater Śilpa O Āmār Kathā* Calcutta 1969 pp. 86–91. O.C. Ganguly eventually wrote over 30 books on Indian art.

6 It was O.C. Ganguly who recounted the story of how Woodroffe junior demolished his father in court one day (above p. 14).

7 *Bhārater* p. 90. By 'Paris' he means France where Woodroffe finally retired. James Woodroffe said the collection was looted during the second world war.

8 ibid p. 90–1.

9 *Kokka* (Tokyo) vol.xix no.223 p. 183.

10 *Much-Maligned-Monsters*, Oxford, Clarendon Press, 1977 (henceforth MMM).

11 ibid pp. 269–72.

12 Guha-Thakurta . . . *a New Indian Art* p. 146–7.

13 ibid pp. 53–64.

14 ibid; Sarkar *Swadeshi Movement* p. 101, 105ff.

15 Guha-Thakurta . . . *a New Indian Art* pp. 149–54.

16 *Rūpam* No.12 p. 144; Mitter *Art and Nationalism* p. 301. *The Bengalee* of 21 March 1905 wondered would students henceforth be taught nothing but designing and moulding clay figurines? 'Are higher branches of art and painting to be banished?'.

17 Sir E. Denison Ross *Both Ends of the Candle* London 1943 p. 139: He (Curzon) 'would not have anything English or quasi-English' at the Delhi Durbar of 1902, since 'India . . . has an art of her own.' (See also Government Art College Centenary Volume p. 29).

18 'British Philistinism' in *The Nineteenth Century* (London) Feb 1903, cited in Guha-Thakurta . . . *a New Indian Art* p. 156.

19 Lipsey *Coomaraswamy* vol.3 ('His Life and Work') Princeton 1977.

20 ibid p. 19–20.

21 Guha-Thakurta . . . *a New Indian Art* pp. 159–62.

22 'He (the image maker) did not choose his own problems but like the Gothic sculptor obeyed a hieratic Canon . . . not (a) . . . philosopher or aesthete, but a pious artisan'. [Coomaraswamy *Dance of Śiva*, quoted by Mitter MMM p. 279].

23 *Myths of the Hindus and Buddhists*, London, Harrap, 1915. Coomaraswamy completed the book which Nivedita had begun before her death.
24 *Essays in National Idealism* (1909 Calcutta) and *Art and Swadeshi* (1911 Calcutta). He placed a divide between cultural and spiritual 'swadeshi' and the more 'crude' political version.
25 *Rajput Painting*, London, OUP, 1916; JISOA November 1961 (Golden Jubilee Number) p. 99; Guha-Thakurta . . . *a New Indian Art* p. 166.
26 ibid pp. 286, 191.
27 MMM p. 269–70.
28 G.D.M. Birdwood *The Industrial Arts of India* Calcutta 1988; first published London 1880.
29 Quoted by Mitter MMM p. 269. (Lipsey *Coomaraswamy* p. 70 explains he was looking at a photograph of an Indonesian stone sculpture of a *dhyāni* Buddha from Borobudur. Its soft features and smooth rounded limbs reminded him of a certain kind of pudding.).
30 Lipsey *Coomaraswamy* p. 60.
31 London 1928 p. 34.
32 Quoted by Mitter MMM p. 245. It was Ruskin who especially taught that 'Nature – natural form – was the source of beauty' (Lipsey *Coomaraswamy* p. 57).
33 *The Theosophist* vol.40/1 (Oct. 1918–March 1919) p. 297 (a reply to a reviewer of his own *The Renaissance in India*). Mitter also makes this connection [MMM pp. 240, 247–8].
34 Cousins *Renaissance* p. 146.
35 Birdwood *Industrial Arts* (1988) p. 2.
36 ibid p. 125.
37 Cousins *Renaissance* p. 119–20; Mitter MMM p. 247–8.
38 Cousins *Renaissance* p. 85–6.
39 ibid p. 107.
40 *Rūpam* No.11 (July 1922) p. 100.
41 *Indian Sculpture and Painting* London 1928, p. 8. 'Indian art is essentially idealistic, mystic, symbolic and transcendental. The artist is both priest and poet' (p. 10).
42 ibid pp. 12–24.
43 S.N. Hay *Asian Ideals of East and West: Tagore and his critics in Japan* Harvard University Press 1970 pp. 21–3, 51.
44 Guha-Thakurta . . . *a New Indian Art* p. 158.
45 'The Aryan Myth and British Writings on Indian Art and Culture' in B. Moore-Gilbert (ed.) *Literature and Imperialism* London 1983. Mitter's paper shows how art theories were linked to notions of race, but his analysis applies more widely. See also Mitter's MMM pp. 263–5: the orientalist notion of India as 'a continually decaying society'.
46 MMM p. 258.
47 Havell's view of the Brahmanical synthesis is similar to that of Dinesh Chandra Sen (see below p. 000). See *Benares the Sacred City*: London 1905 p. 61; *History of Aryan Rule in India from the earliest times to the Death of Akbar* London 1918 pp. 148–57, where he manages to claim Akbar as an 'Aryan'! On p. 179–80 he interestingly disagreed with Fergusson by saying the *śikhara* of the Hindu temple was an 'Aryan' feature precisely *because* he viewed it as a Śaiva symbol. (Compare this with L.D. Barnet below p. 127–8). See Guha-Thakurta pp. 177–9, 181; on p. 181 she calls this view of Havell's 'orientalist' and 'essentialist' – no doubt, but it was how many Hindus also saw things.
48 *Dance of Śiva*, New York, 1981, p. 21–2; 'The Theory of Art in Asia' in *The Transformation of Nature in Art*, New Delhi 1974 pp. 3–57.

49 H. Zimmer *Artistic Form and Yoga in the Sacred Images of India* Princeton 1984 pp. 21–64; see below p. 133.
50 V.K. Pal *Tantrāchārja Sivacandra*, Cooch Bihar, 1972, p. 105–6. See below chapter 6.
51 *Benares the Sacred City* p. 112–3. This of course was long before Avalon's books were published. Havell's account of Śāktism in the 2nd edition of *Indian Sculpture and Painting* (1928) draws on Woodroffe's *Garland of Letters* (1922).
52 MMM pp. 272–3, 274, 277–8; Guha-Thakurta . . .*a New Indian Art* p. 158.
53 Havell *Indian Sculpture and Painting* (1928) p. ix–x. This recalls a similar statement by Woodroffe (below p. 000).
54 Woodroffe would not, like Havell, have urged that the British Empire should become 'Aryan' in order to save itself [Guha-Thakurta p. 18].
55 MMM p. 268.
56 Guha-Thakurta . . .*a New Indian Art* p. 154ff.
57 They still used perspective, and *chiaroscuro* to give the illusion of solidity, for example, until a time when they deliberately abandoned these to produce flat 'decorative' art believed to be a more truly Indian style [Mitter *Art and Nationalism*]. Guha-Thakurta lists six ingredients of Abanindranath's style including Pre-Raphaelite and Art Nouveau trends [. . .*a New Indian Art* p. 227].
58 Guha-Thakurta . . . *a New Indian Art* pp. 211ff.
59 ibid pp. 243, 258–60.
60 A.K. Bhattacharya 'The Indian Society of Oriental Art in Retrospect' in JISOA 1981–3 (75th Anniversary number) p. 148.
61 ibid; also the Golden Jubilee Number (1961): 'The Indian Society of Oriental Art: Its Early Days' pp. 96–103.
62 *Modern Review* vol.19 (February 1916) p. 255.
63 JISOA 1961 p. 99. A reproduction in *Modern Review* (February 1909) of Surendranath Ganguly's 'Ganeṣa writing the Mahābhārata' was from a painting in the possession of Woodroffe. It had been taken by him to England, but its present whereabouts are not known. For Ramananda Chatterji's important influence see Mitter *Art and Nationalism*.
64 JISOA 1961 p. 96–7. (Extract from Tagore and Chand *Joṛāsānkor Dhāre*). Abanindranath describes the enthusiasm with which Woodroffe collected articles from all over the Indian subcontinent. The exhibitions are described in Mitter *Art and Nationalism* pp. 317–28.
65 Lipsey *Coomaraswamy* p. 87; *Rothenstein Papers*, Houghton Library, Harvard University, bms ENG 1148 (1638): letter from Woodroffe to Justice H. Stephen, 24 July (1910).
66 K. Datta & A. Robinson *Rabindranath Tagore: the Myriad-Minded Man* London 1995; M. Lago *Imperfect Encounter: Letters of William Rothenstein and Rabindranath Tagore 1911–1941* Harvard U.P. 1972 p. 19–20: Havell's lecture to the Royal Society of Arts was the beginning of a 'cultural chain reaction' that brought Rabindranath to the attention of the West (ibid p. 2). Rothenstein's visit is recorded in his *Men and Memories* London 1932–39.
67 Mitter *Art and Nationalism* pp. 324–6.
68 Rathindranath Tagore *On the Edges of Time* Calcutta 1981 p. 90.
69 Quoted in JISOA 1961 pp. 101–3. For Cousins' enthusiastic promotion of the society and the cause of 'Indian art' see Mitter *Art and Nationalism* pp. 328–30.
70 JISOA 1961 p. 102 (quote from Cousins' biography *We Two Together*).
71 Woodroffe expressed the hope that the Indian people would 'regain their artistic heritage and realise that their duty is not to borrow from others but to give of their own.' Quoted in Mitter *Art and Nationalism* p. 315. Curiously, this stricture did not seem to apply to 'imitation' of Japanese style.

72 Gangopadhyay *Bhārater* p. 101–2.
73 JISOA 1961 p. 98.
74 *Ānanda Bāzār Patrika*, 18 March 1944 (short obituary notice).
75 A. Tagore & R. Chand *Joṛāsānkor Dhāre* Calcutta 1985 p. 116.
76 JISOA 1961 p. 96.
77 Guha-Thakurta ... *a New Indian Art* p. 278: 'Such an organisation [ISOA] underlined the extent to which the whole phenomenon of 'national art' had come to rely on the support and accolades of the European Orientalists'.
78 Guha-Thakurta ... *a New Indian Art* p. 174–5. See for example *Modern Review* Jan–Feb 1907 'The Function of Art in Shaping Nationality'.
79 'Reminiscences' in JISOA 1961 p. 45–6.
80 Woodroffe lectured to the Vivekananda Society in Calcutta (see below chapter 11) and his name is on a list of past Presidents at the Society's headquarters there. For Nivedita see B. Foxe *Long Journey Home: a biography of Margaret Noble (Sister Nivedita)* London 1975. Woodroffe is not mentioned in Nivedita's published letters.
81 Guha-Thakurta ... *a New Indian Art* p. 169; Y. Horioka *The Life of Kakuzo* Tokyo 1963. Okakura had been influenced by an American professor of Philosophy, Ernest Francisco Fenollosa, who had combined a personal conversion to Buddhism with a passion for Japanese art as collector and connoisseur rather in the mould of Woodroffe himself in India, and of Havell.
82 S.N. Dhar *A Comprehensive Biography of Swami Vivekananda* Calcutta 1975, p. 1392–3 and p. 1476 footnote 92.
83 Horioka *Kakuzo* p. 48; Guha-Thakurta pp. 167–9.
84 *Viśvabhārati Quarterly* New Series II/2 (1936) pp. 65–73 (Okakura Number).
85 Guha-Thakurta ... *a New Indian Art* pp. 170–5.
86 ibid p. 168. Two Japanese painters were sent in succession by Okakura to teach the students of Abanindranath. The master himself returned for a second visit in 1913, just before his death. [Tagore and Chand *Joṛāsānkor Dhāre* pp. 135, 137].
87 K.R. Towndrow 'Sir William Rothenstein and his Indian Correspondence' in *Indian Art and Letters* vol.xxv no.1 (1951) pp. 14–32, p. 17.
88 J. & M. Cousins *We Two Together* Madras 1950 p. 316.
89 *Sorabji Papers* OIOC Mss Eur F165/21–5: letter to Harrison Faulkner Blair, dated 15 March 1906. She reminds her correspondent that she has already described the Woodroffes' house 'last year' but alas the letter in question seems not to have survived.
90 A. David-Neel (ed. M Peyronnet) *Journal de Voyage: Lettres à mon Mari* Paris 1976 p. 97 (Letter dated 21 January 1912).
91 ibid pp. 110–13. (Letter dated 14 March 1912). As a contrast to this social world she had described a more formal garden party given by a Maharani to entertain the Viceroy Lord Hardinge, which David-Neel attended with Mrs Woodroffe and Mrs Moeller. Here she found 'no cordiality', the Indians bored, the English preoccupied with preserving their dignity as 'whites'. Mrs Woodroffe, she said, 'didn't look as if she was enjoying herself' (ibid p. 103–4).
92 Tagore and Chand *Joṛāsānkor Dhāre* p. 73.
93 H. Keyserling *Travel Diary of a Philosopher* London, 1925, vol.1 p. 335. He is full of the 'romantic orientalist' idealization of Hinduism.
94 Lipsey *Coomaraswamy* p. 79.
95 *Zetland Papers* OIOC Mss Eur D609/1:Marquis of Zetland *My Bengal Diary* vol.1 p. 107.
96 Sir E. Montagu *An Indian Diary* London 1930 p. 85.
97 Tagore *On the Edges of Time* pp. 89, 90–1.
98 W. Rothenstein 'Gaganendranath Tagore', *Viśvabhārati Quarterly* New Series IV/1 (1938) p. 4.

99 Towndrow: 'Sir William Rothenstein . . .' p. 15. Letter dated Aug 6 1910.
100 *Men and Memories* vol.2 (1934) p. 249–50.
101 *Rothenstein Papers*: letter from Woodroffe to Rothenstein 16 December (1910) and letter from Woodroffe to Justice Stephen 24 July (1910).
102 Rothenstein *Men and Memories* vol.2 p. 249. James Woodroffe recalled many Indians visiting their home in Calcutta, including Rabindranath Tagore, but in 1930 when the poet visited Oxford and both James and his father were living there, he could not remember them meeting.
103 Communication of Dr Saumaren Bhaumik, Rabindra Bharati University.
104 Communication of Mr Sobhun Ghose.
105 Denison Ross *Both Ends* . . . p. 131 quoting his wife's record of her stay with Sir Denzil and Lady Ibbetson in 1905.
106 Tagore *On the Edges of Time* p. 91.
107 See below pp. 75–6.
108 Tagore *On the Edges of Time* p. 8; Nirad Chaudhury *Autobiography of an Unknown Indian* New Delhi 1976 p. 403–4. Pavitra Gangopadhyay does not name his host but calls him a 'baṛa sahib' and a judge of the High Court. There were few Indian High Court judges at this time.
109 Sarkar *Swadeshi Movement* p. 171–2 records that Asutosh Chaudhury and Hirendranath Datta (also reported to be a friend of Woodroffe) were prominent in the swadeshi movement and were leaders in the National Education Movement; but they threatened to disaffiliate schools that had links with the (more revolutionary) Samities. For Rabindranath's disillusion, see ibid p. 62–3. See *Modern Review* vol.cviii, no.1 (July 1960) pp. 52–4: an article on Asutosh Chaudhury which mentions his *soirées* at his house in Ballygunge.
110 Zetland: *My Bengal Diary* vol.2 p. 66–7: entry for 27 November 1921. Asutosh Chaudhuri was released from his Presidentship of the Bengal Legislature because he wanted to organize opposition to Gandhi at the forthcoming Congress at Nagpur.
111 Communication of Dr Saumaren Bhaumik at Rabindra Bharati university. As a very young man he was a student of Abanindranath.
112 Ronaldshay: *Essayez* London 1956 p. 129–30.
113 Ronaldshay *The Heart of Aryavarta* London 1925 p. 148–9.
114 Ronaldshay *Essayez* pp. 124–7. *Zetland Papers*, OIOC Mss Eur D609/5: letter from Gaganendranath Tagore, June 1919.
115 Cousins *Renaissance* p. 89 gave the war as the reason for their being a gap in the annual exhibitions.
116 A.K. Bhattacharya in JISOA 1981–3 p. 151.
117 Zetland: *My Bengal Diary* vol.1. p. 257. Entry for 7 September 1919.
118 See *Rūpam* No.12 (Oct. 1922) p. 144.

CHAPTER 5

1 *Bhārata Shakti* [henceforth BS] (3) p. viii (Preface to 1st edition).
2 ibid p. ix (Preface to 2nd edition).
3 S. Sarkar *The Swadeshi Movement in Bengal* New Delhi 1973, pp. 150ff, especially p. 154. The charge against Western education was that it did three things: it denationalized; it secularized and alienated from religion; and it made servants of the Raj and imitators of the West. Criticism of the official system 'had been mounting for more than a generation before 1905'.
4 E. Stokes *The English Utilitarians and India* Oxford 1959, p. xiii.

5 BS(3) pp. 75–83.
6 *Seed of Race* [henceforth SOR] (2), p. 5.
7 See Ashish Nandy *Intimate Enemy: Loss and Recovery of Self under Colonialism* Delhi 1988. W. Halbfass *India and Europe: an essay in understanding*, New York, 1988.
8 BS(3) p. 50.
9 'Education, Patriotism, Freethinking': BS(3) pp. 62–72. Reprinted from *The Bengalee* 21 April 1915 p. 2.
10 See D. Kopf *The Brahmo Samāj and the Shaping of the Modern Indian Mind* Princeton USA 1979.
11 Seal was first a Brahmo, later a secular humanist. David Kopf calls him 'a very convincing advocate of the religion of humanity' (ibid p. 62). His book on Ram Mohun Roy 'the Universal Man' was published in 1933. For Woodroffe's use of writings by Seal see below chapters 9 and 11.
12 Because it was said to represent a 'reformed' Tantrism. See below chapters 7 and 8.
13 ibid p. 63–4. With regard to his religious views he said the Raja was 'like a piece of shot silk which shows a different colour according to its position and the light'.
14 ibid p. 66.
15 ibid p. 69–70 The real moral of this story is that each must be allowed to be true to his own nature and not be distorted by standards imposed by others. He cites it as a plea for tolerance, but also uses it to question the idea of social reform.
16 ibid p. 71–2.
17 See Nirad Chaudhury '*Autobiography*... p. 110: 'We were little Hindu Protestants', & pp. 139, 203 on the Brahmo Samāj as 'Hindu Protestantism'.
18 IOR L/R/5/43, Reports on Indian Newspapers, Bengal, Report nos. 4–10 (for January and February 1916) refer to a series of incidents involving Mr Oaten, leading up to the college being closed and the setting up of a commission of inquiry .
19 BS(3) p. 49.
20 'Imitation and Independence' BS(3) pp. 46–53.
21 ibid p. 48.
22 T. Raychaudhuri *Europe Reconsidered* Oxford 1988, p. 252 on Vivekananda. 'After his return from the West he preached a gospel of manly virtues, an ideal of western-style worldly achievements, as the first step towards national regeneration.' See also Heehs, *The Bomb in Bengal*, cited in Chapter 4 above.
23 *pravṛṭṭi*, 'turned towards' or 'forward' refers philosophically to the outward phase of creation (of the world) and *nivṛṭṭi* to its reabsorption in the godhead. Hence the latter's equation with ascetic withdrawal in the individual.
24 BS(3) p. 59–60.
25 ibid p. 58.
26 Sir E. Denison Ross *Both Ends of the Candle* London 1943, p. 97.
27 'Indian Islamic Culture' BS(3) pp. 84–7.
28 R. Kumar *Annie Besant's Rise to Power in Indian Politics* New Delhi 1981, p. 110.
29 S.N. Dhar *A Comprehensive Biography of Swami Vivekananda* Calcutta 1975, p. 972 and ftnt 153.
30 In *Bhārat Varṣa* (for reference see below chapter 11, note 1).
31 It is quoted in Sanskrit in SS(DP) where the *sandhi* is wrong. It should read: *striyo devas striyaḥ prāṇaḥ*.
32 'Education of Women' BS(3) pp. 91–5.
33 See Nandy, *Intimate Enemy*...
34 See above p. 14.
35 *Modern Review* vol.22/1 (July 1917), p. 110. He 'gave some very wise and much needed advice to the managers of that orthodox school for girls'.
36 BS(3) pp. 1–34.

37 *Amrita Bāzār Patrika* 7 July 1919, p. 7: a Note on the condition of cattle in India by Nilananda Chatterji. A report by Woodroffe on the society's work to date was published in the same paper on 2 July.
38 Chatterjee Nilananda (ed): *The Condition of Cattle in India* Calcutta 1926, preface.
39 ibid, preface.
40 Communication of James Woodroffe.
41 *Bulletin of the Indian Rationalist Society* [henceforth BIRS] vol.1/1 (June 1919), p. 1. See Kopf *The Brahmo Samāj*, p. 48 for the ethical values which the idea of science represented for Bengali thought in the nineteenth and early twentieth century.
42 BIRS vol.1/5, p. 102.
43 ibid vol.1/4, pp. 57–71.
44 'The Gayatri as an Exercise of Reasoning', reprinted in GOL pp. 287–310.
45 ibid p. 295.
46 BIRS vol.3/10 (April 1922), p. 277.
47 ibid vol.3/6 (November 1921): p. 169–70.
48 *Modern Review* vol.23/11 (Nov. 1917), p. 534. 'Sir John Woodroffe by his straightforward, altruistic and courageous exposition reminds one of the race of thinkers headed by Spencer and the positivists of the last century – a race which is now prominent by its absence'.
49 'Indian Education' (BS(3) pp. 75–83), p. 78.
50 BS(3) p. 56.
51 See above p. 35–6.
52 BS(3) p. 54–61.
53 The date (June 1916) and heading have been omitted in the 3rd edition.
54 ibid p. 55–6.
55 See below p. 167.
56 SOR (2) p. 8–9.
57 *Asian Quarterly Review* (London) vol.16/47 (July 1920), p. 532–3.
58 SOR pp. 17–19.
59 In the sense of holding *Brahman* as the supreme principle.
60 See P. Robb (ed.) *The Concept of Race in South Asia* Delhi 1995, especially Jaffrelot pp. 327–54 on the idea of the Hindu race; and Indira Chowdhury-Sengupta pp. 282–303 'The Effeminate and the Masculine in Bengal' where she describes how the idea of a 'common Indian race' was developed in Bengal from the mid-nineteenth century. Peter Robb's introduction 'South Asia and the Concept of Race' discusses the question as to whether there was a pre-colonial idea corresponding to 'race' in India, pp. 1–76.
61 *Modern Review* vol.10 p. 222–3 (August 1911) and p. 277 (September 1911) contain extracts from Brajendranath Seal's speech.
62 ibid vol.10 pp. 60–4, and p. 276 (emphasis added).
63 SOR(2) p. 16–17.
64 IIC(3) pp. 121, 136.
65 Woodroffe however sees the 'degeneration' in terms of weakness and dependence on the West, from which India needs to learn only to the extent that doing so enables her to become free.
66 See Chowdhury-Sengupta in Robb *The Concept of Race* . . . p. 284–5; Partha Mitter 'The Aryan Myth and British Writings on Indian Art and Culture' in Moore-Gilbert B. (ed.) *Literature and Imperialism* London 1983, pp. 69–89, especially p. 81 on Birdwood. Compare Ernest Wood: *An Englishman defends Mother India* Madras 1929, p. 315, 324. Annie Besant believed in an idealised caste system promoting the development of the Aryan 'type' [Kumar *Annie Besant's Rise* . . . p. 57–8].
67 See above p. 30.

68 He should not be confused with the William Archer who was an ICS officer and wrote on folk arts in the 1920s.
69 London 1917. His visit was in 1914, but his book wasn't published until 1917. This was considered particularly insensitive timing as many Indians were at that time fighting for the empire in the war.
70 Quoted in IIC(3) p. 1. Vivekananda for his part had already called European civilization barbarian [Raychaudhuri *Europe Reconsidered*, p. 273].
71 Mr Oaten, the teacher at presidency College who had been attacked by students, had used the word 'barbarian' in its technical sense but this had been 'misunderstood' by the students. [*Papers of Sir Asutosh Mukherji* National Library, Calcutta. Letter of 11 May 1916 from O'Malley, Bengal Secretariat].
72 For example, he does not think *Bānde Mātāram* seditious and 'it should be the motto not only of the schoolroom but of the secretariat'; and he noted the need for widespread *primary* education, not always considered important (*India and the Future*, p. 268–9).
73 *India and the Future* p. 223.
74 See 'Press Reviews' in GOL(1) pp. v–xi; SOR(2) pp. 74–8. In London *The Times Literary Supplement* commented 'While the neo-Hindu and Nationalist papers almost exhausted the language of eulogy, Anglo-Indian journals unfavourable to the Montagu reform proposals charged the author with obscurity, extravagant abstraction, and the making of unworthy attacks on Western civilization.' [4 September 1919, p. 475(c)].
75 *Indian Philosophical Review* vol.2/3 (January 1919), p. 274.
76 'Cultural assimilation is thus a perfected form of conquest initiated by force of arms . . . The cultural assimilation acts as a compensation for lost political control. . . The cultural conquest is so complete as to render political control . . . unnecessary. . .' [IIC(3) p. 93–4].
77 See above on Ashish Nandy (note 7) .
78 IIC(3) p. 120 (He is quoting the sociologist Benjamin Kidd).
79 ibid p. 268–9.
80 See in *Shakti and Shākta* the chapter entitled 'Bharata Dharma' [SS(DP): chapter 1]. The use of the theme is to get away from narrow, usually negative, definitions of 'Tantra'.
81 IIC(3) p. 22.
82 ibid p. 346.
83 ibid p. 68.
84 ibid p. 272.
85 '. . . incarnations of the Humane Ideal in and evolved by man's mind, have taught the unity of all being and have anticipated in their presence the yet unfolded future of mankind.' ibid p. 115.
86 Altruistic love hardly ever features in his books on Tantra. Where ethical injunctions from the Tantras on individual practitioners to do good are occasionally quoted it is part of his apologetic purpose – to argue that the texts are not *un*ethical. Eg KT 12:63 translated in SS:93 which says that the *Sādhaka* 'should to good to others as if they were his own self'.
87 Selfless action without desire.
88 IIC(3) p. 346–7.
89 See Kopf *The Brahmo Samaj*, especially pp. 182ff.
90 WAP p. 57 (though here he disagrees with him.) See Raychaudhuri *Europe Reconsidered*, pp. 26–103 (his section on Bhudev). 'His purpose was to protect his society from servile imitation and inform it with self-confidence based on sober appraisals of western life in relation to traditional Indian values' (p. 26).

91 For example, the writer of the review in *Bharat Varṣa* quoted in chapter 8 below (see p. 000). Reviews of Woodroffe in *Modern Review* are usually favourable, but Annie Besant comes in for criticism.
92 CWN vol.xxvi (1921–2), p. 162.
93 N.C. Sengupta 'Sahitye Jatīyata' in *Yuga Parikrama* Calcutta 1961, p. 136–7. For this reference I am grateful to Mr Satyakam Sengupta. Ram Mohun Roy was unfashionable in the Hindu revivalist atmosphere of Woodroffe's times.
94 Reprinted in GOL(1): p. vii.
95 This latter information was supplied to me by Mr Keshab Sircar in Calcutta, but unfortunately I do not have the reference. See J. Sarkar *India Through the Ages: a survey of the growth of Indian life and thought* Calcutta 1928, p. 139.
96 IIC(3) p. xxv. Preface to the third edition.
97 ibid p. xiii.
98 See chapter 6, note 2.

CHAPTER 6

1 Desai *Erotic Sculpture: a sociocultural study* New Delhi 1975.
2 O.C. Gangopādhyāy *Bhārater Śilpa O Amār Kathā* Calcutta 1969, p. 91. There are other contemporary examples of Europeans wearing Indian dress. Ernest Wood (a Theosophist and principal of Sind National College) did so when he bathed in the Kistna river with pilgrims at a festival; he also did so on the railway and claimed to have been turned out of first class compartments through being mistaken for an Indian. [*An Englishman Defends Mother India*, pp. 279, 343]. Mrs Kate Tibbits, another Theosophist, "donned the ascetics' dress" when she joined a group sitting around a pandit on the *ghats* at Benares [*Veiled Mysteries of India* London 1929, p. 67]. This British woman, who was married to an ICS officer, was devoted to a woman guru in the city [*Voice of the Orient*, London 1909 p. 203]. The incomparable Alexandra David-Neel not only wore the sari and the saffron robe, she even claimed to have lain on a bed of nails and presented herself to a group of astonished tourists [*L'Inde Aujourd'hui, hier, domain*, Paris, 1954 pp. 28, 201–2].
3 *Bhārater* p. 91.
4 Tagore and Chand *Joṛāsānkor Dhāre* Calcutta 1985, pp. 172, 174–5.
5 *Bhārater* p. 89–90.
6 ibid.
7 V.K. Pal *Tantrāchārya Sivacandra* Cooch Behar 1972 (1379 BE), [henceforth 'Pal'].
8 *Bhārater* p. 90.
9 Pal p. 82 says that Woodroffe wore this dress. I am grateful to Mr Krishna Ghose of Calcutta for having a copy of this photograph made for me.
10 The Sanskrit edition of SCN (TT/2) was first published in 1913. Thackers Directory gives Middleton Row as Woodroffe's address in 1911–12. ('Alexandra Court' has been inserted in his handwriting on the letter above 'Middleton Row' which is printed.).
11 An Asiatic Society of Bengal Council minute for 31 March 1915 records that Johnson & Hoffman had provided the Society with a list of albums containing photos of Indian architecture. (Archives of the Asiatic Society of Bengal, 1 Park Street, Calcutta.).
12 This was also told to me at the High Court at Calcutta.
13 *Baśumati* vol.14/2 (1342 = 1936), p. 700–2; *Bharat Varṣa* vol.23/2, pp. 461–4.
14 Quoted by Pal p. 83.

15 P. Mangal *Bhārater Śilpi Nandalāl*, Calcutta, 1389 (BE), p.66. *puruṣa* and *prakṛti* are the male and female polar opposites in the dualist metaphysics of *sāṁkhya*. But they also stand for the God and Goddess and sometimes the human male and female. Their union in an inner, mystical sense is the object of *kuṇḍalinī yoga* but this was sometimes attained through practices involving a sexual partner.
16 Tagore and Chand *Joṛāsānkor Dhāre*, p. 113; Mangal, *Nandalal*, p. 67.
17 B. Datta *Swami Vivekananda Patriot–Prophet* Calcutta 1954, p. 310.
18 ibid p. 312.
19 Pal p. 178. See also below and chapter 11.
20 Volumes 16–19. See below chapter 11.
21 The former revolutionary and Aurobindo's brother mentioned in chapter 3 above, now returned from exile.
22 *Viśvabhārati Quarterly* vol.34/1–4 (May 1968–April 1969), p. 17. Also in Datta *Vivekānanda* p. 309, where it is stated he practised *mantra sādhanā*.
23 See below chapter 11.
24 Datta *Vivekananda* pp. 309–13.
25 *The Bengalee* 1 April 1914.
26 Calcutta 1985, pp. 290–346.
27 S.N. Bagchi 'Aghaṭan Ghaṭaner Alaukik Rahaśya – Woodroffer Dīkṣā' in *Bhāvmukhe* (Calcutta) vol.36–9 (1982–5). The story about the 'Judge and the Peśkar' retold in my chapter 3 was original to Mr Bagchi. Some other elements in his story seem to be imaginary.
28 *geruyā, kāṣāy*. In his book Pal claims only that Woodroffe wore this dress in private, at home. See below.
29 J. Sarkar: *India Through the Ages: a survey of the growth of Indian life and thought* Calcutta 1928, pp. 121–3.
30 Vol.23/2 pp. 461–4, p. 462.
31 His best-known volume of poetry was called *Gitāñjali*. See Ray *Bhārater Śādhak*, p. 313 for a list of his publications.
32 Raychaudhuri *Europe Reconsidered*, p. 35; Kopf *The Brahmo Samāj and the Shaping of the Modern Indian Mind* Princeton USA 1979, pp. 219ff.
33 Pal pp. 82, 146.
34 ibid p. 54.
35 ibid.
36 ibid p. 69.
37 *Bhārater Śādhak*, p. 329.
38 ibid p. 330.
39 See below p. 213.
40 *Bhāvmukhe* Vol 36, no 7. (All references to these articles are to offprints in my possession where the pages are not always numbered clearly.).
41 ibid vol.36/8, pp. 259–60. Bagchi's title (see above, endnote 27) 'Woodroffe's initiation: an unusual mysterious, supernatural occurrence' stresses the unusual nature of the event – unusual in Mr Bagchi's view because Woodroffe was a foreigner and a 'Christian'.
42 ibid.
43 Pal p. 55. The visitors are treated with slightly more honour in Bagchi's account for they are given special seats and allowed to watch the pūjā [*Bhāvmukhe* vol 36/9].
44 Pal p. 58. *tejas* means 'splendour', 'glory'.
45 See SP:84/ft.2. *Vedhadīkṣā* – whereby the disciple swoons under transference of power from the guru – such a guru is hard to find [Also KT:14:37].
46 S.N. Dhar *A Comprehensive Biography of Swami Vivekananda* Calcutta 1975, p. 93–4: 'The touch at once gave rise to a novel experience. With my eyes open I saw that

the walls of the room along with everything within it was whirling away till they vanished into naught and the whole universe with my individuality was rushing out as it were to merge itself in some all-encompassing void'.

47 *Bhāvmukhe* vol.6/9, quoting Gopiṇath Kaviraj: *Tāntrika Sādhanā O Siddhānta.*

48 Pal pp. 58–64, 67; Ray *Bhārater Śādhak* pp. 333–6. Bagchi is the only author to give a date for these pilgrimages: the long vacation of the High Court in 1907 *(Bhāvmukhe* vol.36/10).

49 Pal p. 67.

50 ibid p. 64. According to Keshab Sircar, who helped me with translations, this indicated the complete Indianization of Woodroffe. The guru was taken into the heart of the couple's marriage.

51 ibid p. 178.

52 'with ten arms' and 'riding on a lion'.

53 ibid p. 65.

54 ibid p. 64–5.

55 ibid p. 90–1 (quoting from 'Tantrācārya Śivacandrer smṛti tārpane' in *Gaurabhāvini,* Māgh–Caitra 1363).

56 ibid p. 172 Pal draws on many sources and one cannot always be sure when he is writing in his own voice or another's.

57 See below p. 193–4 for Sivacandra on the divine form.

58 Pal p. 105–6.

59 S. Sarkar *Swadeshi Movement,* p. 70.

60 Pal p. 103.

61 Hemendraprasad Ghose's *Baśumati* was a weekly journal in 1914 but copies of it from that time are hard to come by and I have not seen it. The monthly journal did not start until 1922–3.

62 ibid p. 103.

63 *Amrita Bāzār Patrika* 2 April 1914, p. 6: 'A Condolence Meeting'. *Bhārat Varṣa,* a literary magazine, started publication in January 1914 (1320BE) but does not report the *śoksabhā..*

64 Pal did not actually state where the meeting was held but said it was organized by the people of Calcutta.

65 Pal p. 104. Woodroffe may have met Vama Khappa. It was he who perhaps told him to seek out the Mother of the Universe. (See above p. 14).

66 ibid p. 118–9. Pañckori Bandyopadhyay's review of Arthur Avalon's book is referred to in chapter 8 below.

67 Pāl pp. 173–9.

68 ibid p. 173. Later Pal adds another witness to the story; a professor of Philosophy at Calcutta University, Dr Gopinath Bhattacharya, also heard it from Mitra.

69 ibid p. 177–8.

70 Pal uses the Sanskrit and translates it in Bengali as *yogyatā,* eligibility or worthiness.

71 *Vāmācār virācārādi tomār calibe nā. . .* ibid p. 175–6.

72 Pal p. 85–6. The photo of the sheet faces p. 86.

73 See above p. 73.

74 As we have seen, others said Woodroffe's worship was performed to an image of Durga, not Kālī.

75 A. David-Neel *Journal de Voyage: Lettres à mon Mari* Paris 1976 vol.2, p. 254 (Letter dated 13 August 1913).

76 A. David-Neel *L'Inde Aujourd'hui, hier, domain* Paris 1954 p. 140–1. (Translation mine).

77 Retention of semen during intercourse is the aim. Agehananda Bharati however disagrees [*The Tantric Tradition* London 1956, p. 278]. Sivacandra, too, had children, but this did not seem to detract from his standing and authority as a tantric saint.

78 *Journal de Voyage* vol.2, p. 258. (Letter of 13 August 1913).
79 B. & M. Foster *Forbidden Journey*, San Francisco 1989 p. 89.
80 She manifests an interesting progress from 'outsider' to 'insider'. Coming from a French protestant background her initial interest in *Theravāda* Buddhism had a rationalist bias and she expresses some typical 'negative orientalist' condemnations of 'superstition' etc. But later in her adventurous life she was a fully initiated Tibetan tantric nun [Foster and Foster, *Forbidden Journey*].
81 See below p. 118 for this 'transgressive' rite of the 'five offerings'.
82 See ITS:120 for a list of prescribed substitutes for the five *tattvas* given in the tantric texts. Sweets are usually a substitute for wine, not meat. MNT 8:171–2 (GLb p. 230) has the 'three sweets' (milk, sugar, honey) as a substitute for wine. Rice wine was one of the three 'excellent' kinds of wine [MNT 6:2 (GLb p. 138)]. The MNT suggests meditation on the Goddess or on the mantra given at initiation in place of the fifth *tattva* for those whose minds are weakened by lust (8:174). The use of substitutes is usually regarded as *paśvacāra* – the practice of the lowest grade (those who are not strong enough for *vīrācār*). In traditional *divyācar* the outward *tattvas* are internalised as various states and attitudes, and is the path of those who have no more need of ritual. (See SS:605).
83 *L'Inde* pp. 146–54. She contrasted this with two *cakras* which she spied on secretly. One was an orgy; the other was equally 'pure' when it came to the fifth *tattva*, but involved the sacrifice of a goat and partaking of real meat and wine [ibid pp. 154ff]. Actual sacrifice of a goat or other animals is prescribed even in the MNT [6:107–8].
84 Qualities, especially the three qualities which make up the phenomenal world: *sattva*, law, harmony, purity, goodness; *rajas*, energy, passion; and *tamas*, inertia, ignorance. [Eknath Easwaran *The Bhagavad Gita* Arkana London 1986, p. 230].
85 SS(2): viii–x, preface to the 2nd edition. (In SS(DP) passages from the prefaces to the 1st and 2nd editions have been changed about.).
86 See SS:17 where Woodroffe gently dissociates himself from what he perceives as Sivacandra's dogmatism. Other aspects of this letter from Sivacandra are discussed in chapter 10 below.
87 See below p. 214.
88 Letter 10 (emphasis added).
89 Communication of James Woodroffe. As early as 1920 she wanted her son to be confirmed.
90 M.P. Pandit *Kuṇḍalinī Yoga: A Study of Sir John Woodroffe's 'the Serpent Power'* Madras 1959, p. 10.
91 *saumya, śānta.*
92 Pal facing p. 86.
93 Vol.23/2, p. 462.
94 K. Chakravarti (trans) *Bhārat ki sabhya?*, Chottogram 1340 (=1946), translator's preface. He is repeating a remark by Biharilal Sarkar, one time editor of *Bangabāsi*.
95 *The Hindu*, Madras, 18 January 1936.
96 See for example Woodroffe (transl. M. Shibata) *Introduction à l'Hindouisme Tantrique: concepts et pratiques* Paris 1983, p. 7 The introduction to this French translation of extracts of *Shakti and Shākta* described Woodroffe as one of the rare Europeans who had received authentic initiations.

CHAPTER 7

1 A. Sanderson: 'Śaivism and the Tantric Traditions' in Sutherland S. (ed.) *The World's Religions* London 1988, p. 660.

2 T. Goudriaan and S. Gupta *Hindu Tantric and Śākta Literature* Wiesbaden 1981 (henceforth HTSL), p. 7.
3 Cited at SS:145. *Śruti* actually means 'what is heard', indicating the divine status of speech in both tantric and vedic tradition. A. Padoux *Vac: The Concept of the Word in Selected Hindu Tantras* New York 1990 (henceforth *Vāc*), p. 34.
4 T. Goudriaan et al: *Hindu Tantrism* Leiden 1979, p. 15ff where the similarities and differences are discussed.
5 HTSL p. 10. See their p. 116 and ftnt 17 for a list of the *ṣaṭ-karma*, which are aggressive or defensive magic powers.
6 ibid pp. 4, 20–2; André Padoux in M. Eliade (ed.) *Encyclopedia of Religion* Chicago 1987 (henceforth ER) vol.14, p. 275.
7 See Goudriaan in *Hindu Tantrism* pp. 7–9 for a list of eighteen characteristic features.
8 'There is a marked tendency to concretize speculative truths and to locate them in present and tangible realities.' [ibid p. 50].
9 This word has many meanings. See below endnote 15.
10 HTSL p. 3.
11 'The supreme, male Godhead (Śiva, Viṣṇu or one of their forms) does not act by himself but only as inseparably associated with – and through – his energy, his śakti, the dynamic power that manifests, animates, sustains, and finally reabsorbs the cosmic manifestation.' [Padoux *Vāc*, p. 43–4].
12 Goudriaan et.al. *Hindu Tantrism* pp. 5–11.
13 Some of the questions around defining 'Tantra' are discussed in chapter 9 below.
14 For different meanings of *tattva* see below p. 164.
15 See MNT:V:22–3, translated at GLb:86. The name for the fourth element, *mudrā*, has many meanings. In Tibetan Buddhism it means 'a seal', or a symbol or sign. It can also mean 'woman'. Its most familiar meaning in Tantra is a ritual hand gesture. It also designates body postures in *kuṇḍalinī yoga*. But I am informed by Francesca Fremantle that its meaning of 'grain' of a certain kind, regarded as an aphrodisiac, is known from vedic times.
16 For a summary of Tantrism see Padoux *Vāc*, pp. 30–57 (his second chapter); also in ER vol.14 pp. 272–80: 'Tantrism'.
17 E. Payne *The Śāktas* London 1933, pp. 1–3.
18 *Religions of India* Boston and London 1896. See pp. 483–92, his chapter on modern Hindu sects.
19 *A View of the History, Literature and Mythology of the Hindus* London 1822 (first published Serampore Mission Press 1811).
20 *Hindu Manners, Customs and Ceremonies* London 1906 (first published in French in 1821.).
21 *The Popular Religion and Folklore of Northern India* London 1896.
22 *Buddhism of Tibet* London 1895. At SS:62 Woodroffe criticises Waddell's statement that 'Tantra' was 'restricted to the necromantic books of the later Śivaic or Śakti mysticism'; At SS:204 he cites his description of yoga as a 'parasite containing within itself the germs of Tantrism' which 'cankered' *mahāyāna* Buddhism (thus producing the 'monster outgrowths' of the *vajrayāna*).
23 Eg PT/1 p. 3. For Hodgson see below.
24 The idea of 'vain repetitions' and 'mere externality' expressed protestant suspicion of ritual. When the Marquis of Zetland (Governor of Bengal in 1919) visited a hermit–Lama residing at Lachen in the Himalayas, he claimed that the Lama 'frankly admitted that *the images, the vain repetitions, the maṇḍalas and all the elaborate externalism* of Lamaism as ordinarily practised meant nothing to him. Such things *were but mummery*'. But the Lama said they were necessary to help ordinary people.

Zetland was very impressed by this hermit–Lama. [*Zetland Papers* OIOC Mss Eur D 609/1 *My Bengal Diary* vol.1 p. 271–2 (emphasis added)].

25 *The Śāktas* p. 1.

26 P. Bishop *The Myth of Shangri-La* Athlone Press London 1989, p. 127.

27 ibid pp. 10–19.

28 W.W. Hunter *A Life of Brian Houghton Hodgson* London 1896. On p. 280 Hunter lists some scholars who drew on Hodgson's work. Abstracts of the Sanskrit texts which he donated to the library of the Asiatic Society of Bengal were published towards the end of the century by Rajendralal Mitra [*The Sanskrit Buddhist Literature of Nepal* Calcutta 1882].

29 W.H.H. Hodgson *Essays on the Languages, Literature and Religion of Nepal and Tibet* New Delhi, Asian Education Services, 1991 (reprint of 1874 London edition).

30 ibid pp. 12, 15. *Upadeśa* were one of twelve classes of Buddhist scriptures he listed. It was some time after acquiring the exoteric scriptures before he was given access to the Tantras. Burnouf (*Le Bouddhisme* p. 466) wonders whether this was from shame or because they were specially venerated.

31 *Introduction à l'Histoire du Bouddhisme Indien*, Paris 1876 (2nd ed.), pp. 1–5.

32 ibid pp. 465ff.

33 '*les livres qui me paraissent le misérable produit de l'ignorance et de la crédulité la plus grossiere*' ibid p. 470.

34 ibid p. 481ff.

35 T. Duka *Life and Works of Alexander Csomo de Koros* London 1885.

36 'On Buddha and Buddhism' in *Works of the Late Horace Hayman Wilson* (henceforth '*Works*') vol.2, London 1862, pp. 229–65, p. 320. *Annales du Musée Guimet* vol.2 (1881) p. 132 (see next endnote).

37 'Analyse du Kandjour: recueil des livres sacrés du Tibet' in *Annales du Musée Guimet* vol.2 (1881), pp. 291–349, especially pp. 291, 295, 309. This is a French translation of de Koros' article in *Asiatick Researches* of 1836.

38 Bishop *Myth of Shangri-La*, p. 19. James Hilton's *The Lost World* was first published in 1933.

39 Wilson *Works* ... vol.1, 'Prospectus'. R. Symonds *Oxford and Empire: the last lost cause?* London 1986, p. 104.

40 H.H. Wilson: 'Notice of Three Tracts Received from Nepal' in *Asiatick Researches* vol.xvi (1828), pp. 450–78. Republished in *Works*... vol.2, pp. 1–39.

41 ibid p. 4.

42 ibid p. 33.

43 'A Sketch of the Religious Sects of the Hindus' in *Asiatick Researches* vol.xvi (1828), pp. 40–136. Both parts were republished in 1862 as *Works* ... vol.1.

44 *Works* ... vol.1, p. 8–9. His main sources were two books in Persian by contemporary Hindu authors, and the popular *bhakta māla* of the *vaiṣṇavas*.

45 *Vāma* means 'left', though it is sometimes also taken to mean 'woman'.

46 ibid pp. 248–50.

47 ibid pp. 254–65. His list is quoted from the *śyāmā rahasya* and translated as: 'Flesh, fish, wine, women, and certain mystical gesticulations'. He adds 'suitable Mantras' as well. He also cites verses from *kulārṇava tantra* and other texts. His description of the actual rite (which he calls the *śri cakra)* he says he has taken from William Ward, but adds quotes from *devī rahasya* to augment Ward's account from oral sources [ibid p. 258 and footnotes].

48 ibid p. 260.

49 'On the Religious Practices and Opinions of the Hindus' in *Works*... vol.2, pp. 40–119. For the section on the Tantras see pp. 77ff.

50 ibid p. 78–9. Emphasis in the original.

51 Symonds *Oxford and Empire*, p. 104.
52 E. Gait *History of Assam* Calcutta 1926 pp. 42, 58, 268. Although the exuberance and devotion of the Durga and Kālī festivals today are many millions of miles away from such associations, memories of the darker side of the history of Kālī still linger, as anyone who talks with people in Bengal can discover. I myself spoke with an elderly woman living in north-east Bengal who claimed that human sacrifice had been practised in her youth in Cooch Behar. The practice has been illegal since 1835. For a fuller and interesting discussion see Rachel Fell McDermot: 'A Tantric Icon Comes Alive: the Creation of the "Orientalist Kālī" in Early-Twentieth Century Bengal' in H.B. Urban (forthcoming), and the references therein.
53 H.M. Monier Williams *Brahmanism and Hinduism* London 1891, p. 181.
54 ibid p. 184–5.
55 ibid p. 185 (emphasis added).
56 H.M. Monier Williams *Hinduism* London 1894, p. 128–9.
57 *The Religions of India* London 1906, p. 204–5.
58 Monier-Williams *Brahmanism and Hinduism* p. 189 with ftnt 1; p. 208.
59 M. Sinclair Stevenson *The Rites of the Twice-Born*, OUP London, 1920. 'For the sake of truth' she declared 'it may be the terrible and austere duty of someone to investigate it...' (p. 419 ftnt.2). She did not know this terrible duty had already been undertaken. By contrast, the account of orthodox brahmanical ritual in this book by a missionary author is a shining example of empathy and objectivity.
60 M. Dyczkowski *The Doctrine of Vibration* New Delhi 1989, pp. 14–17.
61 ibid p. 16. See note 52 above, and on Rajendralal Mitra below.
62 The *pāśupatasutra* specifically enjoins behaviour contrary to accepted norms, such as making lewd gestures, so as to provoke social ostracism [Dyczkowski *Doctrine of Vibration* p. 8].
63 D.C. Sen *History of Bengali Language and Literature* Calcutta 1911, p. 250–1.
64 Compare Havell's view, above p. 67). The same theory to account for the origin of Tantrism was put forward in *Prabuddha Bharata* by an unnamed writer and reproduced in PT/2 p. 11ff.
65 See below p. 214.
66 *My Bengal Diary* vol.2 p. 23–4.
67 J. Taylor (trans.) *Prabodhacandrodaya: The Moon of Intellect, an allegorical drama* London 1812.
68 'If at any time in the history of India the mind of the nation as a whole has been diseased it was in the Tantric age'. B. Bhattacharyya *An Introduction to Buddhist Esotericism* London, OUP 1932, preface.
69 R.G. Bhandarkar *Vaisnavism, Saivism and the Minor Religious Systems* Strasbourg 1913, pp. 144–7.
70 R. Mitra *Indo-Aryans* Calcutta 1881 vol.1, p. 403.
71 ibid p. 404ff. In a chapter on 'Spiritous Drinks in Ancient India'.
72 ibid vol.2, pp. 105–12.
73 'Is Śakti Force?' SS:188–191. In Woodroffe's time there were many scholars of Tantra in Bengali, who were 'insiders'. Pañcānan Bhattachāryya, Ghose's collaborator in some later editions of *Tantrik Texts* was a prolific writer and influential philosopher. The foremost Indian authority on Tantra, who combined the role of scholar with personal initiation, was Gopinath Kaviraj, Principal of the Sanskrit College in Benares from 1924. His many influential books in Hindi, Bengali and English started to appear just a little later than those of Arthur Avalon [G. Kaviraj, *Aspects of Indian Thought* Burdwan 1966. G.G. Mukhopadhyay *A Great Savant: MMP Gopinath Kaviraj* Calcutta 1990].
74 L. de La Vallée Poussin *Bouddhisme* Paris 1909, his 5th chapter.

75 Quoted in PT/1 p. 25 and SS:77.
76 *Études et Textes Tantrique* Gand (Belgium) 1896.
77 *The Saktas* pp. 128ff.
78 D. Kopf: 'Sexual Ambivalence in Western Scholarship on Hindu India' in *Comparative Civilizations Review* vol.13 pp. 143–57, p. 144.
79 'In India there is no twilight before the dawn. . .' The people of the Vedas had not had to struggle through the intermediary stage of 'barbarism', they were civilized from the beginning [*Antiquities of India* p. 1].
80 ibid p. 3. Barnett's analogy of the head and feet recalls the famous *purūṣa sukta* in the Rg Veda [X:90].
81 N.N. Bhattacharyya *History of the Tantric Religion* New Delhi 1982, p. 168ff.
82 P. Mitter 'The Aryan Myth and British Writings on Indian Art and Culture' in Moore-Gilbert B. (ed.) *Literature and Imperialism* London 1983, pp. 69–89. The 'Aryan myth' led to perceptions of later Indian history as one of degeneration due to racial intermixture, see above p. 67.
83 *Antiquities of India* p. 4.
84 ibid p. 17.
85 See P. Kumar *Śakti Cult in Ancient India* Varanasi 1974.
86 See eg SS:140 and 103–13 (note by Brajalal Mukherji).
87 The claim was that it had been superseded by *Shakti and Shākta* and *The Serpent Power*. See GLb(2): ix–x (preface to the 2nd edition).
88 A translation by Jñanendralal Majumdar of the *īśā upaniṣad* with a tantric commentary was also published around 1917 under the aegis of 'Arthur Avalon' with an introduction by Sir John Woodroffe. In 1971 Ganesh and Co. published this along with the two translations by Arthur Avalon in the TT series in one book under the name of Woodroffe. See bibliography.
89 TT/1 preface p. vi–vii.
90 TT/2 pp. 1–3.
91 TT/19 Introduction, p. 1.
92 For the meaning of this term, and *bindu*, see below p. 167.
93 Goudriaan and Gupta HTSL pp. 130–4. See below chapter 11 for Woodroffe's problems with this issue.
94 That is, followers of the *kula* path. For the meaning of these terms see below p. 162.
95 'The Ocean of Kula' translated by Arthur Avalon (unpublished). For a succinct summary see HTSL pp. 92–6. The KT is discussed again in chapter 11 below.
96 HTSL p. 134–5.
97 *śri-cakra-sambhāra tantra* in Sanskrit.
98 TT/7 pp. viii, xvii–xviii.
99 TT/7 p. iii.
100 TT/15 was a vaisnavite text (*brahmasaṁhitā*). For a full list of the *Tantrik Texts* see bibliography.
101 Apart from the introductory volume of the series, by J.C. Chattopadhyay (see p. 223 below).
102 H. Zimmer *Artistic Form and Yoga* p. 253ff. See next note.
103 Translated as *Artistic Form and Yoga in the Sacred Images of India* Princeton University Press 1984. (First published in German in Berlin, 1926).
104 ER vol.15, p. 569 ('Zimmer').
105 'Yoga and the Figurative Sacred Image' in Zimmer *Artistic Form and Yoga. . . .* pp. 21–64. Zimmer writes (p. 23–4): 'Here we can discover how an Indian initiate views the meaning and role of the sacred image and we can above all comprehend the spiritual world in which the images of the Hindu divinities are rooted.' He acknowledges his debt to chapters 15–20 of *Principles of Tantra* volume 2.

106 The repetitiveness is mostly the result of its having originated in lectures and articles where Woodroffe covered the same ground on different occasions.
107 Theosophists and other occultists had heard of *kuṇḍalinī* and the *cakras* but appropriated them to their own systems. Such writings are criticised in *The Serpent Power*, especially Charles Leadbeater's *The Inner Life*, published in 1910 [SP:6–10].
108 See eg. Swami Sivananda Radha: *Kuṇḍalinī Yoga for the West* Shambala, Boston & London 1985. (Swami Sivananda Radha is American, but it was her guru Sivananda who recommended her to *The Serpent Power*.).
109 SS:ix refers to an early French translation of *Hymns*. A French translation of extracts of SS together with Woodroffe's own lectures in that language, was published in 1983: (M. Shibata (trans) *Introduction à L'Hindouisme Tantrique*, Paris). The translator also mentions translations of GOL and SP in the 1970's and a full translation of SS was promised. A German translation of SS was published in 1962.
110 C.G. Jung *Collected Works* vol.16 London 1966, p. 334–5. Jung also often cited *Shakti and Shākta*.
111 *Psychological Commentary on Kuṇḍalinī Yoga*, Lectures One, Two, Three and Four, 1932 (from the notes of Mary Foote) published in *Spring* New York 1975–6. See H. Coward *Jung and Eastern Thought* SUNY Press New York 1985 for Jung's use of Indian ideas.
112 Evola's *L'uomo Come Potenza* (1925) was renamed *Lo Yoga della Potenza* ('the Yoga of Power') in its 3rd edition in 1949. See *The Yoga of Power: Tantra, Śakti and the Secret Way* (trans: Guido Stucco), Inner Traditions International, Rochester Vermont, 1992, pp. ix–xv (translator's introduction). Evola unfortunately is associated with neo-fascism.
113 See below chapter 9.
114 *The Śāktas* p. 18–19. He commented: 'We know enough now about the laws of the mind to understand how such things can appeal to…the untutored and credulous'.
115 See his *Brahma and Buddha* Berlin 1926, pp. 156–9 and 'Tantrismus and Śāktismus' in *Ostasiatische Zeitschrift* vol.22 (1936), pp. 120–33, which show the influence of Woodroffe. Glasenapp was in touch with Woodroffe and Ghose. One of Woodroffe's letters reveals he had been asked to write an introduction to a volume of the TT series.
116 In Chantepie de la Saussaye *Lehrbuch der Religionsgeshichte* vol.2, Tubingen, 1925 (4th edition), pp. 178–81.
117 Pyarelal *Mahātma Gandhi* vol.1 book 2 'The Last Phase' Ahmedabad 1966, p. 228.

CHAPTER 8

1 An earlier English translation of the MNT had appeared in Calcutta [GLb: v-vi].
2 See SS(3) pp. iii–xxvii.
3 Lévy, though mainly a Sanskritist, was one of the last of the old type of 'orientalist' who studied a whole range of Asian languages. He visited India in 1897, and again in 1921, when he visited Tagore at Santiniketan. He wrote on the history of Sanskritic culture and the Sanskrit literature of Buddhism. (J. Bacot (ed.) *Mémorial Sylvain Lévy* Paris 1937).
4 Sylvain Levy in *La Revue Critique*, translated at SS(3) p. iii.
5 For a summary of questions around the date of the MNT see Hugh Urban: 'The Strategic Uses of an Esoteric Text: the Mahānirvāṇa Tantra' in *South Asia* vol.xviii

no.1, pp. 55–81. Arthur Avalon claimed to have seen a manuscript of the complete text which was 'some 500 years old' [GLb(2):viii. The actual age was not supplied in the first edition]. J.M.D Derrett argues for a late eighteenth century date. ['A Judicial Fabrication of Early British India, the Mahānirvāṇa Tantra', in *Essays in Classical and Modern Hindu Law* vol.2 Leiden 1977] Arthur Avalon's translation used an edition published in 1888 [GLb:ix).

6 MNT:III (GLb:33ff). Many Tantras acknowledge the absolute Brahman and are monistic in philosophical outlook, but tantric worship itself is not logically directed to the impersonal Brahman, which is beyond form and imagery [Urban 'The Strategic Uses...' p. 21–2]. In the later chapters of the MNT the Goddess comes into her own.

7 MNT:vi:195–7 (GLb:182) and MNT:vi:14 (GLb:140).

8 viii:171–4 (GLb:230) In neither of these latter features was it unique, but the MNT emphasizes these injunctions.

9 The old manuscript of the MNT, which Avalon claimed to have seen (see above note 5) but which he had not been allowed to use, included the *ṣaṭ-karma* in a second part [GLb(1):xiii].

10 Lévy cited at SS(3):iii.

11 J.N. Farquhar: 'Recent Advances in the History of Hinduism' in *International Review of Missions* vol.iv no.13 (January 1915), p. 145.

12 ibid. Later on Farquhar entered the controversy over the MNT's date, supporting the theory that it was actually composed by Ram Mohun Roy's guru [*Outline of the Religious Literature of India*, London, 1920]. Woodroffe replied to him at SS:133–5.

13 Eric J. Sharpe *Not to Destroy but to Fulfil: the contribution of J.N. Farquhar to Protestant missionary thought in India before 1914* Uppsala 1965.

14 F.O. Schrader *An Introduction to Pāñcarātra and the Ahirbuddhyna Samhitā* Adyar Library Madras 1916, Preface.

15 *The Theosophist* vol.35/I/i (October 1913), pp. 138–41.

16 ibid p. 138.

17 ibid pp. 141–4.

18 Rathindranath Tagore's reminiscences of his father paint a vivid picture of this adulation on the second European tour [*On the Edges of Time* Calcutta 1981].

19 'Dons de Sir John Woodroffe' in *Bulletin de l'Association Francaise des Amis de l'Orient* vol.1/1 (June 1921), p. 57–8. [Translation mine].

20 W. Halbfass *India and Europe* New York 1988, p. 142.

21 *Bulletin de l'Association Francaise* vol.1/2 (December 1921), p. 10–11.

22 SS:vii–viii (preface to 3rd edition).

23 Tagore *On the Edges of Time*, p. 154.

24 M. Winternitz: 'Die Tantras und die Religion der Śāktas' in *Ostasiatische Zeitschrift* vol.3 (1915–16), pp. 153–63.

25 'The Tantras and the Religion of the Śāktas' [SS:115–35].

26 'Winternitz 'Die Tantras...' p. 154. Translated at SS:119.

27 ... die in dem Begriffe "Mutter" den höchsten Ausdruck für das göttliche Prinzip gefunden hat...' [ibid p. 163 and SS:131].

28 'Durch die Anwendung aller dieser Mittel macht sich der Verehrer die Gottheit willig, er zwingt sie in seinen Dienst und wird zum Sādhaka, zum Zauberer. Denn Sādhanā, "Zauberei", ist ein Hauptziel, wenn auch nicht des letzte Endziel der Devi-verehrung' [ibid p. 156, translated at SS:122].

29 ibid p. 163; SS:131–2.

30 SS(2) p. viii–ix (Preface to the 2nd edition).

31 ibid p. viii.

32 Above p. 107.

33 P. Bandyopadhyay: 'Sahayogi Sāhitya' in *Sāhitya* vol.24 (Srāvan 1320 = 1913), pp. 363, 364. Translated at SS(3) viii–ix.
34 SS:18–26 and PT/2 pp. 16–23.
35 B.C. Mazumdar in *Modern Review* vol.14/6 (December 1913).
36 Quoted from *Pratibhā* at SS(3) p. xv.
37 Quoted at SS(3) p. viii.
38 SS(3) pp. xiii and xx. The reviewer in the former paper reacted strongly to the deification of the Feminine, calling Śākta Tantra 'a religion of suffragette monists'. Woodroffe replied to this too in *Shakti and Shākta* (see below p. 179).
39 M.P. Pandit *Kuṇḍalinī Yoga: A Study of Sir John Woodroffe's 'the Serpent Power'* Madras 1959, p. 10. This author also cites other contemporary appreciations of Woodroffe.
40 In later editions it has become 'Creation as Explained in the Non-dualist Tantras'. See SS:379–409.
41 R. Symonds *Oxford and Empire: the last lost cause?* London 1986, p. 189.
42 'The Tantrik Creation' in *Amrita Bāzār Patrika* Tuesday 19 January 1915, p. 7.
43 30 March 1915, in an announcement that the lecture had been reprinted in *The Hindu Spiritual Magazine* where it was 'given pride of place'.
44 Frederick Eden Pargiter (1852–1927) was a judge of the Calcutta High Court from 1904–6. Before that he served in the ICS Judicial Service. His Indological work included a translation of the *Markandeya Purāṇa* on which he laboured for twenty years, and several books on ancient Indian history, especially *Dynasties of the Kaliyuga*, based on Puranic sources. This book was popular in India because it took Indian tradition seriously as a historical source [British Biographical Index; JRAS vol.xxiv (1928) p. clxiv–clxv].
45 See below pp. 165.
46 'Creation in the Tantra' is described on a leaflet of publications of the *Āgamānusandhana Samiti* as Woodroffe's first public lecture on Tantra.
47 D. Kopf: 'Sexual Ambivalence in Western Scholarship on Hindu India' in *Comparative Civilizations Review* vol 13 (1986), p. 146.
48 A.S. Pandulipi: 'Abhinav praṇalir varṇabodh' *Bhārat Varṣa* vol.4/1 (1916), pp. 137–9.
49 ibid. This translated passage is from 'Press Notices' in TT/19 p. iii.
50 Reprinted at SS:718.
51 *Idylls of the King* Macmillan, Golden Treasury ed. 1904, p. 416.
52 The painting is reproduced in M. Harrison M. & B. Waters *Burne Jones* London 1989.
53 James Woodroffe said that his mother was a Theosophist. The name Mrs N. Woodroffe occurs in the lists of new members in Calcutta in 1910 and although the initial is wrong "Ellen" might have sounded like 'N'.
54 Cousins in his article refers to Madame Blavatsky's *Voice of the Silence* where she calls Tantrikas sorcerers (SS:720).
55 C. Leadbeater *The Inner Life* (1910) reprinted as *The Cakras: a monograph* Adyar 1927, to which Arthur Avalon refers in the passage in question.
56 The title of Louisa Finn's article (above p. 00).
57 P. Gangopadhyay *Calaman Jīban* Calcutta 1956. For pointing out this I am grateful to Satyakam Sengupta.
58 SS(2) p. x. This is the wording in the second edition, but SS(DP):xv places it under the preface to the first edition. The wording in the first edition ran:

> refer ... to other works ... which I have published under the name 'Arthur Avalon' with the assistance of others and, in particular, in co-operation with my friend R.R.: to give him his Rashi name, for his modesty will not permit me to mention any other. [SS(1)p. i)].

This emphasises even more that it was one friend in particular.

59 SS:223 reprinted from *The Theosophist* July 1919.
60 One case where it did arise concerned Dr Thibaut, supposed translator of the *vedānta sutras* and their commentaries. Thibaut was a member of the Sanskrit Examinations Board of Calcutta University in 1915, but an article in the Bengali press complained that both he and Asutosh Mukherji, the President of the Board, were ignorant of Sanskrit. Of Thibaut the article claimed: 'Everyone at Benares knows that he translated those commentaries with the help of MMP Rammisra Sastri of the city. Many old men of our country who are learned in both Sanskrit and English still say that from conversations with Dr Thibaut they have come to the conclusion that his knowledge of Sanskrit is very meagre' [IOL L/R/5/42 Indian Newspaper Reports, Bengal, 1915, No.21/32, *Baśumati* 15 May]. Woodroffe's colleague F.E. Pargiter (see note 44 above), unlike Woodroffe himself, studied Sanskrit academically – he held the Boden Sanskrit Scholarship at Oxford in 1872 while training for the ICS. Whether this would be sufficient for him to have translated without assistance we do not know.
61 In 1935 he does so again – in his review of Payne's book on the Śāktas (for reference, see below chapter 9 note 18).
62 See for example GOL:xii.
63 TT/1 (1937) p. i (preface to the second edition); TT/20 p. i.
64 As recounted in my preface, I was assisted in this by Mr Keshab Sircar of the Ramakrishna Mission in Calcutta, to whom I owe much gratitude for his help, friendship and encouragement.
65 See Appendix: letter 12.
66 Though even here the author can clearly make use of Sanskrit technical terms and phrases. See below chapter 11.
67 Slight hints as to how they viewed Woodroffe *might* be detectable in certain references. For example, Sylvain Lévy quoted above, thought that Arthur Avalon had not made 'even the least demand on European learning' and had 'dispensed with it'. This might suggest Lévy suspected the pseudonymous scholar was not a Western academic. Masson Oursel, when referring to works on Yoga by both Zimmer and Avalon, calls the former only 'an Indologist' [Oursel *Le Yoga* Paris 1954, p. 71].
68 Obituary of Sir John Woodroffe in *Baśumati* vol.14/2 (1342 = 1936), pp. 700–2.

CHAPTER 9

1 A. Padoux *Vac: The Concept of the Word in Selected Hindu Tantras* New York 1990.
2 A. Sanderson 'Purity and Power Among the Brahmins of Kashmir' in Carrithers et al (ed.) *The Category of the Person: Anthropological and Philosophical Perspectives* Cambridge 1985, pp. 199ff (henceforth 'Purity and Power');
——'Śaivism and the Tantric Traditions' in Sutherland S. (ed.) *The World's Religions* London pp. 660–704 (henceforth 'Saivism').
3 D. Sen Sarma *The Philosophy of Sādhana with special reference to the Trika Philosophy of Kashmir* New York 1990; G. Flood *Body and Cosmology in Kashmir Saivism* San Francisco 1993; M. Eliade *Yoga: Immortality and Freedom* New York 1958; L. Silburn *La Kuṇḍalinī, L'Energie des Profondeurs* Paris 1983. There are also the standard surveys cited in chapter 7 above.
4 In the sense of holding *Brahman* as the highest principle. See SS:1–5 and above p. 89.
5 A. Padoux: 'A Survey of Tantric Hinduism for the Historian of Religions' in *History of Religions* vol.20/4, pp. 345–60, p. 350.
6 ibid.

7 The second and subsequent editions interpolate a passage on the derivation of the word 'Tantra' from the root *tan* 'to spread'. At first 'Tantra' was used for any kind of treatise; it gradually acquired the meaning of a religious text of a particular kind.

8 The Bengali translator of *Tantratattva* ('Principles of Tantra') was apparently happy with the term and it is used by Arthur Avalon in his preface to the first volume. In his first public lecture on Tantra Woodroffe himself still used the terms 'Tantric' and 'Tantra' but in the version of that lecture in SS(DP) chapter 19, these have been mostly replaced by 'Śākta' and 'Śākta Tantra' respectively. See SS:379ff. The title of the lecture was originally *Creation in the Tantra*, retained in the first edition of SS.

9 *Prabuddha Bhārata* vol.22, p. 39 (March 1917), underlining added. 'Left wing' refers to *vāmācāra*. The original article makes comparisons here with other 'antinomian' sects in the West in a passage which in later editions of SS is removed to a special chapter on the *pañcatattva*.

10 ibid p. 72 (April 1917). This passage has not been changed in SS. As is often the case the editing is clumsy and the junction of the two articles makes for repetitiveness.

11 Eliade *Yoga* p. 200.

12 D.R. Brooks *An Introduction to Hindu Śākta Tantrism*, University of Chicago Press, 1990, pp. 55–71 lists the 'principal generic features of Hindu Tantrism shared across sectarian lines'. T. Goudriaan, S. Gupta, D.J. Hoens *Hindu Tantrism* Leiden 1979, pp. 7–9 lists eighteen characteristic features.

13 See above p. 122.

14 Padoux 'A Survey of Tantric Hinduism', p. 351.

15 Sanderson 'Śaivism' p. 675.

16 This is the *varṇamāla*, the 'garland of letters' which is the source of mantras. This image of Kālī is thought to have originated in the seventeenth century with the tantric king Agamabagis, who also instituted Kālī pūjā. See Rachel Fell McDermot in Urban (ed.) (forthcoming) for a history of the process whereby Kālī emerged from the visionary *dhyānas* of the tantric texts into general Hinduism through public temple worship and the *Kālī pūjā* festival, in which process her image was eventually 'sweetened'. This is an example of 'exotericization'.

17 *The Śāktas* London 1933, p. 23.

18 In his own review of Payne's book in JRAS, 1935, pp. 385–7.

19 Compare Abhinavagupta's description of the 'cosmic cemetery' where the individual ego is incinerated: *Tantrāsāra*:29:183–5, translated in Flood *Body and Cosmology* p. 274.

20 Sanderson 'Purity and Power'; G. Flood: 'Techniques of Body and Desire in Kashmir Śaivism' in *Religion* vol.22 (1992), pp. 47–62.

21 Sanderson 'Purity and Power'. See his description of the fearful Kāpālika ascetic, smeared with ashes and adorned with human bones at p. 201.

22 'The general trend...was to purify the rites by taking in everything except the elements of impurity. This left the essential structure [of a tantric sect] intact: one worshipped the same deity, with the same complex of emanations or subordinate deities, *mantras*, deity-enthroning diagrams (*maṇḍalas*), and ritual gestures and postures (*mudrās*). The spread of the tantric cults in Indian religion is largely the history of this process of domestication and exotericisation.' ['Saivism' p. 661–2].

23 ibid p. 668.

24 ibid p. 700; 'Purity and Power' p. 205 ftnt.125.

25 Sanderson 'Saivism' p. 661.

26 He quotes it in Sanskrit from *kulārṇava tantra*:11:83 but its origin is Jayaratha's *tantrālokaviveka* [Sanderson 'Purity and Power' p. 205]. Woodroffe – rather timidly? – acknowledges that this might refer to 'secrecy and adaptability to sectarian form' but interprets it to mean that outward forms are irrelevant to one who has pierced to the heart of all sects. For Kaulas, see below.
27 Citing KT:2:7–8.
28 The term *paśu* is one of the three fundamental realities in Śaivism: *paśu*, the individual soul, *pāśa* the bonds which limit it, and *paśupati*, the Lord of the Bound, or Śiva.[M. Dhavamony *The Love of God According to Śaiva Siddhānta: a study in the mysticism and theology of Saivism* Oxford 1971, p. 119].
29 Sanderson 'Saivism' p. 669.
30 ibid p. 661; Goudriaan et al *Hindu Tantrism* p. 112–3, and photographs following p. 156.
31 Sanderson 'Saivism' pp. 670ff.
32 '. . .the Śaiva entered a world of ritual in which these last restraints on *Śakti* dissolved. He was consecrated in the cults of deities who presided in their *maṇḍalas* over predominantly female pantheons and who passed as he ascended to the left from Bhairavas with consorts, to Goddesses above Bhairavas, to the terrible Solitary Heroines (*ekavīrā*) of the cults of Kālī.' [ibid p. 670].
33 ibid p. 675.
34 She represents: 'the ultimate Self which the 'I' cannot enter and survive' [ibid].
35 Flood 'Techniques of Body and Desire' p. 55–6.
36 Padoux *Vac* p. 36. The autochthonous origin of tantric deities is noted by most writers on Tantra, but this in itself is not an explanation for their retention through time or their role in the evolving tantric cults.
37 Sanderson 'Saivism' p. 671, 679ff. *Kula* also referred to the body and from this acquired a philosophical meaning where it was equivalent to the totality of phenomena and thus, more or less, to Śakti. Hence it was eventually seen in a polar relation to *akula* meaning Śiva [Goudriaan and Gupta HTSL p. 44–5].
38 Sanderson 'Saivism' p. 679–80; 'Purity and Power' p. 202–3.
39 Flood *Body and Cosmology* p. 82.
40 ibid p. 269ff. Flood's chapter on the two ritual systems summarises Abhinavagupta's chapter. See also Silburn *La Kuṇḍalinī* pp. 207–39.
41 Sanderson 'Saivism' p. 681–2.
42 See above p. 118. The word *tattva* means 'element' or 'true thing'. It also has a cosmological meaning (see below).
43 Sanderson 'Purity and Power' p. 202–3.
44 ibid pp. 690ff.
45 'The innate dynamism of the divine nature', Dyczkowski *Doctrine of Vibration* p. 20–1; Sanderson 'Saivism' p. 694.
46 'Recognition' of one's identity with Śiva [Sanderson 'Saivism' p. 695]. Its core text was *pratyabhijñāhṛdaya*: 'Concise Verses on the Recognition of the Deity' by Utpaladeva.
47 *Body and Cosmology* p. ix.
48 Padoux *Vāc* p. 77; Sen Sarma *The Philosophy of Sādhana* p. 17–18; Dyczkowski *Doctrine of Vibration* p. 26; at p. 233 note 101 Dyczkowski points out that these two terms, along with the symbolism of light, are almost entirely confined to the *pratyabhijñā* system.
49 Sen Sarma *The Philosophy of Sādhana* p. 21–2.
50 ibid pp. 22–4, 32–7. *Icchā* (will) includes *sankalpa* (imagination or conception). *Jñāna* (knowledge) refers to knowing objects as being in Himself – ie. nondual knowledge. *Kriyā* (action) is the act of objectifying, ie manifesting, all that

makes up the world as an object outside of Himself. In Śiva this is a deliberate act of will. In Brahman agency in this sense is only apparent, part of the illusion of *māyā*.

51 ibid pp. 24, 38. The divine identity is quite different from the human ego-sense for it is characterised by absolute Freedom (*svātantryā*) beyond the limitations which define the individual soul (*jīva*). There are five characteristics of the Divine Nature of Śiva which are restricted in the human soul by five corresponding limitations (*kañcukas*). But these limitations are part of the process of cosmic evolution which is the progressive diminution of divine fullness.

52 ibid p. 30. See also the same author's 'The Conception of Tattva, A Study' in *MM Gopinath Kaviraj Memorial Volume* Varanasi 1987, pp. 199–202.

53 Flood *Body and Cosmology* p. 46.

54 Not atheistic in the modern scientific sense, for mind and consciousness were still anterior to, and causes of, physical matter. See G.J. Larson: *Classical Sāṁkhya: an interpretation of its history and meaning* New Delhi 1969.

55 The *tattvas* are described in a detailed and rationalized form in J.C. Chattopadhyay *Kashmir Saivism* Srinagar 1914. The 36 divided into 3 groups, the 'pure' (divine), the 'mixed' (or intra-psychic), and the 'impure' (material or perceptible). The Sāṁkhyan series of 24 constitute the last group, the additional 12 in the Tantras belong to the first 2 groups. See Sen Sarma 'Tattva: a study'; M. Khanna *Yantra* p. 74; and Padoux *Vāc*.

56 *ābhāsavāda* : 'objective appearances are fundamentally grounded in consciousness, which causes them to 'shine forth'...' [*Vāc* p. 92 ftnt.17].

57 Dyczkowski *Doctrine of Vibration* New Delhi 1989, p. 25.

58 See above p. 145–6.

59 These are loose translations of the terms. For a fuller explanation see Larson *Classical Sāṁkhya*.

60 See SS:379–408; 348–64; 365–78; in SP chapters 2 and 3, and in GOL chapter 10, and throughout his books.

61 In this he was following the Kashmiri philosophers of the *spanda* and *pratyabhijñā* schools who, though Idealist, stressed the reality of this world 'and the common commerce of daily life (*vyavahāra*)'.[Dyczkowski *Doctrine of Vibration* p. 25.].

62 Padoux *Vāc* p. 84: 'Each phoneme is related to an aspect either of Śiva's energy (the first 16 *tattvas*) or of the cosmic manifestation (the remaining 20)'.

63 See GOL:257ff, a chapter on *bīja-mantra*; and M. Khanna *Yantra: the Tantric Symbol of Cosmic Unity* London 1979, pp. 34–9.

64 But, like all tantric divinities, she has her terrible aspect too.

65 Sanyukta Gupta: 'The Religious and Literary Background of the Navāvaraṇa-Kirtana of Muttusvāmi Dikṣitar' in E. Te Nijenhuis and S. Gupta *Sacred Songs of India: Dikṣitar's Cycle of Hymns to the Goddess Kamalā*, Winthertur/Switzerland 1987, pp. 1–23, especially p. 18; Khanna *Yantra*, p. 43–4.

66 It is reproduced on the covers of all of Ganesh's editions of Woodroffe's books. See plate 7.

67 Padoux *Vāc* pp. 89–91; GOL:175ff, 205ff (chapters on *kāmakalā* and the *kalās*). The number sixteen is related to the divinities of the phases of the moon, the *nityās* (see Khanna *Yantra* p. 65–6).

68 'The first resonance of the Supreme Word'. [*Vāc* p. 97].

69 ibid p. 106 and ftnt.56. *Nāda* is the *ardha-candra*, the crescent, below the dot (*anusvāra*) in the *praṇava* [GOL:121].

70 Padoux *Vāc* pp. 78–9, 94.

71 ibid pp. 96–119. Avalon writes on these at GOL:114–42 (on *nāda* and *bindu*) and pp. 175–84 (on *kamakalā*).

72 GOL:114. *Bindu* is also the white drop, the semen, and *bīja* the red drop, menstrual blood. See *kāma-kalā-vilāsa*:6 (Rawson's translation) in P. Rawson *Tantra* (Catalogue to the Arts Council Exhibition) London 1971, p. 127–8. Arthur Avalon denies this association angrily at GOL:129, but accepts it at SP:46.
73 Especially in *kāma-kalā-vilāsa* (see previous note). This is an extremely succinct text describing this cosmic symbol in 55 verses. 'In this brief, often cryptic but widely respected Tantra the whole mechanism of yantra, mantra, Devatā and the meaning of Sādhana are summarized' (Rawson *Tantra* p. 128). See also Padoux *Vāc* p. 113–4.
74 GOL:175ff. The triple Goddess is will, knowledge, action; the three lights – fire, sun, moon; the three times – past, present, future; and so forth.
75 Or it is like the pattern of ring-like waves moving outwards when a stone is thrown in water. See Sanyukta Gupta 'The Religious and Literary Background.... p. 19.
76 ibid. See M. Khanna *Yantra*, and the illustrations therein.
77 *Parā*, *paśyantī* and *madhyamā*, and *vaikhārī* respectively. See M. Khanna *Yantra* p. 37; KKV: vs.22–32. At GOL:32 they are four *śaktis* of *Śabda* (Speech).
78 For the worship of the *śrī yantra* see Sanyukta Gupta 'The Religious and Literary Background... pp. 1–23; and Khanna *Yantra*. GOL does not deal with the full *śrī yantra* but it is dealt with in Avalon's Introduction to the *tantrarāja tantra* (published Madras 1954 under the name of Woodroffe). GOL:205–13 is a chapter on the *kalās*.
79 GOL:154, 220. *śabda* ('Speech') is related to *artha* the object denoted by it, which in *Śabda Brahman* are identical, thus uniting the opposites of perceiver and perceived. Śiva-Consciousness here is identical with *Śabda Brahman*.
80 Eliade *Yoga* p. 244.
81 Silburn *La Kuṇḍalinī* p. 41ff. The wheels are set turning by the ascending *prāṇa* through the *suṣumṅā*. Silburn's sources are the Kashmir Saivite texts and especially Abhinavagupta, where the system is slightly different from the SCN.
82 See plates I–VII accompanying the translation of SCN from SP:317ff.
83 Eliade *Yoga* pp. 233–6. Padoux *Vāc* p. 124–5.
84 Flood *Body and Cosmology* pp. xiv; 1–6.
85 This emphasizes the male bias of Tantra noted above.
86 The mind is called the *antahkarana* ('inner vehicle') and it is composed of *buddhi*, *ahaṁkāra* and *manas*, which can be taken to correspond (very approximately) to consciousness, ego-sense and perception. G.J. Larson *Sāṁkhya* ... gives a full description.
87 See table at SP:125.
88 See table at SP:141–2.
89 See SP:115–42, especially pp. 138–40 and the table at p. 141–2.
90 SP:35 explains more about why she is coiled.
91 Silburn *La Kuṇḍalinī* p. 29–30.
92 Eliade *Yoga* p. 246. SP:241–2 says intense heat is evoked on her awakening. The original title of SP was to have been 'The Six Cakras and the Serpent Fire'.
93 Eliade *Yoga* p. 248–9 (the relation of breath to semen).
94 *Śāradā tilaka*:1:13 is cited several times: 'It assumes the form of Kuṇḍalī and abides in the body of all breathing creatures manifesting itself by letters in the form of prose and verse' [SP:100 and ftnt.5].
95 SP:147. For the cosmic dimension see also Eliade *Yoga* p. 235.
96 See the chapter on 'Practice' in SP, esp pp. 203–15 (the various *āsanas*, *mudrās* and *bandhanas* as well as *prāṇāyāma*), and see the illustrations of the *bandhas* in the appendix to SP.
97 See also Eliade *Yoga* p. 245. *Prāṇa* is drawn upwards through the *suṣumnā* like a needle draws a thread.

98 ibid p. 243. In other texts the highest *cakra* is either at the crown of the head or at a place twelve finger lengths (*dvādasānta*) beyond it. See Silburn *La Kuṇḍalinī* p. 47–8.
99 SP:13 and ftnt 1; and p. 19.
100 V.G. Rele *The Mysterious Kuṇḍalinī* Bombay 1939 (1927), Foreword by Sir John Woodroffe.
101 Flood *Body and Cosmology* p. 258; Padoux *Vāc* p. 144–5 and ftnt.168. A slightly different system is given in the *śāradā tilaka* which has only four *cakras* correlated with the four levels of speech [*Vāc* p. 142]. The texts cited by Liliane Silburn had five (excluding the *svādhiṣṭhāna*). There were other schemes that had nine, twelve or even sixteen *cakras*. At SP:152 Avalon notes one with over twenty.
102 Dzykowski *The Canon of the Śaivāgama and the Kubjikā Tantras of the Western Kaula Tradition* New Delhi 1989.
103 Delhi 1958. First published as an appendix in B.K. Sarkar's *Positive Background of Hindu Sociology*, Allahabad 1914, from where Avalon took his notes. Another example of contemporary interest in this topic is Vasant G. Rele's book to which Woodroffe wrote the Foreword mentioned above (note 101).
104 *Calcutta Review* vol.xi (1849) no.xxii pp. 436–40.
105 Seal *Positive Sciences* p. 218–9.
106 Flood *Body and Cosmology* p. 259 citing Bharati *The Tantric Tradition* London 1965.
107 *Yoga* p. 239.
108 Flood *Body and Cosmology* p. 257.
109 Yet readers might recognize a striking parallel between *kuṇḍalinī* and DNA: each is spiraline and 'spells out' a blueprint for the body. Such analogies need not be taken too far.
110 Silburn refers to *manthana* which she translates *barattement des soufles* [*La Kuṇḍalinī* p. 60].
111 This is described in the PST. See introduction to TT/19.

CHAPTER 10

1 Woodroffe's name is on the list of Presidents at their Society headquarters in Calcutta.
2 SS(1) p. i (preface to the 1st edition). The lecture was '*Shakti and Shākta*' discussed below. Two of the magazine articles have been discussed in the last chapter.
3 S. Chatterji 'Swami Vivekananda's Neo-Vedantism and Its Practical Application' in R.C. Majumdar (ed.) *Swami Vivekananda Centenary Memorial Volume* Calcutta 1963, pp. 260–83.
4 'Give up this filthy Vāmācāra that is killing your country'. [*Complete Works of Swami Vivekānanda* Calcutta, Advaita Ashram 1922 vol.3, p. 340). 'We must stem this tide of Vāmācār which is contrary to the spirit of the Vedas' [vol.7 (5th ed.1958), p. 174]. Vivekananda distinguished this from the 'real' purpose of the Tantras which was 'the worship of women in a spirit of divinity' [ibid p. 215].
5 W. Halbfass *India and Europe* New York 1988, pp. 378–403.
6 ibid p. 400; he calls Woodroffe 'a kind of British neo-Hindu'.
7 A. Bharati *The Tantric Tradition* London 1965, pp. 15, 31. In fact Bharati does identify distinctive tantric innovations in doctrine and sees the polar nature of divinity, or of Buddhahood, as one of them [ibid, p. 18–19].
8 H.P. Alper (ed.) *Understanding Mantras* Delhi 1991, 395. Alper has himself just pointed out that the influence of Woodroffe on tantric studies may be greater than realised [ibid p. 394 with ftnt].

9 A. Padoux *Vac: The Concept of the Word in Selected Hindu Tantras* New York 1990, p. 53 and ftnt.50.
10 A. Padoux: 'A Survey of Tantric Hinduism for the Historian of Religions' in *History of Religions* vol.20/4, pp. 345–60, p. 347.
11 H. Von Glasenapp: 'Tantrismus and Śāktismus' in *Ostasiatische Zeitschrift* vol.22 (1936), pp. 120–33.
12 J.J. Kripal *Kālī's Child: the Mystical and the Erotic in the Life and Teachings of Ramakrishna* University of Chicago Press 1998.
13 L. Nathan and C. Seely *Grace and Mercy in Her Wild Hair* Boulder Colorado 1982.
14 Above p. 82.
15 It was a review in *The Nation* of New York cited at SS(3):xxi. In the background of these remarks was the American social philosopher F. Lester Ward's theories on the primacy of the female principle, from which Woodroffe here distances Śāktism.
16 PT/1 pp. 14, 30–1. Woodroffe frequently criticises intolerant attitudes. At SP:287 he quotes: 'To dispute the religion of another is the mark of a lower mind. O Lord! O Great Magician! with whatever faith or feeling we call on Thee, Thou art pleased'.
17 Eg PT/2 p. 3. '... the Indian mind rightly apprizes as of the highest value the world of ideas, deeming the question of their "historical" origins and development to be, as in fact it is, of much inferior importance. To the Western ... Sanskritist the position is, in general, reversed.' He claimed this was because they believed Indian civilization had little intrinsic value.
18 There follows a long list of names of the Goddess in many ancient cultures.
19 SS:137ff. E. Sellon *Annotations on the Sacred Writings of the Hindus* London (privately printed) 1865.
20 He is citing the *Sarvollāsa*, a tantric compilation by Sarvanandanātha. SS:251 indicates that Woodroffe had just been introduced to this text in 1917, the year when he delivered this lecture.
21 The tantric side, as opposed to the *Smārtas*, was 'represented by the general body of present-day Hinduism' [SS:149].
22 N.N. Bhattacharyya *History of the Tantric Religion* New Delhi 1982; D. Chattopadhyay *Lokāyata* New Delhi 1959, who favoured Tantra and Śāktism as evidence of a religion of 'the people' over and against Brahmanical philosophy.
23 For example: 'A man with a taste for drink will only increase his thirst by animal satisfaction. But if when he drinks he can be made to regard the liquid as a divine manifestation and have thought of God, gradually such thoughts will overcome and oust his sensual desires.' [SS:602–3].
24 SS(DP):628, has 'spiritual advance' in place of 'attainment of liberation', thus making it a more this-worldly aim.
25 Sumit Sarkar: "'Kaliyuga', 'Chakri' and 'Bhakti': Ramakrishna and His Times" in *Economic and Political Weekly* July 18 1992.
26 H. Zimmer: *Philosophies of India*, New Delhi, 1989 pp. 560–602.
27 See the very interesting article by H.B. Urban: 'The Cult of Ecstacy: Tantrism, the New Age and the Spiritual Logic of Late Capitalism' in *History of Religions* 39/3 pp. 268–304.
28 Vivekananda approved the worship of *śakti* as the Mother, and claimed this was the real '*dharma* of Westerners'. 'Protestantism is not very important in Europe...the worship is for the Mother...with the child Jesus in her arms...' [*Complete Works* vol.5 (7th ed. 1959) pp. 505–7].
29 This is an odd way of putting it. It sounds as if Woodroffe means by 'vehicle' the mind-and-body in which the transmigrating soul is incarnated in one particular life. But that would imply the exact reverse of what he says, because then the Virgin Mary *would* herself be the incarnation (*avatāra*) of God. 'Vehicle' is not a

term of Christian theology, but it sounds as if Woodroffe is thinking of the Virgin Mary as *Theotokos* ('God-Bearer') in Eastern Orthodox theology.

30 The Sanskrit term *adhikāra* is used in Tantra to apply to personal spiritual – sometimes physical – qualities which made an individual suitable for a particular initiation [KT:13:16–17, 20, cited at SS:575]. However according to the rules of the Brahmanical *Mīmāṁsā* school to have *adhikāra* for a ritual meant to be entitled to perform it by your caste and station in life, that is, within the system of *varṇāśrama dharma*. [Van Buitenen *The Bhagavadgitā in the Mahābhārata*, University of Chicago Press 1981, p. 19] For Arthur Avalon the residual idea of qualification by caste is translated into qualification by race and culture.

31 See the description of the twelfth century *ars notoria* summarized by A. Faivre ('Occultism' in ER vol.11, p. 37). There is even the same debate over whether to define Occultism in terms of a belief-system or merely as a ritual system (ibid p. 36). [See also ibid vol.5, pp. 156–63 'Esotericism'].

32 ibid vol.11, p. 38; vol.5, p. 156.

33 B. Campbell *Ancient Wisdom Revived* Berkeley & London, 1980.

34 F. King *The Magical World of Alisteir Crowley* London 1977; and I. Regardie *Golden Dawn* London 1970.

35 *yadihāsti tad anyatra: yannehāsti na tat kvacit* [SS:277].

36 'According to this principle, things that are similar exert an influence on one another by virtue of the correspondences that unite all visible things to one another and to invisible realities as well.' [A. Faivre in ER vol.11, p. 36].

37 D. Sen Sarma: 'The Conception of Tattva, A Study' in *MM Gopinath Kaviraj Memorial Volume* Varanasi 1987, pp. 199–202.

38 *Encyclopedia of Magic and Superstition* London, 1974, 'Introduction' p. 12.

39 A. Faivre in ER vol.5, p. 157 ('Esotericism').

40 The same statement is made at SP:85 ftnt.2.

41 *Prabuddha Bharata* vol.6 (1901), pp. 25ff. There were many articles and notes on the 'New Thought' in this periodical of the Vivekananda movement. See also vol.10 (1905), pp. 150–3.

42 William Walker Atkinson *The Message of the New Thought*, Holyoke Mass., 1911. 'Yogi Ramacaraka' was another example of a pseudonym being used to cover the collaboration of a Western writer and an Indian teacher, here Atkinson and his guru, Baba Bharata. See A. Rawlinson *The Book of Enlightened Masters: western teachers in Indian traditions* Chicago 1997, p. 618. Rawlinson calls Atkinson's books 'an East-West hybrid' that was 'only tangential to Hinduism'.

43 Also SS:494: 'The creative power of thought is now receiving increasing acceptance in the West... Because they have discovered it anew, they call it "New Thought"; but its fundamental principle is as old as the upanisads...'.

44 Atkinson *New Thought* p. 14.

45 Compare WAP:147. 'The Mind...is a radiant and transparent and light Substance and can travel like a ray of light out through a sense organ'.

46 PT/1 chapters 4–7.

47 PT/1 pp. 234ff and beginning of chapter 5, p. 237.

48 'Herself' when the Goddess is seen as the primary divinity beyond the trinity of Brahmā, Viṣṇu, Śiva.

49 In later editions these were re-phrased as 'the Consciousness' and 'the Psycho-Physical' aspects respectively [SS:250, 290].

50 *Modern Review* vol.17/1 (January 1915), p. 62.

51 F.M. Turner *Between Science and Religion: The Reaction to Scientific Naturalism in Late Victorian England* New Haven & London 1974, p. 15.

52 ibid pp. 247, 249.

53 ibid p. 12.
54 Gustave Le Bon *The Evolution of Matter* London 1907; L. Houllevigue *The Evolution of the Sciences* London & Leipzig 1909; E. Haeckel *Monism as Connecting Religion and Science: The confession of faith of a man of science* London 1894; *The Riddle of the Universe* London 1913. For Haeckel see also David De Grood *Haeckel's Theory of the Unity of Nature* Amsterdam 1982.
55 F. Capra *The Tao of Physics* London 1976, pp. 62ff.
56 S. Kern *The Culture of Time and Space 1880–1918* London 1983, p. 154.
57 Capra *Tao of Physics* p. 67–8.
58 *Daily Chronicle* 11 February 1913, quoted in *The Theosophist* vol 34/2, p. 1. Articles about the new discoveries from the popular press in 1906 are also noted by Kern . . . *Time and Space* p. 184.
59 Le Bon *Evolution of Matter* p. 10 'It [intra-atomic energy] is characterised by its colossal greatness . . .'.
60 Perhaps slightly later than this lecture. In his preface to the paper *Power as Matter* (1921) Woodroffe mentions a book by Professor Lewis Rongier which had just been drawn to his attention, in which the Ether theory was declared to be defunct. He welcomes the new theory claiming that it makes 'the notion of *Māyā* at least intelligible even to those who have hitherto derided it.' [WAP pp. 173–4, and 188–90].
61 Kern *Time and Space* p. 154.
62 ibid; Capra *Tao of Physics* p. 62.
63 *Ether and Reality* London 1925, p. 52.
64 ibid p. 162.
65 Quoted in G.F. Sander *The Riddle of the Ether,* preface p. xii.
66 In the *Sāṁkhya*, gross matter is the last of the *tattvas* to emanate out of *prakṛti*; *ākāśa* or space/ether is the first of these to evolve. See G.J. Larson *Classical Sāṁkhya,* Delhi 1969.
67 Compare Le Bon *Evolution of Matter* pp. 11–12, 313.
68 In later editions he has 'Spirit, *Mind* and Matter' [SS(DP) p. 290] thus disrupting the polarity of Haeckel's idea, although as we shall see Haeckel too included the concept of mind or 'sensation' as a third element.
69 De Grood *Haeckel's Theory* p. 44; Haeckel *Monism* p. 17–18.
70 Haeckel *The Riddle of the Universe* p. 16.
71 De Grood *Haeckel's Theory,* pp. 40–3.
72 Haeckel claimed to be a pantheist, his 'Substance' midway between 'matter' and 'spirit'. De Grood comments that 'the tables could be turned on Haeckel if the qualitative essence of force and energy were interpreted in terms of psychical activity. . . Then the outcome would be pan-psychism in which it would be as reasonable to reduce matter to God as God to matter' [*Haeckel's Theory,* p. 67]. In effect this is what Woodroffe did to him.
73 Turner *Between Science and Religion* p. 12.
74 ibid p. 26.
75 He was quoting here de Houllevigue *The Evolution of the Sciences*, p. 112–3.
76 'An immaterial living spirit is just as unthinkable as a dead, spiritless matter; the two are inseparably combined in every atom.' [Haeckel *The Riddle* p. 58.].
77 DeGrood *Haeckel's Theory* p. 38.
78 ibid p. 45; Haeckel *The Riddle* p. 183–4.
79 De Grood *Haeckel's Theory* p. 40.
80 ibid p. 45–6; Haeckel *The Riddle* p. 73.
81 B. Mitra *Jagadish Chunder Bose: a biography for students* London 1982, see pp. 27–30, 29–39, 57.

82 Quoted ibid p. 57.
83 He is quoting Le Bon *The Evolution of Matter* p. 251.
84 Houllevigue *The Evolution of the Sciences* p. 289.
85 *Modern Review* vol.17/1 (January 1915), p. 62.
86 Kern *Time and Space* p. 177.
87 ibid p. 204.
88 This is not the original Conclusion of the first and second editions.

CHAPTER 11

1 *Baśumati* vol.14/2 (1342 = 1936), p. 702. *śāradā tilaka, prapañcasāra, kulārṇava, tantrarāja* and *tantrābhidāna* were stated to be his work.
2 ibid pp. 700–2.
3 See above p. 106.
4 *Bharat Varṣa* vol.23/2, pp. 461–4.
5 *Indian Culture* vol.2/1–4, p. 841; *Samsad Bāngāli Caritābhidhan* Calcutta 1988 (2nd ed.) 'Atal Bihari Ghose'.
6 See above p. 103.
7 Copy in my possession.
8 *Occult Digest* (Chicago?) April 1930, p. 6 "The Teachings of the Tantra" by Babu Atal Bihari Ghosh. Copy in my possession.
9 For the contents of the articles, see below p. 231.
10 The originals are now located at OIOC Mss Eur F285/4,5 & 7 where the numbers on the individual letters are different from those in Appendix 1.
11 See above p. 95.
12 'I hope you will go very slowly yourself with the work until some other pundits are appointed to help you'. [letter 7].
13 Because it mentions his daughter's illness. See below.
14 *An Introduction to the Tantrarāja Tantra* Madras 1954.
15 'My Italian friend' – possibly Julius Evola.
16 Communication of James Woodroffe.
17 Not in the appendix.
18 TT/18–19, first published as TT/3.
19 This seems already to have been done with the Introduction to *śāradā tilaka*.
20 His letters were typed or handwritten by others from about 1930 onwards. A letter of March 1935 mentions the excess salivation due to his paralysis.
21 The two letters in question, from Helena Hopkins Zak and someone who signs himself Bernard, have not been included in the appendix as they are quite long. The note mentioned above on p. 205 was also from Helena Hopkins Zak. They are to be found at OIOC Mss Eur F285/7.
22 Translation mine. See letter 14 for a transcription of the original. Sadly, in Germany in 1936, this compliment is ambivalent.
23 2nd ed. London 1948 (henceforth TBOD) pp. lxv–lxxxiv. (1st ed. 1927). Evans-Wentz wrote in his preface: 'I have been really little more than a compiler and editor... To the deceased translator' (2nd ed. p. xx). Lama Kazi Dawasamdup died in 1923 in Calcutta.
24 This correspondence is at OIOC Mss Eur F285/1,2,3 & 6. The Lama's son did not know what became of the manuscripts.
25 In TBOD, however, he writes more respectfully of Lama Dawasamdup's scholarship (p. lxxxiv).
26 In TBOD he seems more ready to perceive differences, eg. p. lxviii.

27 Pandit Satiscandra Vidyabhusana. See TT/7 p. viii.
28 ibid and p. xviii; SS:650.
29 Charles Bell *The Religion of Tibet* Oxford 1931, pp. 200, 206–7.
30 2nd ed. p. xx.
31 Letter dated April 1927 in OIOC Mss Eur F285/7 (Letters to Atal Bihari Ghose from various persons). In his diary he mentioned that Ghose was 'critically examining and annotating' Milarepa. [Bodleian Library, Oxford, Mss Eng misc.f.826, pocket book entry for 26 December 1926.].
32 A letter from James Woodroffe after his father's death reveals that he was not certain about this.
33 Letter 5 suggests there was another sponsor of *śāradā tilaka.*
34 I learned that large numbers of unsold copies of the series accumulated in Darbhanga. Sales mentioned in the letters do not seem to amount to much.
35 Zetland Papers OIOC MSS D609/1: *My Bengal Diary* vol.2 p. 97 (July 14 1921): 'I asked [Emerson] if he thought the erotic ritual was much prevalent. He said he thought no, except at the temple of Kāmākhya near Gauhati in Assam. . . . It stands on a summit of a hill and the Maharaja of Darbhanga, a notorious Śākta, is a great patron of it and has built a house on the hilltop.' His son's secretary said that he worshipped the Goddess at Kāmākhya in order to gain a son and heir.
36 *Tantrācarya Sivacandra* pp. 53–5, 72–3, 78.
37 J.N. Farquhar *Modern Religious Movements in India* New York 1919, pp. 317–21.
38 Conversation in Darbhanga with Mr A.K. Mishra, former secretary to Rameshwar Singh's successor, Kameshwar Singh.
39 *The Englishman*, Calcutta, 23 December 1918, p. 5 (on the inter-caste marriage bill). S. Henningham *A Great Estate and Its Landlords in Colonial India: Darbhanga 1860–1942* OUP 1990. Henningham's history of Darbhanga chronicles the reign of Rameshwar Singh and his successor Kameshwar Singh but nowhere mentions that either of them was a Tantric.
40 B. Ramusack *The Princes of India in the Twilight of Empire 1914–39* Colombia Ohio c.1978, p. 50.
41 M. Hoffman *A Sculptor's Odyssey* London 1936, pp. 169–70.
42 K.C. Sarkar: 'A Forgotten Historian and Antiquarian' *Modern Review* vol.113/2 (February 1963), pp. 159–62. See also *Journal of the Varendra Research Museum* vol.7 1981–2 (A.K. Maitra Number), University of Rajshahi.
43 A.K. Maitra: 'The Stones of Varendra' *Modern Review* vol.7/6 (June 1910), p. 590.
44 Sarkar 'A Forgotten Historian. . .' p. 161.
45 SS(1) p. i (preface). Under 'Preface to the First Edition' in the Dover Press edition, this information has been omitted.
46 The preface to the second edition is dated October 1918, but it does not seem to have been published until 1920 (perhaps because of the war).
47 SS:vi (preface to the fifth Edition), and SS:viii (preface to the third edition). The French lectures are to be found in Woodroffe: *Introduction à l'Hindouisme Tantrique*, Paris 1983 (Translated M. Shibata). Two were delivered to Ellen Woodroffe's French Literary Society in Calcutta; and one was his address of 1921 in Paris, mentioned above p. 141.
48 OIOC: Miscellaneous pamphlets P/V 55–68.
49 *Autobiography of an Unknown Indian* New Delhi 1976.
50 SP:xii (Preface to the first edition). The only earlier publications were two translations from *Hymns to the Goddess* which appeared in *The Theosophist* in 1912. The Samiti's pamphlet states that Woodroffe's *début* was his public lecture to the Dalhousie Institute – ie his 'Creation' lecture. If he had produced anything earlier, his admirers would certainly have retrieved and published it.

51 An anonymous writer in the *Rationalist Review* calling himself 'Vidura' had strong views on this matter. A draft article in Ghose's house shows that this was he.
52 *Bhārata Shakti* (3) p. xx, 'Postscript'.
53 TT/1 p. 1.
54 For obtaining a copy of a tape of this interview I am grateful to Mr Gautam Sengupta then of All India Radio Archives, Calcutta.
55 B. Mallick (ed.) *Suniti Kumar Chatterji (1890–1977) Commemoration Volume* Calcutta 1981, preface.
56 *Hymns to the Goddess* (2nd ed. 1952) p. viii–ix.
57 See above pp. 145–6.
58 Copy in my possession.
59 For example, Woodroffe at first seems to have thought of *prakṛti* in more material terms than in later editions. There are also the changes in the use of the word 'Tantra' referred to in chapter 9 above.
60 See for example 'Imitation and Independence' address to Friends Union Club BS(3) p. 53. Also his address to the Rationalistic Society (see GOL:288).
61 See M.P. Pandit's remarks quoted in chapter 8. That Woodroffe could recognize concepts in Sanskrit terminology rather than English is actually stated in one of his letters to Dawasamdup.
62 See OIOC P/V 63. The articles which became chapters 19 and 20 were the first to be published of the *Studies* series. This first offprint was published in July 1917 by the Ramakrishna Mission in Madras. It contained chapters 19, 20 and 10 – in that order. In the second of these, the first is said to have been published 'last December'.
63 GOL:201ff. Woodroffe has heard of Abhinavagupta: at SS:396 he calls him 'the great Kashmirian Tantrik'.
64 Ganesh's transliteration is not always accurate. GOL(1) used 'sh' for both dental 'ś' and palatal 'ṣ'. *suśira* I am informed should be *suṣira* ('hollow'). Ganesh do not indicate *visarga* by a subscript dot. *Vyāptākāśaih* is translated wrongly by Woodroffe and should mean 'which pervade ether'.
65 As often in the Avalon/Woodroffe style, in the passage quoted the author does not translate all the Sanskrit words but only some of them. He assumes the reader knows that *Samvit* (or, in its root form *samvid*) means 'Consciousness' (see WAP:113 ftnt. 1)), in which he then distinguishes two forms, the first of which is 'Void-Consciousness' (*Śūnya-samvid*); his second form, *Utpatsuh samvid utpattya-vasthā sūkṣmā* seems to be three categories: consciousness about to manifest, in the manifest state, and subtle, which Avalon amalgamates into one. *bhānam* means 'light' not 'experience'. For corrections to Avalon's passages I am indebted to Dr Dermot Killingley.
66 See J.C. Chattopadhyay (ed.) *Śiva Sutra* (Kashmir Series of Texts and Studies vol.1) Srinagar 1911, preface p. ii. He says he has 'not allowed a single sentence' to go out without checking with the pandit, 'who has made a deeper study than any other pandits in the department'.
67 He refers to 'my friend Jagadisha Chandra Chattopadhyaya Vidyavaridhi' in his article published in *Prabuddha Bhārata* vol.22 Feb–March 1917, p. 38, and in the same passage republished in SS(1) p. 3. In later editions of SS the personal reference is omitted.
68 In H.V. Guenther *Yuganaddha, the Tantric view of Life*, Chowkambha Sanskrit Series, Varanasi 1952, preface p. iii. (This preface is not included in other editions of the book.).
69 Eg GOL:107, where the quotes from *Prayogasāra* and *Vāyavīya Saṁhitā* occur in a passage taken from Raghava Bhatta's commentary on ST:1:7. A reference from PST paraphrased at GOL:125 and at SS:399–400 is also from the same.

70 In the DP edition it has been referred to in parenthesis: 'See also Vayu Samhitā. . .' [p. 56].
71 It is one of the two articles published in *Prabuddha Bhārata* discussed above p. 155.
72 D.L. Lorenzen *The Kāpālikas and the Kālamukhas: two lost Saivite Sects* Berkeley, University of California Press 1972.
73 In *Shakti and Shākta* there are about 30 references altogether to *mahānirvāṇa* and about the same number to *kulārṇava* (though these are rarely referred to in *Serpent* or *Garland*). By way of comparison, the next most frequently cited text in *Shakti and Shākta – sammohana tantra* – had 12.
74 Above pp. 137–8.
75 Eg its 'grand opening chapter' quoted in two places, and the famous saying that man may rise by that through which he falls [SS:592–3, 633]; in other places he refers to the moral qualities of a disciple [SS:575; KT:13:16–17:20] and of a guru [SS:593, no reference]; and the injunction to do good to others [SS:93; KT 12:63 – the *sādhaka* 'should to good to others as if they were his own self.'] Most of the citations of KT illustrate its philosophical non-dualism.
76 KT:8:57 (Ghose's translation).
77 ibid (ftnt). In a later chapter however he acknowledges that they could also be meant 'physically'.
78 In another place he suggests it was only intended to be read by the initiated [SS:586].
79 It was *sarvollāsa* which provided Woodroffe with his saying 'Women are life itself' in his speech to the Hindu girls' school in 1917.
80 See above p. 000, and bibliography.
81 R. Anantakrishna Śāstri *Ānandalaharī* (the first forty-one verses of *saundaryalaharī* – 'Wave of Beauty') *with yantras and commentaries* Palghat, 1899 (but Avalon appears to be using a second edition of the whole text published by Ganesh and Co. for which I do not know the date). The translation of *Śrī Lalitā Sahasraṇāma with Bhāskararāya's commentary* was published in Madras in 1899 (2nd ed.).
82 His review of Avalon's books is referred to above pp. 139–40.
83 See Foreword to TBOD p. lxxx–lxxxi and TT/7 p. xviii.
84 SP:144–7; 178–80; 246–54.
85 Calcutta 1916.
86 *Modern Review* vol.19/5 (May 1916) p. 559, a review of Chattopadhyay's *Hindu Realism.*
87 David Kopf *The Brahmo Samaj and the Shaping of the Modern Indian Mind* Princeton USA 1979, pp. 60ff. Kopf calls him 'a very convincing advocate of the religion of humanity' (p. 62).
88 *Modern Review* vol 17/1 (January 1915), p. 63.
89 See SP:254–6 and footnotes.
90 SP:167 (and ftnt.3); 171 (and ftnt.2).
91 Pandit Anantakrishna Sastri worked for the Theosophical Society but his opinions on the *kaula* sects also reflected those of Laksmidhara, whose work he translated. The *kaula* sects are associated with *vāmācāra.*
92 See above p. 204.
93 Varendra Research Society Monograph No.6 (March 1935) Rajshahi, pp. 12–16.
94 Lokesvarananda (ed.): *Studies on the Tantras* Ramakrishna Mission Institute of Culture Calcutta 1989. Here Ghose is described as 'One of the Founders of the Āgama Anusandhāna Samiti'.
95 Eg chapters 24–6 in the 9th edition: 'dhvani', 'sun moon and fire', and 'bija-mantra'.

96 'White and Gold' in *Shama'a* January 1921 pp. 237–9.
97 JISOA November 1961, p. 99.
98 'Tantrik Ritual: Early morning rites' (parts 1 & 2); 'Pūjā; 'Snana'. See *Vedānta Keśari* vol.10 (March–April 1924) pp. 873–9, 922–5; and vol.11 (May–June 1924) pp. 12–15, 61–5.
99 *Vedānta Keśari* vol.9/4 (August 1922) pp. 134–6. See appendix 2 below.

CONCLUSION

1 IIC(3) p. 354.
2 Nandy A: *Intimate Enemy: Loss and Recovery of Self under Colonialism* Delhi 1988.

APPENDIX I

1 The Sanitarium in Park Street was near Free School Street crossing. It was either a restaurant, or perhaps a health club (where Woodroffe took his bath?).
2 According to Thacker's Directory, A. Hirsch was a Partner of Cohn Bros & Fuchs, hides & skin merchants, at 5 Mission Row from 1913–16 inclusive. What its connection was with the work of Woodroffe and Ghose I do not know, unless they rented the premises.
3 Barrackpore was a suburb of Calcutta where the Viceroys had country residences. (See D. Dilks *Curzon in India, London 1970*).
4 The date looks as if it has been altered either from 10 to 20 or vice versa. But 1920 is more likely for many reasons. Woodroffe's handwriting has noticeably deteriorated since the other Calcutta notes, and generally his handwriting gets worse. The Avalon/Woodroffe books had not been published in 1910, and so members of the public would not be sending him unsolicited works; and in 1920 Woodroffe was on furlough in England, which could account for the reference to his 'return'.
5 It does not look like one of the five official *Śankarācharyas* of India. The five are: Śrngeri, Kānchipuram, Badari, Puri, Dwaraka. Possibly the title Shankaracharya was a mistake, or else *Trivikrama* was the name of the manuscript.
6 This letter is undated, but he mentions his daughter Barbara, who died in 1925, and the forthcoming publication of the second part of TRT (1926).
7 The divine bird, or goose, symbol of the soul, also of breath.
8 Perhaps the name of his Italian friend though it looks more like an Indian name. His desire for consistency suggests he takes the symbolism very literally.
9 A cult founded by the American "Tantric" Pierre Bernard, also called "Oom the Omnipotent", which was reputed to hold sexual orgies. The Tantrik Order of America produced a journal, but only one issue of it is extant. See Andrew Rawlinson *The Book of Enlightened Masters: western teachers in Indian traditions* Chicago 1997 for an entry on this organization.
10 '*not really*' scribbled in another hand.
11 '*and if BC says anything*' crossed out.
12 The Sanskrit text of the *māhānirvāna tantra* was published in the *Tantrik Texts* series in 1929. So this letter must be from that date or before.
13 Maharaja of Darbhanga.
14 The Maharaja of Patiala.
15 Presumably, of the Samiti, but there is no reference in any of the organization's literature to his having ever been its president.
16 Signature almost invisible.

BIBLIOGRAPHY

ARCHIVES AND ARCHIVAL COLLECTIONS

OIOC, British Library, London:
Ameer Ali, Sir T: 'Echoes of British India' draft in *Ameer Ali Papers*, Mss Eur C336/3
—— *Judicial and Public Department Annual Files*
Government of India
—— *Indian Newspaper Reports, Bengal*
—— *Chelmsford Papers* Mss Eur E264
—— *Curzon Papers* Mss Eur F111
—— *Havell Papers* Mss Eur D 736
—— *Morley Papers* Mss Eur D573
—— *Sorabji Papers* Mss Eur F 165
—— *Sir John Woodroffe Papers* Mss Eur F285
—— *Zetland Papers*:
Lord Ronaldshay: *My Bengal Diary.*
Mss Eur D 609/1/2
Letters to Lord Ronaldshay, Marquis of Zetland D 609/5
Cambridge University Library:
Hardinge Papers
Archives of the School of Oriental and African Studies, London:
Denison-Ross Papers PPMS 8
Bodleian Library, Oxford:
Evans-Wentz Papers
National Archives of India, New Delhi,
Home Department (Judicial Branch) Proceedings
National Library, Calcutta
Sir Asutosh Mukherji Papers
Houghton Library, Harvard University, USA
Rothenstein Papers

PRINTED BOOKS AND SECONDARY SOURCES

Alper, Harvey P. (ed.) *Understanding Mantras* Delhi, Banarsidass, 1991.

Anantakrishna Sastri, R. *Lalitāsahasraṇāma with Bhāskararāya's commentary* Madras, Thompson & Co, 1899 (1st ed. 2nd ed. Adyar 1925).

—— *Ānandalaharī, with yantras and commentaries* Palghat, T.S. Subramania & Co 1899 (2nd ed.).

Archer, William *India and the Future* London, Hutchinson, 1917.

Ashe, G. *Gandhi: a study in revolution* London, Heinemann, 1968.

Atkinson, William W. *The Message of the New Thought* Holyoke Mass., Elizabeth Towne & Co, 1911.

Aziz, K.K. *Ameer Ali, his life and work* Lahore, Publishers United Ltd, 1968.

Bagchi, Samarendranath: 'Aghaṭan Ghaṭaner Alokik Rahaśya – Woodroffer Dīkṣā' in *Bhāvmukhe* vols 36–9 (1389–92 = 1982–5).

Bandyopadhyay, P: 'Sahayogi Sāhitya' in *Sāhitya* vol.24 (Śrāvan 1320 = 1913) pp. 363–8.

Barnett, L.D. *Antiquities of India: an account of the history and culture of ancient Hindustan* London, Warner, 1913.

Barth A. *The Religions of India* London, Kegan Paul Trench & Trübner, 1921 (first published Paris 1881).

Beck G.A. (ed.) *The English Catholics 1850–1950. Essays to commemorate the restoration of the Hierarchy of England and Wales* London, Burns Oates, 1950.

Bell, Charles *The Religion of Tibet* Oxford, Clarendon 1931.

Bhandarkar R.G. *Vaisnavism, Saivism and the Minor Religious Systems* New York, Garland Publications 1980 (1st ed. Strassburg 1913)

Bharati A. Foreword to Guenther H.V. *Yuganaddha, the Tantric View of Life* Varanasi, Chowkambha Sanskrit Series, 1952 (2nd ed.).

—— *The Tantric Tradition* London, Rider, 1965.

Bhattacharje, S.B. *Encyclopedia of Indian Events and Dates* New Delhi, Sterling, 1995.

Bhattacharyya, N.N. *History of the Tantric Religion* New Delhi, Manohar Publications, 1982.

Birdwood, G.C.M. *The Arts of India* Calcutta, Rupa paperback 1988. (First published as *The Industrial Arts of India* London, 1880).

Bishop, P. *The Myth of Shangri-La: Tibet, travel writing and the western creation of sacred landscape* London, Athlone Press, 1989.

Brooks D.R. *An Introduction to Hindu Śākta Tantrism* University of Chicago Press, 1990.

Brown, J. *Gandhi's Rise to Power: Indian Politics 1915–1922* London, Cambridge U.P. 1972.

Burnouf E. *Introduction à l'histoire du Bouddhisme Indien* Paris, Maisonneuve, 1876 (2nd ed.).

Campbell, Bruce F. *Ancient Wisdom Revived: a history of the Theosophical Movement* Berkely & London, University of California Press, c.1980.

Capra F. *The Tao of Physics* London, Fontana/Collins, 1976

Carmichael M.H.E. *Lord Carmichael of Skirling: a memoir prepared by his wife* London, Hodder & Stoughton, 1929.

Chatterjee, Nilananda *The Condition of Cattle in India: being an enquiry into the causes of the present deterioration of cattle with suggestions for their remedy* Calcutta, All India Cow Conferences Association, 1926.

Chatterji, Satischandra: 'Swami Vivekananda's Neo-Vedantism and its Practical Implications' in Majumdar R.C. (ed.) *Swami Vivekananda Centenary Memorial Volume* Calcutta, 1963, pp. 260–83.

Chattopadhyay D. *Lokāyata* New Delhi, People's Publishing House, 1959.

Chattopadhyay, J.C. *Kashmir Saivism* Srinagar, Kashmir Series of Texts and Studies vol.2, 1914.

—— *Hindu Realism: being an introduction to the metaphysics of the Nyaya-Vaisheshika system of philosophy* Delhi, Swastika Publications, 1975 (first published Allahabad, Government Press, 1912).

Chaudhury, Nirad C. *Scholar Extraordinary* London, Chatto & Windus, 1974.

—— *Autobiography of an Unknown Indian* Bombay, Jaico Publishing House, 1976 (1st ed. 1951).
—— *Hinduism* London, Chatto & Windus, 1979
Chichester, C.R. *Schools* London, Burns & Oates, 1882.
Chirol, Valentine *The Indian Unrest* London, Macmillan, 1910.
Chowdhury-Sengupta I: 'The Effeminate and the Masculine: Nationalism and the concept of race in colonial Bengal' in P. Robb (ed.) 1995 pp. 282–304.
—— 'Reconstructing Spiritual Heroism: The Evolution of the Swadeshi Sannyasi in Bengal' in J. Leslie (ed.) 1996 pp. 124–42.
Coomaraswamy A.K. *Rajput Painting* London & Milford, OUP, 1916.
—— 'The Theory of Art in Asia' in *The Transformation of Nature in Art* New Delhi, Munshiram Manoharlal, 1974.
—— *The Dance of Śiva* New York, Dover, 1985 (first published 1920).
Cousins, J.H. *The Renaissance in India* Madras, Ganesh, 1918.
—— 'The Āgamas and the Future' *Modern Review* vol.23/1 (1918) reprinted in *Śhakti and Śhākta* (DP ed. pp. 718–72).
—— and Cousins, M. *We Two Together* Madras, Ganesh, 1950.
Coward, H. *Jung and Eastern Thought* New York, SUNY Press, 1985.
Crooke, W. *An Introduction to the Popular Religion and Folklore of Northern India* Allahabad, Government Press, 1894.
Csomo de Koros, A. 'Analyse de Kandjour: recueil des livres sacrês du Tibet' in *Annales du Musée Guimet* vol.2 (1881) pp. 291–349. (Translated from *Asiatick Researches* 1936).
Datta, Bhupendranath *Swami Vivekananda Patriot–Prophet: a study* Calcutta, Nababharat, 1954.
Datta, K. and Robinson, A. *Rabindranath Tagore: the Myriad-Minded Man* London, Bloomsbury, 1995.
David-Neel, A. (ed. M. Peyronnet) *Journal de Voyage: Lettres à mon Mari* Paris, Libraire Plon 1976.
—— *L'Inde Aujourd'hui, Hier, Demain* Paris, Libraire Plon, 1954 (1st ed. 1951).
De Grood, D.H. *Haeckel's Theory of the Unity of Nature: a monograph in the history of philosophy* Amsterdam, Grüner, 1982.
Derrett, J.M.D. 'A Judicial Fabrication of Early British India, the Mahānirvāṇa Tantra' in *Essays in Classical and Modern Hindu Law* vol.2, Leiden, Brill.
Desai, Devangana *Erotic Scupture: a sociological study* New Delhi, Tata McGraw–Hill, 1975.
Dhar S.N. *A Comprehensive Biography of Swami Vivekananda* Madras, Vivekananda Prakashan Kendra, 1990 (1st ed. 1975).
Dhavamony, M. *The Love of God According to Śaiva Siddhānta: a study in the mysticism and theology of Saivism* Oxford, Clarendon, 1971.
Dubois, Abbé de (trans. H.K. Beauchamp) *Hindu Manners, Customs and Ceremonies* London, Clarendon, 1906 (3rd ed. first published in French in 1821)
Duka, T. *Life and Works of Alexander Csomo de Koros* London, Trübner, 1885.
Dyczkowski, M. *The Canon of the Śaivāgama and the Kubjikā Tantras of the Western Kaula Tradition* New Delhi, Banarsidass, 1989.
—— *The Doctrine of Vibration* New Delhi, Banarsidass, 1989.
Eliade, Mircea *Yoga, Immortality and Freedom* New York, Bollingen Foundation, 1958.
—— *Autobiography vol.1 1907–1937: Journey East, Journey West* San Francisco & London, Harper & Row, 1981
—— (ed.) *Encyclopaedia of Religion* New York, Macmillan, 1987.
Elwes, W. & R. *Gervase Elwes: the story of his life* London, Grayson & Grayson, 1935.
Encyclopedia of Magic and Superstition: alchemy, charms, dreams, omens, rituals, talismans, wishes Octopus Books, London, 1974.

Evans Wentz, W.Y. *The Tibetan Book of the Dead* London & Oxford, OUP, 1948 (2nd ed.) (1st ed. 1927).
Farquhar J.N: 'Recent Advances in the History of Hinduism' in *International Review of Missions* vol.iv no.13 (January 1915), p. 145.
—— *Modern Religious Movements in India* New York, Macmillan, c.1915.
—— *An Outline of the Religious Literature of India* London, OUP, 1920.
Finn, L.M. *Was the Scholarly Advocate a Secret Adept?* unpublished paper c.1980.
Flood, Gavin D: 'Techniques of Body and Desire in Kashmir Śaivism' in *Religion* (1992) vol.22, pp. 47–62.
—— *Body and Cosmology in Kashmir Saivism* San Francisco, Mellen Research U.P. 1993.
Foster, B. and M. *Forbidden Journey* San Francisco, Harper & Row, 1989.
Foster, Father S: 'An Educational Genius' *Catholic Herald* 24 August, 1984
—— 'The Thirteenth Lord Petre' *Essex Journal* Winter 1984, pp. 69–71.
—— 'A Pillar of Downside: Lord Petre' reprinted from *The English Benedictine Historical Symposium* (no date) pp. 24–33.
Foxe, B. *Long Journey Home: A biography of Margaret Noble (Nivedita)* London, Rider, 1975.
French, P. *Younghusband: the Last Great Imperial Adventurer* London, Harper & Collins, 1994.
Gangopadhyay, O.C. *Bhārater Śilpa O Āmār Kathā* Calcutta, A. Mukherjee, 1969.
Gangopadhyay, P. *Calaman Jīban* Calcutta, Vidyoday Library, 1956.
Ghose, Atal Bihari: 'The Teachings of the Tantra' in *Occult Digest* (Chicago ?) April 1930, p. 6; May 1930, p. 13.
—— *Śiva und Śakti* Rajshahi, Varendra Research Society Monograph, 1934
—— 'The Spirit and Culture of the Tantras' in Lokesvarananda (ed.) *Studies on the Tantras* Calcutta, Ramakrishna Mission Institute of Culture, 1989.
Ghosh, Binoy Jiban *The Murder of British Magistrates*, Calcutta, 1962.
Glasenapp, Helmut von *Der Hinduismus* Munich, Kurt Wolff Verlag, 1922.
—— *Brahma und Buddha*, Berlin, Deutsche Buch-Gemeinschafft, c.1926.
Gorman *Converts to Rome* London, Sands & Co, 1910.
Goudriaan T. and Gupta S. *Hindu Tantric and Śākta Literature* Wiesbaden, Harrassowitz, 1981.
—— and Hoens D.J. *Hindu Tantrism* Leiden, Brill, 1979.
Green, V.H.H. *Religion at Oxford and Cambridge* London, SCM Press, 1964.
Gupta, Sanjukta: 'The Religious and Literary Background of the Navāvaraṇa-Kirtana of Muttusvāmi Dikṣitar' in Te Nijenhuis E. & Gupta S. *Sacred Songs of India: Dikṣitar's Cycle of Hymns to the Goddess Kamalā* Winthertur/Switzerland, Amadeus, 1987, pp. 1–23.
Government College of Art and Craft: *Centenary Volume,* Calcutta, 1966.
Guha-Thakurta, T.G. *The Making of a New 'Indian' Art: artists, aesthetics and nationalism in Bengal c.1850–1920* London, Cambridge U.P. 1992.
Haeckel, Ernst (trans. J. Gilchrist) *Monism as Connecting Religion and Science: the confession of faith of a man of science* London, Adam & Charles Black, 1894.
—— (transl.J. McCabe) *The Riddle of the Universe* London, Watts & Co, 1913.
Halbfass, W. *India and Europe: an essay in understanding* New York, SUNY Press, 1988.
Hardinge of Penshurst *My Indian Years 1910–1916* London, John Murray, 1948.
Harrison, M. & Waters, B. *Burne Jones* London, Barrie & Jenkins, 1989.
Havell, E.B. *Benares the Sacred City: Sketches of Hindu Life and Religion* London, Blackie & Son, 1905.
—— *History of Aryan Rule in India: from the earliest times to the Death of Akbar* London, Harrap, 1918.
—— *Ideals of Indian Art* London, John Murray, 1920 (1st ed.1911)

—— *Indian Sculpture and Painting* London, John Murray, 1928 (1st ed. 1908).
Hay, Stephen N. *Asian Ideals of East and West: Tagore and his critics in Japan* Cambridge Mass., Harvard University Press, 1970.
Hees, P. *The Bomb in Bengal: the rise of evolutionary terrorism in India 1900–1910* Delhi, OUP, 1993.
Henningham S. *A Great Estate and Its Landlords in Colonial India: Darbhanga 1860–1942* Delhi, OUP, 1990.
High Court, Calcutta *The High Court at Calcutta: 125th Anniversary Souvenir*, Calcutta, 1987.
Hodgson W.H.H. *Essays on the Languages, Literature and Religion of Nepal and Tibet* New Delhi, Asian Education Services, 1991 (1st ed. 1874).
Hoffman, M. *A Sculptor's Odyssey* London, Charles Scribner's Sons Ltd, 1936.
Hopkins E.W. *Religions of India* Boston and London, Ginn, 1896.
Horioka, Y. *The Life of Kakuzo* Tokyo, Hokuseido Press, 1963.
Houllevigue, L. *The Evolution of the Sciences* London & Leipzig, T. Fisher Unwin, 1909.
Hunter W.W. *A Life of Brian Houghton Hodgson* London, John Murray, 1896.
Inden, R: 'Orientalist Constructions of India' in *Modern Asian Studies* 20/3 (1986), pp. 401–46.
—— *Imagining India* Oxford, Blackwell, 1990.
Jaffrelot C: 'The ideas of the Hindu race in the writings of Hindu nationalist ideologues in the 1920s and 1930s: a concept between two cultures' in P. Robb (ed.) 1995, pp. 327–54.
Jung, C.G. *Collected Works* vol.16 London, Routledge & Kegan Paul, 1966.
—— 'Psychological Commentary on Kuṇḍalinī Yoga (from notes of Mary Foote)' in *Spring* (Zurich) 1975 & 1976.
Kern, S. *The Culture of Time and Space 1880–1918* London, Weidenfeld & Nicolson, c.1983.
Keyserling, Count H. (trans J. Holroyd Reece) *Travel Diary of a Philosopher* vols 1 & 2 London, Jonathan Cape, 1925.
Khanna, M. *Yantra: the Tantric Symbol of Cosmic Unity* London, Thames and Hudson, 1979.
King, F. *The Magical World of Alisteir Crowley* London, Weidenfeld & Nicolson, 1977.
Kopf D. *British Orientalism and the Bengal Renaissance: the dynamics of Indian modernization* Berkeley, University of California Press, 1969.
—— *The Brahmo Samaj and the Shaping of the Modern Indian Mind* Princeton U.P. 1979.
—— 'Sexual Ambivalence in Western Scholarship on Hindu India' in *Comparative Civilizations Review* vol.13 (1986), pp. 143–57.
Kripal, J.J. *Kālī's Child: the Mystical and the Erotic in the Life and Teachings of Ramakrishna* University of Chicago Press, 1995.
Kumar, Pushpendra *Śakti Cult in Ancient India (with special reference to the Puranic Literature)* Varanasi, Bharatiya Publishing House, 1974.
Kumar R. *Annie Besant's Rise to Power in Indian Politics* New Delhi, Concept Publishing Co, 1981.
Lago M. (ed.) *Imperfect Encounter: Letters of William Rothenstein and Rabindranath Tagore 1911–1941* Harvard U.P. 1972
Larson G.J. *Classical Sāmakhya: an interpretation of its history and meaning* New Delhi, Banarsidass, 1979.
La Vallée Poussin L.de *Études et textes tantriques: Pañcakrama* Gand, H. Engelcke, 1896.
—— *Bouddhisme: opinions sur l'histoire de la dogmatique* Paris, Beauchesne, 1909.
Le Bon, Gustave (trans. F. Legge) *The Evolution of Matter* London, Walter Scott Publishing Co, 1907.
Leslie, J. (ed.) *Myths and Mythmaking* London, Curzon Press, 1996.

Leslie, K. *The Red Judge and other anecdotes* Rangoon, Rangoon Times Press, 1934.
Lipsey, R. *Coomaraswamy* vol.3 'His Life and Work', Princeton U.P. 1977.
Lodge, Sir Oliver *Ether and Reality* London, Hodder & Stoughton, 1925.
Lorenzen, D.L. *The Kāpālikas and the Kālamukhas: two lost Saivite Sects* Berkeley, University of California Press, 1972.
Maitra, A.K: 'The Stones of Varendra' *Modern Review* vol.7/6 (June 1910), p. 590–1.
Mallik, B.P. (ed.) *Suniti Kumar Chatterji (1890–1977) Commemoration Volume* Calcutta, Burdwan University, 1981.
Mangal P. *Bhārater Śilpi Nandalāl* Calcutta, 1982 (1389 BE).
Marshall P. (ed.) *The British Discovery of Hinduism in the Eighteenth Century* London, Cambridge U.P. 1970.
McClelland V.A. 'The Liberal Training of England's Catholic Youth: William Joseph Petre (1847–93) and Educational Reform' in *Victorian Studies* March 1972, pp. 257–77.
McDermott, Rachel Fell 'A Tantric Icon Comes Alive: the Creation of the "Orientalist Kālī" in Early-Twentieth Century Bengal' in Urban (ed.) forthcoming.
Meade M. *Madame Blavatsky: the Woman behind the Myth* New York, G.P. Putnam's Sons, 1980.
Mitter, P. *Much Maligned Monsters: a history of European reactions to Indian Art* Oxford, Clarendon, 1977.
—— 'The Aryan Myth and British Writings on Indian Art and Culture' in Moore-Gilbert, B. (ed.) *Literature and Imperialism* London, Roehampton Institute, 1983, pp. 69–89.
—— *Art and Nationalism in Colonial India 1850–1922: occidental orientations*, London, Cambridge U.P. 1994.
Mitra, B. *Jagadish Chunder Bose: a biography for students* London, Orient Longman, 1982.
Mitra, Rājendralāla *Indo-Aryans: contributions towards the elucidation of their ancient and medieval history* vols 1 & 2, London, Edward Stanford, 1881.
—— *The Sanskrit Buddhist Literature of Nepal* Calcutta, Asiatic Society of Bengal, 1882.
Monier Williams, H.M. *Brahmanism and Hinduism* London, John Murray, 1891.
—— *Hinduism* London, SPCK, 1894.
Montagu, Sir Edwin *An Indian Diary* London, Heinemann, 1930.
Nandy, A. *Intimate Enemy: Loss and Recovery of Self under Colonialism* Delhi, OUP, 1988.
Newman, J.H. *The Letters and Diaries of . . .* (ed. with notes and introduction by C.S. Dessain & Thomas Gornall) vol.xxvi Oxford, Clarendon Press, 1974.
Pandit, M.P. *Kuṇḍalinī Yoga: A Study of Sir John Woodroffe's 'the Serpent Power'* Madras, Ganesh, 1959.
Padoux, André: 'A Survey of Tantric Hinduism for the Historian of Religions' in *History of Religions* vol.20/4 (1981), pp. 345–60.
—— 'Tantrism' in Eliade (ed.) *Encyclopedia of Religion* vol.14, pp. 273–80 (1987)
—— (trans. J. Gontier) *Vac: The Concept of the Word in Selected Hindu Tantras* New York, SUNY Press, 1990.
Pal, Vasanta Kumar *Tantrāchārya Sivacandra* Cooch Behar, Trivṛta Prakāśinī, 1972 (1379 BE).
Pāndūlipi, A.S: 'Abhinav praṇālir varṇabodh' *Bhārat Varṣa* vol.4/1 (1916), pp. 137–9.
Payne E. *The Śāktas* London, OUP, 1933.
Petre, The Hon. & Rev. W.J. *The Position and Prospects of Catholic Liberal Education* London, Burns & Oates, 1878.
Provence Belge de la Compagnie de Jésus *La Mission du Bengale Occidental du Archidioces de Calcutta*, Bruges, 1921.
Pyarelal *Mahātma Gandhi: the last phase* vol.2, Ahmedabad, Navajivan, 1966.
Ramusack, B. *The Princes of India in the Twilight of Empire: dissolution of a patron-client system 1914–39* Colombio, Ohio State U.P. c.1978.

Rawlinson, A. *The Book of Enlightened Masters: western teachers in Indian traditions* Chicago, Open Court, 1997.
Rawson, P. *Tantra* (Catalogue to the Arts Council Exhibition) London, 1971
Ray, S.N. *Bhārater Sādhak* vol.2, Calcutta, Karūṇa Prakāśinī, 1985 (1392 BE).
Raychaudhuri, T. *Europe Reconsidered. perceptions of the West in nineteenth century Bengal* Oxford, OUP, 1988.
Ray Chowdhury, Ranabir *Calcutta a Hundred Years Ago – excerpts from The Statesman* Bombay, Nachiketa Publication, 1987.
Regardie, Israel *Golden Dawn: an account of the teachings, rites and ceremonies of the Order of the Golden Dawn* Saint Paul, Minn., Llewellyn Publications, 1970.
Rele, Vasant G. *The Mysterious Kuṇḍalinī (with Foreword by Sir John Woodroffe)* Bombay, D.B. Taraporevala Sons & Co, 1939 (4th ed. 1st ed. 1927).
Rich, P.J. *Chains of Empire* London, Regency, c.1991.
Robb, P. (ed.) *The Concept of Race in South Asia* Delhi, OUP, 1995
—— 'Introduction' in P. Robb (ed.) 1995, pp. 1–76.
Ross, Sir E. Denison *Both Ends of the Candle* London, Faber, 1943.
Rothenstein, W. *Men and Memories 1900–1922* vol.2 'An Indian Pilgrimage', London, Faber, 1934.
Said E. *Orientalism* Penguin Books, 1995.
Sanderson, A: 'Purity and Power Among the Brahmins of Kashmir' in M. Carrithers et.al. (eds) *The Category of the Person: Anthropological and Philosophical Perspectives* London, Cambridge U.P. 1985, pp. 190–216.
—— 'Śaivism and the Tantric Traditions' in S. Sutherland et.al. (eds) *The World's Religions* London, Routledge, 1988, pp. 660–704.
Sarkar, J. *India Through the Ages: a survey of the growth of Indian life and thought* Calcutta, M.C.Sarkar & Sons, 1928.
Sarkar K.C: 'A Forgotten Historian and Antiquarian' in *Modern Review* vol.113/2 (February 1963), pp. 159–62.
Sarkar, S. *The Swadeshi Movement in Bengal 1903–8* New Delhi, Peoples Publishing House, 1973.
—— 'The Kalki-avatar of Bikrampur: A Village Scandal in Early 20th Century Bengal' in Guha R. (ed.) *Subaltern Studies* VI, Delhi & Oxford, OUP, 1989, pp. 1–53.
—— '"Kaliyuga", "Chakri" and "Bhakti": Ramakrishna and His Times' in *Economic and Political Weekly* 18 July 1992.
Schrader, F.O. *An Introduction to Pāñcarātra and the Ahirbuddhyna Samhitā* Madras, Adyar Library, 1916.
Seal, Brajendranath *The Positive Sciences of the Ancient Hindus* Delhi, Banarsidass 1958, (1st ed. Ahmedabad 1915).
Sellon E. *Annotations on the Sacred Writings of the Hindus* London, privately printed 1865 (1902).
Sen, D.C. *History of Bengali Language and Literature* Calcutta University, 1911.
Sen, Rāmaprasāda (trans. L. Nathan & C. Seely) *Grace and Mercy in Her Wild Hair* Boulder Colorado, Great Eastern Book Co, 1982.
Sengupta N.C. *Yuga Parikrama* Calcutta, Sengupta Trust, 1961.
Sen Sarma, D.B: 'The Conception of Tattva, a Study' in *Navonmeṣa: MM Gopinath Kaviraj smṛti granth* Varanasi, MM Gopinath Kaviraj Janamaśhthābdi Samiti, 1987, pp. 199–202.
—— *The Philosophy of Sādhana with special reference to the Trika Philosophy of Kashmir* New York, SUNY Press, 1990.
Sharpe Eric J. *Not to Destroy but to Fulfil: the contribution of J.N. Farquhar to Protestant missionary thought in India before 1914* Uppsala, Swedish Institute of Missionary Research, 1965.

Silburn, L. *La Kuṇḍalinī, L'Énergie des Profondeurs* Paris, Les Deux Oceans, 1983.
Stevenson, M. Sinclair *The Rites of the Twice-born* London, OUP, 1920.
Singh, K. *Prophet of Indian Nationalism: a study of the political thought of Sri Aurobindo 1893–1910* London, Allen & Unwin, 1963.
Sinha, N.K. *Asutosh Mookerjee: A biographical study* Calcutta, Asutosh Mukherji Memorial Committee, 1966.
Symonds R. *Oxford and Empire: the last lost cause?* London, Macmillan, 1986.
Tagore, A. and Chand, R. *Joṛāsānkor Dhāre* Calcutta, Viśvabhāratī Granthanavibhāg, 1985 (1391 BE).
Tagore, Rathindranath *On the Edges of Time* Calcutta, Orient Longmans, 1981 (first published 1958).
Tattvabhusan, Sitanath *Autobiography (with details of philosophical study and spiritual endeavour)* Calcutta, Brahmo Mission Press, (no date).
Taylor, Anne *Annie Besant: a biography* Oxford, OUP, 1992.
Taylor, Kathleen: 'Arthur Avalon, the Creation of a Legendary Orientalist' in J. Leslie (ed.) pp. 144–63.
Tennyson, A: 'Morte d'Arthur', *Idylls of the King* London, Macmillan, 1907.
Thackers Indian Directory 1887–1961 Calcutta, Thackers Press and Depository.
Tibbits, Kate *Cities Seen in East and West* London, Hurst & Blackett, 1912.
—— *Veiled Mysteries of India* London, Nash & Grayson, 1929.
Towndrow, K.R: 'Sir William Rothenstein and his Indian Correspondence' in *Indian Art and Letters* vol.xxv no.1 (1951), pp. 12ff.
Turner, F.M. *Between Science and Religion: The Reaction to Scientific Naturalism in Late Victorian England* New Haven & London, Yale U.P. 1974.
Urban H.B: 'The Strategic Uses of an Esoteric Text: the Mahānirvāṇa Tantra' in *South Asia* vol.xviii no.1 (1995), pp. 55–81.
—— 'The Cult of Ecstacy: Tantrism, the New Age and the Spiritual Logic of Late Capitalism' in *History of Religions*, vol.39 no.3 (February 2000), pp. 268–304.
—— (ed.) *In the Land of Tantra: Contextualizing Eroticism, Secrecy and Power in the Tantric Traditions of Bengal* (forthcoming).
Van Buitenen, J.A.B. *The Bhagavadgītā in the Mahābhārata*, University of Chicago Press, 1981.
Van Manen, J: 'A Tibetan Tantra' in *The Theosophist* 1919, reprinted in *Śhākti and Śhākta* (DP ed. pp. 213–25)
Vivekananda, Swami *The Complete Works of Swami Vivekananda* Calcutta, Advaita Ashram Press, 1922 etc.
Ward, William *A View of the History, Literature and Mythology of the Hindus* London, Kingsbury Parbury & Allen, 1822 (first published Serampore Mission Press, 1811).
Wedderburn W. *A Life of Alan Octavian Hume: Father of the Indian National Congress 1829–1912* New Delhi, Deep & Deep, 1988 (first published 1913).
Wilson, H.H: 'Notice of Three Tracts Received from Nepal' in *Asiatick Researches* vol.xvi (1828), pp. 1–39.
—— 'A Sketch of the Religious Sects of the Hindus' in *Asiatick Researches* vol.xvi (1828), pp. 40–136
—— 'A Sketch . . . etc, part.2 in *Asiatick Researches* vol.xvii (1832), pp. 169–314.
—— *Works of the Late Horace Hayman Wilson* vols 1 & 2, London, Trübner, 1862.
—— *Religious Sects of the Hindus* New Delhi, Asian Publication Series, 1976.
Wood E. *An Englishman defends Mother India* Madras,Ganesh, 1929.
Zetland, L.J.L. Dundas, Lord Ronaldshay (Marquis of) *The Heart of Aryavarta: a study of the psyychology of the Indian unrest* London & Bombay, Constable, 1925.
—— *Essayez: the memoirs of . . .* London, John Murray, 1956.

Zimmer H. *Artistic Form and Yoga in the Sacred Images of India* Princeton U.P. 1984 (first published 1926).
—— *Philosophies of India* Delhi, Motilal Banarsidass, 1989 (first published London 1952).

NEWSPAPERS AND JOURNALS

Amrita Bāzār Patrika, Calcutta
Baśumati, Calcutta
The Bengalee, Calcutta
Bhārat Varṣa, Calcutta
Bhāvmukhe, Calcutta
Bulletin de l'Association Francaise des Amis de l'Orient, Paris
Bulletin of the Indian Rationalistic Society, Calcutta
Calcutta Weekly Notes, High Court, Calcutta
Comparative Civilizations Review, Chicago
The Englishman, Calcutta
History of Religions, Chicago U.P.
Indian Art and Letters, London, India Society
Indian Culture (Journal of the Indian Research Institute), Calcutta
Indian Philosophical Review, Baroda
International Review of Missions, London
Journal of the Indian Society of Oriental Art [JISOA], Calcutta
Modern Asian Studies, Cambridge U.P.
Modern Review, Calcutta
Prabuddha Bhārata, Calcutta
Religion: a journal of religion and religions, London
Rūpam, Calcutta (ISOA)
Sāhitya, Calcutta
The Statesman, Calcutta
The Theosophist, Adyar, Madras
Vedānta Keśari, Madras, Ramakrishna Mission
Viśvabhārati Quarterly, Santiniketan, West Bengal.

THE BOOKS OF ARTHUR AVALON/SIR JOHN WOODROFFE

A Books and articles published by Arthur Avalon:

1913: *Tantrik Texts* (ed.) Vols 1–21, London, Luzacs; Calcutta, Thacker Spink & Co.
1924: 'Tantrik Ritual' (parts 1,2,3 & 4) in *Vedānta Keśari* March–April, pp. 873–9, 922–5; May–June pp. 12–15, 61–5.
—— with Ellen Avalon 1913: *Hymns to the Goddess* London, Luzacs; 2nd ed. 1952 Madras, Ganesh & Co.

B Books published originally under the name of Arthur Avalon and subsequently reprinted or revised under the name of Sir John Woodroffe:

1913: *The Great Liberation* (*Mahanirvanatantram*) (trans.) London, Luzacs; 6th ed. 1985, Madras, Ganesh.

1914: *Principles of Tantra* (ed.) vols 1 & 2, London, Luzacs; 6th ed. 1986 Madras, Ganesh.
1917: *Wave of Bliss (Ānandalaharī)* (trans. & commentary) London, Luzacs;
Greatness of Śiva (*Mahimnastava* of Puspadanta) (trans. & commentary) London, Luzacs;
Īshā Upanishad (with commentary of Sadānanda) (ed.) London, Luzacs;
Reprinted 1971 as: *Īṣopaniṣad, Wave of Bliss, Greatness of Śiva*, Madras, Ganesh.
1918: *The Serpent Power* London, Luzacs.
2nd ed. 1922, Madras, Ganesh.
3rd ed. 1928, Madras, Ganesh.
14th ed. 1989, Madras, Ganesh.
1952: *An Introduction to Tantra Sastra* (original introduction to MNT) Madras, Ganesh.
8th ed: 1990 Madras, Ganesh.
1954: *An Introduction to the Tantrarāja Tantra* Madras, Ganesh (Reprint of introduction to TT/8).

C Books and articles on Tantra originally published under the name of Sir John Woodroffe:

1918: *Shakti and Shākta* London, Luzacs.
2nd ed. 1920, London, Luzacs.
3rd ed. 1927, Madras, Ganesh.
6th ed. 1965, Madras, Ganesh/1978, New York, Dover.
9th ed. 1987, Madras, Ganesh.
1922: *Garland of Letters*: London, Luzacs; Madras, Ganesh;
9th ed. 1989, Madras, Ganesh.
—— with P.N. Mukhopadhyay 1922–3: *The World as Power*, Madras, Ganesh;
6th ed. 1981, Madras, Ganesh.
—— with P.N. Mukhopadhyay 1929, *Mahāmāya* Madras, Ganesh.
2nd ed. 1929, Madras, Ganesh.
1973: and M.P. Pandit: *Some Readings in the Kulārṇava Tantra*, Madras, Ganesh.
1983: (transl. M. Shibata) *Introduction a l'Hindouisme Tantrique: concepts et pratiques*, Paris, Éditions Trismégiste.

D Books by Sir John Woodroffe on Indian culture

1917: *Bharata Shakti*, Calcutta, S.C. Chowdhury
2nd ed. 1918, Calcutta
3rd ed. 1921, Madras, Ganesh.
1918: *Is India Civilized?*, Calcutta ?
2nd ed. 1919, Madras, Ganesh.
3rd ed. 1921, Madras, Ganesh.
1919: *The Seed of Race: an essay on Indian Education*, Madras, Ganesh.
2nd ed. 1921, Madras, Ganesh.

E Other books and articles by Sir John Woodroffe

1900: *The Law Relating to Injunctions in British India*, Calcutta, Thacker Spink & Co.
1903: *The Law Relating to Receivers in British India*, Calcutta, Thacker Spink & Co.
1908: *Civil Procedure in British India: commentary on Act V of 1908*, Calcutta, Thacker Spink & Co.
1912: 'Introduction' to M.M. Ganguly *Orissa and Her Remains: Ancient and Medieval*, Calcutta, Thacker Spink & Co.

1921: 'White and Gold' in *Sha'ama* (Bombay, ed. Mrinalini Chattopadhyay) vol.1/1 (January 1921), pp. 237–9.
1922: 'The Wise Childhood' in *Vedānta Keśari* vol.9/4 pp. 134–6.
1927: 'Foreword' to W.Y. Evans Wentz *The Tibetan Book of the Dead* London, OUP, 1927.
1927: 'Foreword' to V. G. Rele *The Mysterious Kuṇḍalinī* Bombay, D.B. Taraporevala Sons & Co.
—— with Sir S. Ameer Ali 1898: *The Law of Evidence Applicable to British India* Calcutta, Thacker Spink & Co.

THE TANTRIK TEXTS

General Editor: Arthur Avalon

1 *Tantrābhidhāna* (Seven tantrik dictionaries) Editor: Tārānātha Vidyāratna Introduction: Arthur Avalon 2nd edition Pañcānan Bhattacharyya (ed.)	January 1913 1937
2 *Ṣaṭ-cakra-nirūpaṇa* by Purnānanda Swāmi Editor: Tārānātha Vidyāratna Introduction: Arthur Avalon	January 1913
3 *Prapañcasāra tantra* (1st ed.) Editor: Tārānātha Vidyāratna Introduction: Arthur Avalon	August 1914
4 *Kulachūdāmaṇi tantra* Editor: Giriṣa Candra Vedāntatirtha Introduction: Aksay Kumar Maitra	August 1915 (Rajshahi)
5 *Kulārṇava tantra* Editor: Tārānātha Vidyāratna Introduction: Arthur Avalon	1917
6 *Kālīvilāsa tantra* Editor: Pārvati Caraṇa Tarkatirtha Introduction: Arthur Avalon	November 1916 (Śrinagar)
7 *Śrīcakrasambhāra tantra* Editor: Kazi Dawasamdup Foreword: Arthur Avalon	September 1918 (Ranchi)
8 *Tantrarāja tantra* part I Editor: MMP Laksmana Śāstri Introduction: Arthur Avalon	November 1918 (Chaibassa)
9 *Kārpūrādistotram* (Hymn to Kālī by Mahākāla) Translated by Arthur Avalon	c.1922
10 *Kāmakalāvilāsa of Pūnyānanda* Editor: MMP Sadāśiva Miśra Translation and notes by Arthur Avalon	c.1922

11 *Kaulopaniṣad, Tripurāmahopaniṣad Bhāvanopaniṣad, Bahvṛīcopaniṣad, Ārunopaṇiṣad, Kāḷikopaniṣad* c.1922
Editor: Śitārāma Śāstri
Introduction: Arthur Avalon

12 *Tantrarāja tantra* part II 1926
Editor: MMP Sadāśiva Miśra
Introduction and summary: Arthur Avalon

13 *Mahānirvāṇa tantra* 1928
Editor: Arthur Avalon

14 *Kaulāvalīnirnayah* 1928
(Compilation by Jñānānanda Paramahaṁsa)
Editor: Arthur Avalon

15 *Brahmasamhitā* and *Viṇusahasraṇāma* unknown
Editor: Arthur Avalon

16/17 *Śāradātilaka tantra* by Laksmanadeśika 1933
Editor: Arthur Avalon
Introduction: Arthur Avalon

18/19 *Prapañcasāra tantra* 1935 and 1937
Editor: Arthur Avalon
Intro: Arthur Avalon

20 *Chidgagana-chandrikā* 1937
Editor: Svami Trivikrama Tirtha

21 *Tārā-bhakti-sudhārṇava* 1940
Editor: Pañcānan Bhattācāryya

INDEX

abhāsavāda 146, 165
advāya 163 (*see* śiva–śakti)
Abhinavagupta 160–3, 221, 222, 287, 288
adhikāra 108, 113, 189, 293
advaita (*see also* non-dualism) 133, 163–4, 174, 175, 177, 184, 194
advaita vedānta 68, 166,
āgama(s) 117, 118, 155–6, 157, 160, 163, 177, 182, 224 (*see also* tantra, tantras, tantraśāstra)
Agamānusandhana Samiti 101, 117, 151, 203, 204, 208, 211–2, 219, 250
All India Cow Conferences Association 16, 45, 83
Ameer Ali, Sir Sayeed 13, 15–16
Ameer Ali, Sir Torick xiii, 15–17, 49, 61, 73, 83, 84
Amoeba (The) xiv, 21, 27, 28, 35, 85,
Andrews, Charles Freer 2, 45, 237
An Introduction to Tantra Śāstra 129, 138–9, 214, 216, 217, 232
antinomianism 185
anuśīlan samitis 42, 46,
Archer, William 38, 82, 87–8,
art (Indian) 60, **61–78**, 88,
and nationalism 61, 68–70, 76
aryans 67, 86, 125, 127–9, 182–3, 268, 282
Asiatic Society of Bengal 3, 6, 36, 120, 121, 126
Association Francaise des Amis de l'Orient 140
Aurobindo 42, 46, 47, 101
Avalon, Arthur xi–xii, 1, 2–4, 5, 11, 15, 36, 38, 51, 58, 59, 65, 67, 71, 79, 80, 87, 99, 104, 117, 119, 137–53, 155–7 et passim, 203–34, 235–8
as pseudonym 2–3, 140, 146, **147–53**, 204, 216, 219; as Woodroffe and Ghose 3, 151–3, 203, 205—8, 219, 230–4, 236–7; image 114, 120, 142, 143, 143–5 et passim, 153, 235–8; influence on orientalists 2, 119, 135–6, 137–43 et passim, 235; reception by Indians 143–5, 147, 236; writings 1, **129–36**, 154–7, 221–3 (*see also* Woodroffe, John George; Ghose, Atal Bihari and individual book titles)
Avalon, isle of 148

Bagchi, S.N. xiii, 50, 98, 99–102, 108, 265, 276
bānde mātāram 44, 46,
Bandyopadhyay, Panchkori 107, 228
Banerjea, Sir Gurudas 145
Barnett, L.D. 1, 119, 126, 127–8
Barth, A 119, 124, 140
bauls 99,
Beatson Bell, Sir Nicholas 145
Bell, Charles 211
Bengal Humanitarian Association 83
Besant, Annie xii, 2, 44–5, 47, 70, 82, 86, 91, 92, 147, 148, 190, 237, 264
bhairavī (female tantric) 96, 97, 100, 109, 178, 204
Bhandarkar, R.G. 126
Bhārat Varṣa 7, 95, 99, 112, 146–7, 203
bhārata dharma 89, 214 (*see also* 'brahmanism')
Bhārata Shakti 39, 47, 70, 78–85, 91, 217
Bharati, Agehananda 175, 223
Bhattacharya, Dineśa Candra 227
Bhattacharya, Pañcānan 130, 206, 281